Created and Directed by Hans Höfer

THE NILE

Edited by Andrew Eames
Consultant Editor: Rowlinson Carter
Main photography: Richard Nowitz and Tor Eigeland

Editorial Director: Brian Bell

Houghton Mifflin

APA PUBLICATIONS

This book is the last of a triumvirate of Insight Guides on Egypt. Following the success of *Insight Guide: Egypt*, which since its initial publication in English has been translated into German, French, Spanish and Chinese, Apa Publications set about commissioning two new books: one on Cairo and the other on the Nile, the life-giving ribbon of water that brings fertility to a part of the world that would otherwise be inhospitable to human beings. The books form part of the series founded in 1970 by **Hans Höfer** and now spanning the world with more than 190 titles.

Höfer

The intention of **Andrew Eames**, project editor of *Insight Guide: The Nile*, was to provide an entertaining, informative and beautifully illustrated ship-board companion for those many thousands of awe-struck visitors who sail up and down the river today, stopping off at monuments which were erected 4,000 years ago with engineering skills that are barely matched even in these modern times.

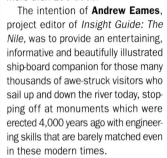

Eames

Of course, most cruises have their own guides on board, but most guides – and most cruises – concentrate on the highly visible slice of Nile history that began 3,000 years before the birth of Christ and ended shortly after Christ's death. Contrary to the impression given by many guides and Egyptologists, the Nile did not suddenly cease to play a key role in the history of the region after that time, any more than it ceased flowing.

This book, while recounting the best stories from pharaonic times, completes the progress of the great river with an account of the history of the Nile in the years since. Some of that history has entered into legend: the meeting of Stanley and Livingstone, for example, and the death of General Gordon at the hands of the Mahdi in Khartoum. All these episodes and more are superbly narrated by **Rowlinson Carter**, this book's consultant editor and a frequent Insight Guides contributor.

Carter, a widely-travelled journalist, documentary-maker and historian, has a liking for historical exclusives; he believes that history is not about dates and events, but a story about people – their glory, bravery, villainy, lechery and greed. He is currently working on his own anecdotal account of the development of western civilisation.

Carter

Harnessing Carter's ideas and turning them into chapters was the task of project editor Eames. An experienced journalist, he writes for Britain's national newspapers and has had two travel books published by Hodder & Stoughton: *Crossing the Shadow Line,* an account of his years in South-east Asia, and *Four Scottish Journeys*.

Thanks to Apa's schedule of Egyptian books, Eames was also able to draw on contributors familiar with the successful Insight Guide approach. **Jill Kamil**, a Kenyan-born journalist and author who has lived most of her life in Egypt, wrote most of the invaluable chapters detailing the river banks and their monuments. Kamil's own books include *Upper Egypt, Sakkara and Memphis, Luxor* and *Coptic Egypt,* all published by Longmans.

Kamil

For the chapter on Cairo, Eames invited **John Rodenbeck**, editor of *Insight Cityguide: Cairo,* to distil the city

J. Rodenbeck

into 4,000 words, which he did admirably. Rodenbeck has lived in Cairo off and on since 1964, working as scholar, writer, actor, and publisher. For nine years he headed the American University in Cairo Press and was the publisher of Egypt's Nobel prizewinner, Naguib Mahfouz. He is a professor of English and comparative literature at the American University.

Max Rodenbeck, John's son, who wrote the section on the Nile Delta, is the Cairo correspondent of the *Economist,* but his name is also familiar to readers of *Middle East International* and the *Financial Times.* He is married to an Alexandrian and reads, speaks and writes Arabic fluently.

M. Rodenbeck

The chapters on flora, fauna, the Nile outside Egypt and the Travel Tips are the work of **Cassandra Vivian**. Vivian, who lived in Egypt for 15 years before returning to her native America, is the editor of *Cairo: A Practical Guide* and author of *Father of Rivers: A Traveler's Companion to the Nile Valley.* Her most recent publication is *Islands of the Blest: A Guide to the Oases and Western Desert of Egypt.*

Vivian

Dilys Powell, veteran film critic for the *Sunday Times* and *Punch* magazine in London, contributed the chapter on the Nile in the Cinema. The short piece on the mummy business was written by **Susanne Pleines**.

Photographs in this book are primarily the work of US-based **Richard Nowitz**, an Insight Guide regular who contributed extensively to the books on Jerusalem, London, Wales and Cairo, and **Tor Eigeland**, a London-based Norwegian photographer well known for his work in National Geographic's *Traveler* magazine.

Nowitz

Other images came from regular Insight Guide contributors, including **Marcus Wilson-Smith**, **Lyle Lawson**, **Eddy Posthuma de Boer** and **Topham Picturepoint**.

Kuoni Travel helped out with transport arrangements. Proof-reading and indexing were completed by **Dorothy Stannard**, and **Jill Anderson** supervised the production process.

Stannard

All the contributors were duly humbled by the awareness that were adding to an already vast literature about the Nile. As long ago as 1360, John Mandeville declared with great conviction that the Nile "comes out of Paradise and runs through the deserts of India, then it sinks down into the earth and runs under the earth a great country and comes up again under a mountain that hat Alloche, the which is betwixt India and Ethiopia… and so all the length of Egypt."

John Lloyd Stephens, one of the first of the modern era of Nile cruisers, enthused in 1837 that "a voyage on the Nile would exceed any travelling within my experience. The perfect freedom from all restraint, and from the conventional trammels of civilized society, form an episode in a man's life that is vastly agreeable and exciting. Think of not shaving for two months, of washing your shirts in the Nile, and wearing them without being ironed."

Now that the river is home to 200 luxury cruise boats, the "episode" of Nile cruising remains as "vastly agreeable and exciting" as it was then, but modern-day travellers may – if they wish – be spared the "exhilaration" of not washing, shaving or ironing their shirts.

CONTENTS

Introduction

The Wonder of the Nile
by Rowlinson Carter **21**

The Search for the Source
by Rowlinson Carter **29**

The Birth of Nile Cruising
by Rowlinson Carter **45**

*Vodka with Pyramids; the Business
of Cruising*
by Andrew Eames **52**

History

An Outline of History
by John Rodenbeck **56**

**Pyramid Builders of the
Old Kingdom**
by Rowlinson Carter **59**

*Pyramidology and
Pyramidiocy*
by Rowlinson Carter **64**

Graverobbers and Curses
by Rowlinson Carter **67**

The Mummy Business
by Susanne Pleines **71**

**Rebel Dynasty of the
New Kingdom**
by Rowlinson Carter **73**

Ramses the Builder
by Rowlinson Carter **83**

Cleopatra and the Ptolemies
by Rowlinson Carter **87**

The Mamlukes
by Rowlinson Carter **93**

The French on the Nile
by Rowlinson Carter **103**

The British on the Nile
by Rowlinson Carter **113**

Encounter at Fashoda
by Rowlinson Carter **122**

The Last Pharaohs
by Rowlinson Carter **129**

Spy Stories
by Rowlinson Carter **142**

Features

The Taming of the Nile
by Rowlinson Carter **147**

Wildlife
by Cassandra Vivian **153**

Flourishing Flora
by Cassandra Vivian **155**

The Nile in the Cinema
by Dilys Powell **159**

Places

Introduction
by Andrew Eames **173**

The African Nile
by Cassandra Vivian **176**

The Voyage Begins: Aswan
by Jill Kamil **185**

Aswan to Luxor
by Jill Kamil **203**

Luxor
by Jill Kamil **217**

Luxor: the West Bank
by Jill Kamil **231**

Discovering Tutankhamun
by Rowlinson Carter **240**

Luxor to Abydos
by Jill Kamil **245**

Middle Egypt
by Jill Kamil **255**

Pigeons and Hippos, Cats and Cattle
by Rowlinson Carter **260**

Memphis, Sakkara and Giza
by Jill Kamil **265**

Cairo
by John Rodenbeck **279**

Dealings with the Natives
by Rowlinson Carter **291**

The Delta
by Max Rodenbeck **299**

The Rosetta Stone
by Rowlinson Carter **302**

Maps

The Nile **30**
The Nile Outside Egypt **176**
Aswan **186**
The Nile in Egypt **202**
Luxor **216**
Cairo **280**

Getting Acquainted

The Place 306
The Climate 306
The Economy 306
Government............................ 306
Geography & Population 306
Etiquette 306

Planning the Trip

What to Bring 307
What to Wear......................... 307
Entry Regulations 307
On Arrival 307
On Departure 307
Health 307
Money 308
Public Holidays 308
Getting There 308
Specialist Tours 309
Special Facilities 309
Useful Addresses 309

Practical Tips

Business Hours 309
Religion & Religious
Services 309
Media 310
Postal Services 311
Telephone 311
Internet 311
Embassies
& Consulates in Egypt 311
Emergencies 311

Getting Around

Orientation 312
From the Airport 312
Public Transport.................... 313
Private Transport 313
On Foot 314
Hitchhiking 314

Where to Stay

Hotels 314

Eating Out

Where to Eat 317
Drinking Notes 318

Attractions

Culture 319
Historical Sites 321
Other Attractions................... 322
Cruising the Nile 324
Festivals 324
Photography 325

Outdoor Activities

Participant 325
Spectator 325

Shopping

What to Buy........................... 326

Language

Conversation 327

Further Reading

The Nile 328
Other Insight Guides 328

Art/Photo Credits 329
Index 330

THE WONDER OF THE NILE

Egypt only exists thanks to a bit of geographical nonsense. The line of least resistance for water escaping from two African lakes 1,000 miles apart, one of them actually straddling the equator, was not a quick dive into the Indian Ocean and Red Sea which lay close at hand. Instead, one went off as if looking to join the Congo river for its immense journey west to the Atlantic. The other went roughly south for hundreds of miles before that, too, proved to be a feint. Between them, the two rivers logged some 3,500 miles (5,600 km) of idle wandering before combining their forces for a 2,000-mile (3,200-km) mercy mission through what would otherwise have been one of the most terrible places on earth.

Replenished by only one tributary and hardly ever by rainfall, a lesser river than the unified streams of the White and Blue Niles would have petered out in the insatiable sands of the desert long before it reached the Mediterranean. The Nile, shedding colour codes where two rivers become one, not only survived but, at the hottest and driest time of every year, conjured up a momentous tidal wave of flood water which could not be contained in the course it had been carving into the desert for more than a million years.

The sheer volume of silt which the flood brought defied comprehension. In any one year it seemed sufficient to have stripped the lands from whence it came to skeletal bare bones, yet there was always more, year after year. Moreover, it was silt of great fertility, capable of turning a thousand miles of useless desert into an agricultural paradise.

In southern or Upper Egypt, the miracle was confined to a narrow ribbon along the banks but, with only 100 miles to go, the river seemed suddenly in several minds about where to surrender to the Mediterranean. The result was what the Greeks recognised as the shape of their letter Delta, seven channels which merged during the floods into a coastal lake which drove the inhabitants on

to high ground and brought out the boats.

Wherever the silt was deposited, all a farmer had to do was wait for the water to subside, scratch seeds into the ground, let his livestock trample them in, and sit back to watch them grow. The feeding of the river people more or less took care of itself. They could settle down in one place and for several months of the year there was very little that they really needed to do.

The Nile made Egypt: The pyramids and all that followed were built on the unique com-

bination of effortless subsistence, efficient communications and transport. Prevailing winds blew couriers and cargo vessels up the Nile, the current brought them down. The engineers who built the pyramids did not have the wheel; as long as they stayed close to the river, they didn't need it.

To be galvanised, however, these ingredients needed a strong, centralised authority, precisely the effect achieved by the union of Upper and Lower Egypt in 3000 BC. The river enabled the government to shepherd far-flung resources: the Aswan granite quarries at one extreme; at the other, the Delta's under-employed *felaheen* or farmers.

Preceding pages: heavy feet at Abu Simbel; lips of Ramses II at Luxor temple; *felucca* sail; sail-cruising at Aswan; the Nile in Upper Egypt. **Left**, and **right**, welcome to the Nile.

The pieces were then in place to undertake the most monumental extravagance the world has ever seen. Standing as they do now without the temples and other structures which once surrounded them, the pyramids appear so outrageously pointless that John Greaves, a 17th-century Oxford mathematician and one of the first Europeans to have seen them since Roman times, felt obliged to give serious consideration to the various views put forward about some secret purpose. Common sense told him that they would have been insanely impractical as granaries, and he did not think much of the theory that one of the Giza pyramids was a monument to a popular prostitute from grateful clients.

All sorts of reasons for the construction of the pyramids are examined in a subsequent section of this book, but the fact is that they and later monuments of Egypt would have been inconceivable without the unprecedented social phenomenon of surplus wealth. That is not to say that a peasant wincing under the lash on some pyramid building site would not have cocked an eyebrow at the mention of surplus wealth. Herodotus said it: "Egypt is the gift of the Nile."

Egypt's fortunes subsequently waxed or waned depending on its ability to ensure that East-West trade passed through the hands of its tax collectors. Whenever Egypt's grip on the trade weakened, Baghdad grabbed it. Portuguese explorer Vasco da Gama's opening up of the African sea route to India was a devastating blow to Egypt's position; it was redressed in time, not without problems, by the Suez Canal.

The Nile ignored: The river which was largely responsible for putting all this into motion faded into the background as the limelight swept west. Once the greatest commercial centre in the world, Cairo became the forgotten outpost first of the bizarre Mamlukes, a self-appointed and self-perpetuating aristocracy of white slaves, and then of the Ottoman Empire.

Tourists in Egypt nowadays get very little help from their guides, or from most guidebooks, if they wish to lift the veil over the thousand years during which the Nile flowed through lands as closed then as Albania has been in modern times. Ironically, Albania produced the tobacconist who at the beginning of the 19th century was fished out of the Mediterranean by a British admiral bobbing about in a small boat. As Mohammed Ali, this man went on to found an Egyptian dynasty, invariably dubbed "The Last Pharaohs", which ended with the gluttonous Farouk choking in exile over an Italian meal with the last of a celebrated line of mistresses. This book consciously tries to fill those gaps of information.

Napoleon's mission: The veil over Egypt was lifted by Napoleon, who was as determined to seize Egypt from the Turks as Britain was determined that he should not. Napoleon sent scholars up the Nile with his army to establish what, if anything, had survived. They found the monuments half buried in sand, the temples taken over by squatters. The temple at Luxor (Thebes), the spectacular capital in pharaonic times, presented the most vivid evidence of how the sand had built up over centuries. The Arabs had built a mosque among the ruins at what was for them ground level. When the sand was cleared away, the mosque was suspended in space, as incongruous as a cow in a tree.

Renewed interest in the Nile, including thoughts of putting a dam across it, produced the absurd situation of engineers being asked to perform the task when no one could tell them about the source. Voyages of discovery had stumbled on places like America and Australia whose existence was only dimly suspected, but here was a river which was not only known but essential to men from practically the beginning of time.

Search for the source: Theories about the river's source abounded, from the obviously crackpot notion that the Nile flowed backwards from some sea, to one which got close to the truth. Ptolemy, the Graeco-Egyptian geographer, produced a map in the 2nd century AD which showed the river rising from two equatorial lakes watered by what he called the Mountains of the Moon.

The search for the source is brilliantly told by Alan Moorehead in his two volumes on the Nile and is treated at some length in this book. The Egyptians themselves certainly reached the confluence of the White and Blue Niles at what is now Khartoum, but until the middle of the 19th century no explorer setting out from Egypt got farther up the White Nile than Gondokoro, which is about half as far again from the Mediterranean. In every instance they ran into insuperable barriers: an oozing swamp on the White

Nile, cavernous torrents on the Blue. It was therefore a case of abandoning boats and walking. Amazingly, the mystery of the source was not absolutely sorted out until the Wright brothers – pioneers of aviation – were growing up, and even today it is possible to follow the Blue Nile back to its source only by air.

As Moorehead says, this was not exploration for the sake of adventure. "In these deserts the river was life itself. Had it failed to flow, even for one season, then all Egypt perished. Not to know where the stream came from, not to have any sort of guarantee that it would continue – this was to live in a state of insecurity where only fatalism or

Egypt feasts on the fruit of the Nile, but it is not Egypt's river alone. The most famous argument about the extent of the Nile is one which saw Speke shot dead before he could have it out with with friend and rival Burton. The matter should have been settled by Henry Morten Stanley, the pugnacious journalist who presumed that a tired-looking man wearing a blue cap and red waistcoat in the middle of Africa was Dr David Livingstone, but there are still those who argue that the two lakes from which the branches of the river demonstrably *do* flow do not take the issue back to its logical roots, the various streams which feed the lakes.

There may well be diehards who won't

superstition could reassure the mind."

When the facts become known, it emerged that for the purposes of comparison with the other great rivers, the White Nile deserves most of the credit in making the Nile as a whole the longest river at 4,150 miles (6,680 km), having chipped in about half. The Amazon is only just beaten but carries a very much larger volume of water. The Blue Nile, which is independently only about 1,000 miles (1,600 km) long, comes into its own during the flood, when it provides more than 80 per cent of the combined volume.

Above, enchanted by the Nile sunset.

give up until the Nile is traced back to clouds in the sky, in which case they may not be satisfied with a list which says the countries of the Nile are pre-eminently Egypt, Sudan, Ethiopia and Uganda. Also party to it in minor roles are Kenya, Tanzania, Zaire, Burundi and Rwanda. The river sustained people wherever it passed, but in a sense it was also divisive. Until comparatively recent times, there were no bridges across the Nile south of Cairo.

The course of the White: Leaving Lake Victoria, the White Nile first calls at Lake Albert and, fortified, makes a triumphant exit over the Murchison Falls. It is the area between the lakes which taxed, as may be seen in the next chapter, the likes of Speke and Grant and the most romantic couple who ever went exploring, the bewhiskered Sir Samuel Baker and his unflappable wife, lovely enough to put deplorable ideas into a tribal king's head and resolute enough to keep her fists clenched and eyes open even when unconscious.

Below the Murchison Falls, the White Nile becomes a stream of little green cabbages bobbing down 80 miles (50 km) of cataracts to Gondokoro. The cataracts made Gondokoro the last outpost of slave traders pushing south from central Sudan. It was a frightful place, a squalid collection of huts in the 19th century, but getting there felt like

tongue-in-cheek commissions by the "Last Pharaohs" to stamp out slavery. It is also where, at Fashoda in 1898, Britain and France were drawn into what would have been the stupidest of all their many wars. These topics, and others are all expanded in various sections of this book.

There is little left at Gondokoro or at Fashoda to remind travellers (who would still have to be dogged, if not so lucky) of these events, but memories are better served in Khartoum, which in the 19th century reminded an Italian of Milan. The town suffered at the hands of the Mahdi's followers but they left intact the palace from whose roof Gordon, shortly before his death, was

reaching safety for explorers struggling up from the south. Going south, Baker thought it the worst place imaginable; on the way back, he mounted an ox, ran up a flag and fired off a gun to celebrate his return.

It is possible nowadays to sail between Gondokoro and Khartoum, a channel having been cut through the cloggy weed of the Sudd, a swamp the size of France and the barrier which prevented all but the most dogged, and luckiest, travellers from getting south even to Gondokoro. This is the world in which first Baker and then General Sir Charles Gordon (pious soldier to some, brandy-and-soda addict to others) were given

firing down on them in his nightgown.

Gordon's murder was avenged at Omdurman by British troops led by Lord Kitchener and including the young Winston Churchill. They sailed down from Egypt in Nile paddle-steamers, requisitioned from Thomas Cook, a company which was successfully bringing up to date a tradition of luxurious Nile travel that dated back even beyond the voyage that had been laid on by Cleopatra for her "older man", Julius Caesar.

The course of the Blue: The Blue Nile arrives at Khartoum, now virtually at one with Omdurman, with the momentum built up during a descent of some 4,000 ft (1,200 metres) from the highlands of Ethiopia. The sharp drop over the comparatively short distance of 1,000 miles (1,600 km) has carved a gorge which is up to a mile deep. In places the gorge allows enough elbow room for human settlement, but this is an infernally hot, malarial option exercised only by people who feared the slave traders.

Nowhere in the heyday of Nile exploration was the Dark Continent darker than in the Ethiopia of the Blue Nile: "a wilder, more barbaric place," says Moorehead, "cannot be imagined." The stories brought back by explorer James Bruce after his visit in 1770 were simply not believed and it remains true now, as it was then, that the Blue Nile in

allowed their appetite for slaves and gold to take them. The place looks and feels African; the Egyptian imprint is left by 200 somewhat dilapidated pyramids around the now deserted ruins of Meroe.

In 1902, the building of the British Aswan Dam began the backwards encroachment of a new lake on the Kingdom of Nubia, and with the completion of the High Dam more than 60 years later the old kingdom had completely gone, its villages under 200 ft (60 metres) of water, the population removed to "New Nubia" in a desert region of the Nile.

Modern times: Convention puts the dawn of "Modern Egypt" at the beginning of the 19th century when the rusty shackles binding the

Ethiopia is no place for tourists. Given the almost unbroken state of civil war, the prospects are not much improved when, 470 miles (760 km) after testing its source at Lake Tana, the Blue Nile crosses into Sudan.

The first whiffs of Egyptian influence on the united Nile begin about 180 miles (290 km) downstream of Khartoum near Shendy, the old slave centre which was thriving when Burckhardt spent some time there in 1814. This was as far south as the northern invaders – Egyptians, Persians, Greeks and Romans –

Left, the prevailing wind means the *felucca* is still effective transport, even for tourists (above).

country to the Ottomans twisted and then snapped. As the century progressed, the Suez Canal was opened and the first paddle-steamer took to the Nile as a cruise ship. The Khedive Ismail was determined to give Egypt the trappings of a modern state and to a large extent he succeeded.

The history of the Nile, as opposed to Egypt, has its own turning point. The construction of the High Dam in the 1960s meant electricity in millions of houses. It also ended the annual inundation. The Nile farmer could flick on a television and sit back, but it was not long before he had to get up and queue for some modern fertiliser.

A large, ginger-haired Scot was standing on a mountain in Ethiopia in 1770 when he suddenly tore off his shoes and went bounding down the slope. He was twice thrown headlong but, undaunted, charged on until he was knee-deep in a small patch of swamp. "I stood in rapture…" – he had a very loud voice – "in that spot which had baffled the genius, industry and inquiry of both ancients and moderns, for the course of nearly three thousand years. Though a mere private Briton, I triumphed here in my own mind, over kings and their armies." James Bruce was exultant because he had discovered the source of the Nile, or so he thought.

Alas, says Alan Moorehead, whose two books on the Nile ought to be compulsory reading for anyone interested in the subject, "he was on the wrong river… He was even on the wrong part of the wrong river." Moreover, he was "utterly mistaken" in thinking that he was the first European to reach that particular spot.

Nevertheless, Bruce's expedition was a remarkable victory over considerable hurdles. To mention just two, he had been attacked by pirates before he even got to Africa and, shortly after setting out on land, he was given food for thought by warriors who showed him how they adorned the shafts of their spears with the testicles of intruders.

Only the race to the moon in modern times has mirrored the kind of excitement which was generated by the search for the source of the Nile. The objective of exploration was clearly defined but infuriatingly elusive. It was not simply a matter of sailing or even walking up the river until it stopped. The ancient Egyptians themselves as well as Persians, Greeks, Romans, Arabs, and sundry Europeans had all tried that, but they all ran into impenetrable barriers.

Before the aeroplane, the source could only be approached methodically from the other side, as it were, and even then it remained to be proved that a particular lake,

spring or indeed Bruce's little swamp was what ultimately flowed past the pyramids. Explorers who started from what they supposed to be the source were all too familiar with the sickening realisation that the river they were doggedly following was turning to go the wrong way. What they had pinned their hopes on as the Nile turned out to be the Congo, Niger or some other river. In the hundred years which followed Bruce's barefoot charge down the mountain, the source of the Nile became, in the celebrated phrase of

the historian Sir Harry Johnston, "the greatest geographical secret after the discovery of America."

Caught up in fierce competition, explorers could be very rude about one another. When it was brought to Bruce's attention that a Portuguese priest named Pedro Paez seemed to have beaten him to his swamp by 150 years, he made a snarling reference to "the lies of a grovelling fanatic". Later rivalry between Burton and Speke, as we shall see, had tragic consequences.

Bruce's mistakes: The Nile divides near Khartoum in the Sudan into the White Nile and Blue Nile, and Bruce's fundamental

Preceding pages: in search of the source (from the film *Mountains of the Moon*). **Left**, 1587 map illustrates the confusion over the river's route. **Right**, Scottish explorer James Bruce.

mistake was in thinking that the latter was the main river, the former merely a tributary. In fact, at the confluence, the White has already flowed for some 2,000 miles (3,200 km), the Blue for only about 500 (800 km). The mistake was easily made because when the Blue floods it builds up such momentum over the 6,000 ft (1,800 metres) descent from the Ethiopian highlands that it causes its more sedate partner to dam back on itself. The effect is discernible because, although not quite blue and white, the waters are distinctly coloured. At normal times of the year, the two streams flow shoulder to shoulder before blending for the remaining 1,750 miles (2,800 km) to the Mediterranean.

Bruce's audiences at home were, as always, curious about the weather. "I call it hot," he told them, "when a man sweats at rest and excessively on moderate motion. I call it very hot when a man with thin or little clothing sweats much, though at rest. I call it excessive hot when a man in his shirt, at rest, sweats excessively, when all motion is painful, and the knees feel feeble as if after a fever. I call it extreme hot when the strength fails, a disposition to faint comes on, a straitness is found round the temples, as if a small cord was drawn round the head, the voice impaired, the skin dry, and the head seems more than ordinary large and light. This, I apprehend, denotes death at hand…"

The cruel reward for Bruce's heroic efforts in such an unappealing climate was that many refused to believe him. They scoffed at the thought of tribesmen who wore rings in their lips rather than ears and smeared themselves with the blood of cows, and at clouds of tiny flies striking terror into animals and humans alike. Total disbelief was reserved for the practice of casually hacking slices of steak off living animals. The skin was pinned back over the wound, Bruce explained, and the beast was driven off to recover as best it could.

His gulping audiences then heard that, while others gorged themselves on raw meat and beer, amorous couples rolled around on the ground. Guests seated on either side of this activity might stretch out a piece of cloth as a screen but, he added, "they seem to think it a great a shame to make love in silence." Bruce assured audiences that "all this passes without remark or scandal, not a licentious word is uttered, nor the most distant joke

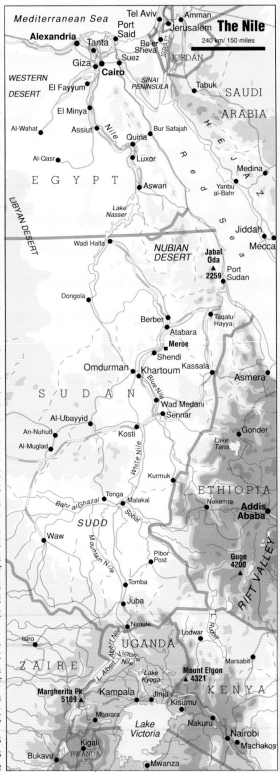

upon the transaction." Bruce did not easily tolerate disbelief of his stories. He lost patience with a fellow diner at a country house weekend who said no one would or could eat raw meat. Storming off to the kitchen, he returned with a slab of uncooked beef, sprinkled it with salt and pepper "in the Ethiopian manner", and rammed it into the sceptic's face. "You will either eat that, sir, or fight me!" The startled guest looked up at the towering figure and tucked in. "Now, sir," Bruce thundered as the last morsel went down, "you will never again say it is impossible." Nevertheless, the arguments went on for long after his death, the result of an accident reminiscent of his charge down the

had to rely on what contemporaries could tell him about the Nile, and he did not believe half their stories either. There were all sorts of theories, including the idea that the Nile flowed backwards from the sea, but the one he found least plausible was ironically closest to the truth, namely that "the Nile flows from melted snow". How could that be, he asked, since it flowed from places which were even hotter than Egypt? He thought it more likely that the sun sucked up water and deposited it on the catchment area. The least he could say was that the Nile entered Egypt "from parts beyond".

Other Greeks investigated, and the Roman Emperor Nero sent an expedition upriver,

mountain; he fell down the staircase of his mansion in Scotland, breaking his head.

In producing his five-volume *Travels to discover the Sources of the Nile, in the years 1768, 1769, 1770, 1772, and 1773, by James Bruce of Kinnaird Esq., FRS,* Bruce had few references to work from. The richest source of material, as had been the case for more than 2,000 years, was Herodotus, but on the source of the Nile even the "Father of History" was suspect.

Visiting Egypt in about 460 BC, Herodotus

Above, cattle-watching by the new Nile where it flows out of Lake Victoria at Jinja in Uganda.

but the hardest information was in a map produced by the geographer and astronomer Ptolemy in AD 150. Based on the work of the Syrian geographer Marinus of Tyre, the map showed the Nile rising from two great lakes in Central Africa which were fed by what he called the Mountains of the Moon.

The intellectuals who accompanied Napoleon's army to Egypt in 1798 managed to get as far as the cataracts at Aswan; they might have gone further because there are navigable stretches above the cataracts. The hopeless difficulties begin where the Sobat tributary joins the river near the town of Malakal in what is now the Sudan – the dreaded Sudd.

"This region is neither land nor water," says Moorehead of the Sudd. "Year by year the current keeps bringing down more floating vegetation, and packs it into solid chunks perhaps 20 ft thick and strong enough for an elephant to walk on. But then this debris breaks away in islands and forms again in another place, and this is repeated in a thousand indistinguishable patterns and goes on forever." The result is "a vast sea of papyrus ferns and rotting vegetation, and in that foetid heat there is a spawning tropical life that can hardly have altered very much since the beginning of the world; it is as primitive and as hostile to man as the Sargasso Sea."

The Blue Nile, it transpired, springs from the snows and monsoon rains which feed Lake Tana in the Ethiopian highlands. The river leaves the lake calmly and unobtrusively, gliding towards the Tisisat Falls 20 miles (32 km) away. There it explodes. Bucking and rearing at the narrow confines of the gorge below, the river begins a furious descent which over a million years has carved a gorge in places a mile (1.5 km) deep and 15 miles (24 km) wide. Tackling it by boat was, and is, out of the question. In a few places where the valley widens there may be the odd village, but they are cut off from one another by the impassable walls of the gorge. Even wild animals steer clear of the malarial torpor in the valley.

Eccentric explorers: The challenge of the Nile attracted some improbable characters. In 1812, Thomas Legh, a British Member of Parliament, went on holiday to Turkey with his friend, the Reverend Charles Smelt. An outbreak of plague drove them to Egypt and, once there, they felt they ought to look around. A slave whom they bought to help with chores as they explored the sites 100 miles south of Philae proved so efficient that they took him back to England. They also offered a passage to Donald Donald, a Scot they ran into, who had been taken prisoner by the Turks, enslaved, circumcised and converted to Islam. He declined the offer, saying he was quite content where and as he was.

Another outbreak of plague persuaded Legh and Smelt to postpone their departure and remain at Minia. They were consoled by girls, "notwithstanding their colour", but bored by life in the Turkish garrison. "When the antiquities that may exist in the neighbourhood have been examined, and any lo-cal interest ceases to amuse, nothing perhaps can be more melancholy than the prospect of a long residence in a Turkish town, where the absolute want of books, the frivolous conversation and the excessive ignorance of the natives, the daily smoking of tobacco and drinking of coffee, form the chief features of the torpid and listless existence to which a stranger is condemned."

The most puzzling acquaintance they made was a certain "Sheik Ibrahim", not least because he spoke perfect English with an upper-crust accent. The mystery was not solved until they returned to England, and established that he was really John Lewis Burckhardt, Swiss by birth but a product of Cambridge University. With a view to becoming an explorer, Burckhardt had read Arabic and toughened himself up by trudging around the English countryside in bare feet, sleeping rough and living exclusively on vegetables and water.

Burckhardt managed to attach himself to an organisation calling itself the Association for Promoting the Discovery of the Interior Parts of Africa. Growing a heavy beard, he first assumed the identity of "an Indian Muhammadan merchant" and then changed to Sheikh Ibrahim ibn Abdullah, an authority on Islamic law. To prove that he had perfected Arabic, he produced a translation of *Robinson Crusoe*.

He spent eight years on the Nile as a solitary nomad, observing tribes like the Shaiqiya, a mysterious people who appeared to be neither Nubian nor Arab and in some respects resembled the Mamlukes. He encountered the few Mamlukes who survived the Battle of the Pyramids against Napoleon's army and the subsequent massacre by Mohammed Ali. They had been able to maintain a luxurious standard of living by systematically plundering villages. Burckhardt found a colony of Mamluke fugitives living on river rafts, their slaves keeping the overhead awnings cool with buckets of water.

For all his preparations in Cambridge, Burckhardt's health could not long withstand the 10 hours per day he forced himself to march. Nevertheless, he entered parts of the Sudan which few, if any, Europeans had seen. One of these was Shendy, known as "The Gates" and a legendary staging post for caravans and pilgrims arriving from as far west as Timbuktu on the way to the Red Sea.

Burckhardt kept a record of Shendy's thriving slave market. About 5,000 slaves were traded each year. Most were under 15 years of age, the boys fetching $15 each and the girls $25. Of the girls, Ethiopians were prized "for their beauty, and for the warmth and constancy of their affection." All boys were circumcised and given Arab names but, in spite of the greatly enhanced value of eunuchs, the Muslims themselves disliked performing the mutilation. If it had to be done – as when Mohammed Ali placed an order for 200 eunuchs whom he wished to give away as presents – the job was passed on to a couple of Christian Coptic priests. It was a rare trader who did not sleep with the girls

typical: "Almost too much was contained here in one man." He was not especially tall – about 5' 11" (1.8 metres) – but he looked and was immensely strong, a brilliant swordsman who did not need even a sword to put down single-handed a mutiny on a ship in which he happened to be a passenger. He had, as the poet Swinburne remarked, the brow of a god and the jaw of a devil, together with an enormous moustache and, most riveting of all, "questing panther eyes".

His erudition was beyond belief; he was an authority on anthropology, history, geography, botany, geology, meteorology, economics and, somewhat notoriously, erotica. He wrote and spoke well over 30 languages and

who passed through his hands.

Burckhardt died in Egypt of dysentery when he was only 33. His letters and notes were published and, in lifting the lid on places like Shendy, stirred the anti-slavery sentiments which gave greater impetus to the big guns of Nile exploration like Burton, Speke, Baker, Livingstone and Stanley.

Burton and Speke: In everything that has been written about Richard Francis Burton, the reader can sense the author taking a deep breath before plunging in. Moorehead is

Above, Burton and Speke, as portrayed in the film *Mountains of the Moon*.

reckoned he could master any new one in six weeks. Not content with obscure languages most people had never heard of, he lived with a troop of monkeys to compile a kind of monkey dictionary.

John Hanning Speke, whose name in the context of the Nile is usually mentioned in the same breath as Burton's, was very different. He was six years younger, tall, fair and elegant. He was passionately fond of hunting, practically the only subject in which Burton could not work up any interest. Although by no means prudish, Speke hardly drank, never smoked, and would never have followed Burton's example of painting his face and wearing disguise in order to examine Karachi low-life.

They were both in the British Indian Army but met by chance in Aden. Burton was passing through on his way to explore Abyssinia and Speke at once changed his plans to go with him. They were lucky to survive the experience. Their camp was rushed by Somali tribesmen at the dead of night, one of their party was killed instantly, but Burton fought like a tiger in spite of massive injuries to his jaw. Speke was first stabbed in the arms and legs and then transfixed with a spear. In the melee he was dragged away unconscious, miraculously to escape certain execution and catch up with Burton some

time later. Both recovered from appalling wounds to volunteer for service in the Crimea and, when that war was over, they put their minds to finding the source of the Nile.

Knowing the futility of trying to sail or walk up the river to its source, they elected to start in Zanzibar and cut across Africa in search of snow-capped mountains, lakes or anything else that might look like a good bet. They travelled in caravan behind a guide in ceremonial headdress and beneath the red flag of the Sultan of Zanzibar. When struck by malaria, as they frequently were, they travelled in hammocks.

Eight months on, the caravan drew up on the shores of Lake Tanganyika. Burton surmised that any river flowing north from the lake could well be the Nile. Travelling in two canoes, they found a river but it flowed into the lake, not out of it, and in any case at 2,535 ft (770 metres) above sea level they were lower than known levels of the Nile elsewhere. They paused to reconsider their position. Burton was not feeling well and anyhow wanted to write up his notes. It was agreed that Speke, just recovered from a bout of ophthalmia which had virtually blinded him, should go ahead to look into reports of a larger lake some three weeks to the north.

The great disagreement: The lake Speke found was the fulfilment of his dreams. "I no longer felt any doubt," he later wrote, "that the lake at my feet gave birth of that interesting river, the source of which has been the subject of so much speculation, and the object of so many explorers." He hurried back to Burton and found him still nursing an ulcerated jaw. Burton was singularly unmoved. According to him, "we had scarcely breakfasted before (Speke) announced to me the startling fact that he had discovered the sources of the White Nile… The fortunate discoverer's conviction was strong; his reasons were weak…"

Speke could not prove that the lake was the source, and until he did so Burton was sticking to his equally unproven theory that the Nile sprang from the Mountains of the Moon, wherever they might be. The most he was prepared to concede was that Speke's lake, which they agreed to call Lake Victoria, flowed into the Upper Nile. As it was one article of faith pitched against another, they agreed to drop the subject for the time being. They undertook the long trek back to the Indian Ocean on reasonably friendly terms. Burton had a few things to do in Zanzibar so Speke took an earlier passage back to England, the agreement being (Burton said) that he would make no reference to their findings in Africa until Burton rejoined him.

In the event, Speke immediately told the Royal Geographical Society that he believed he had found the source. The news caused a sensation. Money was made available so that without delay he could lead another expedition to confirm his findings, and he was well-advanced in planning the expedition, with no role for Burton, when the latter returned. He was lean, haggard – and ignored. No one was terribly interested in his carefully compiled report on Lake Tanganyika or his objections to Speke's claim. His place on Speke's next expedition would be taken by another Indian Army officer, Captain James Grant.

Speke and Grant took a year over the journey inland from Zanzibar, spending a month with a convivial king whose fat wives were turned one way and another so that Speke could measure their impressive dimensions with a tape. When it was time to go they were advised that the country ahead was in a state of civil war and that it would be necessary to receive permission to progress from a King Mutesa whose court was a six-week walk away. While Speke went ahead to

nest, caught a trout, or done any other boyish trick… There appeared no curiosity to know what individual human being the urchin had deprived of life." The king reciprocated with gifts of young girls whom Speke passed on to his porters as wives. To complete the picture, the mother of the queen was an alcoholic who drank on all fours from a trough of beer.

Search for Speke: Mutesa withheld permission to proceed for nearly five months, a delay which prompted Sir Roderick Murchison at the Royal Geographic Society in London to get in touch with Samuel Baker, then big-game hunting in the Sudan, to ask him to search for Speke and Grant. Baker has been characterised by Moorehead as "almost

negotiate, Grant, who had hurt his leg, remained with the king and his fat wives.

Etiquette at the court of King Mutesa was unpredictable. Speke was required to shoot four cows to prove that his presents of pistols actually worked. A rifle required more stringent testing. The king handed it to a boy and told him to find some man to try it on: "which was no sooner accomplished than the little urchin returned to announce his success, with a look of glee such as one would see in the face of a boy who had robbed a bird's

Left, the unpredictable King Mutesa. **Above**, Mutesa's capital, Buganda.

a caricature of the professional Victorian, the solid, whiskered clubman-figure who is absolutely fixed in his habits and his loyalties, but equally determined to enjoy himself." He was certainly enjoying himself in the Sudan with his much younger, Hungarian-born second wife and with provisions supplied by Fortnum & Mason of Piccadilly, but when the call came, he responded.

In the meantime, Speke and Grant went off to investigate reports they had picked up at Mutesa's court of a large river flowing north from Lake Victoria. If true, it would lend considerable weight to Speke's theory. With his bad leg, Grant could not keep up with the impatient pace of the march and agreed that Speke should again go ahead. On 21 July 1862, Speke was finally convinced by the discovery of a broad river about 40 miles north of the lake. It was, he wrote, "the very perfection of the kind of effect aimed at in a highly developed park, with a magnificent stream, 600 to 700 yards wide, dotted with islets and rocks..." The countryside abounded in crocodiles, hippopotamuses and herds of hartebeest. He told his porters that they were looking at the very cradle of Moses and ought to shave their heads and bathe in it. They reminded him that they were Muslims.

It was still necessary to establish that the river in question did indeed flow from the lake. Marching upstream for a week, Speke was at last satisfied. The river made a spectacular exit, rushing out of the lake over what Speke named the Ripon Falls after an earlier president of the Royal Geographical Society. "It was a sight that attracted one for hours," he wrote. "The roar of the waters, the thousands of passenger-fish leaping at the falls with all their might; the Wasoga and Waganda fishermen coming out in boats and taking post on all the rocks..."

Instead of going back the way they had come, Speke's plan was to head directly north, which meant they would leave the meandering course of the river from time to time. They would pick it up again to meet a boat which by prearrangement had been sent south from Khartoum to await them, always assuming they were still alive. The rendezvous had to be vague because the proposed route through what is now Uganda was uncharted territory.

More than two years after their departure from Zanzibar, Speke and Grant heard welcoming rifle shots and the sound of a drum and fife band. On the strength of rumours of two white men in the vicinity, a column of Egyptian and Nubian soldiers in Turkish uniform had come out to meet them. Speke's priority was to get a cable to London: "Inform Sir Roderick Murchison," it said, "that all is well, that we are in latitude 14'30" upon the Nile, and that the Nile is settled."

At Gondokoro, he ran into Baker and his wife preparing themselves for their rescue mission. Baker was disappointed to call it off, and even more so when Speke said he had positively identified the source. Think-

ing that Speke and Grant might be dead, he had been nursing that ambition himself. Speke confided, however, there might be a second source, a large lake known locally as Luta Nzige, and he gave Baker a map of their route. Baker immediately began to recruit porters who were willing to run the risk of a war raging along the proposed route.

Tragic debate: Speke and Grant returned to a rapturous reception in England. Speke addressed a capacity audience at the Royal Geographical Society, was widely interviewed by the newspapers and rushed his preliminary findings into print. Burton disputed his discoveries, but was willing to concede, as before, that the Nile flowed from Lake Victoria. He pointed out that Speke had not circumnavigated the lake to find out whether it was itself fed by a river, in which case the source of the Nile lay wherever that river originated; that there was another river, Burton was sure, and of course that it would flow from his Mountains of the Moon.

Burton's objections had some supporters, one of whom was Dr David Livingstone. "Poor Speke," the doctor wrote, "has turned his back upon the real sources of the Nile." Others joined the Burton bandwagon, one reviewer in particular tearing into Speke's account of his journey. The careful measuring of the fat wives, he said, was disgusting, not what Speke called "engineering". "We believe none of our readers ever met with or ever heard of such a piece of 'engineering' as this, and we dare say will never wish to meet with such another."

The acrimony built up over a solid year. An announcement that Burton and Speke would appear on the same platform at a meeting of the British Association for the Advancement of Science in Bath stirred the sort of excitement associated with prize fights, Burton having earlier said, for example, that "I don't wish to have any further private or indirect communication with Speke".

Several hundred geographers and scientists gathered in Bath for the debate which was due to start at 2 p.m. on 16 September 1864. Burton himself recorded what happened on the day: "Early in the forenoon fixed for what silly tongues called the 'Nile Duel' I found a large assembly in the rooms of Section E (Geography and Ethnography). A note was handed round in silence. Presently my friend Mr Findlay broke the tidings to me. Captain Speke had lost his life on the yesterday, at 4 p.m., whilst shooting over a cousin's grounds. He had been missed in the field and his kinsman found him lying upon the earth, shot through the body close to the heart. He lived only a few minutes and his last words were a request not to be moved."

According to those present, however, Burton did not receive the news as stoically as his account suggests. He staggered visibly about the platform and sank into a chair "with his face working". He was heard to moan "By God, he's killed himself!" But he managed to pull himself together long enough to deliver a hastily-substituted paper on Dahomey. On getting home, his wife said, "he

them and rampant malaria, but they were suspected wherever they went of being slave traders, although matters improved when Baker started wearing a tweed suit. In African eyes he now resembled Speke, and him they trusted.

The suit worked wonders. "I climbed up a high and almost perpendicular rock that formed a natural pinnacle on the face of the cliff, and waving my cap to the crowd on the opposite side I looked almost as imposing as Nelson in Trafalgar Square... Upon landing through the high reeds, they immediately recognised the similarity of my beard and general complexion to that of Speke, and their welcome was at once displayed by the

wept long and bitterly". All she could make out was the same word repeated over and over again: "Jack".

Baker's progress: Deep in the heart of Africa, Baker and his wife did not hear of Speke's death, which was officially "accidental", the coroner allowing the possibility that Speke was standing on a low wall when he lost his balance and, in falling, discharged the gun.

Conditions were worse than they feared. Not only was there a war swirling around

Above left, John Speke. **Above right**, Richard Burton, a partnership that ended in tragedy.

most extravagant dancing and gesticulating with lances and shields, as though intending to attack, rushing at me with the points of their lances thrust close to my face, and shouting and singing in great excitement."

Mrs Baker's waist-length blonde hair was as mesmerising as her husband's tweed suit. Tribesmen brought their families to watch when she washed it, and it gave the trigger-happy King Mutesa ideas. The king had stubbornly refused to supply porters as long as he had reason to believe that Baker, who had already given him shotguns, beads, carpets and so forth, had more presents up his sleeve. "We shall be nailed for another year in this abominable country," Baker despaired, "ill with fever, and without medicine, clothes or supplies." Thus Mutesa one day appeared to have had a complete change of heart, Baker could have his team of porters and proceed. Moreover, he wanted him to take an attractive virgin for company. The quid pro quo was simply that the king should have Mrs Baker.

Baker drew his pistol and, holding it at the king's chest, threatened to shoot him there and then. Mrs Baker, admired by her husband above all because "she was not a screamer", was dreadfully ill with malaria, but on learning of the king's proposition she rose from her sick-bed and "withered him

"with teeth and hands firmly clenched, and her eyes open, but fixed."

Mrs Baker was unconscious for three days; when she came round, she was off her head. Baker nursed her for a week – "a little wild honey and a guineafowl or two" – before he, too, collapsed. When he recovered some hours later so had she; she could at least recognise him. They recuperated for two days and pressed on. On 13 March 1864 their guide promised that on the following day they would see beneath them the lake that Speke had sent them in search of.

Baker had promised to allow himself three cheers on reaching the lake but in the event he was dumbstruck. "I led the way, grasping

with an outburst of furious indignation." Faced with the combined wrath of the Bakers, the king dropped the idea. Porters and a guide – but no attractive virgin – materialised the following day.

Never would Mrs Baker's ability to suppress a scream be more tested than in the days which followed. Crossing a stretch which was half-river and half-swamp, Baker looked back and was horrified to see her "sinking gradually through the weeds, while her face was distorted and perfectly purple. Almost as soon as I perceived her, she fell, as though shot dead." It took eight or ten men to drag her to safety. She was apparently dead

a stout bamboo. My wife in extreme weakness tottered down the pass, supporting herself upon my shoulder, and stopping to rest every twenty paces... A walk of about a mile through flat sandy meadows of fine turf interspersed with trees and bush, brought us to the water's edge. The waves were rolling upon a white pebbly beach: I rushed into the lake, and thirsty with heat and fatigue, with a heart full of gratitude, I drank deeply from the Sources of the Nile." He named it Lake Albert, after Queen Victoria's consort.

Next to him, Mrs Baker stood "pale and exhausted – a wreck upon the shores of the great Albert lake that we had so long striven to reach. No European foot had ever trod upon its sand, nor had the eyes of a white man ever scanned its vast expanse of water. We were the first and this was the key to the great secret that even Julius Caesar yearned to unravel, but in vain."

It took them two months to return to King Mutesa and, in case he had dreamt up some other evil in their absence, Baker thought it prudent to put on a show of force. Off came the tweed suit; on went a kilt, sporran and Glengarry bonnet. Their arrival produced a bizarre twist: the "king" was actually some-one else; the man with designs on Mrs Baker was merely a stand-in who had been given the job as long as suspicion remained that the Bakers were, after all, slave traders bent on capturing the king.

The Bakers returned to Gondokoro after an absence of two years. They rode into town on oxen with guns firing and a Union Jack fluttering – but there was no one to meet them. They had long been presumed dead. A warmer welcome awaited them in Khartoum, but it was not until reaching Cairo that Baker was able to realise a dream that had haunted him for the past five years he had been in Africa: a decent glass of Allsopp's pale ale.

On the voyage back to England he wondered whether it had all been a dream, but "a witness sat before me; a face still young, but bronzed like an Arab by years of exposure to a burning sun; haggard and worn with toil and sickness, and shaded with cares, happily now past; the devoted companion of my pilgrimage, to whom I owed success and life – my wife." Before even reaching England, he was awarded the Geographical Society's gold star and a knighthood soon followed. Officially he became Sir Samuel Baker; to the public "Baker of the Nile".

Dr Livingstone: Baker's discovery of Lake Albert actually confused the issue of the true source of the Nile. Were the lakes Albert and Victoria in any way connected? On 22 May 1865, Sir Roderick Murchison ended a eu-logy of Speke with the announcement that the Society had resolved to clear matters up once and for all. The man they had chosen for the job was a 52-year-old missionary, Dr David Livingstone.

Livingstone said that he did not really want to go back to Africa. He had gone out as a medical missionary 22 years earlier and carried out prodigious exploration in the southern and central regions. On the other hand and for all the fame his books had given him, he felt no compulsion to remain in Britain. Both his wife and eldest son were dead; the younger children were taken care of. He was physically fit with only occasional bouts of stiffness in the shoulder where on a previous expedition he had been attacked by a lion.

The invitation from the Society had the appeal, perhaps, of the old dog prevailed upon to show the youngsters a few tricks.

Personal considerations apart, the trip would give him another opportunity to advance his crusade against slavery. On the specific matter of the source of the Nile, he had liked Speke as a person more than Burton but, like Burton, he leaned towards Herodotus and the theory of the river rising from fountains at the bottom of high mountains.

Like many of the other explorers before him, Livingstone chose to start from Zanzi-bar and planned to travel through unexplored country below Lake Tanganyika, south of the usual caravan routes. "Never can there have been a journey which was founded upon so many misassumptions as this one,"

Left, Samuel Baker and Mrs Baker on the move. **Right**, Baker dressed as a pasha.

says Moorehead. "It was a search for the source of a river in a region where it did not exist; it was an anti-slavery expedition that had no power whatever to put down slavery; it was the march of a man who believed that he alone, unarmed and unsupported, could pass through Africa, and that was almost impossible." One way or another, Moorehead concludes, "it is astonishing that he did not die much sooner."

Three years down the line, most of Livingstone's teeth had fallen out, he had contracted malaria which could not be treated because he had lost all his medicines, and nearly all his men and animals, and he had achieved next to nothing. A river he reached after incredible hardships was not the Nile but the Congo.

"The impression of being in Hell" destroyed Livingstone's will to continue. He was reduced to begging for food, his only comfort was the Bible, which he read over and over again. He was in these desperate straits when one of his porters "came running at the top of his speed and gasped out, 'An Englishman! I see him!'"

Famous moment: The visitor himself should now be allowed to take up the story. "As I advanced slowly towards (Livingstone) I noticed he was pale, looked wearied, had grey whiskers and moustache, wore a bluish cap with a faded gold band around it, had on a red-sleeved waistcoat, and a pair of grey tweed trousers. I would have run to him, only I was a coward in the presence of such a mob – would have embraced him, but that I did not know how he would receive me. So I did what moral cowardice and false pride suggested was the best thing – walked deliberately up to him, took off my hat, and said, 'Dr Livingstone, I presume?' 'Yes,' he said, with a kind smile, lifting his cap slightly."

The background to this famous meeting was a journalistic assignment. Henry Morten Stanley, the English-born *New York Herald*'s man in Paris, had been assigned to cover the opening of the Suez Canal in 1869 and to write a piece on Nile cruises such as would interest American tourists. He was then to proceed to Jerusalem, Constantinople, the Crimea, the Caspian Sea, Persia and India. Only after all this should he think of "looking around for Livingstone", whom most people had by now given up for dead. This he duly did.

Having been rescued, it did not occur to Livingstone to turn back home. Instead, the two of them went off to investigate a few ideas that Livingstone had concerning the source of the Nile. This involved a walk of some 600 miles (960 km). Only then did Stanley seem to feel the pressure of a deadline and go home.

Livingstone had to wait several months for the reinforcements which Stanley had promised to arrange at the coast. Within days of their arrival, however, he was on the go again, now hoping to establish that the source of the Nile was a stream which ran into Lake Bangweolo.

Eight months into his investigations, Livingstone began to fear that the river concerned was again the Congo, not the Nile. He did not have to live long with the doubt: on 1 May 1873 his boys entered his hut. Apparently kneeling across his bed in prayer, Livingstone was dead.

Final proof: On learning of Livingstone's death, Stanley resolved to settle the issue of the Nile source personally.

Africa had never seen anything quite like the expedition he put together: 365 men, 8 tons of stores and a steel boat which came apart in sections. It was conducted like a military campaign. The column did not pause for casualties, and there were many of those. Any hint of African opposition was put down with force. The boat was assembled and lowered into the water as soon as they reached Lake Victoria. After a voyage of 1,000 miles (1,600 km) lasting 57 days, Stanley had conclusive proof that the lake had only one outlet, Ripon Falls.

There were still a few loose ends to attend to, but for all practical purposes the argument was eventually over and it remained only to award the garland to the solver of the great geographical secret. "Speke," Stanley wrote, "has now the full glory of having discovered the largest inland sea on the continent of Africa, also its principal affluent as well as its outlet. He also understood the geography of the countries we travelled through better than any of those who so persistently opposed his hypothesis…"

Unfortunately for Speke himself, this recognition was posthumous.

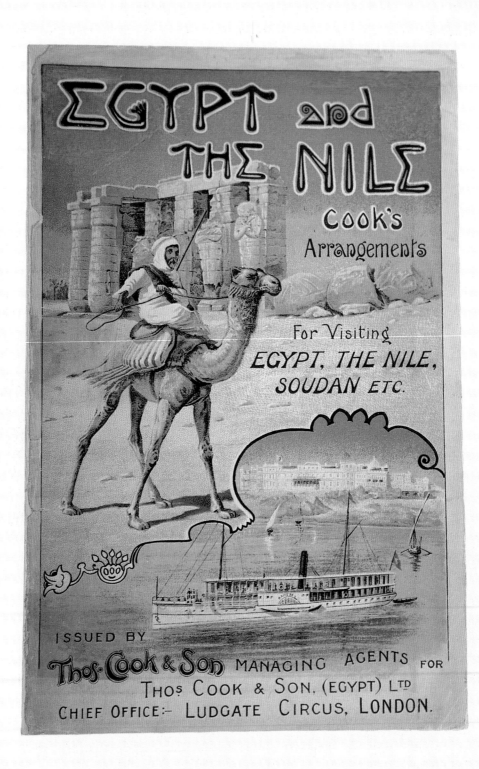

EGYPT and THE NILE

Cook's Arrangements

For Visiting
EGYPT, THE NILE,
SOUDAN ETC.

ISSUED BY
Thos. Cook & Son MANAGING AGENTS FOR
Thos. Cook & Son. (EGYPT) Ltd
CHIEF OFFICE:- LUDGATE CIRCUS, LONDON.

Thomas Cook, a somewhat strait-laced printer from Leicester in England who went into tourism in the 1840s as a means of diverting people away from drunken idleness, recognised in 1869 that by far the best way to see the sites of Egypt was by boat. It was only along the river that Egypt had ever been really habitable, and where everything was built. Ordinary houses depended on bricks made out of Nile mud. The pyramids and temples used limestone and granite, and hauling the huge blocks over desert sand did not bear thinking about.

The Great Pyramid of Cheops had in fact been in existence for more than 1,000 years before Egyptians were introduced to refinements in land transport. The chariots of the invading Hyksos in about 1600 BC demonstrated the possibilities of the wheel, an invention which the Egyptians had taken only as far as the potter's wheel.

Even so, the wheel had its limitations. To stray from the Nile was to enter a formidable desert better suited to horses. The camel, curiously, was either a much later import from Asia or not highly rated. In general, then, the Egyptians still concentrated on boats, not land transport. They built canals – notably at Suez – not roads. If they wanted to see more of the country, and Thomas Cook hoped they would, it would best be from a boat.

The Egyptian nobility had always treated themselves to grand river craft; lesser beings travelled more modestly. The modern cruise ship is in the tradition of the former, the ubiquitous *felucca* of the latter. It is still possible to hire a *felucca,* an Italian term applied loosely to any kind of pleasure boat, and explore the Nile independently, but to do so is to miss out on the grander scale of things. The Nile has its famous hotels in Cairo, Luxor and Aswan, but long stretches of the river remain as they always have been.

Cruisers: Perhaps inspired by the example of Gustave Flaubert in 1850, the novelist William Golding tried an independent cruise

in present times and ended up writing a bad-tempered book about the experience. His crew were forever jumping ship to look up relatives, and his skipper was argumentative about where they should moor.

Flaubert and Maxime du Camp, the photographer, went as far as Wadi Halfa, although they were as interested in brothels as in ancient monuments. Flaubert was particularly struck by a certain Kuchiouk Hanem: "a regal-looking creature, large-breasted, fleshy, with slit nostrils, enormous eyes, and mag-

nificent knees; when she danced there were formidable folds of flesh on her stomach." Both caught venereal diseases.

Thomas Cook, a militant abstainer, would not have approved. In his eyes, the secret of a good holiday was the absence of haggling over prices. He therefore charged his clients a lump sum for passage, accommodation, board, the services of a guide and so forth. Naturally, he made no provision for alcoholic drinks, a policy seemingly set in stone for packaged holidays ever after.

Cook introduced the paddle-steamer, romantic in retrospect (with no small thanks to Agatha Christie's *Death on the Nile*) but at the time scorned by traditionalists who preferred the elegant *dahabiyya*, an Arab sailing vessel. Napoleon commandeered *dahabiyyas* for his Nile expedition and named his flagship *L'Italie*. Nearly a century on, Lord Kitchener commandeered Cook's paddle steamers for his expedition to avenge the murder of General Gordon in Khartoum.

Amelia Edwards's *A Thousand Miles up the Nile* did for the *dahabiyya* what *Death on the Nile* later did for the paddle-steamer. The redoubtable Miss Edwards joined a Miss Marianne Brocklehurst and nephew Alfred of Macclesfield, Cheshire, for her voyage to Abu Simbel, the two parties travelling in their separate boats. They made leisurely

applying plaster to take a cast. These were touched up with coffee, "gallons a day".

Books like hers caught the popular imagination and soon hundreds of *dahabiyyas* were plying for trade on the Cairo waterfront: "boats with six cabins and boats with eight; boats provided with canteen, and boats without; boats that can pass the cataract and boats that can't; boats that are only twice as dear as they ought to be." Miss Edwards ploughed back the royalties from her book into the Egypt Exploration Society and an Egyptology chair at Cambridge University.

Modern style: The present type of cruiseship was introduced in 1959. There are now around 200 large vessels in operation. Some

progress, pausing to collect innumerable objects and to allow Alfred to pursue his futile dream of bagging a crocodile. "Too clever for him," Miss Edwards remarked.

The two spinsters managed to acquire a mummy, but even stuffing it into a tight locker could not contain the smell. Worried about being caught in illegal possession, they gave up after a week and tipped "the dear departed" over the side. At Abu Simbel Miss Edwards cleaned the faces of the statues of Ramses II, "one of the handsomest men not only of his own day but of all history." The noble features had acquired unsightly white spots as the result of an artist

cabins may be small bordering on claustrophobic, but in general the standards of accommodation, food and entertainment are reliable. Most have swimming pools, and the bar staff cheerfully go without sleep for as long as passengers are likely to be in need of their attention.

The short cruise between Aswan and Luxor takes three days, often with extra days tacked on at either end. It would be a criminal waste to allow fewer than three days for Luxor (Thebes), both for its own attractions and as the starting point for day-trips to, among others, the Valley of the Kings and Hatshepsut's temple at Deir el Bahri, as well as the "modern" village of Quornah, home to the shifty Rassul family. Seven-day cruises continue as far north as Nag Hammadi; in summer, others go all the way between Aswan and Cairo, in which case it is possible to visit Tel el Amarna, the setting for the extraordinary tale of the heretical pharaoh Akhenaten, the most famous face in Egyptian history, Nefertiti, and the strange beginnings of Tutankhamun.

Travel in a cruise ship is as self-sufficient as passengers want it to be. The ships always moor at night and all meals may be had on board, but by Western standards Egypt is cheap and the additional cost of trying out places ashore is unlikely to hurt. In any case,

ploring ancient Thebes, and the ghosts of men like Howard Carter still hover in the bar.

The Cataract in Aswan has a glorious view from its eyrie on a granite bluff. It opened in 1899 and was immediately so popular that overflow guests had to be put up in tents. The showpiece was and is the dining room, the ceiling rising in four sweeping arches in the style of Mamluke architecture to form a 75-ft (22-metre) dome. Both the Winter Palace and the Cataract have splendid gardens.

Most sadly missed of Egypt's historic hotels is Shepheard's in Cairo with its famous terrace and a ballroom modelled on the pillars of Karnak. A guest once wrote that "even the lavatories have something monumental

romantics would certainly wish to relive the age of the *dahabiyya* when well-heeled passengers decamped to hotels like the Winter Palace and the Cataract.

Grand tourism: The Winter Palace on the waterfront at Luxor was opened in 1905 and became almost as famous as any landmark in the city. In addition to an unbroken stream of suitably qualified guests in the royal suite – in their present absence, a quiet word with the manager may produce the key – the hotel was the headquarters for archaeologists ex-

Left, solar boat in the tomb of Ramses I. **Above**, *Rameses*, one of the first Nile paddle steamers.

about them…you feel as if you were sitting in the central chamber inside a pyramid." It was destroyed during riots in 1951: the mob ripped down curtains and smashed furniture to make a bonfire; the coloured glass dome of the Moorish Hall crashed in flames, and two members of an Italian opera company tore out in their underwear clutching their jewellery. A woman died when flames forced her to jump from the fourth floor. The present hotel bearing the name is a state-owned operation on a different site.

The cruise-ship deckchair between excursions ashore is a fitting place to reflect on such facts as that sailing is never easier than on the Nile. The prevailing wind blows a craft upstream, the current brings it back. Ancient Egypt did not need the wheel to enjoy efficient transport and communications. These two elements, added to the agricultural windfall provided by the annual inundation, were the key to the creation in 3000 BC of the kind of nation-state that was still suffering teething troubles in 19th century Europe.

Transport: In those days navigation on the Nile was efficient but not foolproof. Barges drifting down from Aswan with granite blocks for the pyramids dragged a sizeable stone from the stern to keep them pointing in the right direction, and broad, upturned prows

brought down as passengers but then faced the prospect of a long walk home.

Thor Heyerdahl of *Kon-Tiki* fame set out to demonstrate that the papyrus raft which was the starting point for Nile craft (the baby Moses occupied a tiny version in the bulrushes) could have been developed into an ocean-going vessel capable of reaching places like Ceylon, a voyage mentioned in Pliny. Heyerdahl's first experiment in the Mediterranean failed when *Ra I* became waterlogged, but in *Ra II* the next year, 1970, he was halfway across the Atlantic before the bindings holding the papyrus together came apart.

Heyerdahl had copied the design from ancient drawings, collected papyrus reeds

evolved to simplify dislodging after inevitable groundings on sandbanks. Sails, originally square but later "latteen", or triangular, under Arab influence (the *nuggar* boats of the Sudan stick to a compromise), had to be disproportionately large or at least set high to catch wind passing above the shelter of high banks. A stiff breeze made them a handful.

The Nile was always a better waterway than, say, the Euphrates. The craft used in ancient times were made of hides stretched across wooden frames, rather like the British coracle. They drifted down to Babylon where they were dismantled, the pieces were transferred to the backs of asses which had been

from Lake Tana (the Ethiopian source of the Blue Nile) and brought in craftsmen from Lake Chad to put the boat together by traditional means. The voyages were not totally successful but he felt he had proved the point. Some experts argue that Heyerdahl set his sights unnecessarily high and that wood, more plentiful in ancient Egypt than at present, would have made up a significant content of craft which nevertheless retained the old, "papyriform" shape.

The early passenger boats on the Nile had a cabin which left enough room on either side for oarsmen. The first sails resembled venetian blinds made of papyrus, but suitable materials were not long coming and sails became works of art painted in rich colours – checks, stripes and flower patterns – and embroidered with the emblem of the soul of the king.

To judge from the amount of deck-scrubbing going on in tomb paintings, a premium was put on cleanliness. Another curiously recurring feature of these paintings is the ship's boy in the process of being thrashed. This could almost be construed as an early form of advertising, a reassurance to passengers that no stone would be left unturned in the interest of their comfort, and that comfort would certainly not be compromised by an inept or lazy crew.

ens, and hence the potentially misleading term "solar boats" – nothing to do with solar energy. No example of the boats known to have been buried with the pharaohs was found until 1954 when the young Egyptologist Kamal el-Mallakh cleared away rubble on the south side of the Great Pyramid at Giza and found the entrance to what proved to be an air-tight boat chamber. On prising it open he was struck by a blast of hot air. "I closed my eyes and I smelt incense," he wrote, "I smelt time... I smelt centuries... I smelt history itself." For the first time in 4,800 years, sunlight broke the darkness of the pit and revealed first the tip of a steering oar and then the magnificent prow.

The boats in most common use were the one-man papyrus canoes used for fishing and fowling (the latter with a throwing stick resembling the boomerang but with the important difference that it did not come back) and "white-water" sport over the cataracts. However, they were not all so small: ships used by the military or for cargo attained lengths of more than 400 ft (120 metres).

The solar boat: The royal boats were in a class of their own, symbolic of the boat which took the sun-god Ra across the heav-

The sealing of the chamber had worked so well that the wood looked "fresh and new". The boat, however, was largely in kit form, 1,224 pieces of wood carefully stacked in 13 layers together with rigging, baskets, matting and all the other accessories. What was singularly lacking, though, were instructions on how to put the thing together. It took several false starts and 10 years to work out the puzzle, and the solution may now be admired in the purpose-built museum at the foot of the Great Pyramid.

Unfortunately, the museum is in the path of heat waves bouncing off the pyramid, and to make matters worse the modern air-conditioning system is quite unequal to what the ancients achieved with slabs of limestone weighing 16 tons each and sealed with gypsum plaster.

The boat has suffered more in the past 40 years or so than in the previous 4,000-plus, yet another example of the dilemma which haunts so much of Egypt's history, the choice between preservation and tourist revenue; exposed to view again after centuries under sand, many monuments have begun to deteriorate and there is serious concern that, a stone's throw from the museum, the Sphinx's head may soon fall off.

The boat is in any event a marvellous sight: 143 ft (44 metres) long and 19½ ft (5.9

metres) wide, it displaces 45 tons and would have had about 15 inches (38 cm) of freeboard amidships, both prow and stern rising well clear of the water. The hull is ingeniously made of boards stitched together with twisted hemp and leather thongs which shrank with water and thus made caulking unnecessary. The captain had a little "cabin" towards the bow, the greater part of the boat being given over to the royal quarters and a long canopy.

It is clear from the way the thongs have cut into the wood that the boat was actually used, but how and why is debatable. Six pairs of oars would not have provided much propulsion, so they might have been used merely

for steering and the boat was either towed by a tug or pulled along by ropes on land. Not being all that practical, it is quite likely that the boat was reserved for state occasions including, perhaps, Cheops' last journey to Giza for embalming and burial. Six boats were subsequently discovered at Senusert III's pyramid at Dahshur. Although products of the later Middle Kingdom, they were both smaller and more primitive than the Cheops example. As Cheops could hardly have spared effort or expense on his pyramid, it may be wondered why he did not actually build a chamber big enough to take the boat whole.

Heavy traffic: By the Middle Ages there were reputed to be 36,000 ships working the Nile, the Italian monk Frescobaldi reporting that "there was such a great quantity of boats that all those that I have ever seen in the ports of Genoa, Venice, and Ancona put together, not counting the double-decked ships, would not come to one third (their) number." Cairo was then one of the great commercial centres of the world, with slaves, gold, ivory, and spices coming down the river to connect with traders operating across the Red Sea.

The Arab historian Abd el-Latif remarked on ships with "a wooden chamber over which is elevated a dome with windows, and in the daytime furnished with shutters, and which give a view over the river in each direction. There is in this chamber a private cabinet and latrines, and they decorate it in various colours, with gilding, and the most beautiful varnish."

In the end, of course, these beautiful designs had to yield to changing circumstances. The modern cruise ship is replacing the paddle-steamer as the paddle-steamer replaced the *dahabiyya*, rare examples of which will now only be seen immobile at what will probably be their final moorings. Steel is more practical than wood, as wood was more practical than papyrus.

The steam engine and then the diesel obviously forced the pace, but in the 1870s, just as Thomas Cook was getting his new business off the ground, something else was going on. Egypt was at last getting proper roads and feeling, for the first time, the full impact of the wheel.

Left, dinner time. **Right,** souvenir in the visitors' book of a contemporary cruise boat (the artist is represented in the illustration as Peter D).

Cruise № 22

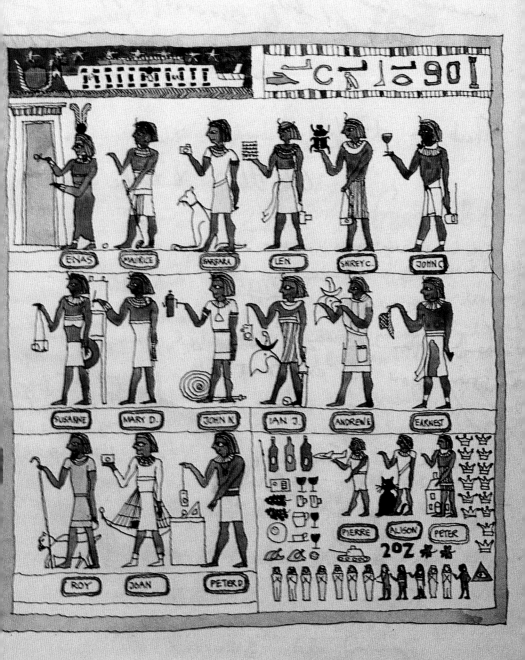

ENAS · MAURICE · BARBARA · LEN · SHIREY C · JOHN C

SUSANNE · MARY D. · JOHN K · IAN J. · ANDREW E · EARNEST

ROY · JOAN · PETER D · PIERRE · ALISON · PETER · 2OZ

🪷 THE BOOK OF THE DEAD
TIRED

VODKA WITH PYRAMIDS – THE BUSINESS OF CRUISING

In the pleasantly cool hours of the evening, as you settle by the pool on the roof of your cruise ship with a glass of something mildly intoxicating in your hand, spare a moment to ponder the industry you are part of – wave cheerily to the line of boats passing downriver – and the nature of the boat you are travelling on.

The pedigree of Nile cruising is as long as that of the temple you'll have been to see today; Egyptian pharaohs cruised up and down the river to survey their kingdom (as well as creating the country, the Nile has long been its main transport artery) and Cleopatra took Caesar for a particularly magnificent river cruise as part of her seduction of the Roman emperor.

The fact is that virtually all of Egypt is visible from the Nile and that here the old philosophical tenet that the world only comes into existence when you can actually see it – if you can't see it then it doesn't exist – is curiously applicable: the world of Egypt *is* only the visible bit; what you see is what there is. Nothing is hiding beyond the horizon except sand, and sometimes even that creeps close to the river bank, squeezing civilisation out into a narrow, thin line of green.

Egypt stretches in a long thin 550-mile (900-

km) fertile line from the southern border with the Sudan up to the metropolis of Cairo, where the line suddenly blossoms into a delta of green that finally approaches the Mediterranean. At the core of the thin line of green is a ribbon of blue – the Nile – and in the off-peak months keen modern-day cruisers can travel the length of the country on its waters, just as the pharaohs did. (In the high season operators concentrate primarily on the run between Luxor and Aswan.)

In 1975 there were only a couple of dozen boats on the river of the size and standard of today's cruisers; by the beginning of the Gulf War in 1991 that total had increased to over 200, and so crowded had the waterway become that the issuing of new licences to operate had to be suspended while the river's facilities were updated to cope with the sheer volume of traffic on the waterway.

Today the principal problems are years of low water levels and the slow and small lock in the barrage at Esna. In low water years the lock can be closed for several days in order to prevent the valuable liquid from draining away; at such times cruise operators are forced to tranship passengers from one boat on the lower reach of the river to another on the upper. Much to the operators' relief a new lock is under construction which will hopefully avoid this necessity and speed up the process of moving from the stretch of lower river to the upper.

It is evident from their shape – like vast floating hotels – that today's cruise ships are made with the passenger in mind. They are not designed for rough weather or choppy seas, and most of them have a draught of less than 3 ft (1 metre) to allow them to operate in the river at all seasons. Some are built overseas in Italy or the UK, but even these do not sail to Egypt under their own steam; they wouldn't cope with the conditions of a sea-journey. Instead they come in pieces as cargo on other, far larger vessels.

Cruisers don't need to be seaworthy: the Nile only experiences rough weather perhaps once a year for a half-hour in May, although one of these half-hours in the 1980s was enough to sink a cruise ship with the loss of many lives.

The more substantial Nile cruisers are of around the same size; 50 to 70 cabins, a staff of 80 for a passenger complement of around 100. Only six or seven of the staff are actually ship's crew, usually distinguishable by their *gallabiyyas*. The captain – many captains come from the same small town and each should know every foot of the river-bed and river-bank – is only in charge of the technical operation of the boat and has no jurisdiction over the passenger areas; his crew are likely to be former fishermen who have settled for a steady job with a reliable income; as you will no doubt appreciate from watching the activities of the small fishing boats, it can be hard work catching anything at all in this great river.

Observant passengers, once they've located the bridge, may notice extraneous goings-on such as the throwing of bread or salt from the bridge area on to the water, or occasional unprovoked hooting of the ship's horn; as with any water-going people, the crews of the Nile boats are superstitious folk, and pay homage to certain key shrines on the river-bank in order to keep luck on their side. Beaching a Nile cruiser is a very embarrassing business, an occurrence that every captain dreads. Scraping the bottom is not infrequent, but just occasionally a boat gets so stuck – usually in the shallows near Edfu – that it has to apply to the Cairo Board of Navigation to have more water released into the river in order to float free. In an incident like this the captain is unlikely to survive in his job unless he has a very good excuse.

Unlike sea-going vessels, the overall master of a Nile cruiser is not the captain. Each ship has the

The crew on the passenger side work shift systems, are paid a salary plus a bonus which depends on the bar takings and room occupancy rate, and as a rule earn better money on cruise ships than they would in the equivalent quality of hotel onshore. Every 45 days they usually have two weeks off; every four weeks a boat on the Luxor to Aswan stretch would expect to do four cruises between the two destinations in the high season (November to March).

The actual costs of running a vessel on the Luxor to Aswan route are surprisingly low, with fuel alone for example only costing some LE150 for a five-day voyage. Average running costs are around LE7,000, or LE20,000–25,000 (£4,000–5,000 sterling) for a week's cruise, which is not much more than what five or six passengers would have

equivalent of a hotel manager, who will have moved into the cruise business from onshore hotels or from the catering industry, and it is to him that the captain answers. The two will come from very different backgrounds, with the hotel manager being urban middle-management and the captain coming from agricultural stock; indeed, the captain is likely to be ranked lower than the chef in the ship's pecking order.

Catering is a prime concern on a cruise ship, just as eating is a prime occupation. The bigger ships have a kitchen staff of around 15, who make all their own bread, cakes, pastries etc on the boat. Most of the meat and groceries are bought either in Luxor or Aswan, and are supplemented by fresh vegetables, fruit and cheese which is sometimes bought at the stops en route.

paid for their holiday.

Staff are the biggest expense. Overall, a cruise operator needs an occupancy rate of around 30–35 percent to break even, and in normal operating conditions will recoup his capital expenditure on the ship within three to five years, which perhaps explains the recent proliferation of the industry. The cruise industry's marketing is deliberately aimed overseas because, other than the advantage of earning valuable foreign currency, overseas holidaymakers pay on average 40 percent more than locals, who are entitled to a discount.

For many poolside drinkers on the top deck in the evening, the combination of dry history, sumptuous self-indulgence, a delicious winter sun, and an endless unrolling of landscape makes the holiday of a lifetime. Vodka with pyramids. ■

AN OUTLINE OF HISTORY

EARLY DYNASTIC PERIOD, 3100-2649 BC
1st and 2nd Dynasties: Memphis was founded (on the site of modern Cairo) as the capital of Egypt. The rulers were buried in tombs at Sakkara, where the first pyramids were eventually built.

OLD KINGDOM, 2649–2134 BC
2649–2575: 3rd Dynasty. Zoser Complex at Sakkara.
2575–2465: 4th Dynasty. Centralised government; pyramids at Dahshur, Giza, and Abu Rawash.
2455–2134: 5th and 6th Dynasties. Pyramids and Sun-Temples at Abu Sir and Sakkara. Tomb reliefs at Sakkara and Gizah. Pyramid texts.

FIRST INTERMEDIATE PERIOD, 2134–2040 BC
7th–10th Dynasties. Collapse of central government; country divided among local rulers; famine and poverty.

MIDDLE KINGDOM, 2040–1640 BC
11th–13th Dynasties. Reunification by Theban rulers; powerful central government; expansion into Nubia (Sudan). Pyramids at Dahshur and Hawarah built by Amenemhet III (1842–1797). Pyramids at Al-Lisht, Mazghunah, and South Sakkara.

SECOND INTERMEDIATE PERIOD, 1640–1532 BC
14th–17th Dynasties. Country divided again. Asiatics ("Hyksos") rule in Delta.

NEW KINGDOM, 1550–1070 BC
1550–1307: 18th Dynasty. Reunification under Theban kings; expulsion of Asiatics in North and annexation of Nubia in South. Period of Egypt's greatest prosperity, with Thebes (Luxor) as main royal residence. Pharaohs include Akhenaton (1353–1335), Tutankhamun (1333–1323).
1307–1196: 19th Dynasty. Ramses II (1290–1224) embodies ideal kingship, builds many monuments, erects colossi.
1196–1070: 20th Dynasty. Invasions by Libyans and "Sea Peoples". Weak kings rule from the Delta.

THIRD INTERMEDIATE PERIOD, 1070–712 BC
21st–24th Dynasties. Tanis is capital, displaced as Egypt is divided among rival rulers.

LATE PERIOD, 712–332 BC
712–657: 25th Dynasty from Kush (Sudan) unites country, begins revival of culture. Assyrian invasions in 667, 663.
664–525: 26th Dynasty rules from Sais in Western Delta. First settlement of Greeks at Memphis.
525–405: 27th Dynasty (Persian). Canal linking the Nile with the Red Sea completed under Darius I (521–486). Fortress called "Perhapemon" (*Babylon* in Greek) built at the Nile end of the canal on the future site of Cairo. Memphis and Heliopolis visited by the Greek writer Herodotus.
404–342: 28th–30th Dynasties. Slow decline.
342–330: 31st Dynasty (Persian). Second Persian occupation.

PTOLEMAIC EMPIRE, 332–30 BC
332–30: Alexander the Great conquers Egypt, founds Alexandria. Ptolemy I rules as governor after Alexander's death in 323 BC, then after 304 BC as first king of dynasty that ends with Cleopatra VII and her children. Decline of Memphis, dilapidation of Heliopolis.

ROMAN PERIOD, 30 BC–AD 324
Rule from Rome. Fortress rebuilt at Babylon in AD 116 under Trajan (98–117). Visits to Egypt by emperors Vespasian, Trajan, Hadrian (twice), Septimius Severus, and Caracalla. High taxation, poverty, alienation, and revolt. Rapid spread of Christianity, despite severe persecution from AD 251 onward.

BYZANTINE PERIOD, AD 324–AD 642
Rule from Constantinople (Byzantium).
324–619: Christianity made state religion, 379. Coptic (Egyptian) Church separates from Catholic Church, 451. Last pagan temple in Egypt (Philae) converted into church, 527.
619–29: Third Persian occupation.
629–39: Re-establishment of Byzantine rule.
639–42: Arab conquest under Amr ibn al-As, who founds new capital, Fustat, next to Babylon, builds first mosque.

ARAB EMPIRE, AD 642–868
Rule by governors on behalf of caliph.
642–58: The Rashidun ("Orthodox" or "Righteous") caliphs.
658–750: The Umayyad caliphs rule from Damascus.
750–878: The Abbasid caliphs rule from Baghdad. Al-Askar built. First Turkish governor appointed, 856.

TULUNID EMPIRE, AD 878–905
Ahmad ibn Tulun, Turkish governor, declares independence, founds Al-Qatai, builds great mosque which carries his name, 876–9.

ABBASID INTERIM, AD 905–935
Reassertion of power from Baghdad.

FATIMID EMPIRE, AD 969–1171
Cairo's first golden age, of which some 30 monuments and a vast number of objects (chiefly in the Islamic Museum) remain as evidence.
969: Al-Qahirah, royal enclosure, founded.
970–72: Al-Azhar built.
996–1021: Reign of al-Hakim, "The Mad Caliph." Mosque of al-Hakim completed.
1085–92: Mosque of al-Guyushi, walls of Al-Qahirah, Bab al-Futuh, Bab an-Nasr, Bab Zuwayla built.
1168: Frankish invasion, Fustat destroyed.

AYYUBID EMPIRE, AD 1171–1250
Saladin (Salah ad-Din) and his successors conduct campaigns against Franks and other invaders.
1174: Crusader invasion repelled.
1187–92: Jerusalem and most of Palestine retaken from the beaten and retreating Crusaders.
1219–21: Frankish invasion by sea; occupation of Damietta and advance on Cairo culminates in

Muslim victory at Mansura ("The Victorious") in the Delta.

1249: Frankish invasion under St Louis culminates in second Muslim victory at Mansura.

BAHRI MAMLUK EMPIRE, 1250–1382

Era of expansion and prosperity, of which over 100 monuments survive.

1260–79: Reign of Baybars al-Bunduqdari ("The Crossbowman"). Defeat of the Mongols, reduction of Frankish states to vassalage, extension of empire from Sudan to Anatolia, from the Euphrates to Cyrenaica.

1279–90: Reign of Qalawun.

1293–1340: Three reigns of An-Nasir Mohammed ibn Qalawun. Period of great architectural splendour in Cairo.

1340–82: Reigns of sons, grandsons and great-grandsons of An-Nasir Mohammed. Pillage and destruction of Alexandria by Franks, 1365.

BURGI (CIRCASSIAN) MAMLUKE EMPIRE, 1382–1517

Continuation of massive building programmes (130 monuments survive) under the rule of 23 sultans. The most important were:

1382–89, 90–99: Az-Zahir Barquq.

1399–1412: An-Nasir Farag ibn Barquq.

1412–21: Al-Muayyad Shaykh.

1422–38: Al-Ashraf Barsbay.

1438–53: Az-Zahir Sayf-ad-Din Gakmak.

1453–61: Inal.

1461–67: Khushqadam (Greek).

1468–96: Qaytbay.

1501–17: Qansuh al-Ghuri.

OTTOMAN PERIOD, 1517–1914

Egypt was a province of the Ottoman Empire with Cairo as its capital.

1517–1798: Ottoman rule was through 106 governors. Cultural decline, commercial prosperity.

1798–1805: French invasion and occupation, followed by chaos.

1805–48: Mohammed Ali Pasha. Enormous programme of modernisation and creation of new empire, both thwarted by European intervention.

1848, 1849–54: Ibrahim Pasha.

1854–63: Said Pasha. Suez Canal concession granted. Cairo-Alexandria rail link, Nile steamship service, telegraph established. Work begun on Suez Canal (1859).

1863–79: Ismail the Magnificent. New programme of modernisation, assertion of autonomy. Assembly of Delegates established (1866), principle of primogeniture accepted by Sultan. Title of "Khedive" granted (1867). Suez Canal opened (1869).

1879–92: Khedive Tewfik. British Occupation begins (1882).

1892–1914: Khedive Abbas II Hilmi. Monuments: Egyptian Museum, Museum of Islamic Art, Rifai Mosque.

POST-1914: PROTECTORATE, MONARCHY, REPUBLIC

1914–17: Sultan Husayn Kamil. British Protectorate declared, martial law instituted.

1917–22: Sultan Fu'ad. Revolution of 1919. Looting and destruction in Cairo.

1922–36: King Fu'ad I. Sovereignty recognised, constitutional monarchy established.

1936–52: King Farouk. During World War II (1939–45), Egypt is neutral, but is reoccupied by Britain. Fires of Black Saturday (1952) lead to military coup.

1952–53: The July Revolution deposes Farouk in favour of his infant son, Ahmad Fu'ad, then declares Egypt a republic. All royal properties are subsequently nationalised. Gamal Abd an-Nasir (Gamal Abdel Nasser) becomes leader.

1956: Nationalisation of Suez Canal. Tripartite Aggression of British, French and Jewish interests against Egypt.

1961: Introduction of Socialist Laws in July Ordinances, plus further nationalisations, sequestrations from foreign residents.

1967: The Six Day War against Israel.

1970: Gamal Abdel Nasser is succeeded as head of state by Anwar Sadat.

1973: The October War against Israel.

1974–77: Open Door Policy, political liberalisation. Riots (1977) over removal of subsidies on food. Sequestrations declared illegal.

1979: Camp David accords in the Unite States lead to peace treaty with Israel. Egypt boycotted by the rest of the Arab World.

1981: President Anwar Sadat assassinated. Hosni Mubarak becomes President.

1994: Two long-dry channels of the Nile discovered in northern Sudan.

1995: Cairo hosts Middle East peace summit between Israel, Jordan, the PLO and Egypt.

1996: In escalation of terrorism, Islamic terrorists kill 18 Greek tourists in Cairo.

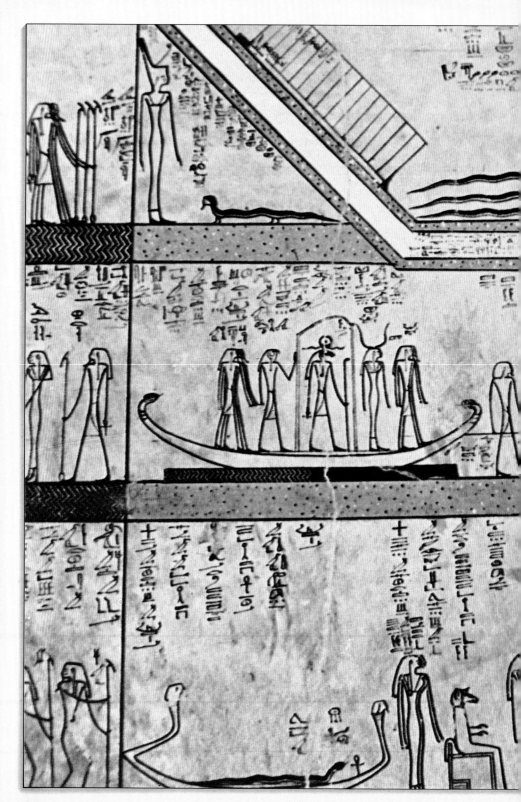

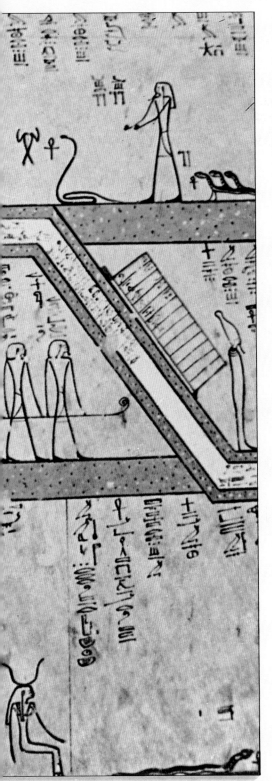

PYRAMID BUILDERS OF THE OLD KINGDOM

Like the egg – or, for that matter, the original Coca-Cola bottle – the Egyptian pyramid has a purity of line which not only makes it instantly and universally recognisable but belies the fact that, as a design exercise, a pyramid is nowhere near as simple as it looks. There are 87 pyramids of different shapes and sizes, as well as in various stages of repair, along a 100-mile (160-km) stretch of the Nile, but it is the trio of large pyramids on the Giza plateau near Cairo that fill the imagination even of those who will never see them in the flesh.

The classic pyramid has four sides, not three, and the sides are not equilateral triangles. After a number of false starts, the builders settled on sides which rise at an angle of 52 degrees, aesthetically more pleasing than the shallower angle one builder resorted to but not so steep as to create concern about earth tremors. For the mathematically-minded, the chosen angle happens to mean that the ratio of the pyramid's height to the perimeter of its base is the same as that of a circle's radius to its circumference.

The more comprehensible statistics of the Great Pyramid of Cheops are awesome: for a start, it covers 13 acres (5.4 hectares) at its base – about seven American city blocks – and is as high as a 40-storey building. It contains more stone than all the cathedrals and churches of England put together and its height as a purely stone structure has been exceeded since by the spires of Cologne cathedral. In its heyday it had a gleaming coat of polished limestone, and Pliny, the Roman historian, mentions locals who slid down the sides to entertain tourists in the interest, presumably, of a little baksheesh. The limestone mantle was all of 8 ft (2.4 metres) thick and the blocks were mated with such precision that the cracks were all but invisible.

As feats of engineering, the pyramids are prodigious beyond comparison, which makes it all the more fantastic that they are not the triumphant summation of ancient Egyptian civilisation but, if anything, the beginning. They are the products of the so-called Old

Left, tomb painting of the pyramid builders.

Kingdom, specifically the Third to Sixth Dynasties inclusively. Generally built in the second half of the third millennium BC, they were historically far more remote from Cleopatra, the last of the Ptolemies and Hollywood's favourite ancient Egyptian, than she is from present times.

First efforts: The pyramids, of course, did not spring up in a cultural vacuum. The pickings of recorded Egyptian history are so rich that satiated historians have, by and large, passed lightly over developments before about 3000 BC when Upper and Lower Egypt were united by conquest under a single king known in legend as Menes but whose real name, from what can be deduced

the same place, and it is still not absolutely clear which was which. It would appear that all eight kings of the First Dynasty and at least some of the Second were buried in tombs cut into rock at Abydos, the centre of the Osiris cult not far from Luxor, while their monuments were erected at Sakkara, near Memphis, but there are experts who argue that it was the other way round.

Either way, the inspiration for the first pyramid was in the mud-brick *mastabas* of Sakkara. Originally large but unremarkable oblong slabs, these developed into monumental buildings, still made out of mud-brick, with stylised facades sufficiently reminiscent of Mesopotamian palaces to encour-

from scanty written evidence, was almost certainly Narmer. Under whatever name, it was he who diplomatically established a new capital at a convenient meeting point between the previously divided kingdoms, at Memphis, not far from modern Cairo.

During the First and Second Dynasties, which is to say for about five centuries after the union of Upper and Lower Egypt, the burial arrangements for the king and nobility became steadily more elaborate. Perhaps because grave robbers were already making a mockery of the most carefully contrived defences, the monument to a departed king and his actual grave were not necessarily in

age the view that the pyramid builders, or at least the architects, were not natives of longstanding but recent immigrants to Egypt. An unresolved argument – not a sensitive subject because Egyptians care far less about this kind of thing than the Greeks – postulates that the brains behind ancient Egypt were foreign, the point being mischievously made that the Egyptians built the pyramids only in the sense that they also built the Aswan dams.

With the arrival of the Third Dynasty, there emerged an architect, Imhotep, of such genius that he was later deified by the Greeks. Imhotep recognised the difficulties but also the advantages of building in stone rather than relatively flimsy mud-brick. One Egyptologist has painted the alluring picture of Imhotep building a square but otherwise fairly conventional *mastaba* slab for his patron, King Zoser, and then, the king being in robust health, wondering whether he would not have time to put a slightly smaller slab on top of it. With the king still in peak condition, there was ample time for another...and so on. When Zoser did die, the Step Pyramid, tiered like a wedding cake, awaited him.

The evolution of the more familiar straight-sided pyramid had to overcome a number of early examples of "back to the drawing board". The dissatisfaction of King Snefru

it in steps and then make the sides come true with polished limestone inserts. In keeping with what became common practice, the pyramid was to have an adjoining mortuary temple. As usual, there is a dissenting minority among Egyptologists, but it seems the incline was altogether too ambitious and the sides collapsed (earth tremors?) while the temple was still under construction. The project was abandoned.

The only part of King Snefru that found lasting peace in the resting places he had so assiduously constructed was (and even this is not certain) his severed, mummified foot. Ironically, the body of his wife, Queen Hetepheres, seems to have been removed

may explain why three pyramids are attributed to him.

At Dahshur, 5 miles (8 km) south of Sakkara, the architect started boldly with sides rising at 54 degrees but, for reasons that may be to do with religious symbolism and aesthetics, let the top tail off at a more manageable 43 degrees – hence the Bent Pyramid. The Northern Pyramid was designed from the outset with a gentle incline.

A precipitous 75 degrees was risked on the Meidum Pyramid, the intention being to build

Left, and **above**, **the Great Pyramid of Cheops and the sadly damaged face of the Sphinx.**

from its tomb by grave robbers and unceremoniously dumped in the desert. Courtiers rescued it and secretly re-buried it in an unmarked grave along with a pile of her scattered possessions. A photographer setting up for a shot of the Great Pyramid in 1925 suffered the ignominy of a tripod that wouldn't stay upright. As he wrestled with the thing, one of the legs disappeared altogether down a hole which proved to be the top of a long shaft down to her grave. The intricate reconstruction of her fragmented bedroom suite by a team from Harvard and the Boston Museum of Fine Art gave the Cairo Museum a priceless masterpiece.

Perfection: If all Snofru's diligence was ultimately frustrated, the preoccupation with pyramid design in his household came to fruition in his son, known to him as Khufu but to posterity by his Greek name, Cheops. Technically a god himself, his secular ambitions evidently antagonised the priesthood, a recurring conflict in pharaonic Egypt which was to boil over practically into civil war in the New Kingdom. The vilification of the priests was so pervasive that, judging by Herodotus, the echoes were still rebounding when he talked to priests 2,000 years afterwards! Cheops, he heard, "plunged into all kinds of wickedness", not stopping at steering his daughter into prostitution to raise

from Aswan on reed barges. However, to be too close to the river would have exposed the building site to annual flooding, so they were kept at a respectful distance and serviced by a canal specially dug for the purpose. The blocks were then dragged along the causeway on sleds.

The building site of 13 acres (5.4 hectares) was first levelled with incredible precision and the floor plan laid out on an equally precise north-south axis. Herodotus maintains that the casing blocks were stacked on top of one another with a kind of derrick, the inner core being topped up with whatever was at hand. The final layer of polished limestone, he says, was started at the top

money for his immortal monument, the Great Pyramid at Giza. It may be closer to the truth to add that Cheops also locked up the temples and put the priests out of business.

The effort that went into the Great Pyramid was immense. Herodotus describes shifts of 100,000 men taking 10 years just to build the causeway, 60 ft (18 metres) wide, from the water's edge to the plateau. Apart from the fact that only the desert nomads ventured any distance from the river, pyramids were always built within easy reach of the Nile to simplify the last leg of the journey which brought blocks of granite, some weighing 70 tons each, 500 miles (800 km) down the river

from a ramp which had gradually been built up. As the mantle progressed, the ramp was whittled down.

On the inside: The internals of the pyramid are a story in themselves. It seems that the original plan was to have a burial chamber beneath the pyramid with access via a descending passage from the north face. The passage had already been lined and polished when it was decided that the chamber ought to be higher, roughly in the centre of the pyramid itself. This entailed a second pas-

Above, the Sphinx and the Great Pyramid as first seen by Napoleon and his team of *savants*.

sage ascending from the first. The ascending passage was enlarged at its extremity into a "Grand Gallery" which in turn led to the burial chamber. Two narrow shafts from the chamber to the outside of the pyramid were at first assumed to be for ventilation, but it now seems more likely that they were aligned for astronomical purposes. Once the king was buried, granite plugs kept in readiness in the Grand Gallery were slid down the ascending passage to seal it off to further visitors. Yet another shaft, just wide enough for a man, served as an escape route for the workers responsible for releasing the granite plugs – if they were lucky.

In Mark Antony's time, Roman tourists were able to enter the descending passage through a hinged stone in the north face and scribble their graffiti on the walls of what was at first intended to be the burial chamber. Very little about the pyramids then appears in print until AD 820 when Abdullah Al Mamun, son of the Caliph of Baghdad, Harun Al-Rashid (the hero of *Arabian Nights*), assembled an army of engineers and labourers to break into the Great Pyramid. They burrowed straight into the north side about halfway between the base and the hinged entrance to the descending passage, which they must have overlooked. Their path eventually crossed that of the descending passage and they arrived at one of the granite plugs. Unable to budge it, they burrowed an extremely difficult and uncomfortable detour which, in the end, delivered them to the burial chamber. It contained nothing but an empty granite sarcophagus. They vented their frustration by hacking at the magnificent granite interior.

The limestone exterior of the pyramid was still intact in the 13th century when Abd-al-Latif, the Arab historian, paid a visit. He was amazed at the spectacle of colour, apparently a combination of original decoration and subsequent graffiti artists. To make copies of the inscriptions, he said, would have filled 10,000 pages. Sadly, his Arab contemporaries were not as impressed by the crowning glory of the limestone. The mantle was ripped off and carted across the river on camel trains to build palaces and mosques in Cairo, amongst which the Sultan Hasan Mosque was one of the notable beneficiaries. The tip of the adjacent Pyramid of Chephren, Cheops' brother and successor, is all that remains to give modern visitors a slight impression of how the whole once looked with mantle intact. Possibly out of filial piety, Chephren kept his pyramid 10 ft (3 metres) lower than Cheops's although, because it is built on slightly higher ground, their relative sizes can be deceptive.

In Mycerinus, Chephren's brother and heir, Herodotus at last finds a good word to say about the Fourth Dynasty: "...he opened the temples and permitted the people, who were worn down to the last extremity, to return to their employments and to sacrifices...he made the most just decisions of all their kings." In any case, he was content with a much smaller pyramid. Colonel Howard-Vyse, whose family sent him off to do some exploring in Egypt to put distance between him and their seat in Buckinghamshire, impatiently used gunpowder to blast his way into Mycerinus's pyramid. He recovered a sarcophagus but it was lost when the ship transporting it to England sank in the Bay of Biscay.

Inscrutable stone: The Sphinx is not now as enigmatic as it famously was when buried in sand up to its eyebrows, but there is still doubt about who the human face on the lion's body belongs to. Because it is carved from a natural outcrop at the foot of Chephren's causeway, it is generally thought to be him. The Egyptians themselves seemed never to rate the beast highly, and the normally punctilious Herodotus does not mention it at all. It was certainly worshipped at one point as a god in its own right: the stela between its paws is a tribute from Tuthmosis IV, a king of the much later 18th Dynasty.

The Sphinx's face has been through the wars: contrary to popular belief, though, the nose was not shot off by Napoleon's troops as target practice, and Egyptians are almost reconciled to the fragment of beard remaining in the British Museum.

After the Fourth Dynasty, the rest of the Old Kingdom is rather anti-climactic. The Fifth Dynasty apparently felt unequal to the task of matching the architectural achievements of their predecessors and to avoid unhappy comparisons chose to conduct their building activities some miles south of Giza. Their pyramids were smaller and slapdash, although any money they may have saved through such economies was swallowed by expenditure on lavish temples devoted to the cult of sun-worship.

PYRAMIDOLOGY AND PYRAMIDIOCY

In about 1850 Pasha Abbas I described the pyramids as "an ugly, useless pile of stones." He was unimpressed or possibly even unaware that the Greeks had ranked them among the Seven Wonders of the World. Medieval Arab rulers were no less disappointed than he that the burial chambers had long been robbed of their treasure, but they were convinced that there were undiscovered chambers which contained maps of unknown parts of the world, navigational charts and the secret of weapons which never rusted. No one, they argued, not even the most extravagantly morbid pharoah, would have invested so much effort in just a tomb.

Abbas, a discredited member of Egypt's last dynasty but nevertheless an indirect descendant of the pharaohs, would not have found many in contemporary Europe who shared his contempt. Following publication of the 24-volume *La Description de L'Egypte* by Napoleon's *savants*, the Egyptian style in jewellery, clothing and furnishing was the rage internationally.

"Pyramidologists" were pursuing all sorts of wonderful theories about the pyramids, although those who pushed their fancy too far risked being demoted to "Pyramidiots". Even the Astronomer Royal for Scotland had to watch his step. "The whole of Professor (Piazzi) Smyth's theory about the Great Pyramid," wrote a fellow member of the Royal Society, "is a series of strange hallucinations, which only a few weak women believe, and perhaps a few womanly men, but no more."

In London, John Taylor, editor of *The Observer*, was caught in a dilemma. A gifted astronomer and mathematician, he had studied the Great Pyramid of Cheops and come to an astounding conclusion. The builders, he decided, "knew the Earth was a sphere; and by observing the motion of the heavenly bodies over the earth's surface, had ascertained its circumference, and were desirous of leaving behind them a record of the circumference as correct and as imperishable as it was possible for them to construct."

Taylor's problem was his profound faith in the literal truth of the Old Testament. He believed that Adam had been created in exactly 4000 BC and that the Flood had occurred in 2400 BC. In marvelling at the sublime mathematics of pyramid design, he was quite ready to accept that the Great Pyramid had been built in 2100 BC. What he could not reconcile was how, in a mere 300 years, the brains and labour required could have recovered from mankind's watery grave.

The pyramid had other peculiar properties too. Patent No. 91304 in Czechoslovakia was rushed through to protect the commercial possibilities of mysterious forces swirling around pyramid-shaped objects. The product in question was a cardboard contraption known as the "Cheops Pyramid Razorblade Sharpener". Sir W. Siemens (as in electrical appliances), on the other hand, was a thoroughly reputable British inventor. He took his guide up a pyramid to prove that a wine bottle wrapped in a moist newspaper and held above his head would emit a shower of sparks. When it did, the official witness let out a howl, hoisted his *gallibiya*, and bolted.

The Curse of the Pharoahs is only one of a long line of demonic powers guarding the sanctity of the royal tombs. They do not seem to have bothered early Roman visitors because Strabo, who took a Nile cruise in 24 BC, described his party crawling down the descending passage of the Great Pyramid by the light of flaming torches.

In the Middle Ages, however, the Arabs were put off by reports of an enormous naked woman with big teeth whose lust no male intruder could decline or escape. If he survived at all, it would be as an insane wreck. It is conceivable that this insatiable woman was loosely based on the daughter whom Cheops, builder of the Great Pyramid, is reputed to have prostituted in order to defray building costs. She was installed in a special chamber and encouraged to charge each of her clients the cost of one block of finished limestone, 2½ million of which were needed before the pyramid was finished.

In 1638 John Greaves, a young astronomer at Oxford University, was prepared to run all these real or imagined risks in order to settle a teasing mystery of the type which would later distress the editor of *The Observer*. The pyramids were too well built simply to have been thrown together, so the architects must have drawn up plans with detailed measurements. What, he wondered, was the unit of measurement they used, and how had the Egyptians arrived at it? Was it essentially practical, like the three grains of barley which originally made up the English inch, or had the Egyptians been capable of arriving at an abstract one like a fraction of a degree of longitude?

Wriggling "like a serpent" down the same descending passage that Strabo and party had followed, Greaves came under attack by bats "so ugly and so large, exceeding a foot in length" that he was driven to firing his pistols, a shattering noise in the confined space. He persevered in his research with a 10-ft calibrated pole. The general idea was to measure anything and everything that

looked like a calculated length. Frequently recurring lengths would therefore be a unit or convenient multiples of a unit. He soon had enough data and observations to fill a book.

Pyramidographia, published in 1646, caught the attention of Sir Isaac Newton. Using Greaves's figures, he arrived at the length of what he called the "profane" or Memphis cubit, which enabled him to interpret the geographical degree as quoted in the classical authors and so move closer to his theory of gravitation. The role of the pyramids in his theory is not as widely acknowledged as perhaps it ought to be.

The search for other examples of applied mathematics in the pyramids then extended to *pi*, the ratio between the diameter and the circumference of a circle. This had traditionally been credited to Pythagoras, the Greek geometrician who lived about 500 BC and coincidentally shared the ancient Egyptians' abhorrence of eating beans. Modern computers have now calculated this incommensurate number to 10,000 decimal places, but it was only 1,100 years after Pythagoras that a Hindu mathematician, Arya-Bhata, worked out the fourth decimal. Mathematicians were agog at what seemed like evidence that the pyramid builders had reached at least the second decimal 2,000 years before Pythagoras even started.

All this was meat and drink to Napoleon's *savants* who cleared sand and rubbish which had all but buried most of Egypt's pyramids in order to measure the external dimensions more accurately and unlock further mathematical sensations. While they pored over their findings, the young general, still some way from crowning himself emperor, insisted on spending some time alone in the Great Pyramid's burial chamber.

He emerged from the chamber white in the face, pointedly refused to answer questions and told his staff that the matter was never to be raised. Only towards the end, when he was in exile on St Helena, did he nearly bring himself to discuss what happened with a trusted companion. He held himself back, however, and shook his head. "No," he remarked. "What's the use? You'd never believe me."

Conjecture about the hidden purpose of the pyramids has never ceased. Some of the discoveries are beyond dispute. Clearing the base of the Great Pyramid has established, for example, that the entire perimeter of the 13-acre site is level to within a tolerance of less than one inch. It has also confirmed that, like most pyramids, the axis is aligned on true north with an astonishing degree of accuracy. Such findings have led a new generation of pyramidologists to suggest that what were long thought to be access or ventilation passages into the centre of a pyramid were actually designed to time the moment of a star's transit across the sky.

In 1971, a reasonably sober study pushed the claims for the Great Pyramid to record levels. The builders, it said, "knew the precise circumference of the planet... the length of the year to several decimals... the mean length of the earth's orbit round the sun... the specific density of the planet... the 26,000-year cycle of the equinoxes... the acceleration of gravity... and the speed of light".

The author concerned, Peter Tompkins, disarmingly conceded the danger of latter-day Pyramidiocy and went so far as to quote (in his *Secrets of the Great Pyramid*) an early sceptic who sighed that in due course he fully expected the pyramid to reveal the distance to Timbuktu, the number of street lights in Bond Street, London, the specific gravity of mud and the mean weight of adult goldfish. ∎

GRAVE ROBBERS AND CURSES

The Curse of the Pharaohs, a built-in feature of almost every B-film about Egypt, is distinguishable from kindred phenomena like the Bermuda Triangle in containing at least a grain of truth. Pharaohs, priests and *felaheen* alike were forever putting curses on people for all sorts of reasons, and in a superstitious way they sometimes worked. But Hollywood's favourite curse, that of Tutankhamun, is another matter.

Tomb curses ranged from short and snappy – "He who enters here will have his neck wrung like chicken" – to colourful and closely detailed. A vizier was not content simply to see the culprit die. He would first have to endure a jet of fire playing on his head, starvation, social ostracism, the death of his children, the violation of his wife before his eyes – and that was just the beginning.

The curse which the film-going public learned about was reputed to have killed more than 20 people involved in the violation of Tutankhamun's tomb in 1922. The first victim was Lord Carnarvon, Howard Carter's patron and partner. His death was attributed to a mosquito bite or, better, a scarab, the belief that the scarab ubiquitous in Egyptian mythology was a kind of scorpion (wrong) rather than a prosaic dung beetle (right).

King Tut's curse: The dread secrets of Tutankhamun's tomb were unmasked in dramatic announcements over a period of five years, and with popular interest running high, newspapers and magazines as well as the film industry made the most of the story. It did not serve their interests to quote doctors who said that Carnarvon had been in poor health for years and died of pneumonia. It was more rewarding to recall the words of a philosophical peasant who was said to have seen loitering at the tomb-site and heard to mumble: "These people are looking for gold but they will find death". A death-bed repentance was put into Carnarvon's mouth and solemn significance attached to a power failure which switched off the lights in his Cairo room 10 minutes before he expired.

Left, Luigi Mayer's illustration of exploring a passage in the Great Pyramid.

Carter ridiculed the whole idea, but even he admitted to a slight shudder when a servant reported that he had gone to investigate the sudden silence of Carnarvon's pet canary, always a lusty singer, and found it fast disappearing down a cobra's throat. An Egyptian official engaged a snake-charmer named Mussa to ensure that there were no further mishaps with snakes. The official dropped dead.

In due course it was virtually impossible for anyone connected with Carter's work to suffer any kind of misfortune or to die without fingers pointing rigidly at the curse. The wording was quite specific: "Death will come on swift pinions to those who disturb the rest of the Pharaoh". It sounded authentic, especially the bit about "swift pinions", but when sceptics asked to examine it, it transpired that no one had ever actually seen the inscription. The disappointing truth was that, while almost all tombs did carry one curse or another, Tutankhamun's did not.

The robbing of tombs is as old as the tombs themselves. Pharaohs who proclaimed their own divinity were not deterred by the posthumous powers of their predecessors. Not only did they empty tombs of their valuables, they sometimes threw out the coffin as well and reserved the space for their own, adding insult to injury by tampering with the previous occupant's cartouche to give the impression that they had built the tomb as well.

The pyramids were a maze of false passages and man-traps designed specifically to foil robbers, but of course the ins and outs could hardly be concealed from the workforce who built them. In claiming that he and he alone supervised the building of Tuthmosis I's tomb – "No one else knew where it was or ever heard about it" – the architect Ineni was referring to the type of unmarked tomb in the Valley of the Kings, a far more modest undertaking whose security lay in its secret location, not its strength or the ingenuity of its defences. Even so it was not done without slaves, and Ineni skips over the point that his 150 slaves were kept isolated in a special compound and murdered as soon as the job was done.

The earlier pyramids could not have been

more obvious targets, either for burglars or for foreign armies who could tackle the task brazenly and not worry about being arrested. The medieval Arabs applied their considerable engineering skills to the challenge presented by the Great Pyramid. They hacked a large hole in the wall and crawled around the inside like ants, but when they finally entered the burial chamber they discovered they were not the first.

Switching to the discreet tombs of the Valley of the Kings was a tacit admission that pyramids could never be wholly secure graves. Self-aggrandisement, an important part of building a pyramid, was achieved instead through funerary temples, obelisks,

Hapi, a water-carrier Kemwese, a peasant Amenheb and a slave Ehenufer who confessed, needless to say under considerable duress, to taking "all the gold from the mummies of the God and the queen" were lashed until their palms and the soles of their feet turned to pulp and then executed. On the other hand, the prefect of East Thebes, a certain Peser, in collusion with the administrator of the necropolis, Pevero, and the vizier of all Thebes, Kamwese, got off similar charges with a slap on the wrist. A coppersmith with the curiously un-Egyptian sounding name of Peichert saved his skin by talking as his interrogators set about cutting off his nose and ears.

mighty statues and wonderfully immodest temple inscriptions. The real burial sites gave away nothing, but once the locations became known they were virtually defenceless.

Crime and punishment: The 20th and 21st Dynasties, by which time the Valley of the Kings was known and the pharaohs were looking about for a new location, seem to have degenerated into a running battle between robbers and loyal necropolis guards who would surreptitiously move the contents of the tombs around to hide them.

When the villains were brought to book, there were two scales of justice. The records show that a carpenter Tramun, a stonecutter

The history of grave-robbing in Egypt reflects the changing value of antique objects. Gold, precious metals and jewels would appeal to any thief in any age, but it is to be wondered whether a serious-minded scholar like the Roman Strabo would have attached the same incalculable value to something like the Rosetta Stone if he had felt inclined to line his pockets with "souvenirs". He reported that at the time of his visit there were 40 empty royal tombs which visitors could enter, and perhaps by then the obvious targets for grave robbers had been exhausted.

Moribund or dead, the business picked up as Egypt was drawn into the European orbit by rivalry between France and England at the turn of the 19th century. The belief that mummies, especially when ground like pepper, had wonderful medicinal properties created a brisk trade in them, so brisk in fact that supply could not meet demand and not a few common criminals in Europe would have been less than flattered to know that their mortal remains were being ground up and passed off as genuine ancient Egyptian. Works by Napoleon's *savants* created a craze for anything Egyptian, and peasants became aware that there was money to be made out of odds and ends in the sand which would previously have been ignored.

"Collectors" like Giovanni Belzoni, the former circus strongman, used his strength (his stage act included lifting 12 people at a time) and knowledge of hydraulics (or, failing that, a battering ram) to cart off supposedly immovable objects like the Young Memnon whose sheer size had left it unmolested on the ground at Luxor for thousands of years. The race to scoop up anything and everything – or pull it down – for sale to collectors and museums in Europe and America resulted in some lurid confrontations between arch-competitors like Belzoni and Bernardino Drovetti, the Italian-born French Consul in Egypt. Drovetti's riposte to Belzoni's battering ram was dynamite. Belzoni's methods left something to be desired, but it is touchingly clear from his writings that he meant well and his acquisitions form a substantial part of the British Museum's vast Egyptian collection.

Resident robbers: The demand for objects of antiquity did not go unnoticed in the village of Quornah, near the Ramesseum on the west bank at Luxor, where certain atavistic instincts ran deep. No one was better acquainted with the nooks and crannies of the Valley of the Kings than the descendants of those who had worked on the tombs to begin with. Save for the flow of free-spending tourists, Quornah was an unlovely place to live but the inhabitants were attached to it.

The appearance of some illustrated papyri on the European market in 1871 worried the Antiquities Service in Cairo. Not only was the quality quite superb, but the papyri appeared to belong to a historical period which

had until then had offered up very little. The natural suspicion was that someone had stumbled on a new tomb about which the Service knew nothing and was keeping it quiet. It was almost certainly near Luxor, so it was to Luxor that an obliging American collector was despatched with a brief to behave rich and hungry for important pieces.

Within days of arrival the agent was tipped off that he could usefully call on the Rassul family in Quornah. After the usual formalities, items for sale were produced, rubbish at first but steadily improving in quality until it was very obvious that the Rassul family had something up its sleeve. What the agent and the Antiquities Service did not then know

was that it had been there for some 10 years, a tomb whose contents were sustaining a large part of the village. Only the Rassuls knew where it was but, acting like wholesalers, they had co-opted the village as their sales team.

The agent's suspicions were sufficient to have the brothers Ahmed and Hussein Abd er Rassul brought in for questioning. It can only be imagined how they would have reacted to the prospect of having their noses and ears chopped off, but whatever happened to them during the three months they helped with enquiries (the *courbash*, or hippo-hide whip, was still then virtually a civil

Left, Belzoni's men removing the head of Memnon from Luxor. **Right**, today's art of imitation.

Superstition 69

servant's badge of office), the brothers emerged tightlipped.

Mohammed, the head of the family, was not as resilient and in due course led an Antiquities Service representative, the archaeologist Emile Brugsch, on a walk which took them past Hatshepsut's temple at Deir el Bahri. Climbing a path up the north cliff, poor Brugsch was assailed by the most appalling smell. This turned out to be the sign that they had reached their destination, the carcass of a donkey left rotting in the sun. Beneath it, or anyway close by, was a hole which the tottering Brugsch squeezed through to begin an unnerving descent of 50 ft (15 metres) at the end of a rope. At the bottom, a passage about 4 ft (1.2 metres) high disappeared into the rock.

Noble gathering: Trying to keep a candle alight, Brugsch felt his way along the passage. In places, chambers had been cut into the sides, and Brugsch gradually identified the contents in speechless disbelief. Almost any coffin would have been an exciting find, but the names on these defied an Egyptologist's imagination: Tuthmosis III... Ramses II... Amenhotep I... Seti I... In modern and more general terms, it would be like joining a dinner party at which the other guests happened to be Napoleon, Nelson, Gordon, Kitchener, Farouk and Nasser, with perhaps Washington, Hitler, Elvis Presley and a few popes thrown in.

The only possible explanation for such a galaxy to be assembled in such an unprepossessing place is thought to have been an especially turbulent period when all the royal tombs were threatened and loyal subjects, either priests or necropolis guards, gathered up as many coffins as they could and removed them in total secrecy to a common grave for safe-keeping.

The gold and funerary objects found with the kings could have put the whole of Quornah into the lap of luxury for the rest of time. As it was, Mohammed was rewarded with £500 and the case against the brothers was dropped. Brugsch arranged a powerful guard of 300 men to see the find safely down to boats waiting on the Nile. The operation took two days and was enlivened by local women shrieking and tearing at their hair. Charitable observers compared their performance with the traditional mourning for a dead king; others ventured that it might have been laced

with despair at the loss of a nice windfall.

Almost 30 years later, in 1902, Carter was the Inspector of Antiquities at Luxor and in that capacity was called upon to investigate a robbery at the tomb of Amenhotep II, the only royal mummy left in its original burial chamber. An armed gang had forced their way past the watchmen, pulled the king's body out of the sarcophagus and dumped it on the floor. Using a police dog, Carter followed footprints from the scene of the crime – to the front door of the Abd er Rassul family! Charges were brought against them, but again unsuccessfully. Ten years after that, Carter had to deal with a gunfight between rival gangs over another tomb, one of

which – he was not totally surprised to note – consisted of Rassuls. He quietened them on this occasion by threatening to push the lot of them into the tomb concerned and lock it up.

Quornah still stands above the coachloads of tourists heading for Hatshepsut's temple and the Valley of the Kings. The authorities have long thought that the villagers would be more comfortable on the opposite bank and have offered alternative accommodation. The villagers say they do not wish to leave, but they do not say why.

Above, Anubis, jackal-headed god of embalming. **Right**, Egyptologist with mummy and case.

THE MUMMY BUSINESS

The Nile Valley is the birthplace of mummification, but visitors will find that mummified human beings are far easier seen overseas than they are in Egypt, where most of them were originally created. Those mummies that still remain in Egypt are no longer on display out of respect for the dead.

They did not always earn such respect. The Egyptians may have thought they were safe for eternity in their hidden stony tombs and sarcophagi, but others were equally clever and very few mummies were allowed to remain in their original tombs (the rather insignificant king Tutankhamun was one of the lucky ones).

Some were hacked to pieces by early tomb-robbers in search of jewel-charms. Others were ground to dust in Europe in medieval times and sold as aphrodisiacs or remedies against "abscesses, fractures, bruises, paralysis, migraine, epilepsy, haemoptysis, coughs, sore throats, high blood pressure, stomach insufficiencies, sickness, liver and spleen illnesses, internal ulcers and poisoning." Even though dealing in mummies was illegal and methods of transport dangerous, many "wholesalers" made a fortune in the trade. It was only heavy taxation that finally stopped the export business in the 17th century.

In fact, a lot has been learned about the early Egyptian from mummification, a process which only came about because of his belief in life after death, for which he needed his body and soul. In a long procedure which took a maximum of 70 days (for nobility), the inner organs were removed and the corpse was first dried with natron and then embalmed to turn the papyrus-like skin into what we would call leather today. In order to maintain its physical presence the body was often filled with mud, saw-dust or sap and covered in thousands of metres of sap-soaked bandages.

When mummification was at the peak of its popularity it was a massive industry, with embalmers working day and night shifts to wrap not only the "upper ten thousand" of society, but also every

little holy bull, ibis, crocodile, pavian, cat, mouse and scarab.

X-rays of mummies have proved that illnesses such as rheumatism, arthritis, polio and even arteriosclerosis were well known in pharaonic days. Not every ancient Egyptian died heroically in a battle; some also suffered heart attacks or died in childbirth, as one mummified foetus which was discovered in the womb of its mummified mother illustrates only too graphically.

Not every Egyptian lived in a pompous palace. Most of them spent their lives in mud-brick huts where they suffered many of the ailments that still haunt us today. Due to their unconventional flour-grinding methods, for example (they added sand to the grain to speed up the process and to produce the first genuine "sandwiches"), their teeth were in a terrible state, themselves ground down.

In the 19th century surgeons and anatomists found a new source of income by unwrapping mummies in front of a big audience. A British anatomist, T.J. Pettigrew, started the show in his own house, but soon moved to bigger venues. On 10 April 1834, a crowd of some 600 people gathered in his town hall to be present at the unwrapping of the "most interesting mummy ever discovered in Egypt". But the mummy proved to be a tough match. Neither hammer nor scissors nor knives succeeded in cutting through the thick protection. After three hours of intense probing, cutting and sawing Mr Pettigrew gave up and announced that "the result of the operation would be published some other time."

At the end of the 19th century, America also tried to turn the mummy trade to gold. August Stanwood had the brilliant idea of making brown wrapping paper from the ancient bandages and shrouds. None of the American housewives ever knew that their vegetables and meat were wrapped in the remains of Egyptian mummies. A cholera epidemic traced back to Stanwood's paper mills marked the end of the trade.

The last person to be mummified in the west was Alexander, the 10th Duke of Hamilton, who died on 18 August 1852. He stipulated in his will that T.J. Pettigrew should embalm and bury him in an Egyptian sarcophagus in a huge mausoleum. ■

By the time Nile Valley cruising became really popular 100 or so years ago, the hunt for "antique souvenirs" even in the remotest spots had become a profitable business for *felaheen* who could unearth or manufacture them. The discovery of some rotting wooden chests filled with small clay tablets was therefore a minor windfall for a peasant woman scraping manure from an abandoned archaeological site known as Tel el-Amarna. The tablets were just what customers wanted, about the same size as a biscuit and therefore easily popped into a pocket or handbag. Many of the tablets chipped or broke as she scooped them into her sack but that hardly mattered: in fact, a bit of wear and tear made them look all the more authentic.

The mystery of Tel el-Amarna: Her find was brought to the attention of experts in Cairo but, overstretched by amazing discoveries pouring in from all over Egypt, they were not unduly excited. The site in question was a mystery. It had been thoroughly excavated by a Prussian team sponsored by King William Frederick IV as early as 1843 when *felaheen* were noticed by an earlier generation of tourists to be in possession of a considerable quantity of glassware, statuettes and pottery, artistically unusual and attractive objects but in nearly every case broken. The Prussians had uncovered the remains of a sizeable city but it, too, had suffered from more than the passage of time. It gave every indication of having been deliberately and comprehensively razed.

The more the skilled Prussian team investigated, the deeper the mystery. To begin with, the site was about halfway between Cairo and Luxor where the uncompromising sands of the Eastern Desert reached all the way to the river. When the Nile flooded, the water broke across the opposite bank; the city side was forever high, dry and barely fit for human habitation, so why was it there? Next, there was clear evidence of temples, palaces, public buildings and private housing of an exceptionally high standard, many with swimming pools. It seemed impossible

that historians had not turned up any references to the site, which as a feat of construction must have been on par with the building of a pyramid.

Most perplexing of all was the fanatical manner in which every pictorial or written reference to the notables who controlled the city had been obliterated. Those notables cannot have been less than kings or queens, yet wherever their names and images had once adorned the interior of ransacked tombs there were only the gouge marks of chisels. In one instance, a chisel had followed the outline of a human figure with such precise malice that it had gone right through the gypsum surface to leave an almost perfect silhouette indelibly in the limestone beneath.

No statue had been spared. The Prussians had found a nose here, a toe there, lips and even a woman's severed breast, but not nearly enough to assemble a likeness. They had admitted defeat, and nothing had happened since to enlighten the resident experts in Cairo.

The tablets uncovered by the woman were neatly and compactly inscribed but mostly in an incomprehensible form of cuneiform. Where there might have been references to a pharaoh the name, if it was a name, made no sense. Thanks to an Egyptian historian named Manetho, who lived at the time of the Ptolemies, the experts had a chronological list of kings since the earliest times.

Although there were hazy intermediate periods between 30 dynasties subsequently grouped together and called the Old, Middle and New Kingdoms respectively, the dates themselves meshed, so creating a system which appeared watertight. To suggest that it would now have to be dismantled to accommodate a previously overlooked king of some ranking was tantamount to taking a group of eminent mathematicians aside and whispering gently in their ears that, on the matter of squares of the sides of a right-angled triangle, dear Pythagoras, alas, had got it all horribly wrong.

The woman's tablets, therefore, were considered to be the work of a forger with insufficient expertise to make his fakes remotely plausible. Back into sacks they went

Left, head of Akhenaten, leader of the rebel Tel el-Amarna dynasty, in the Luxor Museum.

and, with official blessing, on to the stalls of unfussy souvenir salesmen.

Rebel King: The ghastly mistake was discovered in time to recover only 377 examples of what have become known as the Amarna Letters. They were in cuneiform because they had been written to the king of the mysterious city by the subject kings of Nineveh, Babylon, Canaan and Mitanni during the 18th Dynasty when Egypt was at the zenith of its imperial power. The king concerned was therefore neither an imposter nor some trifling monarch of an intermediate period. The question remained: who was he, and what was he doing in Amarna rather than in Thebes (Luxor), whose dominance of con-

temporary Egypt was a distinguishing feature of the 18th Dynasty?

The letters unlocked the world's best kept secret. The king concerned was Amenhotep IV (afterwards Akhenaten) who, like some of Stalin's rivals after the Russian revolution, had been simply purged from the pages of history. In his case, though, the illusion lasted more than 3,000 years. Those responsible were remarkably efficient. As borne out by the evidence at Amarna, every public reference to him was smashed. The hole in the 18th Dynasty caused by his summary expulsion was papered over for historical purposes by doctoring the dates of a succes-

sor. The odd mention in subsequent records went no further than dark and nameless hints of unspeakable heresy.

As a fuller picture of the facts emerged, the reprieved Amenhotep IV was given a tumultuous welcome by the academics. Some scholars drew parallels with Jesus Christ, others opted for the Prophet Mohammed. "The first individual in history," declared another. While theologians pondered the implications of the monotheism Amenhotep propounded – a single God with definite ideas about right and wrong – the imagination of a broader public was captured not so much by the king but by his queen and his younger half-brother.

They were Nefertiti, the immortal beauty, and the boy-king Tutankhamun. The special irony in Nefertiti's case was that her face – gouged and smashed in a frenzied campaign to ensure that it went irrevocably into oblivion – has survived as the most durable and recognisable Egyptian, queen or commoner, and has overtaken even the Sphinx as the biggest money-spinner in the tourist-based souvenir industry.

Lasting as long as it did, ancient Egypt inevitably had high and low fortunes, and in retrospect they were never higher than during the 18th Dynasty, the mainstay, together with the Setis and Ramseses of the 19th and 20th, of the New Kingdom. It was during the 18th Dynasty that the normally placid, often cowed and hitherto inward-looking Egyptians were fired by imperial dreams which they pursued as determined warriors. The military assertiveness tailed off after a few generations and stopped completely, if it did not actually go into reverse, under controversial Amenhotep III. Thereafter the New Kingdom went into decline, although not without some brisk rearguard actions waged by the Ramseses.

United by the invader: The impetus for the growth of militarism was the humiliating occupation of the country by the Hyksos for three centuries. They came, as far as the Egyptians were aware, vaguely from "somewhere in the east". Nor was there, it seems, the familiar historical phenomenon of invaders being seduced into the superior culture of the conquered. The Hyksos kept to themselves in fortresses, not so much administering the land as helping themselves to whatever they wanted through the long arm of raiding parties. They ventured out on horse-drawn chariots and armed with bronze swords, neither of which the Egyptians had seen before. Any reluctance to meet their wishes was settled with brutal finality. The Egyptian pharaohs continued to live in their palaces in Thebes but were left in no doubt that they were under sufferance. One was ordered to do something about the hippopotamus in the palace pool. Its infernal bellowing, the Hyksos leader complained, made life at his headquarters intolerable. The headquarters in question happened to be in the Delta, several hundred miles away!

Having inspired Egypt's scattered and fractious noble families with a sense of common

In any case, Amose's ultimate victory depended on chasing the Hyksos well beyond Egypt's northern border, and this campaign seems to have opened his eyes to the possibilities of turning the tables. Put simply, harassed kings would quite soon pay large sums to persuade the Egyptians to go home and not come back.

The immense wealth of the 18th Dynasty, and hence the means to turn Thebes into the grandiose capital of the world, was based on a subtle form of international blackmail which recognised the price which a victim would pay before insurrection became a more attractive alternative.

Tuthmosis III applied this principle to the

purpose, Amose I (also Kamose) managed to nurse popular resentment through what must have been a difficult and dangerous gestation until he had an army capable of engaging the Hyksos. If the much later examples of the Vandals and other belligerent barbarians in North Africa are anything to go by, the task may have been made easier by the tendency of those who are forced by harsh realities at home to live by the sword or die.

Left, the bust of Queen Nefertiti where it now rests in the Berlin Museum. **Above**, coloured mosaic from Tel el-Amarna which illustrates the very different style of the rebel dynasty's art.

hilt. Between 1490 and 1486 BC, he swept through all the neighbouring countries and advanced into Asia Minor. The titles he accumulated reflect his progress: first the "Hero of Seventeen Campaigns", then "Conqueror of Three Hundred and Sixty-Seven Cities", finally "Founder of the Egyptian Empire". His awed subjects heard tales of the intrepid king wrestling personally with an enraged elephant. There was harder evidence of his success in the arrival of barges and caravans at Thebes loaded with booty and the tribute negotiated with newly subject kings. Tuthmosis paused between conquests to erect monuments commemorating his trail of victories. Some of these, incidentally, still stand, although not where he intended or could possibly have imagined: one is in Central Park, New York, behind the Metropolitan Museum, with others in London, Rome and Istanbul.

Royal usurper: Preoccupied abroad, Tuthmosis failed to pay sufficient attention to what was happening at home. The treasures he repatriated were put into the custody of the priesthood of Amon, a provision which conferred power as it nurtured ambition. He eventually returned to discover that in his absence he had been usurped.

The usurper, moreover, was his aunt, the dowager Queen Hatshepsut, who preferred now to be known as "King" and, to that end, had taken to wearing male clothing and a false beard, albeit the gold variety which was a traditional symbol of royal authority. She evidently liked the look of the beard because she is seen wearing it in a number of official portraits. She also ordained a statue which put her face, cum beard, on the body of a scaled-down sphinx. "The world's first feminist," a modern biography notes approvingly.

The "Napoleon of Egypt" took this sudden reverse sitting down. He applied himself to pottery and, on the evidence available, seems to have become adept at it. His formidable aunt remained on the throne for a further 18 years, time enough to build what many regard as the Nile Valley's most awesome temple, the one which bears her name at Deir el Bahri on the west bank opposite Luxor. She may in the end have died of natural causes or, more likely, Tuthmosis's patience ran out and he meted out what was forever hovering over pharaohs like an occupational hazard, the careless sip from a poisoned chalice.

Hatshepsut's death released Tuthmosis's coiled energy. While one set of workmen embarked at top speed on belated monuments to himself, others went about pulling down everything related to her. He spared the temple, but was unhappy about her two enormous obelisks inside. When no amount of heaving could budge them, he settled for a wall which at least plastered their repulsive presence out of sight, and the obelisks did not see the light of day again until modern times.

Luxor fiesta: Tuthmosis introduced an annual "Feast of Victory" as a belated celebration of his earlier triumphs. The festivities lasted 11 days in what must have been an already tight calendar of public holidays. Thebes' Day of the Dead, for example, carried on through the night. The occasion marked the joyous reunion of the dead with their descendants and in several respects resembles Halloween. Oil lamps were hung on every door to help groggy spirits who might otherwise have difficulty locating their graves afterwards.

The most prolonged celebrations were in honour of Thebes's favourite goddess, Opet the hippopotamus, which goes some way to explaining why the Hyksos chief's little joke about the racket in the palace pool would

have hit a raw nerve. The climax of a month of revelry saw the image of Amon, who had assumed the position of the supreme god in Thebes, leave his sanctuary in the Karnak Temple for a fantastic procession through the city by river to the "Harem of the South" temple (the Temple of Luxor). What happened when god and royal retinue disappeared into the temple was a secret known only to those entitled to be there.

It seems, though, that Amon underwent a curious transmogrification into Min, a god whose powerful sensuality was credited to eating large quantities of lettuce. The proceedings were enlivened by young priestesses who, in costumes designed around tiny kilts and much larger top hats made out of reeds, formed a chorus line and performed a dance which honoured, if it did not imitate, the revered hippopotamus.

The time and money needed for such extravagant public entertainment was provided not only by the wealth flowing in from abroad but also by the relatively effortless availability of life's necessities. As long as the Nile flooded reliably every year, the cultivation of crops required no more than short bursts of activity at the appropriate times of the year. Landless peasants might not have sung praises to their good fortune, but those on the higher rungs of the economic scale would

not have regarded everyday life as taxing.

Godly hierarchy: The strict observation of religious obligations, on the other hand, could have been made daunting by weight of numbers. Beliefs evolved with regional variations from the basic conception of a father-sun and mother-earth (later expanded to include a son, thereby forming a trinity) whose divinity permeated everything, animate and inanimate, which had been created out of a watery nothingness. While a rock was in this sense semi-divine, attention was focused on

Left, Queen Hatshepsut with the beard of royal authority, and **above**, Hatshepsut's mummy.

some 2,000 gods with whom a more rewarding relationship could be maintained.

The Nile had its own roster of gods, principally the aforementioned hippopotamus and the crocodile. Towns along the river adopted their own favourites from lesser echelons. These creatures were given temples where, soothed by hymn-singing, they slithered or wriggled about with rings in their ears (if they had ears) and jewelled bracelets round their legs (if they had legs). At the end of their pampered lives they were put to rest in a private cemetery. Local loyalties could lead to conflict; war was declared between neighbouring towns over the status of a particular fish. Sacred in one, in the other it was blasphemously caught and eaten.

"The Egyptians are religious to excess, beyond any other nation in the world," Herodotus reported. His visit was very late in the day, but he took into account ancient practices. "They all wear linen cothes which they make a point of continually washing... The priests shave their bodies all over every other day to guard against the presence of lice or anything else equally unpleasant while they are about their duties."

The priests had every reason to insist on strict religious observance. They were the necessary medium through which dealings with the gods were conducted. To grant or withhold that service from petitioners could in certain circumstances be construed as power over life or death.

The priests naturally demanded payment for each and every transaction they concluded and this, together with the sale of magic charms for every conceivable purpose, constituted colossal revenue. The rewards awaiting a priesthood able to attract adherents to its particular god were as handsome and enticing as modern businesses find the prospect of a significantly larger market share. It was the manner in which the priests of Amon promoted their vested interest that was to bring about the confrontation which convulsed the 12th Dynasty.

Perhaps the real explanation for Tuthmosis III's lame surrender to his bearded aunt was that she had cultivated the backing of the priesthood while he merely commanded the army. The fear of the authority of the priesthood increased over the generations and communicated itself to the children who were growing up in the palace nursery in the days of Tuthmosis's great-grandson. The children were the future Amenhotep IV and Nefertiti, the daughter of the then king's principal architect.

Romantic novelists and even some purportedly serious biographers can be sensed as near swooning over their word processors as they tackle a plot involving a young prince (shy, sensitive but good at games) and the daughter of a commoner ("a golden slip" with "wide and innocent eyes"). At first they play together like brother and sister. With the furtive exchange of childish kisses they experience, deep inside, a pubescent premonition of love. And so it comes about that they ascend hand-in-hand to the throne and are proclaimed King and Queen of Egypt. "The will of the sun!" declares a biographer bringing her chapter to a breathless close.

The gruffer version of events simply states that the prince Amenhotep was crowned in 1369 BC at the age of 16, his wife Nefertiti was a year younger, and they already had a child. They were initially co-regents, sharing the throne with the ailing Amenhotep III. According to some interpretations, the king later discarded Nefertiti in favour of a homosexual half-brother, although there is a possibility that the apparent half-brother was in fact Nefertiti in some kind of light disguise. This, in turn, could imply a weakness for transvestism reminiscent of Hatshepsut, Tuthmosis III's aunt.

Change of god: Amenhotep IV was no warrior king, but to a questioning frame of mind he added fearless tenacity of purpose. He began by chipping at the authority of the priesthood with the ordering of modest temples to a lesser god, better known in the northern city of Heliopolis than in Thebes, with whom he felt a close affinity, Aten. Although Amon had associations with the sun, Aten's were exclusively so, and the god was portrayed with a sun-disc on his head. One of the last glimpses of the young king (with his queen Nefertiti) before the storm broke was included as a painting in the preparation of a tomb for the vizier Ramose in the Valley of the Kings, where it can still be seen today.

At 18 years of age, Amenhotep IV probably did not feel quite ready to confront the priesthood head-on, preferring instead to build a haven where he could worship Aten as he saw fit. The site chosen was halfway between Thebes and the Old Kingdom capital of Memphis. It was, of course, Tel el-Amarna, the first city to be designed and built from scratch. It was laid out against the barren backdrop of the desert in an oblong about two miles long and a half-mile wide. It included palaces, temples, a grid of streets broad enough to allow four carriages abreast and – a major innovation much imitated since – a working-class neighbourhood of neat, identical little houses.

This immense undertaking required the concerted effort of most of the craftsmen and artisans living in Thebes, a haemorrhage which could not have gone unnoticed by the priesthood of Amon. Barges brought sandstone down from Aswan and timber up from the Mediterranean. The king seems to have restrained himself while his father remained in Thebes, probably too old and ailing (and perhaps still too loyal to Amon) to decamp to the new city. On his death in 1361 BC, however, an undeclared war broke out between pharaoh and priests.

The first shot fired was the declaration that the king would henceforth be known as Akhenaten in honour of the sun-god. This was quickly followed, possibly as a preemptive measure, by orders that all the temples to Amon and other gods in Thebes were to be closed, the priests dismissed and public references to all gods but Aten removed. One of the pillars at Karnak still shows signs of the defacement of Amon's name, an inadequate indication of what was evidently an orgy of destruction by troops who were loyal to the king.

The new order: A stalemate lasting several years followed. The priests, denied the right to wear their traditional leopard-skin capes and deprived of a living, went underground. Akhenaten, for his part, was content to retire to Tel el-Amarna and forget about them. His rejection of the old religious order brought about a comparable revolution in the arts. Instead of the highly stylised presentation of the human form, artists experimented with distortions of the body, sometimes grotesque, which would not have been out of place in the 1920s.

This artistic licence extended even to the way in which the royals were portrayed: Akhenaten seen slouching on his throne or standing with a fat belly and spindly legs; his eyes heavily lidded, his lips bulbous. The most intriguing – and leading to speculation that Amarna might have tolerated sexual licentiousness – show the naked king without male sexual organs but with pendulous, almost female breasts. It was the radical departure in all departments of art which produced the puzzling "antique souvenirs" in the early part of the 19th century.

Diversions at court seem to have deprived Akhenaten of the will to rule in all but a token way. It was either that or a pacifist nature which caused him to ignore letters from his subject kings in the north warning him of encroachments on the empire and imploring him to lead his army against them. These, indeed, are the letters which, when found by

the date on which Haremhab, a former army general, seized power, and fitting it some years after his death.

On the precise circumstances of Akhenaten's death, the trail runs cold. He may have been poisoned; he may have died young (he was probably 32) of a complaint, according to theories based on the elongated shape of his head, associated with excessive inbreeding. In any event, the state in which the Prussian team found Tel el-Amarna at the beginning of the 19th century and what was discovered by archaeologists who rushed back to the site to sift through the evidence ever more finely, leaves no doubt about the ferocity with which the supporters of Amon

the peasant woman in 1887, were very nearly lost again through the failure to recognise the import of the cuneiform script.

Once the letters had rescued Akhenaten from the oblivion into which the avenging priests had conspired and very nearly managed to thrust him after his death in about 1353 BC, Egyptologists were able to piece together a more rounded biography. The gap in the chronology of kings had been papered over, it was discovered, by bringing forward

Above, King Akhenaten and Queen Nefertiti depicted in the slightly grotesque Tel el-Amarna style, playing with three of their children.

sought to redress the balance.

It was left to the Swiss archaeologist Ludwig Borchardt and a Briton, Howard Carter, to fit the most spectacular pieces to a fascinating jigsaw. Borchardt was aroused from an afternoon nap on 6 December 1912 by his foreman who had caught a glimpse of flesh-coloured plaster on an object buried in the sands of Amarna. It was a magnanimous gesture on the part of the foreman towards a man who was about to realise the fruits of a two-year search. As Borchardt's practised hand flicked away grains of sand, Nefertiti's features slowly, triumphantly emerged from a 3,000-year-old grave.

All the representations of Ramses II – and they far outnumber those of any other pharaoh – are of squared shoulders, a head held high, and an expression of immense self-satisfaction. It is all the more ironic, therefore, that it should have been an unrecognised statue of him, toppled face down in the sand, that the poet Shelley should have immortalised as an ignominious example of a god with clay feet. The poem, of course, is *Ozymandias*, Ramses's coronation name:

I met a traveller from an antique land who said:
Two vast and trunkless legs of stone
Stand in the desert…
…And on the pedestal these words appear:
'My name is Ozymandias, King of Kings:
Look on my work, ye mighty, and despair!'
Nothing beside remains. Round the decay
Of that colossal wreck, boundless and bare
The lone and level sands stretch far away.

Shelley was wrong because a great deal remained: Abu Simbel, the Ramesseum, the temple of Karnak, the temple of Abydos, parts of the temple of Luxor, six temples in Nubia (before the building of the dams), and others which Ramses usurped in his name. Recent excavations have uncovered a string of fortresses which he built along the Mediterranean coast. All were lavished with statues and fulsome tributes to himself, an exercise in self-aggrandisement which makes the combined personality of 20th-century despots look coy.

It cannot be denied that Ramses II led a full life. He ruled, initially as co-regent, for 67 years, lived for 90 or so, waged 20 wars, oppressed the Israelites (it was he from whom Moses fled), married officially three times but maintained an active harem of more than 200 women, had more than 100 sons and about 60 daughters, and by the girls he added to his innumerable grandchildren.

"One of the handsomest men not only of his own day but of all history," gushed the normally reserved spinster Amelia Edwards, a 19th-century Nile traveller. She devoted

some time to removing white spots from the faces of his enormous statues at Abu Simbel, but even on such close acquaintance she would have been pushed to recognise the features when his coffin was opened some years afterwards. Admittedly well beyond his prime when he died, Ramses II had rotten teeth and a large, hooked nose which sculptors scrupulously overlooked. His heart was evidently in a bad way and he had serious arthritis in a hip.

His greatest battle was fought against the

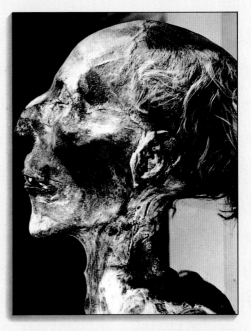

Hittites near Aleppo in Syria in the fifth year of his reign, about 1285 BC. Pentaour wrote a Homeric epic which dwelt on Ramses's single-handed battle with 2,500 Hittite chariots, and the king liked the thought so much that he recorded the details of the Battle of Kadesh over and over again on his various monuments, most graphically on one of the walls of his temple at Karnak. Of course it was a wild exaggeration but it made good reading.

Ramses permitted himself to be quoted as follows: "I became like the god Mentu. I hurled the dart with my right hand, I fought with my left hand; I was like Baal in his fury

Preceding pages: Ramses's greatest monument, the temple at Abu Simbel. Left , the king's head in stone at the Ramesseum. Right, his mummy.

against them. I had come upon two thousand five hundred pairs of horses; I was in the midst of them; but they were dashed to pieces before my steeds. Not one of them raised his hand to fight; their heart shrank within them; their limbs gave way, they could not hurl the dart, nor had they strength to thrust with the spear. As crocodiles fall into the water, so I made them fall; they tumbled headlong one over another. I killed them at my pleasure, so that not one of them looked back behind him, nor did any turn round. Each fell, and none raised himself up again."

References to the (unnamed) Ramses in the Bible are less flattering. He made Israel

That much was known, and Napoleon's troops thought they had located the palace city near the Delta town of San el Hagar, but because of the connection with the Old Testament and in particular the forced labour and subsequent exodus of the Hebrews, confirmation of the site became a matter of archaeological excitement towards the end of the 19th century. The Egypt Exploration Fund (later "Society") offered one mudbrick, the product of Hebrew hands, for every £1 subscription to their newsletter. Money poured in.

Ramses's fame as a builder is associated not with the New World he sought to establish in the Delta but from the "Old" he

"sigh" and "groan" (Exodus ii.) and in so doing attracted the unfavourable attention of God. He put the Hebrews to work in the fields "with rigour" and it is supposed that they made up a substantial part of the forced labour which built his monuments.

Ramses II, son of Seti I, was of the 19th Dynasty (New Kingdom). His rule followed the religious upheaval fomented by Akhenaten and the boy-king Tutankhamun. His father was instrumental in the drift away from Luxor towards the Delta, and Ramses accelerated the process by building a permanent palace at what had been a summer residence in the old Hyksos capital of Tanis.

strained to leave. He was only a contributor to the temple of Karnak – from the New Kingdom onwards many kings added their personal touches – and tried to magnify his work by usurping the hypostyle hall, which was actually begun by Ramses I and completed by his father, Seti I. The usurpation can be seen in the way his cartouche has been superimposed. It is on a wall outside the hall that Ramses emblazoned his account of the Battle of Kadesh.

He was similarly only a contributor to the temple of Luxor, but he assumed pride of place with the front pylons (another report on the Battle of Kadesh) and four colossal statues, two standing and two seated. The obelisk which is now in the Place de la Concorde in Paris was one of the pair which originally stood near the statues. As in Karnak, Ramses usurped the work of one of his predecessors, in this instance of Amenhotep III.

On the west bank at Luxor is the Ramesseum, a temple serving the cult of Ramses II and containing, therefore, an account of the Battle of Kadesh! This rendition is embellished with the wretched Hittite prince being dangled upside down by his ankles, apparently to shake out water swallowed when he was dumped in the Orontes. The most striking piece in the Ramesseum, thanks to

Shelley, is the broken statue, "Ozymandias" being Ramses's coronation name. It is estimated that in its pristine state, the statue, the largest ever cut from a single piece of granite, weighed 1,000 tons.

At his father's limestone temple at Abydos, Ramses was busy again, imposing pictures of himself as a young prince fraternising with all the kings from Menes onwards and, on a series of pillars, with the gods. He could justly claim all the credit, however, for temples in Nubia and, in particular for his mas-

More Ramses heads. Left, at Memphis and above, at the Temple of Luxor.

terpiece on the island of Abu Simbel which, as may be anticipated, celebrated the victory at Kadesh: Ramses charging a fortress, Ramses spearing an enemy, Ramses inspecting severed hands of the enemy, and so on and so on.

Abu Simbel was famously the subject of an international rescue operation when the site would otherwise have been drowned by the construction of the High Dam. Four colossal statues of the seated king guarded the entrance to a 180-ft (54 metre) hall cut out of solid rock. In the sanctuary within were four more statues: Ramses, of course, this time in the company of Egypt's greatest gods.

A second temple at Abu Simbel, also saved, is a clue to some of the political reality of Ramses's ostentatious reign. It was dedicated to his Great Royal Wife, Nefertari, who was actually one of the despised Hittites. He married her 13 years after the Battle of Kadesh and some historians are inclined to read into the marriage that the Egyptian victory was not as conclusive as the temple ornamention endlessly proclaims. The marriage was in reality a gesture of conciliation, they say, towards people whom he found himself unable to subdue. Indeed, a version of the Kadesh peace treaty in the Hittite capital Baghazkoy claimed victory for the home side!

Ramses II had inherited the vast Egyptian empire built up by Thutmosis III and consolidated by his father. "From and after the conclusion of peace and alliance between Ramses and (the Hittites)," says George Rawlinson, "Egyptian influence in Asia grew vague, shadowy, and discontinuous… we may say that her Asiatic domination was lost, and that Egypt became once more an African power, confined within nearly her ancient limits."

If, as now appears fairly certain, Ramses did preside over the dissolution of the Egyptian empire, Shelley's poem may make an unintended point rather well. But perhaps the ultimate irony for a king whose fantastic building activity should at least have provided a secure and dignified grave, was that his coffin had to be hastily removed from his tomb in the Valley of the Kings to save it from robbers. It was later recovered from what amounted to an anonymous mass grave in the cliff above Queen Hatshepsut's temple at Deir el Bahri.

CLEOPATRA AND THE PTOLEMIES

In October 48 BC, Julius Caesar had the world at his feet. The only obstacle between him and total control of the Roman Empire had been removed with the defeat in Greece of rebellious elements of the army. Their leader, Pompey, had slipped away with the thought of rallying support in Egypt, an independent kingdom, and it was to tie up this loose end that Caesar sailed into the Great Harbour of Alexandria with a fleet of 35 vessels carrying what remained of his two legions of infantry and 800 cavalry.

In the event, Caesar need not have bothered. Pompey had been murdered as soon as he stepped ashore and, according to some accounts, Caesar was presented with his severed head when he arrived shortly afterwards. Caesar might then have turned at once to deal with pressing business in Rome but he was concerned – he said in his official despatches – about contrary winds at that time of year and also about a royal squabble in Egypt which he ought to look into.

Ardour for conquest: Caesar was then 54 years old and, appearances apart, was in his prime. His hair was thinning and his features were beginning to look gaunt, a bitter pill for one who by repute "appeared among all victories to value most those over beautiful women." These conquests were, it seems, his "necessary relaxations in the course of the most arduous public affairs."

His decision to linger in Egypt may have owed more to gossip about the young Queen Cleopatra than to contrary winds. Still only 21, Cleopatra badly needed an ally in struggles with her family, preferably a powerful foreign one. A Roman ambassador passing by the previous year had found himself in her arms being coaxed round to her point of view. It is not hard to imagine what crossed Caesar's mind. Writing a century later, the pious St Chrysostom was down to earth about it. Cleopatra was "exceedingly beautiful", had "the sweetest of voices" and "every charm of conversation". In his opinion, "enough to ensnare even the most obdurate and elderly man."

Left, Cleopatra before Caesar, having emerged from a rolled-up carpet. Painting by Jean Gérôme.

While Cleopatra is fixed in many minds nowadays as a bewigged Elizabeth Taylor in a bathful of asses' milk, her contemporaries always mentioned first the seductive voice and witty repartee. It seems she was an accomplished linguist, capable of conversing with Ethiopians, Hebrews, Arabs, Syrians, Medes, Parthians and – in whatever they spoke – troglodytes who lived in holes.

As for her looks, the debate has included faint praise (Plutarch said that it was quite possible to gaze upon her without being bowled over) and some uncomplimentary conjecture about the size of her nose. "All that we can feel certain about," wrote a Victorian historian with impatient finality, "is that she had not a short nose."

She was certainly wily. "While it was on her sex that she relied when she desired to effect a great stroke," one study decided, "she never neglected the possibilities of bribery combined with an occasional assassination, when it seemed safe to employ the assassin's aid." As she was implicated in the death of two brothers and a sister and spitefully executed a harmless old Armenian king whom she had held captive for several years, Cleopatra "well merited the title of murderess". The author concerned thought her crimes were mitigated by her being a particularly good mother to her children.

"If the Ptolemies at this period in their history had been able to produce a good woman," a critic sighed, "it would have been a miracle." Her father was recognised as one of the very worst examples of a consistently rotten dynasty. He cavorted in female dress, danced in public to the sound of cymbals and, on waking up, thought of nothing but getting drunk again as quickly as possible.

Greek dynasty: The Ptolemies are said to have produced just two kings "at which history can point with pleasure", yet during the 300-year dynasty Egypt was undoubtedly the richest country in the world. When Alexander the Great died in Babylon, his Egyptian conquest passed on to one of his generals, who was crowned in 305 BC and became "Ptolemy the Saviour". He and his successors wanted the best of both worlds: they readily accepted the divinity that went along with the Egyptian crown, but in other respects they remained resolutely Greek. Alexandria was a Greek capital with Greek institutions and a fleet manned by Greek mercenaries.

The one criticial function which the Ptolemies could not perform as expatriate Greeks, however, was collect taxes. The priests had that sewn up, so in religious matters the Ptolemies were ardently orthodox. They ingratiated themselves with the priesthood by building some of the finest temples still to be seen in the Nile Valley, at Dendera, Edfu, Kom Ombo and, especially, on the island of Philae. A few Greek flourishes intruded on the traditional design, but the Ptolemies took pains to be depicted on the walls in Egyptian costume rather than in the Greek dress which they customarily wore. Their cartouches were in hieroglyphs, which in general they could not read. Cleopatra seems to have been unique among the Ptolemies in being able to speak Egyptian. At the tail end of the dynasty, she was unfortunately too late to be depicted on the temples in more than one or two places.

History has two popular versions of how Cleopatra and Caesar came to meet. One has her being carried and dumped at his feet in a kind of sack, a trick to evade hostile pickets surrounding the palace where Caesar was staying. The other prefers her choosing a seductive outfit and bursting in on him in the middle of the night. One way or another, though, all agree that by morning Caesar was firmly on her side.

The problem, as Cleopatra would have explained it, was that she and a younger brother had inherited the throne jointly. She was then 18, her brother was 11. It was normal among Egyptian royals that they also happened to be husband and wife, a form of institutionalised incest designed to keep the royal blood pure. Cleopatra was herself the product of perhaps as many as a dozen consecutive incestuous unions and seemed none the worse for it, although there was more than a touch of insanity among her relatives.

The marriage was a disaster from the outset, and on reaching his majority (at 14), her brother Ptolemy XIV, as he was, reneged on the principle of a shared throne. Caesar agreed with Cleopatra that this was wrong and had the boy brought before him. On being told that Cleopatra was being reinstated, Ptolemy

went reeling through the streets, howling cries of "Betrayal!" He tore his crown from his head and smashed it to the ground.

Royal cruise: Caesar's own history describes what happened next as some kind of disturbance in Alexandria which he dutifully suppressed. In fact, it seems that the population were for Ptolemy and against Cleopatra, but he scarcely mentions her. Nor does he say anything about taking time off to visit the sites of Egypt. According to Appian, he went off "to explore the country and to enjoy himself with Cleopatra in other ways."

With an escort of 400 ships, they cruised in a double-decker floating palace, 300 ft (90 metres) long and 45 ft (14 metres) wide, propelled by banks of oarsmen and a 100-ft (30-metre) linen sail fringed in purple. Meals and entertainment were provided for up to 60 guests who were stretched out on couches in a saloon panelled in cypress and cedar. Guests had private cabins and, as the mood took them, the use of chapels to Aphrodite and Dionysos. The lower deck contained a mock cave made out of slabs of stone and lined with gold.

M. Henry Houssaye gave 19th-century French readers the benefit of his scholarship and imagination on how the couple passed their time. "With Caesar, Cleopatra instinctively played the part…never ceasing to be the charmer, but joining dignity to grace, hiding the courtesan under the queen, showing an even temper every day, expressing herself in chosen language, talking of politics, art, and literature, lifting without an effort her wonderful faculties to the supreme level of the Dictator's intelligence."

The cruise lasted nine months, at which point Caesar decided he really had to get back to Rome. He was not long gone when Cleopatra gave birth to a son, whom she named Caesarion. Caesar never formally acknowledged paternity, although it is thought that an interest in seeing the child was partly the reason for inviting Cleopatra to Rome soon afterwards. Travelling with her was her youngest brother and new husband, Ptolemy XV, who was at that time aged about 11.

Roman society took to Cleopatra as the English did to Mrs Simpson's designs on King Edward VIII, or Americans to Aristotle Onassis's on the widowed Jacqueline Kennedy. "I detest the queen," wrote Cicero after meeting her. "Her insolence...I cannot recall without a pang." Young Ptolemy was "an unprincipled rascal". Caesar rubbed salt into these misgivings by placing a statue of Cleopatra next to the temple of Venus. It was whispered that he intended to discard his loyal wife, marry Cleopatra, assume the title of King of Egypt and move the imperial capital to Alexandria. Caesar's assassination on the Ides of March, 44 BC, was not unconnected with these rumours. Cleopatra left Rome in a hurry, evidently poisoning the "unprincipled rascal" her brother and leaving him in her wake. She defiantly made Caesar's illegitimate son co-regent and named him Ptolemy Caesarion.

from one of the victorious generals. He was tied up in Syria, he said, so he suggested she visit him there.

Plutarch describes her arrival at Syria in a ship with purple sails and a gilded stern. The oars were plated with silver and glinted as they moved to the music of flutes, pipes and harps. She was stretched out on the deck "like Aphrodite... reclining under an awning bespangled with gold, while boys like painted Cupids stood on either side fanning her. Marvellous odours from many censers wafted to the land..."

The general who savoured this agreeable sight was Mark Antony, and, yes, he was certainly free for dinner aboard. "Every dish

Mark Antony: The Egypt to which Cleopatra returned was suffering from a low flood, always a calamity, and though she may not have realised it, tales of Egypt's incredible wealth had thoroughly whetted Roman imperial appetites. This presented a greater threat than squabbles with her family, but for the moment Rome was preoccupied by a civil war between forces loyal to Caesar's memory and republicans. As the war moved to a conclusion in favour of the former, Cleopatra received an intriguing invitation

Above, the *Feast of Antony and Cleopatra*, painting from the studio of Francesco Trevisani.

was golden and inlaid with precious stones, wonderfully chased and embossed... She, smiling, said she made him a present of everything he saw." Would he like to come again? Indeed he would and he did, night after night.

When it was time to reciprocate, Antony's hospitality was comparatively pathetic. Cleopatra recognised that this was no polished courtier like Caesar but a rough and ready soldier. No matter, it seems; "she fell at once freely and boldly into the same manner toward him." His interest in public affairs, says Appian ominously, "began to dwindle." Octavian, the future Augustus and one of

Antony's partners in the triumvirate, put it more bluntly: "He has been bewitched by the accursed woman."

It seems that Antony's invitation to Cleopatra to join him in Syria may have had a longer history than her now well-known weakness for representatives of Rome. He had evidently never forgotten seeing her as a young girl when he was on an assignment to Egypt, then a junior officer with huge personal debts and a propensity for debauchery. His successful handling of the mission had patched up an unpropitious reputation and set him on course for better things.

Even enemies conceded that Antony had good points. A handsome brute, said Cicero, built like a gladiator, an impressive beard, broad forehead and an aquiline nose which his family claimed showed their descent from the demi-god Herakles. Antony cultivated the glorious connection, keeping the image alive by hoisting his tunic high to accentuate bulging thighs and by wearing an unusually large sword. Shakespeare later made him a subtle orator, but at the time Plutarch had reservations. A student of oratory at the University of Athens, Antony had developed Greek tendencies: "boastful and swaggering and full of empty pride."

Having narrowly rescued his reputation once, Antony seemed strangely careless about risking it again. He was 40 when he courted Cleopatra. He had just married for the third time although, it was noticed in Rome, this had not meant giving up his coterie of actresses nor Rome's leading courtesan, Cytheris. Rome was never noted for blind marital fidelity, but his new wife was a popular figure. "Energetic and daring," someone called her.

Indiscretion with Cleopatra, however, was quickly compounded by the strings attached. She was bothered by her sister Arsinoe, she told him, and would like her murdered. Antony agreed to make the necessary arrangements.

Marital problems: While Antony was being drawn into Cleopatra's personal difficulties, the triumvirate's position in Rome was deteriorating fast. His colleagues' appeal for help fell on deaf ears. "He suffered himself to be carried off by Cleopatra to Alexandria," wrote Plutarch, "there to stay and amuse himself like a boy in holiday-time."

At last – and "with difficulty, and like a man aroused from sleep and a drunken debauch" – Antony agreed to lead a campaign against the Parthians in Asia Minor. He was shocked on calling at Athens to find his wife, the popular Fulvia, looking for him. He apparently accused her of abandoning her duties in Rome and they parted on bad terms. She was soon dead – "a willing victim to disease on account of Antony's anger." Antony seems to have accepted the blame and was by all accounts "much saddened by this event".

He did not see Cleopatra for three years and in the meantime remarried. The new wife was Octavia, sister to Octavian. It was evidently a happy marriage and relations with his brother-in-law were good. They split the empire between them, Octavian taking the western half and Antony the eastern. Egypt naturally fell within Antony's sphere of responsibility. Ominously, "that great evil which had long slept, the passion for Cleopatra which seemed to have been lulled and charmed into oblivion by better considerations, blazed forth."

Antony and Cleopatra's reunion saw their earlier positions reversed. It was he who was lavish. She deserved a little something, he said, and made her a present of Cyprus, Phoenicia, the Arabian shores of the Red Sea and chunks of Syria, Cilicia and Judaea. Her response was to ask if she could not have a little more of Syria, a bit that belonged to King Herod. Antony thought not, but made up for the disappointment with the Gardens of Jericho.

The interlude ended with Antony again called away to war, this time in Syria. The war went badly, and he was driven back to the beaches near Beirut, demoralised, unable to pay his troops and drinking heavily. Both women in his life set out to rescue him with money and reinforcements. Cleopatra got there first and, learning that Octavia was en route, "pretended to be desperately in love with Antony." The source, Plutarch, says she went on a hunger strike, assuming an expression of strong passion whenever Antony was near and of great dejection when he had other things to do. In any case, Octavia received word in Athens that she was to proceed no further and go directly home.

The insult to his sister aggravated Octavian's fury over Antony dishing out huge chunks of the empire which were not his to give away. Then there was the news that Antony, safely back in Egypt with Cleopatra, had a staged a triumph in Alexandria (to celebrate an earlier victory over the Armenians), whereas triumphs were exclusively the prerogative of Rome. Cleopatra had watched the triumph from a golden throne and in a preposterous costume, hawk head and cow horns, which convinced Octavian that they were both mad.

Tragedy looms: The last straw was a letter from Antony not only discarding his wife Octavia but ordering her out of their house. Octavian declared war but first had to find Antony and Cleopatra, who had gone off, with the Egyptian army, to winter in Greece.

The eventual battle was a fiasco, Antony deserting his men and taking refuge aboard Cleopatra's ship where, apparently realising what he had done, he is said to have sat in silence on the prow for three days with his head in his hands.

Antony was still miserable when they reached Alexandria. Instead of going to the palace where he usually stayed, he locked himself in a hut on a mole in the Great Harbour. Octavian did not immediately pursue him and gradually the cloud lifted. Cleo-

Above, the *Death of Cleopatra*, oil panel by Baptiste Regnault.

patra, on the other hand, seemed to sense that things could get rather worse. She experimented with poisons, testing them on condemned prisoners until she settled on the asp whose bite "brought on drowsy numbness, with no spasms or groans, but with a gentle perspiration over the face and a dulling of the senses." She took her preparations to the logical conclusion by building a tomb for herself near the temple of Isis Lochias in Alexandria.

The final act has been portrayed with so many twists – for example, with the asp's fangs lost in Miss Taylor's ample bosom – that it may be worth recounting the historical version, as best can be established.

Octavian's army eventually burst through Alexandria's defences with minimal opposition although Antony personally fought bravely. Antony left the battlefield partially redeemed only to be told that Cleopatra had already committed suicide and been interred in her two-storey tomb. He went straight to his chambers, handed his sword to his servant Eros and asked to be run through with it. The faithful Eros could not do it; instead he fell on the sword himself, as if to demonstrate how it ought to be done. Antony followed his example but made a mess of it. He was writhing on the floor when word came that Cleopatra was, after all, still alive.

Antony was carried to the tomb and winched up to the window in a litter. "Never was there a more piteous sight," wrote Plutarch, who claimed to have spoken to an eyewitness. "Antony was hauled up, stained with blood and wrestling against death, stretching out his hands towards Cleopatra as he hung in the air." She pulled him in and he died in her arms.

Cleopatra did not then clasp the asp, as the legend runs. In fact, it seems she attended Antony's funeral and lived for some weeks or even months afterwards.

She did in the end commit suicide, possibly through fear of the triumph that Octavian was likely to hold and which could well feature her in chains, and possibly availing herself of the asp. Before doing so, she had the chance to discuss matters with Octavian. According to Plutarch, she hoped right to the end that, if only Octavian would come into her arms, she would be able to bring him round to her point of view. He wouldn't, so she couldn't.

The Mamlukes are remembered today, if at all, for the heroic futility of their performance at the Battle of the Pyramids in 1798, where they charged Napoleon's artillery and were mown down. Their obscurity is undeserved and surprising because, in the words of the soldier-historian Glubb Pasha John Bagot, for example, the empire they created in Egypt was "a historical prodigy, a unique curiosity among civilised states." It was, in short, a sequence of some 50 military dictators drawn from an ever-replenished pool of young white boys kidnapped or imported as slaves from distant foreign lands.

In this system there was no conception of hereditary succession, or rather none that worked. Whenever one of the former slaves who had worked himself up to ruler or lord died, his wealth went to the treasury and his land was redistributed. His succession was determined by the most telling combination available of ambition, ability and ruthlessness. Death in bed was, for Mamlukes, practically unknown and hardly expected. "But by far the most amazing factor in this extraordinary story," in Glubb's opinion, "is that all these unique peculiarities made no difference at all to the rise and fall of their empire." It lasted, in fact, longer than the British Empire.

Dying days: By the time Napoleon invaded Egypt, the Mamlukes were ostensibly out to grass. They were no longer rulers as such because the country had long been under Ottoman pashas, although behind the scenes they still exercised considerable influence as landowners backed up by private armies. However, French invasion stirred powerful atavistic instincts in the Mamlukes and only they showed any determination to resist it. They had not fought a major battle for nearly 300 years but they were acutely conscious of their traditions. In their time they had been one of the finest fighting forces in the world, an elite body of cavalry who had only one idea about going into battle, and that was the charge. The rules of modern warfare may have changed; theirs had not.

Left, Mamluke at war in the Battle of the Pyramids. **Right**, the Mamlukes dressed in silk and satin.

At 2 p.m. on 21 July 1798 they trotted on to the battlefield of Imbaba, under the steady gaze of the Sphinx, resplendent as Mamlukes always had been in silk and satin robes, riding on gold saddles, armed with gold-inlaid weapons, and carrying their personal wealth in money and jewels in their saddlebags. About 6,000 of these medieval warriors faced several times their own strength of Napoleon's infantry supported by artillery.

Mamlukes and French had met in very similar circumstances on the banks of the

Nile more than 500 years before. On that occasion Crusaders under King (later St) Louis IX of France ("his whole life was a prayer – his whole aim to do God's will") had squared up against a Mamluke army under the last hero of the Saladin dynasty, Al-Salah-Ayyub. The French were annihilated and Louis saved his life only on payment of a colossal ransom of 1 million gold dinars.

Ayoub had uncharacteristically remained unseen in his tent throughout the action. It transpired that he was, and for some time had been, dead, a victim of tuberculosis. The extreme measures taken to conceal his death – meals delivered regularly to his tent, written orders over a signature forged by a eunuch, and so on – were indicative of the Achilles heel in the Mamluke system.

At the repeat performance in 1798, the odds lay impossibly with the French. Their infantry squares interspersed with artillery rolled forward. Murad Bey, the Mamluke commander, waited until they were within striking range of his horses and sounded the charge. Mamluke cavalry at full tilt had once overwhelmed even the Mongols, but times had changed. The leading horses crashed into the French squares with tremendous force but the squares did not yield. Riders galloping up close behind piled helplessly into the melee. Others wheeled and made

Power and glory: Conditions had been very different when the Mamlukes came to power six centuries before. Egypt, then under the Fatimid Arabs, had managed to sit out most of the protracted struggle between Muslims and waves of European Crusaders in Asia Minor and on the eastern shores of the Mediterranean. In fact, the country had profited from the turmoil around Baghdad by inheriting, and then monopolising, the lucrative oriental trade route. The concomitant of booming prosperity, though, was the covetous attention of predators. The Crusaders, who never let their religious mission cloud commercial opportunities, were beaten to Egypt by their illustrious enemy, Nur-ad-

straight at the mouths of the cannon where they were blown to pieces. "The first wild charge having failed to break the squares," wrote Glubb, no mean desert commander himself, "there was nothing else the Mamlukes could do but ride from square to square, being shot."

The carnage over, the French troops broke ranks to scoop up booty which exceeded a soldier's wildest dreams. Only a thousand or so of the Mamlukes survived, but their place in Egypt's history was not quite finished yet; when that day came about some years later, the treacherous circumstances stripped their departure of every vestige of dignity.

Din. The army he despatched to occupy Cairo in 1169 included a Kurdish mercenary destined for even greater renown, Saladin.

Saladin's career in Egypt is chronicled elsewhere in this book; what is pertinent here is that his bodyguard, conspicuous in yellow tunics, were the first Mamlukes. In Arabic, Mamluke means "owned" or "belonging to", and indeed the Mamlukes were slaves, albeit of an unusual kind. They were bought or stolen at six to ten years of age from nomadic tribes living on the steppes of Asia Minor and the shores of the Black Sea. In either

Above, Mamluke on horseback.

case, they were distinctively white children who grew up to serve as bodyguards not only to the ruler but also to many of the Arab or Saracen nobles.

The demand for Mamlukes in these troubled times was such that a special class of merchant scoured the likely areas for suitable boys who were then sold on to the emirs of Egypt (and Syria). Added to their natural ability as horsemen, the boys were given intensive training in the use of the bow, lance, sword and mace. As soon as they were old enough to fight, they were given their freedom, took their master's name as a cognomen, and were provided with weapons, armour and horses. Far from wishing to escape, then, a Mamluke's prospects in Egypt seemed immeasurably brighter than they if they'd stayed on the austere steppes.

Code of honour: In return, a Mamluke was expected to fight and if necessary to die for his patron. The obligation was exclusively to the patron concerned, not to the army, the state or even to the patron's heir when he died. In the latter event, a Mamluke was free to join someone else's army (without the same binding terms of service) or give up soldiering altogether, possibly to go into business. While they remained in service, the only limit to advancement was ability.

Mamlukes thus rose to the highest posts in the land, acting as cup-bearers (i.e. tasters) and masters-of-the-horse. Eventually, Mamlukes could even become masters and owners of other Mamlukes, and those with units of 10, 100 or 1,000 men bound to them as they were to their patrons were given the appropriate rank. An "Emir of a Thousand", who might be either an Arab noble or an elevated Mamluke, was roughly what would now be called a colonel. A private Mamluke army was essential for anyone seriously engaged in the complex struggle between powerful families. Only Mamlukes were without the family and tribal ties which invariably compromised a native soldier's loyalty. (At other periods in Egyptian history, Nubian troops from the south found employment in Egyptian armies for similar reasons as well as for being more aggressive by nature.)

Al-Salah-Ayyub, who used his Mamluke army to such devasting effect against King Louis IX's Crusaders, had brought the system to the peak of efficiency. He had imported boys from various markets, but the best were 1,000 Qipchaq Turks whom he installed in a castle on Rawdah, an island opposite Cairo. They were thenceforth known as the Bahri Mamlukes, or "white slaves of the river". It was they who, in the unusual circumstances of their patron's death in 1249, demonstrated the intrinsic flaw in the system as originally implemented, and that was the danger of servants turning gaolers.

Ayyub's heir, Turan Shah, was in the opinion of the Mamluke officers an intolerable lout who drank too much and boasted of plans to promote some dubious Syrian cronies over their heads. Such talk was unwise because he was not protected by the loyalty which had been his father's due. He had only been in office a few months when a Mamluke burst into his tent and ran him through with his sword. A shocked Turan Shah somehow survived the thrust and was trying to wade to safety across, or at least into, the Nile when he was overtaken by other Mamlukes and finished off.

The leaderless Mamlukes, who seem to have had a relatively relaxed attitude towards women, were rather in favour of recognising Ayyub's widowed queen, a former slave-girl named Spray-of-Pearls. It was she who, forged signature apart, had drawn up the battle orders while Ayyub lay dead in his tent. The more conservative Arabs were appalled. "If you have no man, I'll send you one," wrote the Caliph of Baghdad, who remembered Spray-of-Pearls as the slave-girl he had sent to Ayyub as a present.

The most distinguished of the Mamluke generals, Aktai, offered to lend the arrangement respectability by marrying Spray-of-Pearls. She agreed but insisted that he first divorce his existing wife. This was done, but Aktai needed or liked more than one woman at a time and Spray-of-Pearls, it transpired, was exceedingly jealous although she could barely stand the sight of her new husband. The impasse ended in a conjugal nightmare: Aktai murdered in his bath by her; she by the slave-girls of the previous wife, who battered her to death with their wooden clogs. Stripped to her underwear, Spray-of-Pearls was thrown over the walls of the Citadel.

In-fighting: In the meantime, the previously disciplined Mamlukes were running riot in Cairo. "This truculent soldiery became a terror to the inhabitants," wrote Stanley Lane-Poole, a rare European authority on the period, "they indulged their licence in atrocious acts of violence, pillaged innocent houses, and raided the public baths for women." What had opened Pandora's box was that on Ayyub's death the Mamlukes considered themselves free agents. "After Turan Shah's murder," Lane-Poole notes, "it was but a short step to the throne, and for the next 130 years the colonels of this celebrated regiment, and their descendants, rapidly succeeded each other as sultans of Egypt."

Rapid the succession certainly was – on average every five years, but sometimes just weeks. Citizens learned to recognise the portents of a power struggle and acted accordingly, shuttering their shops, rushing home and locking themselves in. Rival Mamluke factions would then open proceedings by attacking the houses of the competition and carrying off the women and children. Pitched battles in the street brought arrows and spears showering down from roofs and windows. "These things were of constant occurrence," Lane-Poole observes, "and the life of the merchant classes of Cairo must have been exciting."

From time to time, a nimble Mamluke was able to play rival factions off against one another. "Among the strange anomalies of Oriental history," according to Lane-Poole, "none perhaps is more surprising than the combination of extreme corruption and savage cruelty with exquisite refinement in material civilisation and an admirable devotion to art." Egypt became a haven for Muslim artists.

The Mamlukes were also keen sportsmen who built a horse-racing course in Cairo and played a robust game of polo. Their records contain apologies for absence from official events because the Mamluke concerned was recovering from injuries on the polo field. The more serious mishaps were treated in the Maristan hospital which, completed in 1284, was far ahead of its time. There were wards for every known disease, laboratories, baths, kitchens and a lecture room for interns. In what seems to have been an intimation of modern-day *muzak*, musicians wandered the wards playing a medley of soothing melodies. Fifty full-time scholars were at hand to recite uplifting passages from the Koran on coping with discomfort and pain.

The system at its best: The most energetic of the Mamluke sultans was Baybars al-Bunduqdari. As a boy he was big for his age but had fetched only a trifling £20 on the market because of a cataract in one eye. He made up for the deficiency in other ways, setting an example to his men with an exhausting daily routine of martial arts on the training field and once swimming across the Nile both ways wearing a breastplate.

Although he enjoyed a drink himself (he probably died of alcoholic poisoning at a victory celebration) and was "suspected of oriental depravity", he closed all the wine shops and brothels, imprisoning prostitutes "until husbands could be found for them". To ensure that his wishes were being observed, he travelled incognito and often alone to every corner of an empire which, owing to his brilliant campaigns against previously invincible Mongols and the various Crusader strongholds, grew to cover a large part of Asia Minor.

His ability to hold the empire together was facilitated by superb communications. He boasted of roads which enabled him to play polo in Cairo and Damascus in the same week. Urgent matters could be expedited with astonishing speed through the use of pigeons whose beaks and legs were branded to identify them as part of the royal mail. Birds were kept in readiness at key positions, especially frontier posts, within comfortable flying range of their home bases, at which point messages written on a special kind of thin paper and attached under their wings, not on their legs, were transferred to another bird for the next stage.

The last relay of pigeons homed in on a loft in the Citadel in Cairo. Their arrival was attended to immediately. The regulations were that messages received by pigeon had to be passed on to the sultan whether he was in the middle of dinner or asleep. The story was told of a sultan who suddenly craved cherries of a kind he had enjoyed on a recent visit to what is now Lebanon. The cherries were ordered by pigeons going one way and delivered by others waiting to take off in the opposite direction. Relays of 600 pigeons at a time, each with a silk bag attached to either foot containing a single cherry, meant that within three days of feeling the urge, the sultan was able to sit down to a bowl of 1,200 fresh Lebanese cherries, courtesy of the first known instance of bulk air freight.

New order: The complexion of Mamluke

rule in Egypt changed from 1382 with the rise of the Circassian or Burgi Mamlukes, many of whom were Mongols and Greeks. They experienced even more difficulty than before, if that is imaginable, in the transition of office. When an emir died – which happened suddenly and frequently – "the son kept the throne warm whilst the leading nobles fought for the succession; and when the best man won, the 'warming pan' was put away." One poor pawn in this process, Timurbugha, was deposed, reinstated and deposed again all on the same day. The presence of large numbers of Mongols and Greeks meant "it was impossible to allow women to appear in the streets" not even, it

ous Turkoman sects known respectively as the Black Sheep and the White Sheep.

Coupled with the threat posed by the combined Sheep, the Portuguese explorer Vasco da Gama sailed round the southern tip of Africa in 1498 and reached India. The opening of the sea route to India killed the Mamluke monopoly over trade passing between Europe and the East, all of which had previously provided handsome tax revenue as it necessarily crossed Mamluke territory. To make matters worse, Portuguese ships entered the Red Sea and began plundering the Egyptian coast just as a naval threat was also growing in the Mediterranean. For the Mamlukes, war at sea (even if there had been

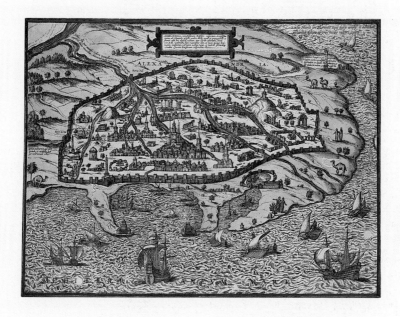

Above, map of Alexandria dating from 1575.

seems, on ceremonial occasions like wedding processions.

"Personally," says Lane-Poole, "some of the second line of sultans (i.e. Circassian Mamlukes) were men of considerable culture... They were also good Muslims, fasted... abstained from wine, made pilgrimages and insured their place in the next world by building mosques, colleges, hospitals." Compared with their predecessors, however, they lacked military prowess, and the northern parts of the empire were under increasing pressure from, among the others, the notori-

timber in Egypt to build ships) was beyond comprehension and beneath dignity.

Decline and fall: The deserts which had for so long sheltered Egypt's borders were thus suddenly inadequate and almost irrelevant to the task. Within five years of Vasco da Gama's historic voyage, the Mamluke government was practically bankrupt. All along the Nile, the anarchistic tendencies of the Mamluke's were exacerbated by the sultan's inability to pay them.

In September 1502, the sultan managed with the greatest difficulty to scrape together 12,000 dinars to calm tempers. The money was sent under guard to Cairo on a mule. On entering the gates of the Citadel, the mule was stolen. The sultan had no more luck when it was decided that the Mamlukes ought at least to look into the possibility of equipping the army with artillery. At the first test firing of guns cast in Egypt, they all disintegrated.

The end was brought much closer by the Battle of Chaldiran between Ottomans and Persians in 1514. The Ottoman army relied on its Janissaries who, like the Mamlukes, were foreign boys specially reared as fighters, with the difference that they were more likely to have been kidnapped Christians who were then required to "take the turban". Although the Janissaries had developed in-

all its treasures to pay the arrears owing to his young Mamlukes but they merely asked for more. "I never wanted to be the sultan!" he cried. "Let me go somewhere else. Choose another sultan!"

Qansuh, then 76, knew his duty, however, and after numerous insults – the heads of friends and relatives being delivered to him in baskets and so on – he led his grumbling army north to engage the Ottomans in Syria. The Mamlukes went into action with one of their thundering charges and were actually acquitting themselves quite well when, in the heat of it, Qansuh was convulsed by a stroke, one side paralysed and his mouth hanging open. In trying to drink some water,

fantry tactics to unprecedented levels of effectiveness, the Ottoman triumph was still regarded as a dazzling surprise. Unfortunately for the Mamlukes, the victorious Ottomans were now free to give them their unwelcome and undivided attention.

The venerable Sultan Qansuh al Ghori, plagued by bankruptcy and mutinous young Mamlukes, indicated in his prayers that he feared the worst: "O Thou, who canst not be an unjust tyrant, have mercy on thy slave, Qansuh al Ghori. O Lord, we have shown ourselves wicked, we are certainly lost unless Thou wilt forgive us, unless Thy pity descend upon us." He stripped his palace of

he fell off his horse. Officers ran to help him but he was already dead. Almost at once, the Ottoman army swept over the position and his body was lost in the heaps of dead.

The Ottoman leader sent a note to Qansuh's hasty replacement in Cairo. "If you do not submit," he promised, "I will come to Egypt and kill all the Turks [a significant indication that he considered the Mamlukes "Turks", his own subjects "Ottomans"] and rip up the belly of every pregnant woman." Not for nothing was he known as Saleem the Grim. The ensuing battle in the centre and surroundings of Cairo was a desperate affair with no quarter given. The streets were said to have been littered with the bodies of thousands of Mamlukes and Ottomans, "all without heads".

Qansuh's successor, the young Toman Bey, resisted fiercely and, rather than accept defeat, retired north to continue a guerrilla campaign. He was not at large long, though, eventually being paraded through Cairo dressed as an ordinary Arab and on a packhorse (a vicious insult to Mamlukes who bred and normally rode magnificent animals) on his way to a gallows erected at the Zuwayla Gate. He recited the first chapter of the Koran three times to the crowd who had followed him through the streets, turned to the hangman and said: "Do your work."

Official end: The Mamluke empire was formally ended by Toman's execution in 1517 but, of course, there were still Mamlukes around when Napoleon invaded in 1898. It seems that about 5,000 Mamlukes survived the Ottoman takeover. Their rehabilitation began with the restoration of their right to appear armed on horseback. With a substantial empire to the north, though, the Ottomans had bitten off in Egypt – which was in a chaotic state – more than they could chew. The Pasha appointed to run it was increasingly grateful for the Mamlukes who, on the right terms, were as willing as ever to provide loyal mercenary services.

Egypt moved further and further away from the focus of Suleiman the Magnificent's titanic struggle with the Habsburg Empire in Europe. "By the 18th century," writes H. Wood Jarvis, "the pasha had grown to be a cipher and the Mamluke Governor of Cairo...was the real master of the land. Disputes between rival beys [as former sultans came to be known] continued as before the Turkish conquest."

As the Ottoman Empire went into steep decline after the death of Suleiman the Magnificent – only his genius could hold it together and his son was a drunkard – French kings began to consider snatching Egypt away. The plan had to wait, however, for the revolutionary zeal of the young Napoleon. The French army landed 38,000 men at Alexandria on 1 July 1798. The elderly Ibrahim Bey had little choice but to ask his Mamluke associate, Murad Bey, if the Mamlukes could be organised to resist them. It was in this context, then, that at 2 p.m. on 21 July and under the gaze of the Sphinx, Murad Bey sounded the fatal charge.

It wasn't long after the Battle of the Pyramids that the French were thrown out of Egypt by the British but, as Britain was not (yet) interested in running the country, the Ottomans resumed control, reasserting their presence with a garrison which consisted mainly of Albanian units, including a certain Mohammed Ali. As the Ottomans now banned the trade in boys who might otherwise have replenished the Mamluke ranks, the survivors of the Battle of the Pyramids were by definition the last of the line.

In July 1805, Mohammed Ali seized power and a Europe preoccupied with the Napoleonic wars was not inclined to intervene. Only the Mamlukes opposed Mohammed Ali, and for a change the nature of their opposition was political. In 1811 the former Albanian tobacconist and future "Father of Egypt" indicated that he was willing to listen to their views at a meeting in Cairo. The invitation was duly accepted. The assembled Mamluke princes entered the Citadel and were filing down one of the narrow streets when the way ahead was suddenly blocked. Before they fully understood what was happening, they were butchered to a man.

Left, Mamluke tombs, Cairo. **Above,** Mohammed Ali had the last of the Mamlukes massacred.

THE FRENCH ON THE NILE

Countless battles have been fought along or for control of the Nile, usually both, but history's "official" Battle of the Nile was actually neither. It was a naval battle between Britain and France in Aboukir Bay, near Alexandria, on the night of 1 August 1798, and although it dragged Egypt out of centuries of political hibernation, the Egyptians themselves were not involved in the fighting and probably did not much care who won. In the event, the result was a resounding British victory which came close to ending Napoleon's promising career before it had properly begun.

Except by his own messianic standards, Napoleon was already a precociously successful general at only 28 years of age who had conquered most of Italy and been compared with Hannibal. Nevertheless, he was not quite yet ready to proceed with his overwhelming objective, which was the invasion of England. India, Britain's imperial crown snatched from France 50 years earlier, was also high on his list but not within reach either. Egypt, in the middle, was perfect. To found a French colony there, he predicted, would make the old enemy England "tremble for the safety of India" and, while it trembled, he could nip back to Paris "and give the enemy its death-blow".

Dream of a historical romantic: Under centuries of Mamluke rule, Egypt (like Greece, also part of the Ottoman Empire) had become an obscure, virtually closed society, the neglected monuments largely buried under drifting sand. As a junior officer, however, Napoleon had devoured scholarly works on the East, his interest spread evenly between erudite mathematical theories about the dimensional ratios of the pyramids and the earthy, conjugal tricks attributed to oriental women. In Milan, he had made a beeline for the famous library's collection of such books, many of which were later found to contain scribbled margin notes made in his handwriting.

He was the supreme historical romantic. Comparisons with Hannibal were satisfying but insufficient: he preferred the vision of another Alexander the Great who, *inter alia*, would liberate noble Egyptians from abominable servitude under the Mamlukes, a military oligarchy of self-perpetuating slaves, a system so bizarre as to be almost beyond belief. Under Napoleon's guidance, the oppressed Egyptians would throb with the French Revolution's clarion call for Liberty, Fraternity and Equality. As the plan evolved

in his head, a personal matter intruded. His wife Josephine was seeing altogether too much of her dancing teacher, Monsieur Hippolyte, and he was not sure whether he wanted to get away from the affront or take her along.

Napoleon's Egyptian campaign was to be financed by unadorned piracy. To top up a fortune in gold and diamonds stolen in Switzerland, his fleet of 13 ships of the line, 14 frigates and hundreds of transports called at Malta, the refuge of the once glorious Order of Crusaders, the Knights of St John. Their glory had faded but they retained the priceless plunder of their campaigns, including the Jerusalem treasures. With the collusion of French knights attached to the Order, Napoleon annexed Malta and popped the treasure into his war chest.

The invasion: A wretched sailor, Napoleon was thoroughly sick all the way to Egypt. The fleet arrived off the now fashionable beach resort in the Bay of Agami and ploughed through violent seas in small landing boats. About 30 troops drowned, and Napoleon himself crawled ashore so wet and exhausted that he passed out on the beach. On coming round, he went to the head of the column and plodded into the sand in the general direction of Alexandria. His orders to the fleet were to find a suitable mooring and wait.

Bedouin manning a coastal fort put up only token resistance, but even so two French generals were knocked out by stones which bounced down on to their heads. The army as a whole fared no more auspiciously on a horrendous, waterless march to Cairo in suffocating heat after taking Alexandria. The Mamluke defenders preparing themselves in the Cairo Citadel imagined that military matters were much as they had been in the Middle Ages, when they had held their own against the Crusaders.

The first reaction of their commander, Murad Bey, to news of the French invasion was evidently outrage. "His eyes became red and fire devoured his entrails", but he soon calmed down and confidently looked forward to slicing up some Frenchmen "like watermelons".

After three days, the French caught first sight of the enemy, a cavalry detachment which Murad had personally brought down the Nile from Cairo in armed *feluccas*. The French troops must have wondered what to make of them. They were mounted on magnificent horses decked out for battle. The Mamlukes themselves were resplendent in yellow turbans, streaming robes over a coat of chain mail, billowing red pantaloons and matching, pointed slippers.

Each man had a pair of pistols tucked into an embroided shawl around his waist, a mace, a scimitar and a carbine. The only disappointment for the amazed French was, perhaps, that Murad failed to live up to the rumour that he went into battle on a white camel. The French for their part were in thick serge uniforms designed for Europe, although at the moment of this first encounter many had stripped and were cooling off in the waters of the Nile.

The Mamlukes broke off quickly on this occasion to mull over the experience of infantry who kneeled to fire muskets while the artillery kept busy over their shoulders. The second encounter a few days later was a combined operation: the armed *feluccas* challenging the gunboats which were keeping pace with the French advance while the wheeling cavalry tried to cancel out the unexpected resilience of the French square with mounting recklessness. The casualties were rather higher than before on both sides, but the action still served as no more than a

rehearsal for the monumental Battle of the Pyramids a week later.

The denouement at Imbaba – "the last great cavalry charge of the Middle Ages" – is referred to in the Mamluke chapter of this book. The Mamluke survivors retired into the desert to fight, as we shall see, a running battle along 700 miles of the Nile, but Napoleon's victory gave him Cairo and an opportunity to put in practice the idealistic side of his mission to Egypt. Having made a grand entrance into the city to a fanfare of trumpets, he installed himself in a sumptuous Mamluke palace on the site of what is now Shepheard's Hotel and began to draft his orders.

Cultural survey: The French contingent included 167 intellectuals and scholars, the "living encyclopaedia" whose task, put simply, was to learn and record as much about Egypt as they possibly could. Their number included every conceivable discipline from astronomy to zoology, and none was more colourful – or destined for greater fame – than Dominique Vivant Denon, impoverished minor aristocrat, failed lawyer, temporary diplomat, antique dealer, archaeologist, interior decorator, street artist, pornographer, friend of Voltaire and also, more relevant to his inclusion in the party, of Josephine, Napoleon's fickle wife.

While these *savants* prepared to immerse

with his fingers, and advising his guests to give equal weight to the Koran and Thomas Paine's *The Rights of Man*. As a concession to the ordinary troops, though, he sent an urgent shopping list to Paris: comedians, ballet dancers, marionettes, 100 prostitutes, 200,000 pints of brandy and one million pints of wine.

As a gesture of cultural reciprocity, bemused Egyptians were expected to wear cockades in their turbans. Although Napoleon had issued orders that his troops were to respect the mosques and refrain from looting, the hands-off policy was impossible to enforce. "Cairo has become a second Paris," an Egyptian complained. "Women go about

themselves in Egyptian antiquity and the study of exotic creatures like the hippopotamus, Napoleon hastened to assure the sceptical Egyptians that, as a product of French revolutionary atheism, he was above the religious differences between Christian and Muslim. "When I am in France I am a Christian," he declared, "when in Egypt a Mohammedan." He tried to drive the point home by appearing in public in Arab costume (because of his size, apparently not a total success), sitting cross-legged at banquets to eat

Left, **Murad Bey, commander of the Mamlukes. Above**, a gathering of the *savants*.

shamelessly with the French, intoxicating drinks are publicly sold and things are committed of which the Lord of Heaven would not approve." Merchants were consoled by the discovery that the French soldier had a lot to learn about doing business in the East: as he tended to pay asking prices, which soared as a result, and gleeful bakers produced a special French loaf which was not only smaller than normal but also contained a fair proportion of sand.

Denon made excursions to Giza to see the Great Pyramid and the Sphinx and to Sakkara. Predictably, he also had a look at Cairo's nightlife, especially the dancing girls. Less predictably, and perhaps a little disingenuously, he was shocked. "Their dance began voluptuously and soon became lascivious, displaying nothing but a gross and indecent expression of the ecstasy of the senses; and what rendered these pictures still more disgusting was that at the moment in which they kept the least bounds, the two female musicians, with the bestiality of the lowest women in the streets of Europe disturbed with a coarse laugh the sense of intoxication that terminated the dance."

Boats burned: Appalling news soon took Denon's mind off ribald female laughter. Exactly one month after reaching Egypt, the French fleet was still lying at anchor in Aboukir Bay and on 1 August Sir Horatio (later Lord) Nelson of the Royal Navy, having searched the Mediterranean high and low, at last caught up with it. He wasted no time, sailing straight at the ships, many of whose crew were ashore.

After a ferocious battle lasting all night, the French fleet was all but destroyed. Worst of all, *L'Orient,* the flagship containing all the stolen Swiss gold and Knights of St John treasure, blew up and sank. Admiral de Breuys went down with it, as did the son of an officer immortalised in the poem which opens with "The boy stood on the burning deck". In the original version, by a Mrs Hemens, it continues with "when all but he had fled", and so on. Royal Navy ratings ever since have provided many variations on the original, most unprintable.

Bonaparte had no way of knowing about the disaster for another week. He had been out riding when the news reached Cairo. A companion described how he dismounted, walked away and was heard to mutter. "So the navy has gone...Is this the end?" The entry in Denon's diary reads: "On the morning of July 31, 1798, the French were masters of Egypt, Corfu and Malta; thirty vessels of the line united these possessions with France." On the following day, he continued, "the Army of the East was imprisoned in its own conquest."

For someone who was suddenly cut off from home and penniless to boot, Napoleon seemed to bounce back with remarkable fortitude. "Oh well," he remarked, "this upset will urge us on to greater things. Egypt used to be the centre of civilization. We shall have to recreate the Egyptian empire..."

A letter to his brother Joseph in France paints a rather different picture. "In two months it is possible that I shall be back in France, so find me a house where I may spend the winter alone. I am sick of humanity: I need solitude and isolation. Greatness wearies me, emotion chills me, my passion for glory has vanished. At twenty-nine years of age I am worn out. I mean henceforth to live in a country house, but never will I share it with her. I have no more reason to live." The "her" in question was of course Josephine. He had just heard the latest from Paris – Josephine, in the words of a popular song, "was at it again".

Not really knowing how long he would be

stuck there, Napoleon set about smartening up Egypt, as he saw it. He thought of relaying the streets of Cairo along Parisian lines, ordered his engineers to dust off plans for a Suez canal, bewildered the locals with a bureaucracy which sought to replace bribery with taxation, stopped people from burying their dead outside their houses, and insisted on a lamp in every doorway at night. One of the *savants* laid on a demonstration of balloon air travel and introduced farmers to the efficacy of the windmill.

Murad, the fugitive Mamluke commander, heard about the loss of the fleet too and took it as the cue for a guerrilla campaign. In order to repair the damage to his military standing, Napoleon felt he needed something more spectacular than a counter-insurgency campaign against a slippery foe. The conquest of Syria appealed; one of his generals, Desaix, could look after Murad and at the same time escort the team of *savants* up the Nile to do their stuff.

Military cruise: The expedition assembled for the Nile trip consisted of 3,000 infantry, 1,000 cavalry, about 100 guns travelling by boat and, where necessary, by camel train. "The scenes they saw along the Nile were not quite the same as those we see now," says Alan Moorehead (*The Blue Nile*). "...The villages, though smaller, have not altered

market. The fallen obelisk was simply another rock."

The military did their best to accommodate the *savants* in their attempt to absorb and record the phantasmagoria and sometimes provided a squad of soldiers while Denon fell behind the column to make the sketches which electrified the 24 volumes of *La Description de L'Egypte,* a runaway success when eventually they were published between 1809 and 1813.

More than once Bedouin looking for stragglers opened fire as Denon sat at his easel. Moorehead describes the interruptions: "No sooner would he begin a sketch or start to trace an inscription than the trumpet would

much in the intervening years, but the ancient temples were then very different. Many were half-buried in sand, and successive generations of Arabs built mud-brick houses among the crumbling walls, throwing out their rubbish everywhere. No one cared for these old columns and statues, no one could read the hieroglyphics on the walls. The mummies hidden in their hundreds in underground caves were of interest solely because the resin with which they were impregnated could be extracted and sold in the Cairo

sound the advance, and he would have to scramble back on to his horse and hurry after the others. "It was intensely frustrating. He was like the enthusiast who, having come miles to see a painting, is turned out of the museum by the closing bell – except that here he never knew whether he, or any other trained observer, would ever be able to come back again."

Murad dropped back along the river all the way to Philae, south of Aswan. The longer the French lines of the communications were stretched, the easier it was for him to double back through the empty desert and cut them. Thieves entered the French camp at night

Left, Dominique Vivant Denon, one of the team of *savants*. <u>Above</u>, Denon measuring the Sphinx.

and even got away with Desaix's horse. He quickened the pace of the campaign and there was less time than ever for Denon and his colleagues to pause in places like Dendera, Esna, Edfu and Kom Ombo.

At Luxor, however, the ordinary soldiers were so impressed by the temples that they spontaneously stopped, grounded their arms and went off to do a bit of sight-seeing. Desaix and Denon themselves rode around the temple site together, little expecting to come under a hail of javelins and stones from troglodytes who were living in the ruins and resented the intrusion. "A war with gnomes," Denon snorted.

The column reached Aswan, 587 miles

as "to tranquilize all the alarms of modesty".

It was not until July, after any number of skirmishes and complaints to Napoleon that "we are naked, without shoes, without anything…" that Desaix felt he had the situation under control. Denon returned to Cairo loaded with drawings and notes but also with some disappointments: he had set his heart on capturing a baby crocodile to take home, but had failed.

Added to his wonderful tales was the excitement created by the discovery of the Rosetta Stone in the Delta. The scholars realised that the Greek inscription at the bottom of the stone was in all probability a translation of the previously unintelligible

(955 km) from Cairo, on 1 February 1799. Murad and the Mamlukes had melted mysteriously away beyond the First Cataract and, if it was true that Sesostris III, a Middle Kingdom pharaoh, had once cleared a passage through the barrier for his punitive expeditions into Nubia, the French could not find it. The French force rested in the town and Denon had more time to look around. The inhabitants of the ruins were no more welcoming than the gnomes of Luxor had been. Denon thought the Nubians exceptionally barbarous – particularly as the men went round stark naked while unmarried women wore no more than mere strips of leather so

hieroglyphs above, but of course it would be some years before the code was finally cracked.

Distractions overseas: News of Napoleon was not nearly so satisfying. His expedition to Syria had been a disaster, and there was disturbing intelligence of an imminent Turkish landing at Alexandria. Murad had reappeared in the vicinity of Cairo and had reportedly climbed the Great Pyramid to signal his arrival to his wife Fatima who, having paid a colossal ransom for her freedom, was on friendly terms with Napoleon. He was furious when a French soldier beat up her chief eunuch.

Murad shadowed at a discreet distance as Napoleon led his men to meet the Turkish threat. The Battle of Aboukir was some sort of consolation for the loss of the French fleet and the setbacks in Syria. The Turks were driven into the sea with huge losses. One of them, actually an Albanian tobacconist turned mercenary soldier, was extremely lucky to be pulled out of the water to safety by Napoleon's *bête noire,* the British admiral Sir Sidney Smith, who happened to be watching from a small boat.

The rescued man was Mohammed Ali, and it was he who, soon to be ruler of Egypt, would drive the final nail into the Mamluke coffin. In the meantime, however, Murad

could think of only one person for the job.

His real destination when he left Cairo was kept secret even from his travelling companions, who included Denon, several of the *savants* and a captured Mamluke whom Napoleon planned to exhibit in France. He promised La Bellilote, a woman who had helped him forget Josephine, that he would be back in a fortnight. Officially, they were embarking on an inspection trip of the Lower Nile, but in Alexandria the passengers transferred to two French frigates for the voyage to France. A month after his arrival home, he was the dictator.

His generals were left behind in Egypt to cope with new Turkish threats as best they

saw that no further help would be forthcoming from the Turks and he quietly slipped back into the desert.

Napoleon's satisfaction was short-lived. The news from France was terrible: political chaos in Paris, the army in retreat in Italy, his garrison in Malta blockaded. His incorrigible opportunism, however, told him that the débâcle could be manipulated to his advantage. If France was in need of a saviour, he

Left, *the Cairo Revolt*, **1798. Detail from the painting by Anne Louis Girodet-Trioson.** <u>Above</u>, **attack by Turkish gunboats in the** *Battle of Aboukir,* **a painting by the Reverend Cooper Willyams.**

could. In 1801, however, Britain was in full cry against France and sent troops to bolster the Turks. There was some French resistance in Alexandria, but Cairo fell without a struggle. Britain offered the French transport back to France but at a price: the Rosetta Stone and one or two other interesting artefacts! The stone still remains in the British Museum.

Having got to know the French and deciding that, on the whole, they preferred the Mamlukes, the Egyptian population wondered what would happen next. British did not try to persuade Egypt that they were there for the country's own good. On the contrary, their presence was just a means to an end.

"The power which becomes the absolute master of the Nile Valley," ran an Egyptian nationalist tract at the end of the 19th century, "becomes virtual sovereign of Africa... the Holy Land and the Red Sea. The Suez Canal is an integral part of Egypt and commands the route to India, China and Australia... England already controls the Mediterranean and it is vital to the Powers of Europe that she should not command also the trade routes of Africa... Thus the British occupation of Egypt is a menace..."

Fifty years earlier Lord Palmerston, the prime minister, had equated Egypt with an inn on the road between Britain and India. There was no wish to own the inn, he declared, merely to ensure that it was "well-kept, always accessible" and able to furnish the traveller with a suitable standard of "mutton-chops and post-horses".

Lord Cromer, the symbol of British occupation of Egypt, produced his own refinement that Britain did not govern Egypt, it only governed the governors of Egypt. The mechanics of government were convoluted. Supreme power lay ostensibly with the Sultan of Turkey, head of the Ottoman Empire. On the ground, it was exercised by the Khedive, one of the Mohammad Ali dynasty and as such not an Egyptian but a Turkish-Albanian who usually could not speak Arabic. British army personnel and civil servants in Egypt were officially on loan to, and paid by, the Khedive, but the Khedive took his orders from the likes of Lord Cromer, whose title (Resident, Consul etc) was anything but Governor.

The occupation: British troops occupied Egypt in 1882, and government records show that in the following quarter century British statesmen said solemnly that Britain had no interest in having – and would shortly be leaving – Egypt on no fewer than 72 occasions. The reason for landing in 1882 was to put down on behalf of Turkey the Arabi nationalist revolt, in which the Khedive himself was also to some extent implicated.

The justification for British involvement in Egypt was extremely flexible, and in the 1860s it bent smoothly to the cause of gaining some international respectability for the Khedive Ismail. He was expecting half of Europe's royalty for the grand opening of the Suez Canal and it could do him no harm to be associated with a crusade against slavery. "My country is no longer in Africa; we are now part of Europe. It is therefore natural for us to abandon our former ways..."

The slavery in mind was being practised in and around the Sudan, one million square miles which the Khedive had inherited from Mohammed Ali, the founder of Egypt's last dynasty. It seemed not to matter that Ismail himself was a massive slave-owner or that he had given state contracts to slave-hunters in the Sudan. The trade was bigger than it had ever been – 15,000 virtually licensed Arabs taking 50,000 slaves out of the Upper Nile every year. The traders ranged from individuals with a couple of donkeys to the commanders of private armies with rights to anyone they could capture in areas as large as 90,000 square miles. There was no doubting Ismail's sincerity in one respect, and that was his willingness to let the anti-slavery drive add large chunks of new territory to his pseudo-empire.

Anti-slavery mission: Ismail met the man he wanted to lead his anti-slavery campaign at a fancy dress ball. He was Sir Samuel Baker, the worthy Victorian explorer whom we have met in the section of this book dealing with the search for the source of the Nile. Ismail offered Baker £40,000 for a four-year contract, the title "Pasha", and virtually unlimited expenses. Within a year Baker had assembled one of the most amazing armadas ever to sail up the Nile: nine steamers and 55 sailing boats to carry a force of 1,700 men, including 200 cavalry, two artillery batteries and a personal bodyguard in scarlet uniforms and fezzes whom he called the Forty Thieves. The Egyptian contingent among the ordinary troops were an unknown quantity, most being criminals released from prison for the purpose. The fleet was accompanied by hundreds of camels loaded with extra equipment. The intention was to establish a base at Gondokoro, which Baker knew and hated from his explorer days.

The armada got only as far as the infernal Sudd. The channel which nowadays enables paddle steamers to negotiate the jungle of swamp, weed and papyrus in three days did not exist. The boats reached a point where they could neither advance nor retreat, added to which the Nile fell suddenly so that they were all left hard aground. Baker ordered his men out of the boats to pack sandbags sufficient to build a dam across the river. Five days later, and at the sound of a bugle, the sacks were dropped in rows between piles and the boats were refloated.

Thereafter, things got worse. While Baker had once been able to overcome tribal suspicion that he was just another slaver himself by donning a tweed suit, the hostility of the tribes and, of course, the Arab traders was implacable. He came under a hail of poisoned arrows at Gondokoro, and before long 1,100 of his men, mostly the jailbirds, deserted with 30 of his sailing vessels. The Forty Thieves and his Sudanese troops, however, proved loyal and efficient. Baker annexed the country around Gondokoro in the name of the Khedive and called it Equatoria.

With greatly reduced forces, Baker was nevertheless able to mount operations deep into what is now Uganda. They frequently saw action ("The Forty Thieves had just the time to grab their rifles and open up a point-blank fire upon the mass of Africans charging down…") but Baker persevered until his contract had been fulfilled to the letter; slavery was overcome.

"A paternal government extended its protection through lands hitherto a field for anarchy and slavery… The White Nile, for a distance of 1,600 miles from Khartoum to Central Africa, was cleansed from the abomination of a traffic which had hitherto sullied its waters. Every cloud had passed away, and the term of my office expired in peace and sunshine. In this result, I humbly traced God's blessing."

Gordon's turn: Baker's campaign against the slave trade was in reality nowhere near as successful as he believed (it simply moved away from the river), nor was Ismail satisfied with his contribution to the size of the Egyptian empire.

Casting around for another European to succeed Baker, his eyes lit on Colonel Charles George "Chinese" Gordon. His nickname was derived from glittering military exploits in China; he was already a legendary figure, a pious and fearless soldier seemingly indifferent to the normal distractions and comforts of life.

He proved his eccentricity at the outset of his dealings with Ismail: offered £10,000 a year, Gordon would not accept more than £2,000. His brief was to establish a chain of forts down the White Nile from Gondokoro to the source in Buganda, annex Buganda and start a steamer service on Lakes Albert and Victoria.

Gordon was fortunate to find an open

channel through the Sudd which enabled him to reach Gondokoro, 1,000 miles (1,600 km) south of Khartoum, after a voyage lasting 25 days. He was dismayed by what he found: in a year, the discipline of Baker's regime had degenerated under Egyptian officials into anarchy. The troops were paid not in money but in spirits and in slave-girls shipped down from Khartoum. Gordon dismissed the Egyptian officials; their European replacements, however, suffered terribly from malaria and the heat. According to Chaille-Long, an American who fell out with Gordon, the latter was frequently depressed, sitting in his tent "with a hatchet and a flag placed at the door to indicate that he was not to be disturbed for any reason whatever; until at least the cloud would lift, the signals would be removed, and the Governor would reappear, brisk and cheerful."

Whether or not Gordon sulked in his tent, with or without the purported brandy and soda, he tackled his assignment with prodigious energy. Where the river proved to be totally unnavigable, he had his ships dismantled and carried around the obstacle piece by piece, and in this way he was eventually able to put two ships on to the waters of Lake Albert, although for the moment Lake Victoria remained out of reach. The forts he built, a dozen in all, formed a chain stretching 600

Ismail Pasha

miles (960 km) from Fashoda almost to the Equator. After two-and-a-half years, perhaps because he felt he could achieve no more in the circumstances, Gordon resigned.

The circumstances which defeated Gordon were associated with Ismail Pasha Ayyub, the Egyptian Governor-General who presided over a system of bribery and extortion that, according to Alan Moorehead, was "wonderfully complete, even by Egyptian standards." Barely a month after Gordon's

Left, the British taking tea on top of the pyramids (1874). **Above**, Ismail Pasha, the corrupt Governor-General who preceded General Gordon.

return to England – long enough for him to be recommended for the post of Governor of Bulgaria – he received a telegram from the Khedive Ismail pleading with him to return as Governor-General of the whole Sudan.

The man he was to replace, Ismail Pasha Ayyub, did not surrender his position gracefully, although it was his sister who smashed every window in the Governor-General's palace in Khartoum and slashed the furniture to bits. Compared with the kind of meal the outgoing Governor-General had laid on, Gordon stipulated that lunch would last no longer than 10 minutes. He lived alone in the palace, "a strange little unpretending man with eyes like blue diamonds."

Gordon worked tirelessly for the benefit of his charges. A channel was cut through the Sudd and his improvements in Khartoum moved an Italian to say that the city reminded him of Milan. His work in and around Khartoum was only the tip of his labours; he was forever disappearing on a camel to settle some distant dispute personally and often alone. He organised punitive expeditions against the Arab slave-lords; one alone resulted in the release of 10,000 slaves. He appointed Europeans to administer the various provinces that made up his domain, one of them later remarking that "only one who had had any direct dealings with negroes… can form a true estimate of what Gordon Pasha has accomplished here."

Gordon himself was especially concerned by news from Cairo, where it was rapidly becoming apparent that the Khedive's well-known financial difficulties were assuming absurd proportions and that his European creditors had run out of patience. In June 1879, his Ismail was deposed, his last act being to scoop up what cash was left in the Treasury, about £3 million, and sail into exile in his yacht.

"Do not fret about Ismail Pasha," Gordon wrote, "he is a philosopher and has plenty of money. He played high stakes and lost… I am one of those he fooled but I bear him no grudge. It is a blessing for Egypt that he is gone." In July, Gordon himself resigned his Governor-Generalship, and few people among the Anglo-French administrators trying to untangle Egypt's financial mess were honestly sorry that he was gone. "Some thought him mad," the pro-Egyptian Wilfred Blunt wrote, "others that he drank, and others again that he was a religious fanatic."

Rebellion: The Arabi revolt that followed (see *The Last Pharaohs* chapter of this book) was the manifestation of long-dormant Egyptian nationalism, although few people admitted it at the time. The British government asked the Ottoman Sultan to send in a Turkish general to restore discipline in the Egyptian army. The Sultan despatched Dervish Pasha, "a tough and unscrupulous old aristocrat with experience in handling rebellious Ottoman minorities", who instantly compromised his authority by accepting a £50,000 bribe from Tewfik, the new Khedive, but in any case he was too late.

A serious riot in the streets of Alexandria led to the death of at least 50 Europeans and several hundred others. Agitators were reported to be roaming the streets with the cry "O Muslims, kill the Christians." On 11 July 1882, the British Navy bombarded Alexandria; on 13 September the Egyptian army was defeated in an hour or two at the battle of Tel el-Kebir.

Rebellion had been brewing in the Sudan, too, first against the Egyptian presence and then decisively against the prospect of rule, direct or indirect, by the occupying British. The unrest centred on a curious figure who had emerged on Abba Island in the Nile, about 150 miles south of Khartoum.

Mohammed Ahmed Ibn el-Sayyid Abdullah, the Mahdi, claimed to be the prophet reincarnate. His family background was uncertain, but all who met him agreed with an Austrian priest who commented on an appearance which was "strangely fascinating... a man of strong constitution, very dark complexion, and his face always wore a pleasant smile." Nor was there any doubt about his ability to inspire his followers. As the British forces were landing at the Suez Canal, he was laying siege to El Obeid, a large town with a strong Egyptian garrison.

El Obeid fell to the Mahdi, and from his new residence in the town he issued a proclamation:

"Let all show penitence before God, and abandon all bad and forbidden habits, such as the degrading acts of the flesh, the use of wine and tobacco, lying, bearing false witness, disobedience to parents, brigandage, the non-restitution of goods to others, the clapping of hands, dancing, improper signs with the eyes, tears and lamentations at the

bed of the dead, slanderous language, calumny, and the company of strange women. Clothe your women in a decent way, and let them be careful not to speak to unknown persons. All those who do not pay attention to these principles disobey God and His Prophet, and they shall be punished in accordance with the law."

The Egyptian government's attempt to bring the Mahdi to heel was a disaster. A force sent up the Nile to deal with him looked good on paper: about 10,000 troops under a competent British Indian Army officer, Colonel William Hicks. In reality, some of the soldiers were jailbirds who were transported in chains, others were wearing chain armour

and exotic helmets, the guides turned out not to know the way, and the entire force was dangerously low on water supplies in the ferocious heat.

This ramshackle troop was wandering almost aimlessly south of El Obeid when it was set upon by 50,000 of the Mahdi's supporters. Only two or three hundred survived, and with that the whole Sudan erupted. The mood in England changed from a reluctance to become involved to the feeling that the whole Nile was threatened and someone would have to do something about it. "If you want some out-of-the-way piece of work to be done in an unknown and barbarous country," Sir C. Rivers Wilson remarked to the British prime minister, "Gordon would be your man."

Mahdi and Gordon: In semi-retirement, Gordon was restless and was looking for action. Jobs in India, China, South Africa and Mauritius had not suited him, and he had gone off to Palestine for Biblical studies. He was on the point of accepting the Belgian king's offer of the governorship of the Congo when the Sudan blew up.

The British government's instructions were not to conquer the Sudan, merely to evacuate the (Egyptian) government that looked as if it might soon be trapped there. Gordon left the Cabinet Office and went directly to the

gates to be flung open and invited anyone who wished to join the Mahdi to do so. Prisoners of war, debtors and men who had long served their sentences were set free from the city jail. Records of old debts were burned. He appointed a "Council of twelve Notables, Arabs" to help him with administration, and started to plan how to "smash up" the Mahdi.

Gordon bombarded Sir Evelyn Baring, his superior in Cairo, with telegrams, 20 to 30 a day, which provided a running and often contradictory commentary on the ideas cascading through his mind. Recoiling under the weight of these telegrams, Baring adopted a policy of allowing them to pile up during

railway station for the journey to Egypt. He was about to board the train when he remembered he had only a few shillings in his pocket. Sir Garnet Wolseley, one of the ministers seeing him off, fished into his pocket for change which, not amounting to much, he topped up with his pocket-watch and chain.

Appointed Governor-General again, Gordon went to work at characteristic full speed. On arrival in Khartoum, he ordered the city

Left, riots in Alexandria in the 1880s prompted rigorous search-patrols by British marines. **Above**, British gentleman trying out a fez.

the day and then, when he had finished other business, going through them all at once. The patent contradictions cancelled one another out, some were answered, and a summary was forwarded to London.

"I am most anxious to help and support you in every way," Baring telegraphed to Gordon after wading through a particularly intimidating pile, "but I find it very difficult to understand what it is you want. I think your best plan will be to reconsider the whole question carefully, and then state to me in one telegram what it is you recommend, in order that I can, if necessary, obtain the instructions of Her Majesty's government."

Under siege: Not even Baring, however, welcomed the day when the telegraph went dead. The tribes north of Khartoum had risen for the Mahdi. Khartoum, and Gordon, were suddenly cut off, and for 10 months – from March 1884 until January in the following year – the wire was silent. The only messages received from Gordon were written on tiny scraps of paper smuggled out of the city by native runners.

The city was besieged by about 30,000 Arabs, but two sides of it were protected by the White and Blue Niles which kept snipers out of range. The garrison in Omdurman fort guarded the northern approach; the southern, facing open desert, had a deep trench which ran four miles between the branches of the river. As the Arabs had bare feet, Gordon sprinkled the southern flank liberally with spikey "crows' feet" and broken bottles. He could send out raiding parties to bring in cattle and maize, and his boats could sail up and down the river with relative impunity. On 22 March, Mahdi envoys were admitted to Gordon's palace to ask whether he would like to become a Mahdi follower and to offer him the necessary costume. Gordon made his response clear by throwing the garment to the ground.

Nevertheless, Gordon's predicament caused considerable consternation in London. "It is alarming," Queen Victoria declared to one of her ministers. "General Gordon is in danger; you are bound to try and save him... you have incurred fearful responsibility." The cry was taken up at mass meetings, prayers were said in churches. The Foreign Office dithered, instructing Cairo to pass on a message to Gordon to the effect that troops would not be sent to Khartoum and that he ought to abandon while he could. If he chose to stay, "he should state to us the cause and intention with which he so continues." Gordon's laconic reply, which took some months to reach London, ended: "I stay at Khartoum because Arabs have shut us up and will not let us out."

Rescue mission: "As the weeks went by," says Moorehead, "Gordon's messages became fewer and fewer like a voice growing fainter in the distance..." In the end the government relented. The general who ws given the job of rescuing Gordon was, with sweet irony, the very same man who had handed over his spare change and pocket-watch at Charing Cross station: Wolseley.

"There is a fated quality about the events of the next six months," writes Moorehead, "an air of pure and certain tragedy that lifts the story out of time and space so that it becomes part of a permanent tradition of human courage and human helplessness... Each of the three main protagonists – Wolseley coming up the Nile with his soldiers, Gordon waiting and watching on the palace roof in Khartoum and the Mahdi with his warriors in the desert outside the town – behaves precisely as he is destined to do, and it is wonderfully dramatic that these three men, who were so perfectly incapable of understanding one another, should have been thrust together in such desperate circumstances and in such an outlandish corner of the world."

Meanwhile Gordon's solitary life in the palace took on a surreal quality. He ate alone and spent hours on the roof with his telescope, monitoring activity in the enemy lines. The long vigil was electrified by news that Wolseley was on his way. Guns were fired, Gordon scampered about renting houses for the English officers and placing orders with butchers and bakers on their behalf.

He smuggled out secret messages advising the advancing Wolseley on the best tactics: "Parties of forty or sixty men, swiftly moving about, will do more than any column... The time to attack is the dawn, or rather before it (this is stale news), but sixty men would put these Arabs to flight just before dawn, which one thousand would not accomplish in daylight... I do hope you will not drag on that artillery: it can only produce delay and do little good."

Meanwhile, however, the ship which had taken away the last European contingent had struck a rock and been disabled, passengers and crew were massacred, and information gleaned from documents taken off the bodies persuaded the Mahdi to close for an attack.

The shelling of Khartoum began on 12 November. Rounds from a gun trained on Gordon's palace generally bounced off the stone walls, but the quickening barrage caused alarm in the city and Gordon found himself surrounded by women begging for food whenever he ventured out. There was still no sign of the relief column and no way of knowing when it would arrive. "Now mark this," Gordon wrote in one of his last communiqués, "if the Expeditionary Force, and I ask for no more than two hundred men, does not come in ten days, the town may fall; and I have done my best for the honour of my country. Goodbye. C.G. Gordon."

Too late: About two weeks after he wrote this message (which had not yet been delivered), the advance guard of the expedition began a final advance on Khartoum. A force of 100 British troops with 2,200 camels were within 100 miles (160 km) on 30 December. On 18 January, after a first contact in which the Arabs suffered 1,100 killed, the British column was 23 miles (37 km) away, but a low river and problems with the steamers' engines delayed the advance. On 28 January

refusing to barricade the palace windows but inviting the Arab gunners to aim at a bright lantern beneath which he had his meals. The unmistakable signs of an imminent assault almost caused Gordon to crack. "What more can I say," he protested, flinging his fez away, "I have nothing more to say, the people will no longer believe me, I have told them over and over again that help would be here, but it has never come, and now they must see I tell them lies." With that he gave the commandant permission to open the gates, if he chose, to let the residents join the rebels. "Now leave me to smoke these cigarettes," he concluded.

Some 50,000 Mahdi crept up on the city

the leading ship ran the gauntlet of heavy artillery fire from both banks to reach the junction of the White and Blue Niles, at which point the town was clearly in view. Ten months after Gordon had first called for assistance it had arrived, although doubts were stirred in the men's minds by Arabs who called out from the bank that they were too late and Gordon was already dead.

Meanwhile Gordon had been putting on a show of defiance by, for example, not only

Above left, the last known photograph of General Gordon. **Above right**, artist's impression of General Gordon's fatal defiance of the Mahdi.

that night, crossing the ditch where it had filled up with mud. In the early hours of morning, they broke in. "Before any sort of resistance could be organised," writes Moorehead, "the streets were filled with a tide of screaming fanatics who hacked with their spears at every human being in their path. No wild animals ever behaved as the Arabs did in that one short hour before the dawn; they killed their victims regardless of whether or not they surrendered, and without distinguishing between men, women and children."

Gordon had stayed up writing until midnight and was woken by the sounds of the fighting. He went up to the roof in his night clothes and lowered a gun to fire at the crowds of Arabs surging towards the palace. He then went back to his room, changed into his white uniform, took up a revolver and sword and stood at the head of the stairs in "a calm and dignified manner, his left hand resting on the hilt of his sword." A mob surged through the palace and up the stairs. To one who cried out, "O cursed one, your time has come," Gordon is said to have made "a gesture of scorn". The General was speared to death.

His head was cut off and sent to the Mahdi in a handkerchief. The Mahdi would have preferred to take Gordon alive, it seems, in

According to prisoners, he retired across the river to Omdurman and grew inordinately fat, pampered in his harem by a selection of women said to represent almost every tribe in the Sudan. It was a style of life which lowered his natural defences, either against some disease or, according to another version, against poison administered by an outraged woman. He outlived Gordon by just five months.

The shock caused by Gordon's death in England was not assuaged when the Mahdi's successor, Khalifa Abdullah, wrote to Queen Victoria summoning her to come to Omdurman to submit and turn Muslim. It was later estimated that during the Khalifa's rule about

order to hold him in chains until he professed the true faith. In the circumstances, his head was put in the fork of a tree, a target for stones thrown by all who passed.

The relief column reached the city three days after Gordon's death and came under furious artillery and rifle fire. Wolseley applied to London for permission to launch a counterattack but, with Gordon confirmed dead, this was refused. The column was ordered to withdraw down the Nile. London's policy, for the moment, was to "let the Sudan stew in its own juice."

With the fall of Khartoum, the Mahdi appeared to lose much of his messianic zeal.

three-quarters of the Sudan's population of about 9 million were exterminated. Nevertheless, Britain could not find the will to avenge Gordon's death until 1895.

Kitchener's turn: One of the first signs of British determination was the requisitioning of all Thomas Cook's pleasure cruisers on the lower Nile for an expedition which was to be commanded by General Herbert Horatio Kitchener, whose features (notably the moustache) were later to be immortalised by the "Your Country Needs You" World War I recruitment poster in Britain.

He was 6ft 2in (1.9 metres) tall, a paler version of the explorer Richard Burton in that he was an excellent horseman, was interested in archaeology and related subjects, and spoke a number of languages. Unlike Burton, he had no interest whatever in women. A famously unemotional man who despised journalists, he led a force of 20,000 which tore apart an attack by Emir Mahmoud, one of the Khalifa's generals, in a preliminary battle, and as he rode along the British ranks afterwards, men raised their helmets in the dark and cheered him. He was, said an officer who watched him closely, "quite human for a quarter of an hour." The words were written by a promising young soldier with Kitchener's army, Winston Churchill.

Kitchener was at Omdurman on 1 September 1898. His men could see the Mahdi's massive tomb and beneath it, on the desert sand, what appeared to be a *zeriba,* a defensive wall made of branches and bushes. "Suddenly," wrote Churchill, "the whole black line which seemed to be the *zeriba* began to move. It was made of men, not bushes. Behind it other immense masses and lines of men appeared over the crest... the whole face of the slope beneath [became] black with swarming savages."

The Arabs held their attack until the following night, when 50,000 warriors, many armed with only spears, charged into the teeth of the British artillery. A war correspondent described the action as "a torrent of death", bodies piling up in mounds so that within an hour or two there were 10,000 casualties strewn all over the battlefield. Of these, the British losses amounted to 400. "At half-past eleven," Churchill wrote, "Sir H. Kitchener shut up his glasses, remarking that he thought the enemy had been given a good dusting."

After a break for lunch, Kitchener examined his conquest. The Mahdi's tomb had already been badly damaged by bombardment, now his body was dug up, decapitated,

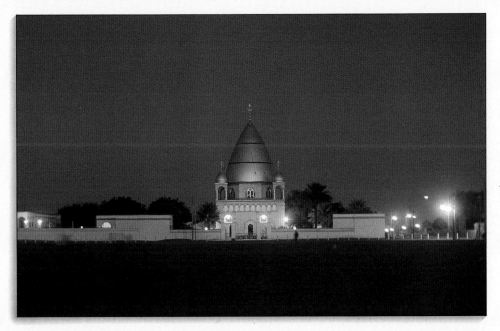

and thrown into the Nile. Kitchener wished to keep the skull to use as an inkstand or perhaps a drinking cup, but he was persuaded to let it be sent to Cairo, where Baring discreetly intervened and had it sent to the Muslim cemetery at Wadi Halfa for a secret burial. Kitchener's plans for the skull were the only blot on the celebrations which greeted news of the victory in England. "Savoured too much of the Middle Ages," sniffed Queen Victoria about the skull episode. If she had thought about it, Victoria could have worked out that, but for one small detail, she now ruled the Nile from the Mediterranean to the Mountains of the Moon.

Left, prisoners at Wadi Halfa. **Above**, the Madhi's tomb in Omdurman.

In 1898, the wounds of Waterloo reopened and England and France were once again baring their teeth at one another. Britain particularly wanted to rule an African corridor from the Cape to Cairo and France yearned for one that cut a swathe on the other axis between the Atlantic and Indian Ocean. They would collide, anyone could see, in the Sudan, but that was a vast territory. The precise point where the two putative corridors met was nothing but a derelict, mudbrick Nile fort on the edge of an indescribably awful

nearest British and French bases, the starting blocks, were at Cairo and Brazzaville respectively, both 2,000 miles (3,200 km) away.

The main British advance on Fashoda was the task of Horatio Herbert Kitchener, Sirdar (i.e. Commander-in-Chief) of the Egyptian army, a towering autocrat immortalised by the moustache and pointing finger of the "Your Country Needs You" World War I poster, and recently celebrated as the defeater of the Mahdi at Omdurman.

His opponent, in Brazzaville, was Jean-

swamp, at a place which was called Fashoda.

Fashoda came to be pinpointed because the French believed that a dam here would present Egypt to France on a plate. Britain had other plans: the opening of the Suez Canal had made the country an attractive proposition and they didn't want the French anywhere near Egypt.

The proposed dam at Fashoda would hold Egypt to ransom. The Nile could be shut off completely or, by suddenly pulling the plug, the waters could be released as a tidal wave to cleanse Egypt of, at least, its repulsive British presence.

The race to occupy Fashoda began. The

Baptiste Marchand, a captain of marines and veteran of several "pacifications" who loathed Englishmen. Marchand moved stiffly, his rigid military bearing slightly hampered by an elbow wound, a legacy of pacification. Restlessly energetic at the best of times, it was said that he twitched in the unforgiving climate of Central Africa.

In 1897, by which time the British had taken Dongola and were extending their railway southwards, Marchand and his team of 12 Frenchmen and 150 Senegalese troops left Brazzaville with 13,000 pieces of baggage, not a few of them taken up by a selection of wines, and travelled by steamer up the

Congo. With the prospect of intermittent rivers and streams ahead, they had packed into their luggage a number of small metal whalers which could be supplemented, if necessary, by native canoes. They had barely started overland when they chanced upon what looked like an enormous stroke of luck. Stranded by falling water in the M'Bomu river they came across a 30-ft steamer called the *Faidherbe*. Marchand decided that they must have it.

The *Faidherbe* did a wonderful job towing them along in their assorted boats. When the keel began dragging on rocks, however, the hard work began, the repeated process of unloading everything, towing the *Faidherbe*

take the *Faidherbe* with them, even if that meant literally cutting it up into portable slices. The cutting and slicing duly followed, but that still left the boiler. If the boiler were cut up, the *Faidherbe* would most definitely never steam again.

"They all gathered around the cylindrical, intractable object weighing over two tons," says Patricia Wright in her book *Conflict on the Nile*. "There was nothing for it: the boiler would have to be rolled. If it were to be rolled then a path would have to be cut and logs laid so as to make a rough road." A thousand dubious porters had to be recruited to negotiate the new track.

After 130 miles of log road they reached

over the obstacle and reloading. There was great relief when the M'Bomu deepened again to take them merrily to within 130 miles of the Upper Sueh, which they believed connected with the Nile.

Marchand may not have known that those 130 miles (210 km) included dense jungle and substantial hills, but in any case he was extremely reluctant to abandon the little boat which had served them so well. They would

Left, the Anglo-Egyptian fleet heading upriver. **Above left**, the *Faidherbe*, Marchand's brave boat, being dragged from the river. **Above right**, British gunboat being hauled up the cataracts.

the Sueh, and they set about reincarnating the *Faidherbe*. But despite starting well, the Sueh widened and widened until it ceased to be a river. "I try in vain to find a horizon," one of the Frenchmen wrote in his journal. "There is not even a tree, nothing but marsh; silent, unforgiving in its terrible uniformity beneath an unyielding sky."

The faithful *Faidherbe* could go no further unless some kind of channel could be found, and even then only when rains brought up the water level. Marchand sent off a party to look for any means through the marsh. The further they went into it, the worse the conditions were, an impossible combination of neither enough water to float a canoe nor firmness underfoot to support a man's weight. "Often there was no water at all, just thigh-deep mud flipping with half-dead fish and reptiles, everywhere enclosed by stifling, airless heat and clouds of mosquitos."

Eventually they spotted a mountain in the distance. "A mountain means land, real earth without marsh, without endless muddy sludge, without reeds, without papyrus," the French officer wrote in his journal. "Land which one can walk on, can sleep on without sinking, on which one can live as a man again." He was emboldened to the conclusion that "the Nile is before me – Fashoda within my grasp!"

it, the worst of the stories they had heard came true. They were lucky to cover a mile in an afternoon through the solid vegetation, and at night the mosquitos descended in vengeful clouds. Only the resourceful Senegalese found an answer to the mosquitos, and that was by sliding into the slime at night with only their nostrils protruding. The hippos, always a problem, also became a constant menace.

In his diary for 10 July 1898, after several weeks of misery, the party's doctor is at last able to make the diary entry they all longed for. "We pass an old Dervish redoubt and then all at once round a bend in the river a group of high, sparse palms appear, behind

After nine weeks in hell the advance party struggled back to the camp, but as there was no question of the main party or the *Faidherbe* trying to go where the reconaissance party had been until the water level rose, they were still stuck. After several weeks of frustration, they set off as soon as the water rose to a level that suited the canoes. The first part of the journey went remarkably well. Game was plentiful, excessively so in the case of hippos, and the chef devised a very acceptable sauce for sautéed elephant trunk.

Their good progress brought them ever closer to the dreaded marsh described by the scouts, the Sudd. When at last they reached

which stretch some imposing but slashed and ruined walls… 5 o'clock, in the name of France, we take possession of Fashoda!"

The former slaving post was in ruins: piles of broken stones, the odd dismembered arch, a cellar piled with rubbish. Nevertheless, they had brought champagne across Africa for the occasion and nothing was going to stop them from toasting Fashoda.

But although Marchand had won the race, it was not inconceivable that with a much larger force at his disposal Kitchener might

Above left, Horatio Herbert Kitchener in Egypt.
Above, Kitchener and Marchand meet in Fashoda.

arrive at any moment, brush them aside, and claim to have got there first. In fact the first enemy were the Mahdi, who attacked the French from two steamboats and were duly repulsed after an exchange of fire.

The French were worried: they had already used much of their ammunition in fighting off the Mahdi, who were certain to return. Four days later someone had spotted the telltale smoke of a vessel approaching. The Mahdi? Kitchener? Neither. It was a sight which brought tears to their eyes. With its siren screeching joyful greetings, there was the faithful *Faidherbe*, with a few welcome reinforcements and resupplies.

A month passed before two wild-eyed and breathless sentries reported that the Mahdi were back. Everyone turned in early that night in readiness for a dawn attack. At 11.30 p.m., however, two couriers approached the camp. They had a letter addressed to "The Commandant of the European Expedition at Fashoda". The letter was signed: "Herbert Kitchener, Sirdar".

The letter from Kitchener was polite and to the point. He wrote that he had come across a group of Mahdi who reported the battle they'd had with Marchand, and, wishing to learn more, he intended to visit Fashoda the following day.

"Mon Général," Marchand replied, "I have the honour to acknowledge receipt of your letter dated 18 September 1898... I shall be the very first to present the sincere good wishes of France to General Kitchener, whose name for so many years has epitomised the struggles of civilisation..." If Kitchener called, he would be happy to welcome him "in the name of France".

In the morning, Kitchener and Marchand got together privately on one of the British boats. Marchand had possession of Fashoda and no intention of abandoning it. Kitchener, on the other hand, had the means to take it from him – five gunboats, 2,500 Sudanese troops, 100 Highlanders, machine guns and artillery – but no wish to use them.

After initial awkwardness, the two men agreed that both sides would occupy the area. Accordingly, the British set up a flag-pole on a mudbank next to the fort, fired a 21-gun salute and ran up not the British flag but the Egyptian. It suited all concerned to maintain that Kitchener was technically there on behalf of not the British but the Egyptian

government, and with the permission of the French – who wouldn't anyway have been able to stop him.

In the French officers' mess Kitchener listened with interest to the story of their hideous journey through the marsh. The French were keen to impress on him how well they had settled in and presented him with a large basket of flowers and fresh vegetables. Kitchener saved his bombshell for the moment of departure. The French government was in tatters, he said, ripped apart by the Dreyfus scandal (the Watergate of its time). He did not believe they would have the time or the inclination to back up Marchand.

The two parties lived side-by-side on the "glob of mud" through the stifling heat of the Sudanese summer. Eventually, word came from the British government insisting on controlling all movement on the river. It also said that a boat was on its way "to undertake the evacuation of Fashoda by French troops." Paris had too many of its own problems to deal with at home.

Marchand could never afterwards bring himself to speak of the evacuation. The British gave a farewell dinner for the French. The two outposts had remained on fairly amicable, albeit wary, terms. There were speeches and a presentation of the flag from the Mahdi gunboat which had opened fire on Fashoda – the only souvenir for the French.

On one point, Marchand was adamant: the *Faidherbe* would leave with them too. The doctor recorded the departure in his diary: "It is done, we have passed by the English camp towed by the *Faidherbe*. Their Sudanese presented arms, the officers saluted with their swords, the band played Marseillaise, we raised our hats, and so we passed, we passed sadly by."

But the wood was poor and the pressure in the *Faidherbe*'s celebrated boiler was low. The engine was tired and the boat was heavily overloaded. At one point a British gunboat had to give them a tow. On reaching rapids, the *Faidherbe* could go no further. The engine expired, the hull was split in a collision with a rock. Two whole days were devoted to constructing a dry dock. The *Faidherbe* was dragged into her final resting place and given a solemn farewell. "Our brave little ship," the doctor noted, "May she rest in peace!"

After an absence of some 2,000 years, pharaonic rule returned to Egypt in the improbable person of a half-dead Albanian tobacconist. The circumstances, obviously, were more than a little curious. They began back in 1799 when Turkey sent an expeditionary force to recover Egypt from Napoleon. The two armies clashed at Aboukir Bay and throughout the engagement, bobbing about offshore in a small boat, was Sir Sidney Smith, a British admiral who seemed to pop up wherever there was trouble in the Eastern Mediterranean.

Sir Sidney thought the Turks might have carried the day had they not succumbed, as usual, to the tactically unsound practice of breaking ranks and dashing forward to collect the heads of fallen enemy. "A barbarous custom," Sir Sidney observed primly. He was not surprised that it produced "a burst of indignation" among the French infantry. The appalled French retaliated with such venom that the Turks were soon driven into the sea, and Sir Sidney found himself suddenly surrounded by shoals of Turkish troops swimming for their lives. He fished out one who reached his gig on the point of drowning and handed him over to one of the crew for artificial respiration. As the man came to, Sir Sidney was struck by the bushiness of his beard and piercing glint in his grey eyes.

It was only by luck, then, that the career of Mohammed Ali, a turbulent Albanian orphan who joined the police to let off steam before going into the tobacco business, later to become a soldier, did not stop there and then. Sir Sidney's act of kindness rescued a maniacal genius, the founder of one of the most eccentric dynasties in all history, not merely Egypt's.

Ali shows his hand: Mohammed Ali's uncomfortable introduction to Egypt did not discourage him from returning, which he did as soon as the country reverted to Turkish suzerainty after the expulsion of the French. He was, as before, in the Albanian contingent of the Turkish army but had risen to second in command. Not for long. In circumstances that have never been satisfactorily explained, his commanding officer's head flew out of a Cairo window and came to rest in a gutter. Automatic promotion made Mohammed Ali the governor of Cairo, and his career changed gear.

In working to establish his authority Ali used guerrilla tactics, as well as more conventional warfare, as he quickly demonstrated with a brilliant cavalry charge on the British force of 7,000 troops sent to deal with him. His resounding victory was perhaps the greatest humiliation the British army had yet suffered "in the east". The worst of it was the grim procession of 500 British prisoners prodded along to the Cairo slave market. The route was pointedly lined with the heads of their dead comrades on poles.

Having disposed of the British threat, Mohammed Ali recognised that doctored coffee was no weapon against the majority of the majestic Mamlukes. The amazing tale of Mamluke rule has its own section in this book; their demise belongs to Mohammed Ali. The Mamluke princes were invited to Cairo from their southern strongholds to join Ali in a glorious send-off for his son Toussoun, who had been given the task of capturing the holy cities of Mecca and Medina. The governor greeted his guests effusively. They arrived on horseback, resplendent as ever in jewelled robes and armour. "After a time," wrote a young Italian mercenary serving with Mohammed's Albanian bodyguard, "according to Eastern custom, coffee was brought, and last of all the pipes, but at the moment when these were presented, as if from etiquette, or to leave his guests more at their ease, Mohammed Ali rose and withdrew."

He had left orders. The Mamlukes were invited to take up the place of honour in the centre of a military procession which was supposed to leave the Citadel and tour the city. Instead, they were trapped between heavy gates and mown down from above.

Overwhelming ambition: The massacre ended an epoch in Egyptian history which stretched back as far as Saladin and the Crusades. It also made Mohammed Ali a dictator, and the way in which he swiftly set about the exploitation of his people was breathtaking. He expropriated all farming land for himself and was therefore able to charge what he liked for the crops. He became the sole proprietor of all factories and hence all manufactured goods, and topped that off by taking exclusive control of imports and exports. As the managing director of Egypt, he launched a crash programme of industrialisation which was supposed to enable the country to catch up Europe in double-quick time.

Lane also described the "violent but naive charm" of Mohammed Ali's notion of justice. A horizontal sweep of his hand meant execution without further ado. A butcher

Ibrahim conquered Arabia, including the holy cities of Mecca and Medina; he sent his younger son Ismail up the Nile with a force of 5,000 men to seize the Sudan, but tribesman sneaked into Ismail's camp and burnt him alive in his tent. His father's reprisals cost 50,000 Sudanese lives.

Egypt was of course part of the Ottoman Empire and to begin with Mohammed Ali was a reasonably loyal subject-ruler. Soon, however, he had ambitions on that empire for himself. The efficient Ibrahim swept across Sinai to take Palestine, Lebanon and Syria right up to the Turkish border. A panic-stricken Sultan issued a *firman* deposing Mohammed Ali as Pasha of Egypt but there

who sold underweight meat had the missing balance carved off his own back. An official who cheated a baker was baked in his victim's oven. The architect friend who built the Mohammed Ali mosque in Cairo, still one of the city's unmissable sights, was executed afterwards to prevent him from building anything comparable for anyone else.

Mohammed Ali's excesses tend to be glossed over because of his revered status as "Father of Modern Egypt", as in one important sense he indeed was. The army he created was genuinely Egyptian rather than a collection of slaves and hirelings and he used it to devastating effect. He and his eldest son

was no stopping the Egyptians. Ibrahim rolled on until he had taken Konia, the ancient Ottoman capital, and was within striking distance of Constantinople. He seemed to be about to achieve the impossible.

When the European powers woke up to these extraordinary events, France and Britain predictably took opposing views. France supported Mohammed Ali, with whom they anticipated arriving at a most useful arrangement if he could only sew up both the Suez and Euphrates overland routes to the east. The British government wished to strengthen the hand of the Ottomans simply to prevent their old enemy, France, from doing just that.

Commodore Napier, Royal Navy, was despatched with six ships to Alexandria, where Mohammed Ali was resident in his newly completed Ras el Tin Palace. "If your Highness will not listen to my appeal to you against the folly of further resistance," Napier began sweetly, "My God, I will bombard you, and put a bomb right where you are sitting!" Ali was robbed of his conquests but soothed with the Treaty of London which in 1841 recognised him as ruler of Egypt, under nominal Turkish suzerainty, with the rights of succession to his eldest son.

A new dynasty: Ali might have lost an empire, but he had founded a dynasty and won respectability. Egypt was back on the tourist

map as it hadn't been since Cleopatra took her Roman lovers up the Nile. Samuel Shepheard, a British farmer's son who had run away to sea, took the first steps towards establishing the famous hotel in Cairo which bears his name in the same year – 1841 – that Mohammed Ali began the construction of his mosque.

The dynasty ran into difficulties when Mohammed Ali's mind began to fail. The co-regent during his debility was Ibrahim,

Far left, Ibrahim, Mohammed Ali's soldier-son.
Left, Abbas, Ibrahim's nephew and successor.
Above, Said, initiator of the Suez Canal.

the soldier-son who had campaigned so well on his behalf, but who met a unique end while his father was still alive. Hot and bothered after a hard day in the saddle, he cooled off under an upturned bucket of iced champagne. The shock gave him pneumonia, but even in this weakened condition he could not resist a young Circassian slave girl who arrived as a present from his mother. Getting to know her finished him off.

Ibrahim was succeeded by his nephew Abbas, a morose recluse. Abbas was a notorious sadist – he enjoyed having loose women either flogged or sewn up in bags and dumped into the Nile – so his eventual strangulation by two slave boys was rather appropriate. Historians have looked long, hard and in vain for a good word to say about Abbas. If modern guides mention him at all it is for his brainwave that the pyramids should be dismantled – "ugly, useless piles of stone" – to provide stones for a Nile barrage.

Abbas's successor, Said, was a fat child who grew up to weigh 25 stone (160 kg). He was as gregarious as his predecessor had been reclusive. True, he decapitated misbehaving sheikhs but he always did it "jovially", and he liked to challenge guests to join him, candle in hand, for a wade through loose gunpowder. He extended railway lines right up to his palaces and had a special coach built along the lines of a house. He would then order the train to stop wherever he fancied living for a while.

Said was open to new ideas, and the idea that appealed to him most was put to him by a glib Frenchman named Ferdinand de Lesseps. It was, of course, the Suez Canal. Almost immediately the scheme went wrong and for the first time in his life Said began to lose weight. He had given De Lesseps a concession without realising that he would have to put up a large proportion of the enormous capital required himself. Nor did he foresee the strenuous objections from Britain; a Suez canal would create a new avenue of trade to the detriment of the Cape sea route to India which Britain had comfortably under control. Said was a skeleton of his former self when he died of worry in 1863, with an overdraft of £10 million.

The creator of Cairo: His successor, Ismail, according to one of Farouk's biographers, Hugh McLeave, was "one of the most bewildering personalities in history," a "depraved ogre" in the eyes of someone like Lord Milner, "a maligned but enlightened spirit" according to kinder critics. His personal charm and prodigal hospitality quickly overcame reservations about his looks and unconventional etiquette. His face, to begin with, was pitted by eczema and sprouted tufts of ginger hair, but it was his eyes that took some getting used to. They pointed in radically different directions and tended to revolve – "keeping an eye on Upper and Lower Egypt", it was said. Perhaps to make things easier for his guests, he generally tried to keep one or other eye closed, but whatever good that might have done was undermined by his habit of removing his boots in company and, sitting cross-legged, playing with his toes.

mium on the price of Eyptian cotton and he could afford massive expenditure on public works. The railway expansion programme added 1,000 miles of track. He built palaces galore, extended canals so that the amount of arable land was greatly increased, opened 6,000 schools, built 60 or so sugar mills and even created a completely new city which, of course, he named after himself: Ismailia.

The appearance of modern Cairo was largely determined by Ismail. It was he who laid out boulevards modelled on the Rue de Rivoli and created out of wasteland and old native quarters the modern city centre. The famous palace on Gazirah Island, sensitively preserved as the heart of the modern Cairo

None of this seems to have inhibited his whole-hearted pursuit of women. His harem contained no fewer than 3,000 Turkish and Circassian women, although it has been suggested that this was "an exercise in self-promotion rather than self-gratification."

Ismail's favourite saying was that Egypt was a part of Europe and, like Mohammed Ali, he also regarded it as his private domain. His preoccuption from the start was with the Suez Canal, but he sought to improve the country in every possible way. Fortunately for him, the American Civil War put a pre-

Marriott Hotel, was built in less than six months for the visit of the Empress Eugenie, one of dozens of foreign dignitaries and royalty expected for the opening of the Suez Canal. The hotel is worth visiting to see what Ismail thought a billiard saloon ought to be.

The Canal and debts: Ismail's extravagance meant that the Canal had to be a commercial success in order to rescue Egypt from financial disaster, but such considerations were not allowed to temper the splendour of the opening. It was a most memorable event, in some respects accidentally. The mountain of fireworks collected for the occasion exploded prematurely and nearly demolished Port Said.

A large rock discovered just below the water level on the eve of the opening was hurriedly dynamited – and the banks collapsed. When a police launch ran aground in the path of the procession of 68 ships (Eugenie to the fore in the French imperial yacht), De Lesseps galloped ahead and personally blew it up. Ismail had commissioned Verdi to write *Aida* for the opening of the Opera House. The house was ready but *Aida* was not; the guests heard *Rigoletto* instead. Nevertheless, the flotilla set off in stately procession down the Canal to the booming of shore batteries and Eugenie declared tearfully that she had never seen a sight so lovely.

The chickens came home to roost six years

tary riot. Britain and France would have none of it and appealed to the Sultan of Turkey, still Ismail's nominal superior, to assert his authority. Ismail did not really need to open the telegram which arrived from the Sultan. It was addressed to "The ex-Khedive, Ismail Pasha". Four days later he boarded the yacht *Mahroussa* for exile in Italy, but not before pocketing all the cash left in the Treasury.

Tewfik, Ismail's 27-year-old weakling son, was quite unequal to the chaos he inherited, least of all to the challenge thrown down by Ahmed Arabi, a relatively junior army officer who, uncannily like Nasser in the following century, was a true Egyptian who

later. With national debts already exceeding £100 million, Ismail could no longer keep his creditors at bay. Britain and France, egged on by their respective citizens and institutions who were owed money, forced him to accept their own financial experts. In order to give them the necessary authority, Ismail's personal powers were reduced to constitutional sovereignty. His last desperate card to retain autocratic rule was to organise a mili-

resented the disproportionate influence wielded in Egypt by foreigners. In 1881 Arabi ringed the Abdin Palace with 2,000 troops and demanded immediate reforms. "I am the Khedive," Tewfik retorted, "and shall do as I please." To which, by his own account, Arabi replied: "We are not slaves and shall not from this day be treated as such." Tewfik placated him with an appointment as Minister of War.

On 10 July 1882, Admiral Sir Beauchamp Seymour sailed into Alexandria and gave Tewfik and Arabi, who were occupying a fort overlooking the harbour, 24 hours for Arabi's resignation. Foreign shipping in the

Left, the Prince of Wales's visit to the Suez Canal in 1869. **Above left**, Tewfik proved unequal to the chaos he inherited. **Above right**, the rebellious Arabi, appointed Minister of War by Tewfik.

harbour hastily got up steam and made for open sea, saluting the British flagship on their way past. The admiral's band returned the compliment with the appropriate national anthem.

At dawn the pleasantries ceased. The bombardment of Alexandria went on all day and by evening there were 2,000 Egyptian dead and the fortifications were demolished. The city itself was blackened, partly by British gunfire but also by looters who took the opportunity to ransack the commercial centre. Tewfik had seen enough. He put himself under British protection and declared Arabi to be a rebel. Thereupon the minister of war was swiftly rounded up by the British army.

Interregnum: Tewfik's vacillations were a portent of the struggle between the Turkish ruling classes and Egyptian nationalism, which manifested itself in the army as well as the streets, but for the moment shopkeepers hastily replaced pictures of Arabi with ones of the Khedive. The British Coldstream Guards became the new garrison in the Cairo Citadel. *The Times* of London reported the celebrations in honour of the victorious British army: "Tewfik in state takes the salute from the 18,000 British who have replaced him on the throne while Arabi from his prison window in the same square watches the defile of the army which scattered to the winds, in twenty minutes, his ambitious labour of the year."

The British presence, which put a cap on Egyptian nationalism for a further 70 years, is dealt with separately in this book. The continuing story of the last pharaohs passed quietly over Tewfik's death in 1892. The outbreak of World War I found his successor, Abbas II, visiting Constantinople in what Britain considered an unsavoury attempt to curry favour with Turkey, which had entered the war on Germany's side. Abbas, and Turkish suzerainty over Egypt, had to go. "Egypt," the Foreign Office announced, "will henceforth constitute a British protectorate." Abbas was deposed the following day, and the British appointed Fu'ad, his sixth son.

Fu'ad married his cousin, Princess Shevikiar – he was strapped for money and she was rich – and both lived to regret it. His obsession with cleanliness, so admired by the British, seemed to have stemmed from an unfortunate incident in the Khan el-Khalili bazaar, when someone had emptied a bucket of slops on his head. He stalked his palace for bad smells. When he cornered one, he attacked it with a burst from an eau-de-Cologne spray. Shevikiar, an outgoing girl who resented being penned up in a harem on becoming his wife, also "found it hard to get used to someone who leapt out of bed at five o'clock as though answering some inaudible trumpet call, and spent half an hour doing physical jerks in front of a mirror. She thought, and others agreed, that Prince Ahmed Fu'ad did not really care for women." Shevikiar decided to run away.

Dangerous engagement: Fu'ad's announcement that he proposed to divorce Princess Shevikiar led to a showdown between him and Shevikiar's hot-headed young brother, Seif ed-Din, who was bent on revenge. On 7 May 1898, Seif ed-Din happened to be passing the Khedival Club in Cairo when he spotted Fu'ad chatting to a fellow member out on the balcony.

The two princes met face to face in, of all places, the Silence Room. This was not the time to observe club rules. Fu'ad took one look at the bristling revolver and took up a flimsy defensive position behind a table. They circled the table warily, the tempo increasing until it became a sprint. Two members dived under the leather sofa, a distinguished Russian visitor backed into a lavatory and locked himself in, the Minister of War literally climbed the curtains.

The macabre dance around the table was punctuated by Seif ed-Din's desperate attempts to get a shot in. One bullet hit Fu'ad in the side, a second in the throat and a third in the thigh. Out of ammunition, Seif ed-Din's rage quickly subsided. The club secretary, an Englishman, put his head into the Silence Room to see what was going on, and a porter was sent off to look for an arresting officer. He returned with a bemused corporal. Offering no resistance, the subdued prince was led away.

Doctors operated on Fu'ad where he lay. They removed two of the bullets but decided the one in his throat was too close to an artery. It remained there for the rest of his life, giving his voice a high metallic whine.

The transcript of Seif ed-Din's trial gives a clue to British imperial attitudes. Not only was the criminal prosecution of a prince unprecedented, but Seif ed-Din's sentencing to five years' hard labour on a rock-pile was sensational. It certainly unnerved him and he was much given to muttering about what he would do to Fu'ad next time. Doctors eventually packed him off to a lunatic asylum in England. His grievance raged unabated for 26 years when, with the help of two of the asylum attendants, he escaped.

Fu'ad was convinced that his life was in danger and the British Foreign Office, concurring, launched an international manhunt. Seif ed-Din managed to evade the net and got as far as Constantinople. Unable to progress from there, he settled for legal proceedings with a view to recovering his fortune, which Fu'ad had long appropriated.

The appropriation of Seif ed-Din's inheritance was only one step in Fu'ad's accumulation of incalculable wealth. By compulsory purchase at a fraction of the market price, or simply by diverting the irrigation canal from the estate of a reluctant vendor, he ended up owning one-seventh of the cultivable land in Egypt. The police manned roadblocks to ensure that his agriculture produce reached the market and was sold before the competition. He had no time for his subjects: "Don't ever expect good faith of the Egyp-

tians," he once remarked. "They don't understand what it is."

King Farouk: Fu'ad's son was brought up in palatial quarantine, in the Kubbah and Abdin palaces in Cairo and in Ras el-Tin and Montazah in Alexandria. Kubah was his principal home: a mile-long driveway through 70 acres (28 hectares) of lakes and exotic gardens to a moated palace of 400 rooms. His doting father spared nothing not only to make the boy comfortable – boats in the lake, camels and horses in the stables, mountains of toys – but also to remove the need ever to go beyond the high palace walls, which might have entailed making contact with other boys of his age or indeed Egyptians in general.

The boy grew up with the idea that football was played by kicking a ball and then waiting while a servant ran after it and replaced it at his feet. When he swam, an escort of sailors paddled along on either side. Given an airgun, he tried it out by smashing every ground floor window in the palace. His mother, Queen Nazli, complained that he was forever locking her maids up in cupboards and hiding the key. "I am trying to punish Farouk for his impertinence and arrogance to me lately," she wrote in an exasperated note to his English governess. "He does not seem to mind anything or anybody, and is getting increasingly selfish every day."

Left, King Fu'ad, whose divorce nearly led to his death. **Right**, the wedding of the young King Farouk and his first wife Farida in 1937.

As his only approved playmates were his sisters Fawzia, Faiza, Faika and Fathia (an Indian fortune-teller once told Fu'ad that F was his lucky letter), Farouk came to frequent the servants' quarters, where many of the occupants were Italians because, it seems, they facilitated his father's dealings with Italian mistresses, for whom he had a penchant. Farouk, a natural linguist and altogether a quick learner, picked up their language and also formed friendships, as with the Italian boy who repaired his electric train, which were to have major consequences.

When Farouk was 14, illness gave his father a brush with death and the heir to the throne's further education became a matter of urgency, so he sat exams to get into English establishments. He would sit nibbling his pencil as he had done in the palace, waiting for someone to supply the answers. The palace tutors had given him a distinction in every subject, but the headmaster of Eton was not convinced. In any case, he did not have Latin. Farouk also failed the entrance exam to the Royal Military Academy at Woolwich but was admitted in the lesser capacity of "Gentleman Cadet".

In the circumstances, Farouk did well at Woolwich, where he was known as Prince Freddie. An 18-roomed mansion in Kingston-on-Thames with a staff of 20 and the occasional reception at Buckingham Palace set Farouk apart from other cadets, but he pitched into their life and cheerfully carried out the most mundane chores, like cutting up oranges for the commandant's wife. The commandant saw potential in his intelligence, good nature and competitive spirit but these were not to be realised, at least not at Woolwich.

Farouk was recklessly putting a horse through its paces around a jumping course in Richmond Park when he was informed of his father's death. "I'll just do three more rounds of jumps..." he said brightly. "You'll do nothing of the sort," replied his English tutor. "We can't have two kings of Egypt dying on the same day." The new King of Egypt was 16 years old.

On his accession, Farouk owned a tenth of Egypt's cultivable land outright and had control over twice as much again. He had £45 million in the bank, five palaces, two sea-going yachts, more than 100 cars including 10 Rolls-Royces, a squadron of aircraft and any number of royal villas and rest-houses throughout the kingdom. Yet, in the opinion of the long-suffering English governess who had tried to contain his childhood excesses, all was not well.

The man in charge: The only life Farouk had seen outside his palace walls was in England. He had never been to Luxor or even to the pyramids when he ascended the throne. The arrangements for him to see his realm were reminiscent of the Nile cruises laid on by Cleopatra for her Roman lovers. Four paddle steamers and two launches sailed up river in stately procession with hundreds and sometimes thousands of tribesmen on camels, horses and on foot keeping pace on either bank. The flotilla anchored at towns and larger villages, Farouk presiding over the games, dancing and feasting in his honour.

Farouk took some of his new responsibilities seriously. He was forever pulling a Koran out of his pocket and quoting from it, but he also revealed traits which were to become legendary. In particular, he was hopelessly, unapologetically unpunctual and he delighted in picking pockets. Handkerchiefs, watches, and cigarette lighters were an irresistible challenge. It all went into a palace treasure trove of handkerchiefs, watches, cigarette lighters – anything he could get his hands on.

Winston Churchill was almost alone in challenging Farouk's licence to help himself. They were sitting together at a dinner during World War II when Churchill, wishing to drop a hint that time was short, reached into his waistcoat pocket for his watch. It had gone! Churchill was in no mood for one of Farouk's little jokes. The watch had been presented to his ancestor, the Duke of Marlborough, by Queen Anne after his victory at Blenheim and was priceless. "Your Majesty," Churchill growled, "I want that watch back as quickly as it can be arranged."

"When did you last see it?" asked Farouk with a show of innocence.

"A little less than an hour ago."

Farouk left the table saying that he could guess who the culprit was. He was back in 10 minutes with the missing watch dangling from his hand.

Once released from the confines of the palace, Farouk ran riot on the roads. He had his entire fleet of cars painted a distinctive shade of red to save the police the trouble of trying to stop him from speeding, general recklessness and the playful practice of taking pot shots with a pistol at the tyres of cars he overtook.

The horns fitted to Farouk's cars simulated the sound of a dog being run over, and the first sign of a royal-red car coming their way had pedestrians and other road-users diving for cover. Farouk thought he was a good driver and had a newspaper editor jailed for printing a story which said that he was followed everywhere by an ambulance to pick up casualties. The only surprise about Farouk's driving was that he did not have a serious accident until 1943, when he put a red Cadillac into a tree and took three weeks

replaced with a fresh tray of 30. And so it went until he felt ready to tackle the subsequent courses, which were permutations of lobster, steak, lamb chops, chicken, quail and pigeons. He was hungry again by mid-afternoon, which meant a lunch as big or bigger than breakfast, followed by dinner at a fairly conventional hour. Hunger between meals was staved off with a bag of toffees which he carried everywhere. Knowing the family tendency towards obesity, Fu'ad had kept him on a diet throughout childhood. Farouk made spectacular amends and was beginning to balloon at 18. Although he bought every slimming device on the market, his girth continued to swell for the rest of his life.

to recover from the injuries.

Those closer to Farouk than fleeing pedestrians were as alarmed by his eating habits as his driving. He seldom went to bed before dawn and never without a bedtime snack of caviar, chicken or steak, several ice creams and a half-gallon of fruit juice. That kept him going until breakfast, which he took around noon. The first course consisted of boiled eggs, 30 at a time. They were brought to his bedside in a tray. By the time he had eaten three or four, the rest were cold, so they were

Above, King Farouk, aged 26, with one of his infamous red cars and the day's bag of wildfowl.

Several theories have been put forward for Farouk's gluttony, but the consensus points at a complaint which has biographers groping for euphemisms: "nature had dealt shabbily with him", "a certain lack of sexual development", and so on.

The determination with which Farouk tried to compensate for his handicap could be jolly – e.g. popping an ice cube down the front of the dress of a woman when she curtsied to him – or lethal. A young army captain was shot dead by Farouk's ADC to prevent him from entering his wife's bedroom when Farouk was within. On more than one occasion, trysts in his car came to grief. He and a lady friend were waylaid by robbers as they were parked in a country lane near Helwan. They were stripped of their valuables and Farouk, whom the robbers had not recognised, was about to have his throat cut when the gang leader told his men to "leave the fat pig – he's not worth the trouble of killing". The gang was duly rounded up and executed, all bar their leader. He was given 100 lashes for calling Farouk "a fat pig" – and £1,000 for having spared his life.

Women in his life: Farouk was certainly not impotent, although there were some conspicuous dissenters among the 5,000 women whom, it was fancifully claimed, Farouk could have called on as expert witnesses. A

insuperable difficulty that she was Jewish. In 1949 his political advisers suggested that a royal marriage would draw public attention away from the military humiliation Egypt had suffered in Palestine. Somewhat reluctantly he agreed, but there was the question of finding a suitable woman.

Farouk's favourite jeweller recognised in one his customers the sort of woman Farouk liked. She had the light skin of a Circassian and a baby face which contrasted with a well-developed body. Unfortunately, she had entered the shop with her fiancé to select an engagement ring. While the couple busied themselves with trays of rings, the jeweller made a furtive call to Farouk's private

number of mistresses quite quickly deserted him and made no secret of the paucity of his performance. A sympathetic aide once tried to comfort him with the assurance that "some people are better endowed by nature than others" and he ought to admit his weakness to himself.

Farouk's long-suffering queen through all of this was Farida, a popular figure whom he had married in 1937. She had given him three daughters but no son. That, coupled with paranoid suspicion that she, too, was having affairs on the side, persuaded Farouk to divorce her. He then took up with a starlet whom he might have married but for the

number. Within half an hour Farouk himself, having peeped at her through the window, raised his fingers in a gesture of approval. The jeweller knew what to do. He removed the chosen ring from the girl's finger and replaced it with a monster diamond. The nonplussed fiancé protested that it was well out of his price range. The jeweller intimated that he was out of luck. "By command of His Majesty," he murmured. Narriman, a girl from Heliopolis, thus became the last Queen of Egypt.

After women, Farouk's great passion was gambling. He frequently spent all night at the casino tables, and as long as he was there no one was allowed to leave. He was a bold gambler, full of bluff, but he rarely won and at times resorted to desperate measures to turn his luck. On one occasion in the Automobile Club, a favourite haunt, he opened the betting at £10,000 on a draw which had given him three kings. The stakes mounted rapidly. When he was called, his opponent laid down a full house. Farouk showed his three kings and set about raking in the chips. "But Your Majesty," the opponent protested, "my hand beats yours. You have only three kings."

"No," replied Farouk, "I am the fourth king." That was the end of the matter.

In the circumstances, it is not altogether surprising that men went into hiding when it was known that Farouk was looking for partners. If necessary, and regardless of the hour, he would drive to some luckless victim's house and park outside, leaning on the car horn until the victim got out of bed and followed the red car back to the casino. A notebook discovered after Farouk was deposed showed that he had lost £850,000 in a single year.

The plots of war: As Farouk became embroiled in one scandal after another, the crown on his head looked increasingly precarious. To begin with, the British government was willing to tolerate young Farouk's foibles. He was under the beady eye of the patrician ambassador, Sir Miles Lampson (later Lord Killearn), whose attitude was typified by one of his exchanges at the bar of the Automobile Club.

"The boy is misbehaving," he remarked to one of the princes. "If we decided to make a change, would you be prepared to take over the Crown?" The prince evidently lit up a cigar, blew a cloud of smoke, and as casually asked whether he too might be replaced if he misbehaved. "I suppose so," the ambassador replied.

The ambassador was less relaxed in February 1942 when the war in North Africa was going badly for the Allies and Farouk, like many of his subjects, began to cover his bets in case Germany took over Egypt. The government was deadlocked, with Farouk favouring a notoriously pro-German candidate for prime minister and Lord Killearn the nationalist Wafdist, Nahas Pasha. As a last resort, Farouk would have to be deposed. With this in mind, Lord Killearn told Farouk that "unless I hear by six o'clock tomorrow (the 4th) that Nahas Pasha has been asked to form a cabinet, your Majesty must expect the consequences."

Farouk rejected the ultimatum and three hours after the expiry British tanks and infantry moved into Abdin Square. Farouk was at his desk when Lampson burst into his study. The ambassador pulled a prepared document from his pocket and pushed it at the King. "Isn't it rather a dirty piece of paper?" Farouk asked. Lampson, squinting

slightly because of a troublesome sty in one eye, told him to read it and sign: "We, King Farouk of Egypt, mindful as ever of the interests of our country, hereby renounce and abandon for ourselves and their heirs of our body the Throne of the Kingdom of Egypt…"

Farouk had his pen on the paper when he looked up almost in tears. "Won't you give me another chance, Sir Miles?" Lampson would have preferred to see the back of Farouk, but in the end he waived the technical breach of the ultimatum to allow the King to ask Nahas Pasha to form a government. The new government duly took its place and

Left, Farouk (centre) opening the partridge season with an invited party of diplomats. **Right**, British ambassador Sir Miles Lampson.

within days Farouk was back at his favourite table in the Auberge des Pyramides nightclub, again on joking terms with the very same British army officers who had so recently been on standby to remove him bodily from the palace.

The final straw: Farouk's submission mortified the officer corps of the Egyptian army, among them Gamal Abdel Nasser and Anwar Sadat. Nasser later wrote that from the moment of submission onwards he was bent on revolution. In the meantime, Nasser and his colleagues had to bide their time while Farouk saw out the duration of World War II and resumed his wily plotting against any Egyptian government which attempted to curb his

increasingly autocratic tendencies.

Nationalist resentment after the war was divided between Farouk and the continued British occupation of the Canal Zone with a force of 80,000 troops. In 1952 the British army moved against the Ismailia barracks of the Buluk Nizam (auxiliary police), which had been the springboard for a number of attacks on British installations. Forty-six policemen were killed.

An argument between a policeman and dancer in the Badia Cabaret club in Cairo started a brawl which was enough to set off the explosive atmosphere in the city. Mobs attacked cinemas with petrol bombs on their

way to the Turf Club, a Mamluke innovation which had become the haughty symbol of British Egypt. Ten members were burnt alive. Lesser symbols of Western decadence – bars, restaurants, nightclubs and, especially, Shepheard's Hotel – were put to the torch in a frenzy of looting.

At the time, Farouk was presiding over a banquet at the Abdin Palace. He was content to let Cairo burn for a while before ordering in the army to restore order, which was a pretence for dumping the government of the day. Farouk thought he had a reliable ally in the army, but he reckoned without Nasser's vision of the future.

American intelligence almost certainly urged Nasser and his "Free Officers" to strike at the "depraved and dissolute weakling (king) who was allowing Communism to take a grip on Egypt."

With British and American assurances that they had no wish to intervene, the coup passed quickly and bloodlessly. Farouk was wakened in the Montazah Palace in Alexandria with the news, but it was too late to do anything about it. For the second time he had an abdication document thrust in front of him and on this occasion there was no going back. His hands were shaking when he signed it so he asked if he could sign it again. He was escorted aboard the royal yacht. "Your task will be difficult," he told his escort. "It isn't easy, you know, to govern Egypt." And he sailed, penniless, for Italy.

On his arrival in Capri, still in admiral's uniform, he bumped into the husband of Gracie Fields, the English entertainer. "Boris, my friend," he said with a broad smile. "I am no longer king and I am here with only one pair of pants. Please take me to your tailor."

Epitaph: On 17 March 1965, Farouk took his latest girlfriend, a hairdresser named Annamaria Gatti, to dinner. As usual, the meal began a little before midnight and, also as usual, he started with a dozen oysters. They were followed by lobster thermidor, a double portion of roast lamb and a huge helping of trifle. He had just lit up a cigar when his face turned purple and he reached for his throat. At 45, he was dead.

Left, Farouk in Naples after his deposition. His companion is an opera-singer whom he had promised to marry. **Right**, Farouk's statue in Cairo, waving goodbye to an era.

SPY STORIES

Cairo was never a city for secrets: the bazaars buzzed. The sheer volume of apparently sensational material swilling about made spying a sinecure, but the spies themselves were victims like everyone else. Even secret Rustum Buildings headquarters of the super-secret British Special Operations Executive, which ran resistance movements in enemy-occupied territory, were nonchalantly familiar to every Cairo taxi driver as "The Secret Building."

Into this cauldron in early 1942 stepped an ostensible Egyptian known as Hussein Gafaar. His real name was John Eppler, he was German, and he was Germany's hand-picked Man on the Nile. He was to experience certain difficulties.

On paper, Eppler's spy credentials were excellent. Born in Germany, he had moved to Alexandria with his mother while still a boy. His mother later married an Egyptian who adopted young John, made him a Muslim and gave him the name Hussein Gafaar. After an education in Europe, he returned to Egypt and on the strength of a generous allowance from his step-father became yet another elegantly unemployed man about town. As a future spy, it didn't matter much that he spoke English with an exotic accent. The Allied forces included so many émigré volunteers that Eppler could, as we shall see, lounge about in a British uniform without arousing suspicion.

Nationalist sentiments were naturally anti-British so there were always plenty of Egyptians, up to and including King Farouk, who were willing to help the Germans, especially when it looked as if they might win. Farouk resisted official British requests to dismiss his Italian servants, who were privy to everything that went on in the palace and accordingly kept Mussolini informed. These were the servants who in his childhood had fixed his train set and slipped him sweets and cakes when he was supposedly on a strict diet.

"Tell Sir Miles," Farouk retorted to pressure from Sir Miles Lampson, the British ambassador, "that I'll get rid of my Italians when he gets rid of his." The ambassador's wife Lady Lampson was half-Italian.

Mussolini had pencilled in Egypt as part of his new Roman Empire. The Italian Air Force was ordered to soften up Cairo in advance of an invasion from Italian forces in Libya, but the order was quickly withdrawn when Churchill threatened to bomb Rome.

With Mussolini out of the way and the German Afrika Korps' entry into the desert war, Eppler's moment arrived. He had been taken to Germany for training and in the spring of 1942 was ready to return, but the only practical route to Cairo began in Libya. This entailed a slog of 1,700 miles (2,700 km) across the Sahara, a jolting prospect for someone whose previous travels had generally been short hops between nightclubs by taxi. Count Ladislous Almasy, a famous desert explorer, was seconded from the Hungarian Air Force to lead Operation Salaam.

Almasy, who had hated the air force and wanted only to return to his beloved desert, steered Eppler and Sandy, his wireless operator, to the outskirts of Assiut on the Upper Nile. There they took their leave, Almasy retreating into the desert while Eppler and Sandy walked into town carrying large suitcases, one stuffed with money and the other with wireless equipment.

In Cairo, Eppler rented a luxurious houseboat on the Nile near the Zamalek bridge. While Sandy set about installing his equipment under a radiogram in the mahogany bar, Eppler nipped off to look up old friends, in particular a popular belly-dancer named Hekmet Fahmy. She was on the friendliest possible terms, she said, with a number of British officers, one of whom worked in intelligence. With that, Eppler thought his job was all but done. It only remained to let the whole belly-dancing sorority know that a suitcase of British and Egyptian currency awaited disclosure of their pillow talk with British military personnel. Eppler could relax. He acquired a Rifle Brigade uniform (limiting himself modestly to the rank of second-lieutenant) and set off for the bright lights.

Back at the houseboat, Sandy, masquerading as an American, laboriously encrypted Eppler's signal to the effect that he was on base and open for business. The code was based on Daphne du Maurier's *Rebecca*, and somewhere out in the desert a German in earphones had his copy of that book open in readiness. The message was tapped out and, via an aerial generously but unwittingly provided by one of Hekmet's "friends", a British Army major, Sandy had the satisfaction of receiving an acknowledgement from the distant desert.

Eppler's second message did not go off as sweetly; at any rate, the vital acknowledgement was not forthcoming. The two agents prodded at their transmitter but could see nothing wrong with it. They decided to seek expert advice and were given the name of a sympathetic Egyptian signals officer. The expert, when he turned up at the houseboat, was a certain Anwar Sadat. The future president of Egypt was appalled at what was going on in the spies' nest. It

seems that Eppler felt he ought to maintain close physical contact with his network of belly-dancer agents. "A place straight out of the *Thousand and One Nights*," Sadat later wrote, "where everything invited indolence, voluptuousness and pleasures of the senses... The young Nazis had forgotten the delicate mission with which they had been entrusted." He told them there was nothing wrong with the transmitter and stormed out, or so he said.

The loyal Hekmet persevered in their interest. According to a fictionalised account of one incident (by Leonard Mosley in *The Cat and the Mice*), she invited a certain "Major Smith" to join her for a drink on the houseboat before he went off on an important mission. One drink led to another and, of course, the major dutifully passed out. Eppler and Sandy rummaged through his briefcase to discover that it contained top secret information which (of course) could have settled the outcome of the war, at least in North Africa.

When the major came to his senses and rushed off to make up for lost time, Eppler and Sandy filtered their windfall through *Rebecca* and triumphantly sent it off. They waited for an acknowledgement from the desert, but none came. They tried again; same result. It later transpired that if anyone was picking up the signal, it was a British counter-intelligence operation a few hundred yards away.

Having exhausted their Egyptian currency, the Germans opened up bundles of English £5 notes. Their crisp condition should have warned Eppler that they were counterfeit, albeit expertly printed in Germany, although he later claimed that he did not know.

With or without benefit of the red-hot information lifted from the comatose British major, Rommel was at that juncture steamrollering towards Cairo.

Rommel's progress was not unmitigated good news for Eppler because the prospect of a British defeat decimated the value of his £5 notes on the black-market. In any case, the British forces in Egypt were paid in Egyptian pounds and British notes, especially crisp (and dud!) fivers, were something of a rarity. Field Security, as British counter-intelligence was known, was soon paddling up the stream of fivers flowing into the city flesh-pots. They then uncovered another clue in two distraught German wireless operators picked up in the desert. Although neither man spoke or could read English, they seemed devoted to the works of Daphne du Maurier, or more particularly a copy of *Rebecca* which was found in their possession. The case against Eppler was clinched by a new girl inducted into Eppler's harem. She was Jewish and worked undercover for Field Security.

The houseboat was raided in the early hours of a morning in mid-July. While Sandy hastened below to open the stopcocks and sink the boat, Eppler grabbed the best weapon he could lay his hands on to repel boarders. Unfortunately, the weapon in question was a pair of rolled-up socks and they were not wholly convincing as the "grenade" which Eppler lobbed at the eager policemen as they battered down the stateroom door.

In the event, the two spies owed their lives to Sadat, but only by default. The British authorities decided that they could hardly shoot them without shooting Sadat as well, and shooting an Egyptian Army officer in the circumstances would have been too provocative. Sadat was nevertheless stripped of his rank and sent to a detention camp. Eppler and Sandy were sent to a prison camp, there to contemplate a sour reverse in their fortunes. ∎

David Roberts, R. A.

146

THE TAMING OF THE NILE

The whole of Egyptian civilisation existed on the paradox that at the hottest and driest time of the year in what would otherwise have been one of the least habitable places on earth the Nile reliably (and mysteriously) broke its banks with an ocean of water and rich silt.

The result was the kind of paradise in which a farmer waited until the flood subsided, scattered a few seeds about, let his pigs trample them into the mud, and sat back to wait for the first of as many as three crops in a season. The Egyptians, wrote Herodotus, "gather in the fruits of the earth with less labour than any other people." With subsistence more or less taking care of itself, the pharaohs had a pool of underemployed labour without which their unparalleled achievements along a 1,000-mile (1,600-km) ribbon of river bank would not have been conceivable.

There were one or two considerations which could upset the system. If the flood was too low, the amount of arable land could shrink disastrously; if too high, it washed away settlements that were supposedly on safe ground. Moreover, the secret of two or three consecutive crops was in having water on hand to refresh silt which would otherwise turn to stone in the searing heat. For these reasons, controlling the Nile exercised Egyptian ingenuity from the start.

Early engineering: A proper understanding of the annual inundation was not realised for fully 7,000 years after the first concerted effort to tame the river. This is credited to Menes, the first king of a united Upper and Lower Egypt, who in about 3000 BC is said to have diverted the river in order to build the new capital, Memphis, on reclaimed land. Another example of early Nile engineering was that of a "native queen" named Nitocris who built a cunning underground apartment with a secret channel leading to the river. She was thus able, it is said, to invite some people to dinner, pull the plug, and drown the lot of them, on suspicion of their having murdered her brother. Immediately after the fateful

Preceding pages: the Nile at Luxor by David Roberts. **Left,** the High Dam at Aswan.

gathering, she committed suicide by throwing herself into a room full of ashes.

The water engineering of the pyramid builders was inspired by more practical considerations. Huge granite blocks were floated down the river from Aswan on reed barges. As the pyramids were generally built high and dry above the flood plain, special canals were dug to reduce the distance over which the blocks had to be dragged on sleds. A curious lapse in the technical precocity which produced the pyramids was the failure to recognise the possibilities of the wheel, an idea already known to potters and shipwrights (as a pulley in rigging), for land transport.

Prisoners taken in foreign wars supple-

is difficult, now that modern dams have altered the level of the river and, of course, caused the annual inundation to cease, to visualise where and how Sesostris did it.

Herodotus, fascinated by contemporary technology as much as salacious gossip, found an ideal subject in Sesostris's son, Amenemhet III, who hurled a bad-tempered javelin at the river and paid the price by losing his sight for 10 years. An oracle advised him that it could be recovered "by washing his eyes with the urine of a woman who had had intercourse with her own husband only." His wife failed the test, as did a long string of women who followed her. He was so relieved when at last he did find a

mented local labour, and this was especially true during the Middle Kingdom (2040–1640 BC) at the tail end of the pyramid period. According to Herodotus, Sesostris III was notably aggressive and showed his scorn for cowardly enemies abroad by depicting them as female genitalia on the columns he left behind as memorials to his conquest. His prisoners were put to work on a network of canals which vastly increased the amount of arable land. His impatience with the enemy in Nubia to the south persuaded him to clear a passage for ships through the First Cataract, through which he mounted successful punitive expeditions. It

loyal wife qualified to restore his sight that he married her himself. The unsuccessful candidates, including the earlier wife, were shepherded into the city of Erythrebolus and burnt – "together with the city".

Canals: The technical side of King Amenemhet's nature appreciated the extra crops that could be wrung out of the silt by efficient irrigation so he initiated an ambitious programme of canals and reservoirs. The 20-mile (32-km) dam wall he threw across the oasis lake in the Fayyum was still functioning to win Herodotus's approval a millennium later. "The water in this lake does not spring from the soil," he noticed. "...It is conveyed through a channel from the Nile, and for six months it flows into the lake, and for six months out again into the Nile."

Herodotus was also impressed by a canal which ran between the Nile and Red Sea. It was wide enough for triremes to pass abreast and reduced the fearsome overland journey to a comfortable cruise lasting four days. Although 120,000 labourers had given their lives to the project, Herodotus noted, it was only completed by Darius, the Persian conqueror, within living memory of his visit.

The Romans, like the Persians and Greeks before them, methodically improved the waterways of Egypt, including a new Red Sea canal which began near modern Cairo.

snake,/Past meads and gardens trails her glittering coil.

The waterways were somewhat neglected by the Mamlukes, and on Napoleon's arrival in 1798 one of his priorities was to clear the canals and repair the hydraulic machine which lifted water into an octagonal tower to supply the Citadel. "The Mamlukes never repaired anything," he complained. Napoleon planned to build a series of dams along the Nile but these, like a proposed Suez Canal, fell by the wayside with his enforced departure.

The good work done by Mohammed Ali, who rose from the French defeat to establish the next and final Egyptian dynasty, was rapidly undone by a succession of incompe-

At the time they considered but rejected the idea of a Suez canal because the Red Sea was thought to be 30 ft (6 metres) higher than the Mediterranean, one of the objections put to Ferdinand de Lesseps when he resuscitated the plan in the 19th century.

The Arabs continued the good work, the Khalig (or "Khaleega") canal dissecting the capital they built at Cairo. As a source of poetic inspiration, this canal was second only to the Nile:

Where bright Khaleega, like a spotted

Left, dam building. **Above**, Abu Simbel temple was relocated above the rising Lake Nasser.

tent heirs, and in the middle of the 19th century a British resident in Cairo was moved to observe that the city's canal was "only pretty during the four months when the Nile fills it, while for the rest of the year 'bright Khaleega' is a gutter of mud and the home of noisome smells."

The entrance to the canal was opposite the Nilometer on the island of Rawdah in Cairo. Nilometers maintained at key points along the river from pharaonic times measured the rise of the water and, in particular, signalled the level (16 cubits) at which the farmers had to start paying tax on the land they worked. "The Government," said the same sour British resident, "of course used to take care to publish a falsified measurement before the due time, and thus induce the peasants to begin payment."

Breaching the Khalig dam: The town crier, accompanied by a boy, would make his rounds with the latest news about the level. "Five digits today," he might cry, "and the Lord is bountiful!" To which the boy would respond with "Bless ye Mohammed!" The real excitement was the day on which the government declared "Full Nile" as a prelude to cutting the dam and letting the water into the Khalig canal. With scores of small boys now forming a procession, the town crier would improvise lines aimed at stirring a rich man's conscience into producing a tip. The boys knew what was required of them as a chorus. "Paradise is the abode of the generous" – "God hath given abundance". An unsympathetic response was likely to bring a quick change of tune. "Hell is the abode of the niggardly".

The annual cutting of the dam was observed with a tradition going back to pharaonic times: a young virgin was thrown into the river as a sacrifice. The victim was later symbolised by an earth tower known as the "Bride of the Nile". It was erected in front of the dam, the river rushing in to consummate the union when the dam was breached.

The eve of the great day was a huge celebration. "All that night nobody sleeps," wrote the long-suffering British resident. "The constant firing of guns…the beating of drums…the discharge of rockets, and general babel of noises would render the desire abortive… It is like Venice in the old carnival time, only the voices and dresses are changed, and we cannot help feeling that, like the carnival, this ceremony belongs to an older state of things and an older religion. As we gaze upon the crowd we feel dimly that the priest of Isis ought to be there."

Early next morning, the Governor of Cairo rode up to oversee workmen responsible for breaching the dam. A holy man was summoned to read a "turgid" document, whereupon purses of gold were flung about. A roar went up as the Nile was at last let in. "Reserve and decency are thrown to the winds," the foreigner noted, "and all the world goes bathing."

In 1833 two Nile barrages were adopted as part of Mohammed Ali's ambitious plans to modernise Egypt, an eccentric Frenchman who took the name Mougel Bey having talked him into a scheme to regulate the water level over the whole Delta. Although barrages were built, the entire scheme was never fully realised because Egypt ran out of money. Enough had been accomplished, however, to be picked up and continued by the British administration who came in to rescue the ailing Egyptian economy from Mohammed Ali's heirs, one of whom suggested that the barrages could cheaply and conveniently be completed by dismantling the pyramids.

Sir Colin Scott-Moncrieff, the canal expert brought in from India to look for another

solution, noted wryly that Mougel Bey's project, idle for 50 years, still employed a large workforce which did nothing but draw their pay, "a duty which they performed with praiseworthy regularity." The relaxed workforce was intrigued by a number of packing cases which arrived from England but not sure how to react when the contents turned out to be electric lighting. Henceforth, Scott-Moncrieff announced, they could look forward to working night and day. The new dams were completed in 1891.

Controversial damming: The next major Nile project on the British agenda caused an outrage: a proposed dam at the First Cataract, archaeologists pointed out, would drown Philae, an island only 500 yards long but nevertheless the site of Egypt's finest Graeco-Roman works, notably the famous Temple of Isis. The height of the dam was lowered to meet these objections, but the English financier who was to put up the money for the dam had also bought some desert near Kom Ombo with the expectation that the new dam would irrigate it. When he realised the revised version would not, the whole scheme hung in the balance.

Over the years, the height of the dam was gradually increased. The island was at first partially under water for half the year; later, all but the tip of the Isis temple remained

submerged. Tourists inspected the site from boats as if it were a coral reef. Ironically, the monuments were made of limestone and therefore impervious to water; with the added protection of a layer of mud, the immersion probably did them good although it did erase some of the wall painting.

The dam meant many more acres under crops and, together with the higher yield produced by perennial irrigation generally, increased revenue easily exceeded the cost. "The reservoir business has been a remark-

Above, ancient irrigation methods, still in use: the Archimedes screw (left) and the *shaduf* (right).

able success here," Lord Cromer, Britain's administrator, reported to Lord Salisbury, the prime minister. "It is by far the most popular step we have ever taken, all the more so because we have done it ourselves, without French or other cooperation."

The decision in 1960 to build the High Dam at Aswan would have sandwiched Philae in destructive currents between it and the older British dam downstream. A rescue operation through UNESCO resulted in the nearby, higher island of Agilka being blasted into a semblance of Philae, after which the monuments were dismantled block by block (47,000 in all) and painstakingly reassembled on their new home.

The High Dam was the culmination of Gamal Abdel Nasser's dream for the economic future of Egypt after regaining control of the Suez Canal. It was an undertaking of pharaonic proportions: 30,000 Egyptians working day and night for 11 years under largely Russian supervision when, piqued by Nasser's politics, Britain and the United States had withdrawn their initial support.

The dam created the world's largest artificial lake and, by reclaiming a vast expanse of desert land and generating cheap power, gave the economy half a chance to catch up with the mushrooming population. On the other hand, it also wiped out Nubia (necessitating the resettlement of 100,000 people), deprived the flood plain of its annual windfall of silt (hence the need now for artificial fertiliser) and increased the salinity of the soil to the point that it now threatens the foundations of many monuments.

For all the unfortunate side-effects, however, a tamed Nile has removed the last in a chain of uncertainties which for 7,000 years, at least, began with not knowing where the river came from or whether it might one day cease. A 12th-century Arab described conditions when the Nile came near to failing: "The air was corrupted, the plague and contagion began to make itself felt, and the poor, pressed by the famine which struck them always, ate carrion, corpses, dogs, and the excrement and filth of the animals... We entered a city and found nothing alive, neither on the earth nor in the air... I heard say from a fisherman from the port of Tennis that he had seen pass close to him, in a single day, four hundred corpses that the waters of the river carried with them..."

WILDLIFE

Despite the great cities and the growing number of dams that harness the river, the Nile still belongs to the flora and fauna that proliferate along its shores and in its waters. The mild weather, the great rural expanse where the river runs free, wild, and unpolluted, offer a wonderful habitat for wildlife.

In parts of Uganda and the Sudan the variety of wildlife remains as it was centuries ago, but in Egypt this is not the case. In prepharaonic times Egypt was a savannah and land leopards, cheetahs, and lions roamed freely. Herds of elephant, buffalo, oryx, and gazelle fed on the wild grasses and drank from the river. In the waters of the Nile, crocodiles and hippopotamuses foraged from source to outlet. But with the continual change in the environment and the growth of the ancient civilisation when man began to dominate the Nile Valley, the animals were pushed further and further south.

The ancient Egyptians seemed to enjoy the natural world around them. Many of their gods were associated with animals: Sobek, god of Fayyum and Kom Ombo, was associated with the crocodile; Anubis, god of the dead, with the jackal; Thoth, god of wisdom with the ibis. The hieroglyphic symbols included animals, birds, flowers, and trees. Houses were decorated with paintings of flowers and public buildings had pillars and colonnades in the form of papyrus and lotus.

By the New Kingdom many of the animals associated with the Nile had already begun to disappear from Egypt. The elephant was gone, so were giraffes and monkeys. The hippopotamus took longer to make its journey south. Hippos outlasted ancient Egypt and the Islamic medieval period and were quite a novelty for European travellers of the Middle Ages who described them vividly for the people back home. They were still in the Delta as late as 1685 and a lone hippo was sighted in Aswan as late as 1816.

By the 20th century only crocodiles remained in Egyptian waters. But today they too are gone. The construction of the High Dam in the 1960s pushed the crocodile south into the Sudan and although a terrified baby

Left, homeward-bound birds.

crocodile occasionally gets churned through the sluice gates of the High Dam, the creatures that once lived in Egypt have gone.

Birds: Not so for the fauna that roams the skies. A tremendous variety of birds inhabit Egypt and their numbers swell each winter as they are joined by additional species migrating to avoid the winters of Europe and western Asia. Officially called the Palaearctic-African Bird Migration, this massive movement begins as early as August and can last until early December. The birds take to the air following a variety of migratory paths which take them over the Maghreb, Egypt, Saudi Arabia, Iraq, Iran and parts of the USSR. Some birds travel nearly 1,240 miles

to Qena along the Nile. At Qena their journey continues south and as they pass Luxor, Esna, and Aswan some birds settle, wintering on the Egyptian Nile. Others continue to lakes nearer the source and some go as far as South Africa.

One of the most common residents of Egypt is the cattle egret. This graceful white bird can be seen in fields, along canals, and at the river's edge foraging for food. A cattle egret sometimes perches on the back of a water buffalo to peck at ticks and other pests. Many people confuse the cattle egret and its cousin the common egret (the former has yellow legs and bill while the latter has black legs) with the sacred ibis. But the ibis, sym-

(2,000 km) before they reach their journey's end south of the Sahara. They come in their thousands and are so exhausted by their journey that they are vulnerable to predators.

Raptors (hawks, eagles and vultures) make their way south following land routes. These paths, sometimes called flyways, begin in eastern Europe and Asia Minor. They follow the eastern shore of the Mediterranean, move south over Israel and Jordan and cross the Gulf of Aqaba to the east of Sinai. From Sinai the migrating birds cut west over the Red Sea Gulfs to the Egyptian coast, turn south and head to Safaga. At Safaga they turn west again and soar over the Red Sea Mountains

bol of Thoth, the god of wisdom, and raised by the thousand as sacrificial birds (4 million mummified ibis were found in one king's tomb), no longer finds the habitat suitable in Egypt. It can still be found in the Sudan.

Doves are also abundant in fields and gardens as are larks, wagtails, warblers, and finches. Two of the most exciting birds to be seen in green areas are the little green bee-eater and the hoopoe. The former enjoys perching on telephone wires looking for insects. Because it is so small its light green

Above, the Nile is a bird-watcher's habitat. **Right**, harvesting the date palm.

154

FLOURISHING FLORA

Although most of the population of Egypt lives in the Nile valley, few towns have been built actually on the rich soil near the river; most are on the fringes of the desert. Thus a trip downriver runs through the heart of agricultural Egypt. Along the river between the acacia and tamarisk trees are fields of sugar cane and groves of banana and the ubiquitous palm trees.

There is a variety of acacia (mimosa) trees in Egypt, all are native to the country and all bloom with tiny yellow flowers. The largest is the Nile acacia which rises above all other trees along the river. The smallest is the sweet acacia known scientifically as the *Acacia farnesiana* because it was grown in abundance in the gardens of the Villa Farnese in Rome. Its flowers are the famous *cassie* flowers used in perfumes and cosmetics and their fragrance fills the air when they bloom in the late autumn. They are particularly abundant around the monuments of Abu Simbel.

The delicate tamarisk, with its bluish-green feathery blooms, the thick-trunked mulberry with its light green leaves and edible fruit, the wind-breaking casuarina with its long pine needles, and the tall eucalyptus with its camphor-producing light green leaves also grace the shore of the Nile, as does the sycamore, the tree of love of the ancient Egyptians.

Sugarcane is not native to Egypt, but a cultivated plant was introduced by Mohammed Ali at the beginning of the 19th century. Cane fields exist all along the Nile and by government decree all farmers must grow sugar cane. The cane is harvested in November and then shipped by special narrow-gauge railways to government-owned factories, also located along the Nile. The cane is processed from December to June and the sweet smell of molasses fills the air. In addition to refined sugar, the single refinery in Egypt produces molasses, alcohol, yeast and vinegar.

The banana is also an import probably brought to Egypt in the Middle Ages. The unusually shaped tree with large helter-skelter leaves has a short life, yielding its well-known fruit for only three years, after which it must be destroyed and a new tree planted.

But the date palm is the most important and prolific tree in Egypt. From Aswan to the Delta, in Sinai and the Western Desert, the palm tree provides food, shelter, and income to the farmers of Egypt. A young tree takes six or seven years to bear fruit, but once mature it will produce for over 100 years. When it no longer bears fruit, it can be revived by transplanting the top and creating another tree.

There are a variety of date trees in Egypt and each bears a different kind of date. Dates are dry, semi-dry, or soft. Dry dates are crimson in colour, crunchy and astringent to the palate. Orange coloured dates are semi-sweet and can often be seen drying in the sun, thousands of them spread on the ground. Brown and black dates are usually soft and sweet.

Palm trees must be pollinated by hand each spring; the female is only susceptible to pollination for two weeks a year. At harvest time (September) the farmer climbs the palm tree harnessed with a sturdy rope and picks each date by hand. By the end of November the harvest is over and the tree is carefully pruned of all dead branches.

The giant fronds, some as long as 20 ft (7 metres) are torn apart. The leaves are given to women who weave them into baskets and mats. The midrib of the leaves are cut and split and made into crates and furniture, including chairs, tables, beds, and closets. The final residue is chopped fine for sawdust.

The fibre that grows at the base of the leaves is combed, kneaded, and woven into sturdy rope and the fruit stock is cut and converted into convenient brooms. One often sees a number of these orange stocks lying on roadways where vehicles pass over them softening the thick, firm branches.

Finally, when a tree is no longer useful the trunk is cut and trimmed to serve as roof beams in mudbrick houses or as pathways and foot-bridges over canals. These days the practice of making the traditional and often highly potent date wine from the sap has ceased, but when a tree is felled the delicious heart of the palm is often still eaten as a special treat. ∎

feathers appear almost brown at a distance, but on closer inspection its delicate lime-green plumage comes into view. The ochre-bodied hoopoe is so spectacularly adorned that it cannot be mistaken at any distance. It has an orange and black feathery crown that opens like a fan when it is excited, and black and white striped wings. It can be seen strutting on garden lawns looking for worms.

Another garden resident is the Nile valley sunbird. Once a year the male, in exotic iridescent purple-green plumage, a yellow breast, a long slender tail feather, goes a-courting. Of African origin, this small bird is found all along the Nile from rain forest to desert. The sunbird is best seen in flower

Some say it once helped the crocodile by cleaning its teeth. Both migrant and resident is the grey heron, a tall, elegant, shy bird that wades knee deep along the river's banks.

It is in the winter, however, that the water birds come. Migrants include the white pelican, white stork, spoonbill, greater flamingo, and numerous species of gulls and ducks. It is a spectacular sight observing these birds flying over the Nile: gulls follow cruise boats foraging for food, flocks of pelicans and storks fly high overhead and the flamingo, graceful long neck outstretched and black striped wings flapping gracefully, flies at eye level past cruise boats.

Among the birds of prey that can be seen

gardens, particularly when hovering around trumpet-like flowers as it pierces the corolla and sips the nectar with its tongue. In the winter the sunbird as well as other resident birds shares the gardens with migrating wheatears, warblers, and finches.

Of the resident birds that enjoy the shores of the Nile, the most colourful and most elusive is the purple gallinule, a stunning bird with blue, purple, and green plumage and a red beak and legs. The purple gallinule is half the size of a duck but just as plump. Another stunning bird about the same size as the purple gallinule is the spur-winged plover which has black, white and brown feathers.

all year round are the kite, black-shouldered kite, and kestrel. If lucky, one can watch one of these birds hunting for field mice or insects. They hover in the air, wings flapping rapidly as they spot their prey. The legs come down, toes spread, talons at the ready. Then they plunge, disappearing into the grass. In a second the kill has been made and they fly off to a safe place to eat their catch. The birds eat most of the rodent, gulping in fur, teeth and entrails. The undigested portions are regurgitated in the form of circular pellets.

Birdwatching places: Crocodile Island in Luxor is a good year-round site. The hotel Mövenpick Jolie Ville has made a special effort to cultivate and preserve the natural environment of the island and a large variety of birds can be seen both winter and summer. Aswan is a nature lover's paradise. Any place along the river's edge is a good spot for watching hundreds of birds, but Saluga Island, now a protected natural area, is the best.

Lake Qarun in the Fayyum is a spectacular natural habitat. The salt water lake is situated in a pastoral environment with desert along its northern shore and farmland to the south. Protected by newly enforced laws, water birds winter in this area in the tens of thousands. Along the northern shore falcons and hawks circle the skies looking for food. In the trees and cultivated areas little green bee-

variety of ducks, they dot the shores. In the winters of 1987–91 flamingos came back to the western shores of Lake Qarun. Hopefully other species will follow.

Hunting: With such an abundance of wildlife, the Nile valley has been the destination of game hunters since the sport began. The great white hunter of Africa with his leopard-banned wide brimmed hat supplanted the explorer and his pith helmet in the first half of this century and the wholesale slaughter of some of Africa's finest animals began.

Today we are wiser and know that animals are a part of our natural world. We still hunt, but with binoculars and cameras, for our curiosity about our fellow creatures is insa-

eaters, crafty bulbul, and the grey shrike can be seen in trees, grasses, and on telephone wires; while flocks of lapwings and swallows, and smaller groups of Senegal thick-knees take to the sky in graceful formations. At the shore of the lake smaller birds from sandpipers to spotted shanks and pips flutter about while a solitary curlew pokes his long curved beak into the sand looking for crustaceans. At night thousands of gulls roost in backwaters, while during the day, accompanied by coots, grebes, and an impressive

tiable. Sadly, there are still a few hunters on the African Nile who kill the animals. Despite restrictions, the need to feed families and the lust for animal skins and ivory overcomes conscience. In Egypt, where game is limited to a few gazelles or oryx on the desert fringes, the hunt is for birds. Gulf Arabs hunger for falcons which they can train as hunters and farmers in the Fayyum, hopeful of meeting their need, set traps with live pigeons as bait. One catch will provide enough money to feed a family for months.

Recently, environmental agencies have stopped European hunters from bagging hundreds of birds on illegal hunts in Egypt.

Left, heron and papyrus today. **Above**, both heron and papyrus were featured in tomb paintings.

There were films about the great past of Egypt in the earliest days of cinema. Mark Antony and Cleopatra were there in the Italian screen before the World War I; Helen Gardner played Cleopatra in 1911, Theda Bara played her in 1917, and everyone in those primitive days was busy with Biblical tales involving the conflict between Egypt and the Children of Israel. Of course, these were silent films in black-and-white. It was when the talkies came, and colour, that the spectacular fictions of history held the day.

It was the stage which led the way. In the restless gap between the wars Bernard Shaw looked with new eyes on the vagaries of history; but his own plays were guarded: he would not abandon them to the caprices of the screen. He was won over at last by the persuasive voice of Gabriel Pascal. Pascal came from Hungary, and he brought a mood of irony new to the British screen; he prevailed on Shaw to yield. *Pygmalion* became a film; so did *Major Barbara,* and in 1945 Pascal directed a version of *Caesar and*

Left, Mankiewicz's *Cleopatra*, with Elizabeth Taylor. <u>Above</u>, De Mille's *Ten Commandments*.

Cleopatra. The lively cast was led by Vivien Leigh as the young Cleopatra; Claude Rains played Caesar; Stewart Granger was there, so was Basil Sydney, and Flora Robson appeared as Ftatateeta. In its day it was the most expensive film ever made in Britain. But it disappointed. If you wanted spectacle it was there, but only in fleeting moments. Shaw is not the place for spectacle: Shaw is the place for irony, for an antidote to romance, and somehow the ironic comment on the absurdities (and the horrors) of history had evaporated in amiable romance. Nor was Egypt in the film; the huge, heartless landscape played little or no part.

The baldness of *Caesar and Cleopatra* as a piece of visual art was to allow irreverence into a story of classical history: theatre was used to it, but cinema, at any rate where Cleopatra was concerned, was the home of romance. In another way, too, the film was making changes. To an Anglo-Saxon audience, if not to Continental watchers, Egypt in close view rather than in the compressed vision of the silent screen was unfamiliar territory. Biblical influence and years of Old Testament teaching had impressed on the public an image of the crossing of the Red Sea under Egyptian pursuit. The cinema, always searching for a good story (and where could it find better narrative material than in the Book of Genesis?) had repeatedly clutched the idea of a hostile Egypt.

Cecil B. de Mille made two versions of *The Ten Commandments*, the first in 1923; the second was to come more than 30 years later; naturally, though, the theme of the enslaving Egyptians still held true. This time there was a new insistence on the background of history; there was emphasis as well on the part played by the Nile itself. The tale of the birth of Moses cannot exclude the presence of the river: the Pharaoh decrees that every newborn Hebrew boy must die, one mother wraps her child in bulrushes and entrusts his cradle to the water, and it is the Nile which carries him away to the rescuing hands of the Pharaoh's own daughter.

The De Mille film was not to be the last of the cinema's famous version of the stories of the Old Testament, and in memory at least it has survived: survived by the force of its convinced maker. It had a distinguished cast: Charlton Heston played Moses; Yul Brynner played the Pharaoh Ramses, and Edward G. Robinson and Cedric Hardwick were among the performers. In publicity the film was described as a record of a struggle for freedom: struggles for freedom were high fashion in the cinema of the time, and the piece was popular.

But tastes were shifting. There was Rome to be considered as well as Israel, there was Egypt itself. In 1934 De Mille made a *Cleopatra* film with Claudette Colbert as the queen, but it made no lasting impression; another name would take over. In 1953 Joseph

in the way of a rendering of the great historical tragedy. Anyway it was Rex Harrison's Caesar which held the critical audience.

The spectacle was splendid; in particular Cleopatra's entry into Rome was admired. But the film was four years in the making. There were endless interruptions, including the illness of Elizabeth Taylor herself; and when at last the opening came the public, too, was beginning to feel exhausted. History and two appalling wars had left audiences ready for another kind of spectacle, a spectacle with reality behind it.

There was something else. Archaeology, once the precinct of the learned, became popular. Discoveries in the Mediterranean

L. Mankiewicz made a version of Shakespeare's *Julius Caesar* with John Gielgud as Cassius and Marlon Brando as Mark Antony; in 1963 he wrote and directed the version of the Cleopatra story which is generally remembered today. It was fabulously expensive and had a dazzling cast: Elizabeth Taylor appeared as Cleopatra and Richard Burton, who was enjoying with her a relationship closer than publicly permitted on the screen, was the Mark Antony. But Miss Taylor, whose physical beauty was sometimes allowed to overshadow her gifts (and they were considerable) as a player, was not at her best; personal preoccupations, perhaps, got

made young people think of excavation; the Tutankhamun discoveries focused interest on Egypt; and fantasies, heavily disguised as learning, occupied the cinemas. Not that they had ever quite vanished. The early years of the 1930s brought Germany's extraordinary horror-thrillers: *The Cabinet of Dr Caligari* came in 1920, but it had followers later on, before Hitler, and in America, too the grip of the dead, grasped audiences. In 1932 *The Mummy*, directed by Karl Freund, was one of the funerary leaders: other mummies equally threatening appeared in Britain, where in the 1970s Hammer horror films had a vogue. In these films there are reminders of the themes of the past. In 1956, for instance, Jean Simmons and Victor Mature appeared in *The Egyptian*; it was a story of a medical student and a military cadet who, centuries before Christ, accidentally save the life of a future pharaoh while lion-hunting. But to touch a pharaoh was a criminal offence. Sooner or later ghosts would rise from the relics of history, the vengeful dead would threaten the incautious living.

It is natural that Egypt should be the most frequent source of these fantasies. Egypt, after all, devoted the most urgent attention to the preservation of the human body in its science of mummification. The daughter of a pharaoh would be rich enough to be sure

by Mike Newell. Egyptian ghosts die hard.

The fantasies and horror tales which linger around Egypt and the Nile should not be taken too seriously. But they persist as an indication of the tastes and interests of the public; and horror, though one may dislike it, is a persistent element of cinema; today the serious critic ignores it at his peril.

The background of contemporary Egypt is less familiar through the cinema than the images of remote history. But the Nile, lodestar of tourists, still haunts imagination, still serves the novelist. Now and then it is the Egypt of the comfortable traveller which we see on the screen – usually with murder thrown in. *Death on the Nile*, say the posters;

that her corpse would be near-immortal.

The burial places of Egypt caught the imagination of the thriller-writer. Bram Stoker wrote *The Jewel of the Seven Stars*, a tale of a man unlucky enough to find the tomb of a murderous Egyptian queen: the spirit of the woman, dead for thousands of years, haunts him and takes possession of his daughter. The story has been used on the screen on two occasions: first in 1971 in *Blood from the Mummy's Tomb*, second in 1980 in *The Awakening*, which was directed

Left, Cecil B. de Mille's *Cleopatra* with Claudette Colbert. <u>Above</u>, *The Cabinet of Dr Caligari*.

the screen has recorded more than one multiple murder, including a case by Agatha Christie, that industrious chronicler of the geography of crime. There was a *Death on the Nile* in 1978, with the popular Peter Ustinov as Hercule Poirot; it was made in Britain, but with an international cast including Bette Davis.

Egypt has also contributed to the list of cinema directors. *The Night of Counting the Years* was an Egyptian film made by an Egyptian, Shadi Abdelsalam; it was produced by Italy's distinguished Roberto Rossellini, who had encouraged the young director; it won France's George Sadoul prize in 1970. The narrative deals with fact; it begins in 1881, when the authorities in Cairo were surprised to find that valuable objects from the 21st Dynasty had been appearing on the black market. They must have come from tombs, and no tombs from that dynasty had been found in Thebes. Archaeologists were sent to investigate; and it was found that a mountain tribe had passed on from generation to generation the secret of the tomb they had discovered; the sale of the objects had proved a valuable source of income in times of need. Now there was disagreement; one of the sons of the family concerned was horrified by what he regarded as sacrilege; and there was murder, a body was thrown into the Nile.

Archaeology thus once again played a part both in cinema and in the history of Egypt. The film was shown in London and at several international festivals; it may not be an outstanding example of cinema, but the source and the facts give it importance. And it belongs to Egypt's own story.

And now the screen moves into another area of adventure: the Nile is still concerned, but not Egypt.

In the 1850s two men set out on a dangerous African expedition. They hoped to find the source of the Nile: astonishing how recently the great secrets of the world have been revealed! One of the two men was John Hanning Speke; the other, Richard Francis Burton, is probably better known as the author of an unexpurgated English version of *The Arabian Nights*.

The first expedition ended in disaster. But the explorers persevered; funds were raised; and the result was the discovery that the great lake named Victoria is now accepted as feeding the Nile. The tale is told in *Mountains of the Moon*, directed and part-written by Bob Rafelson in 1990. It is a tale of adventure, but it is also a record of history. It enquires into the lives of adventurers, it examines character, it contributes to the annals of cinema. In these days of air travel it is easy to forget the explorers of little more than a century ago. The cinema reminds us, as it reminds us of ancient history, as it revives for us the fantasies as well as the poetic truths which human minds have woven around the terrors of the past.

Peter Ustinov as Poirot in *Death on the Nile*.

162

PLACES

Most Nile cruises travel the historically-rich stretch of river between Aswan and Luxor, a basic cruise of 130 miles (208 km) which
takes three days to complete but which is often supplemented with
a trip further down-river to Abydos and Dendera. In the summer, it
is possible to cruise the whole length of the river to the south of Cairo
(upriver, because the Nile flows due north), a total distance of 558
miles (900 km). No cruise boats travel north of Cairo into the Nile
Delta, both because of the difficulties of navigation and because the
ancient monuments which once undoubtedly stood on these lands
have since been washed away by centuries of Nile flooding, and
little remains that is worth seeing.

The river bank varies from parched desert near Aswan – which
can be as much as twice as hot as Cairo – to highly fertile agricultural
land in Middle Egypt and the Delta. Because of the river's history
of annual floods, few of Egypt's towns outside Cairo are built on its
banks, but instead are situated on raised land on the edge of the
floodplain. As a result, the impression that the cruise passenger will
get of Egypt is of a green and pleasant land occupied by farmers and
fishermen, temples and tombs. Pumping stations, occasional factories – built since the upriver dams stopped the flooding and provided
electricity – and rare road bridges only hint at the rest of the
country's contemporary economy.

Aswan is a crossroads and market town, and Luxor a very
extensive village which has grown with the tourist industry; both
have a flavour of stylish, early tourism. But Cairo, the Mother of the
World, is where contemporary Egypt and the Nile cruise passenger
are most likely to meet. Cairo is a monument to Islamic architectural
achievement in which 15 million Egyptians struggle to live; the
history of Cairo begins where the temples and tombs of the Nile
river leave off, and the city's history is still in the making. While the
pharaonic tombs along the river are empty tourist destinations, the
Islamic tombs of Cairo – the cities of the dead – are homes to one
million of the living.

Upriver, south of Aswan, the Nile disappears behind the dam into
the Sudan and beyond, dividing into White and Blue Niles at
Khartoum. Between them, these rivers complete another 3,500
miles through inaccessible territory into the heart of Africa. For
most travellers this has to be a journey of the mind; accordingly the
chapter that follows this introduction provides a helicopter ride
down the beginnings of this great river.

Preceding pages: cool granite of a Nile temple; fishermen; seed-beds on
the riverbank; harvesting sugarcane. **Left,** a welcoming caretaker.

THE AFRICAN NILE

The Nile outside Egypt is another river. In Egypt, the Nile is a river of civilisation, a navigable waterway making its way north to the Mediterranean Sea. Cairo and the resort towns of Luxor and Aswan sit on its eastern shore vying for space with shipbuilders, sugar refineries, and brick factories. But south of the Egyptian border is an African Nile, mostly wild and untamed. In Khartoum the Nile still overflows its banks in a yearly flood. In sub-Saharan Africa the Nile continues to be home to crocodiles and snorting hippopotamuses.

In many places the river remains very much as it has been since the dawn of time. In general, this is not a region that welcomes travellers, both for political and for physical reasons; travel here, as the early explorers discovered, is too much hardship and too little pleasure. This is one reason why man only found the river's source at much the same time as he was learning how to fly. Even today, in an era of space travel and spy satellites, the true source is still a matter of debate.

The source: Modern geographers maintain that the Nile does not begin at **Lake Victoria** as their 19th-century counterparts supposed, but originates in the most remote headstreams of the **Kagera River** in the southern highlands of Burundi. If measured from that source to the outlet of the Rosetta branch on the shores of the Mediterranean, the Nile (including the Blue Nile) is over 4,100 miles (6,600 km) in length, making it the longest river in the world.

But for the romantic the White Nile is born where John Speke said it was, at the place he named **Ripon Falls**. Today the industrial town of **Jinja** sits near the shore where the river emerges from the lake, and the Owen Falls Dam, 2,725 ft (830 metres) long and 100 ft (30 metres) high, straddles the water, completely obliterating Ripon Falls. There were two falls here when John Speke arrived in July of 1862, the fall at the source

Preceding pages: tribesmen at the source of the Nile. Below, the river at Jinja.

which he named Ripon and an additional one, further north and separated by an area which came to be called Napoleon's Gulf. The dam at Jinja, opened in 1954, sits over Owen Falls, but the waters have backed up into Lake Victoria, obliterating both Napoleon's Gulf and Ripon Falls.

From Jinja the White Nile moves north and after some 60 miles (96 km) enters **Lake Kyoga**, a shallow swamp, congested with thick papyrus clumps and a haven for snakes, crocodiles, and water birds. The river moves west through Lake Kyoga turning north as it leaves the lake. A short distance later it turns west again and enters **Kabalego National Park**, a game reserve founded in 1952 under the name of Murchison Park.

The reserve, covering an area of 1,483 sq. miles (3,840 sq. km), straddles the White Nile. In this area the river is wild and appears much as it must have done before it was touched by modern development. In the past this was white rhino country, one of the few places left in the world where this nearly extinct animal

lived. But Idi Amin's modern armies slaughtered game in Uganda with submachine guns, not only for food, but for sport. Today buffalo and hippo can still be seen in Kabalego National Park, having slowly recovered, but the white rhino have disappeared.

Another natural wonder in danger in this reserve is **Kabalego (Murchison) Falls.** As late at 1990 the Ugandan government was planning to build a dam at this site obliterating yet another outstanding natural feature. Here the river is forced into a channel only 20 ft (6 metres) wide and then pushed over three cascades to fall through a rocky gorge.

The sight is not only spectacular, but a natural demarcation line for a variety of fish and animals. Try as they may the fish to the north cannot climb the steps of the falls and the species here vary greatly to those in Lake Victoria only a few miles away. Most of the fish that come over the falls are eaten by crocodiles who ply the waters below awaiting a good meal. The river continues west beyond the park and dips into **Lake**

Right, hippo at the Murchison Falls.

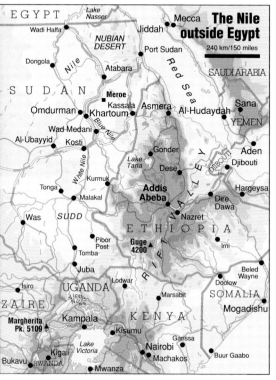

Mobuto Sese Seko, formerly Lake Albert before it moves north toward the Sudan, over 100 miles (160 km) away.

Into the Sudan: The saying goes, "When God made the Sudan, he laughed." Hot, dusty and poor, it is the largest country in Africa. The northern portion of the Sudan is Arabic-speaking and Muslim, intellectually linked to Egypt and the Middle East; while the southern portion of the Sudan is sub-Saharan Africa, pagan, Christian, and linked in temperament and culture and customs to its southern neighbours.

The White Nile enters the Sudan in the African south at Nimule where it is surrounded by lush tropical forests. It slowly flows north to Juba, a small town with a frontier atmosphere. By the time the river reaches **Gondokoro** it has lost the placid pace that is its hallmark for most of its long journey. Instead cataracts twist and churn the waters into an unnavigable stream. After this merciless beating the slack-watered Nile waters are subjected to the opposite extreme. They enter the Sudd.

The **Sudd** is the most awesome natural barrier on the river. It is the end of tropical Africa and the beginning of the savannah and desert of the north. It is hot, humid and steamy. Full of snakes and billions of insects, the Sudd breeds disease. The area is so overgrown with grass and papyrus that navigation is nearly impossible and it is the main reason why explorers in the 19th century had to travel overland from Zanzibar in their search for the source of the Nile. The first Europeans to try to navigate the dreaded Sudd were the explorers Samuel and Florence Baker, who nearly perished in their attempt. Then General Gordon pushed an army through the terrifying maze.

There seems to be no channel to follow in the Sudd. For those who know, there are in fact three channels meandering between and around the grassy islands. They finally break free of the choking grasses, merge into one main channel, and continue the journey north.

Few people live in the Sudd, but in this century it, too, has been transformed.

Jebel Aulia Dam.

178

The **Gebel Aulia Dam** has been constructed 31 miles (50 km) south of Khartoum and new channels have been cut through the Sudd. These two projects will turn the Sudd into a reservoir.

For nearly 2,000 miles (3,200 km) the only means of travel down the spine of Africa has been the river itself. Finally at **Kosti** the first paved road joins the river on its way to Khartoum. This newly developed stretch of metalled road is the only tarmac transport route along the entire course of the African Nile.

The White Nile has travelled 2,265 miles (3,700 km) by the time it reaches Khartoum and has 1,880 miles (2,900 km) to go before it empties into the Mediterranean Sea. In **Khartoum** and **Omdurman** Europe meets Africa. Khartoum, on the east side of the river, is haunted by the ghosts of General Gordon who met his death here, Colonel Kitchener who brought an army south to avenge the British defeat, and colonialists who built whitewashed bungalows surrounded by carefully tended gardens.

Omdurman, still a city of mudbrick buildings and native housings, was the native quarter during the British occupation of the Sudan. Across the river on the west bank of the Nile, it contains the tomb of the Mahdi, the man who fought against the British occupation and the man who was responsible for the defeat and death of Gordon.

The two Niles join: It is in Khartoum that the **Blue Nile** joins the river. The Blue Nile, 1,007 miles (1,600 km) long, has its source at **Lake Tana**, a crater lake in the highlands of Ethiopia. It spills out of Lake Tana over Tissisat (Big Smoke) Falls and charges through a spectacular 400-mile (650-km) long gorge down to the flat, hot, desert plains of Sudan. The river is so turbulent it is unnavigable. The country is so remote that the deep gorge was not mapped until the 1960s.

The Blue Nile is the most important river to the Sudanese. It irrigates 70 percent of the potentially irrigable land and its flood keeps the Nile flowing in the hot, arid, desert summers. In fact, even though this is the shorter of the two

The Mahdi palace on Abba Island, near Omdurman.

rivers, the force of the Blue Nile is so strong when it hits at Khartoum that it holds back the waters of the White Nile and does not merge with the more docile river for many miles.

Just north of Khartoum the terrain turns to desert and the river plunges into the first of six cataracts. Hard granite bedrock thrusts awesome barriers into the heart of the river which twists, stumbles, and pushes its way between these immovable outcrops, polishing them as smooth as steel. The cataracts are numbered north to south, thus the first is at Aswan, the second (now submerged) south of Wadi Halfa, the third above Dongola, and the fourth and fifth between Merowe and Atbara.

Over 30 miles (48 km) north of the trading centre of **Shendy** stand the ruins of the Kushite capital of **Meroe**. At last, after more than 2,500 miles (4,000 km), the Nile meets the first civilisation to build monuments in stone. Meroe is not to be confused with the village of **Merowe**, a modern Sudanese village further downstream. Meroe is a ruin. Its monuments run for almost a mile along the east bank of the river and the cemeteries, where over 40 generations of royal tombs lie exposed in the desert sun, are dominated by dozens of black stone pyramids.

Meroe thrived for over 1,000 years and was the largest community of ancient Kush, a civilisation whose rise to power was due to its location on the Bayuda Road, a trade route that ran from Egypt to the south. Just above Atbara the Nile makes a gigantic S-curve and the Bayuda Road dissects the desert in a straight line, cutting many miles off the upriver journey. Meroe thrived as long as this route was in use, but today the only signs of life are passing trains and the solitary Bedouin tent housing the guard and his family.

Atbara, where the Nile is joined by its final tributary, the Atbara River, is the centre of the Sudanese railway. Although there are few roads in the country, the Sudan does have a good rail system, the longest in Africa. Tracks radiate north, east, and south from the **Worshippers on Abba Island.**

busy terminals. The Atbara stockyards are an impromptu museum of rolling stock as no car or engine is ever destroyed, but is simply moved to an unused track. Since the railway dates from the 19th century, the stock includes many rare items.

Land of the pharaohs: Beyond Atbara the river enters Nubia, a desert land only habitable because of the great flow of the Nile. The river swings west, then south, then north in an S-curve passing the desert towns of Karima, Ed Debba, and Dongola. Scattered along the banks of the river are more and more ruins of past civilisations: Gebel Bakal, the Kurru tombs, and the Nurri pyramids at Karima. All else is wasteland. The blistering summer sun beats relentlessly on this land, whose only salvation is that the Nile keeps flowing. The spring floods in Ethiopia provide the river with enough water to counter the tremendous evaporation caused by scorching summer temperatures. Here the Nile is truly the gift of the gods.

By the time the river arrives at **Wadi Halfa** it is in the land of the pharaohs and surrounded by the stone ruins of ancient Egypt. Wadi Halfa, founded by the British in 1884 as the capital of the Northern Province of the Sudan, is linked to Aswan by boat, train, and dirt track. But the original town, abandoned in 1964, now lies under the waters of Lake Nubia. What exists today is the new Wadi Halfa, a gutsy town of merchants and, some say, smugglers. The *souq* is filled with electronic equipment illegally brought into the Sudan from Egypt.

A ferry service links Wadi Halfa to Egypt. The steamer travels north on Lake Nubia, the man-made expanse of water that flooded most of Nubia in the 1960s and 1970s. As the steamer travels north it moves over ghost towns and ancient monuments that lie beneath the waters, and quietly enters the **High Dam Lake** or Lake Nasser, the Egyptian name for the same waterway. Then Abu Simbel appears on the west bank, and finally the Saad al Ala, the High Dam, comes into view. This is Egypt and the African Nile is left behind.

Sayed el Hussein Mosque, Wadi Halfa.

THE VOYAGE BEGINS: ASWAN

In the eyes of many, Aswan is the most beautiful of Egypt's riverine cities. It became known for its healthy climate amongst turn-of-the-century tourists, who used to come in the winter, when the air was said to be as refreshing as in Switzerland. Summer temperatures in Aswan can reach 48° C, but the winter nights here can be decidedly chilly.

Aswan is a border town, situated 400 ft (132 metres) above sea level, 558 miles (900 km) south of Cairo. The governate of Aswan covers 341 sq. miles (850 sq. km) with a population of 1 million. Before the High Dam was built, only 40,000 or so people lived in the town, but the industrialisation that followed has swollen the population to 200,000 and significantly changed its character from the place the early tourists used to love.

Unlike Luxor, which can be overrun by tourists and tourist interests, Aswan manages to shoulder the burden of tourism without letting it dictate its character too much. The market streets are often filled with visitors from the Sudan or tribes from the Eastern Desert as well as with Europeans on package holidays.

There are no bridges over the Nile here, so the town has grown almost exclusively on the east bank, behind a long riverside promenade, the **Corniche**, which is habitually lined with cruise boats, *feluccas* and restaurants on the riverside, and by travel offices and tourist shops on the landside. Several river barges offer meals which, though not necessarily inspiring in cuisine, have the added advantage of Nubian folkloric music and dancers for entertainment. Inland, running parallel to the Corniche, are the *souq* or market streets, which are particularly active at night.

Aswan is situated where modern Egypt begins; to the north the river flows down through Egypt to Cairo and out through the Delta to the Mediterra-

Preceding pages: cruising from Aswan. **Left,** the river and Cataract Hotel, Aswan.

nean; to the south it extends behind the High Dam into Lake Nasser, which disappears deep into the Sudan.

The Nile at Aswan is thick with river vessels of all kinds and studded with islands of granite. **Elephantine Island** is the largest, hosting various monuments, a Nubian settlement and the rather unappealing tower of the Oberoi hotel at one end; **Kitchener's Island** (also known as Botanic Island or Plantation Island) hidden behind it hosts the botanical gardens, an excellent green oasis when the heat becomes too unbearable.

On the shores, date palms grow down to the river's edge, but beyond them, the hinterland of Aswan is bleak, hot and arid: the sandstone hills of the Eastern Desert are tinted with iron ore and the Western Desert has ochre dunes and limestone hills. The Nile becomes unnavigable above Aswan, even though some noticeboards on the Corniche still advertise boat services into the Sudan. Three hundred and fifty miles of lake, two dams and a cataract (now dried up thanks to the dams) separate the river in the Sudan from the Egyptian Nile.

Early tourism: Aswan has been a famous tourist site for thousands of years.

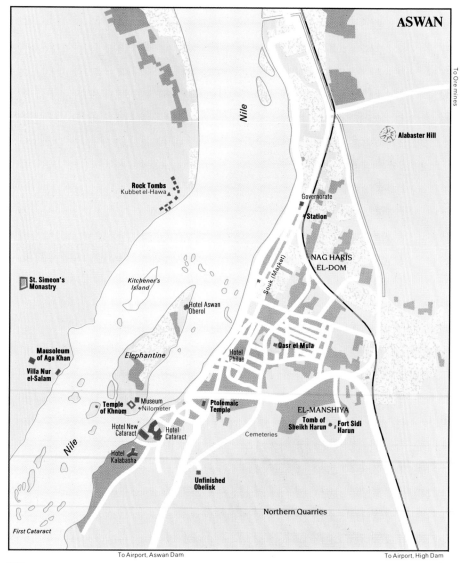

Greeks, Macedonians, Romans and Egyptians fell under the spell of its beauty. Among those who wrote about it in glowing terms were Strabo the Roman geographer, Ibn Khaldun the historian-diplomat of medieval times, and Shelley and Keats the 19th-century Romantic poets. The finest relic from colonial times is the **Pullman Cataract** (formerly Old Cataract) hotel, at the southern end of the Corniche. The interior is a fabulous Moorish palace and it is almost traditional amongst visitors to have a drink in the terrace bar, overlooking the river. Even if you are not staying at the Pullman Cataract, it is worth poking your head into the hotel's dining room, Club 1902, which is to the left of the main entrance.

Lord Kitchener, British Consul of Egypt, was deeded Kitchener's Island at Aswan by the Egyptian government for his campaigns in the Sudan, and imported and planted a large variety of rare African and Indian plants there. Kitchener's mark is also to be seen in graffiti to do with his Sudan campaign

on the walls of the temple of Philae, on Agilka island behind the Aswan dam.

Lady Duff Gordon set a fashion when she travelled to Upper Egypt to seek a cure for tuberculosis in the mid 1800s. After her, came many of Europe's notables who sought a retreat from Europe's cruel winter. The late Aga Khan, leader of the Ismaili community, a sect of Islam, found such peace and beauty in Aswan that he chose a site on the western bank, on a peak overlooking his favourite part of the river, for his mausoleum. It is said that he used to bury himself neck-deep in warm sand as a cure for the "terrible rheumatism" from which he suffered.

In antiquity Elephantine, the largest of the islands, situated immediately opposite Aswan, was known as *Abu* or Elephant Land, because it was the trading post for ivory – although another theory for the island's name points to the shapes and textures of the rock formations, which seem elephantine. The island commanded the First Cataract that formed a natural boundary to the south, and its noblemen bore the title "Guardians of the Southern Gate".

Furious floods: Before the dams, the cataracts were obstacles to the smooth flowing of the river Nile. They were granite-toothed boulders that had been torn from the mother rock by countless floods to lie strewn along a 4½-mile (7-km) stretch of the river. At low Nile the water was sluggish, and would flow around these obstacles. But during the annual flood it hurled over them with a roar that classical writers described as loud enough to cause deafness.

When the river flowed through Nubia, lying between the Sudan and Egypt, the water was confined by sandstone hills. But once it passed the region of the First Cataract and approached Aswan, the waters became quiet. The confining hills on both sides of the river spread out, and as the water found its level on the floodplain, it lost its velocity and was able to deposit a heavy layer of rich alluvial soil on the land.

It was this annual replenishment of vital minerals that rendered Egypt so fertile. Little wonder that the ancient

Nubian house, Elephantine Island.

Egyptians, although well aware of the barren and inhospitable land of Nubia lying to the south, saw the churning water around the cataracts at Aswan as the point at which the life-giving waters arose from the eternal ocean. In other words, the cataract region was the edge of their world.

They believed that three gods guarded the cataracts: Khnum, the ram-headed god of Elephantine, Satis, his wife, and Anukis, his daughter. Welcoming the flood was Hapi the Nile-god, who was believed to live in a grotto at Bigeh Island in the midst of the cataracts. Hapi's role was to receive the water with outstretched arms and channel it north to Upper and Lower Egypt, finally to flow into the eternal ocean (the Mediterranean) to the north. Hapi is depicted on temple walls as a simple fisherman with good round belly and drooping breasts, symbolising plenty. On his head are aquatic plants and papyrus, and in his hands are the fruits of the land.

Aswan's name derives from the Greek word *Syene* (from which the Coptic *Suan* is derived) and stems from the ancient Egyptian *Swenet* meaning "making business" or trade. Indeed, this is the very character of Aswan. In its market places are Nubians and Egyptians as well as tribes from the surrounding deserts, especially the fuzzy-headed Bisharin of the Eastern Desert. They exchange their produce the same way as they have for thousands of years, amidst the stringent smell of spices. Among the much sought-after products by Westerners today are dry *Aswani* dates, and *foul sudani*, peanuts roasted in the hot sand. Bedouin clothing, saffron (now very expensive in the West) and *kakaday* (dried hibiscus flowers for tea) are also good buys. Bargaining here is a more low-key and less aggressive process than it is in many Egyptian towns, and many products – notably the spices – are actually fixed-price.

Nubian migration: Aswan has been the link between two cultures, Egyptian and Nubian, for thousands of years. In fact, there is evidence that Nubia – the region between Egypt and the Sudan – was populated in prehistory by tribes under regional chieftains, much as the earliest settlers in Upper Egypt. Nubia, as vast a landmass as Egypt itself, was a country in its own right, inhabited by attractive black-skinned, fine-featured people, of Nilotic extraction rather than African. That is to say they are similar in appearance to the people of the sources of the Blue Nile, the Ethiopians, rather than those of Africa south of the Sahara. The excavation from Nubian tombs of objects of Egyptian origin indicate that there was cultural exchange between Nubians and Egyptians.

When, therefore, the population of Lower Nubia had to be resettled in Egyptian territory because their land was destined to disappear beneath Lake Nasser on completion of the High Dam in Aswan in 1971, it was natural for many to choose to live in an area closest to their native territory – in other words, around Aswan. The Egyptian government also provided for large-scale community resettlement further north, at Kom Ombo, particularly for the Beni Kanz or Kenuz tribe, who are of mixed Arab blood.

The population of Aswan today is, consequently, largely Nubian, with the notable exception of the police force and the officials of the High Dam Authority, who are Egyptians. Most of the hotel staff, all the sailors and a large percentage of the population are Nubians, who live in concentrations on Elephantine Island and in Garb (West) Aswan. "The Nubians have taken a vow not to intermarry with Egyptians," said the late Labib Habachi, an Egyptologist who worked among them for many years. "They are extremely gentle people, and honest, which is why the Antiquities Organisation recruit so many of them as *ghaffirs* (guards) at the archaeological sites."

A state of mutual respect has existed between Nubians and Egyptians for a long time. Nubians were also recruited, on occasion, to help Egyptian troops suppress rebellious desert tribes, and it is significant that Nubian was the language used by the Egyptian army for secret communications in its conflict with Israel in 1973. Modern Egyptians, particularly those from Cairo, will denigrate Nubians as lazy and stupid, but Aswan's pleasant atmosphere is in part due to their relaxed attitude.

Excursions south: During ancient Egypt's first peak of cultural development, the Old Kingdom (2686–2181 BC), Egypt seems to have had a loose sovereignty over Nubia. The Nubians, moving with their herds of sheep and goats, relied on Egypt for grain and vegetable oil. And, aware of the rich veins of gold-bearing quartz and iron ore in the seemingly impoverished land to the south, the Egyptians were only too happy to supply their needs. A decree by Pharaoh Pepi I (*circa* 2300 BC), refers several times to "the peaceful Nubians", and inscriptions in many of the noblemen's tombs on **Qubbet el-Hawa** make reference to them.

Qubbet el-Hawa or "Dome of the Wind" takes its name from a small domed structure on the summit of a hill on the western bank of the Nile opposite Aswan. This landmark is not, as is popularly believed, the tomb of a sheikh. It was built in the 19th century as one of several signal posts, most of which bore the name of a saint or sheikh.

Qubbet el-Hawa was the burial ground of the noblemen from Elephantine. The tombs were hewn out of rock about halfway up the hill facing the river, approached by a narrow ledge. The group of Old Kingdom tombs is especially interesting because the door-jambs bear autobiographical texts written by ancient Egyptians who explored the darkest reaches of the African continent 4,000 years before any medieval explorer.

One of these tombs (No. 34) belongs to a nobleman called **Harkhuf** who lived in the reign of the 6th-Dynasty pharaoh Merenre (*circa* 2280 BC). Harkhuf styled himself a "caravan leader" and went on various journeys southwards – perhaps as far as the Sudan and beyond, because he was able to record that "never had any companion or caravan-leader... done it before."

On each of his travels, Harkhuf brought back precious products: gold, ostrich feathers, animal skins, ivory,

Cruise boats in the Corniche.

ebony, incense and gum. He also, on his fourth expedition, successfully brought back a "dancing pygmy" for his Pharaoh, the young Pepi II, successor of Merenre, who came to the throne at the age of six. In his record of the event, Harkhuf states that he sent his messengers ahead of his convoy to inform His Majesty of his gift, to which Pepi wrote back, with enthusiasm, that the pygmy should be guarded so as not to let it fall overboard.

Another example of pioneering spirit and filial devotion can be found in the Qubbet el-Hawa tombs of **Mekhu** and his son **Sabni**. Mekhu was a nobleman of Elephantine in the reign of Pepi II, about 2280 BC, and while on an expedition in Lower Nubia his convoy was attacked by desert tribes, and he was killed. When his son Sabni received the news, he quickly mustered a convoy of troops and pack-donkeys to march southwards and recover the body. The text on Sabni's tomb relates how he duly punished the tribe responsible for his father's death, recovered the body and started his journey home.

Meanwhile the pharaoh, who had been informed by Sabni of his intention, had despatched a whole convoy of royal embalmers and mortuary priests along with the necessary oils and linens for the mummification and internment of Mekhu. In an expression of gratitude Sabni delivered the spoils of Mekhu's convoy to the pharaoh at Memphis.

Looking north: The inscriptions in tombs such as these clearly indicate that although Aswan was situated at the farthest limit of Egypt, it was spiritually closer to Memphis, the capital, than any other city. This was not only because, during the Old Kingdom, the noblemen of Elephantine held responsible positions that answered to central government, but also because Aswan was the starting point for caravan routes south.

The noblemen of Elephantine were a proud and independent breed who lived at a time when the pharaoh encouraged initiative and responsible action; a time when many Lower Egyptians travelled to Upper Egypt to find work, just as, today, Upper Egyptians travel to Cairo and the Delta. With the passing of the Old Kingdom, Aswan's time of glory was over. It was never again to have such prestige. In fact, it was not until the Graeco-Roman period that it regained its importance when, in the reign of Ptolemy II (285–246 BC) the popular cults of Osiris, Isis and Horus were brought to Aswan.

West of Qubbet el-Hawa, hidden in the flanks of the Western Desert, is the **Monastery of St Simeon**. It is large and well preserved and dedicated to a local saint who lived in Aswan in the 5th century. The present construction dates from the 7th century, and there is evidence of restoration in the 10th century, but the building is thought to have originated from much earlier times. The monastery was abandoned in the 13th century, either because of lack of water or the threat of roving nomads.

The surrounding wall of the monastery is fortress-like, at over 18 ft (6 metres) high. The view from the upper level, which is actually built over the northern wall, is one of the most picturesque of Egypt's desert scenes. The

Tourist *feluccas* crossing the river at Aswan.

windows look out from the steep cliff over a desolate wilderness which has undeniable mystic appeal.

The **Mausoleum of the Aga Khan**, also in the Western Desert, is another landmark of Aswan. The Aga Khan, the spiritual leader of the Ismaili sect of Islam (he claimed direct descent from Fatimah, the daughter of the Prophet Mohammed) used to winter in Egypt seeking relief from rheumatism. His tomb was built in the Fatimid style with a single dome, the dome being one of the important innovations of Islamic architecture between the 10th and 12th centuries (the tombs of the Fatimids at Aswan are on the eastern bank, north of the granite quarries). The mausoleum is constructed of rose granite and the inner walls are of marble embellished with verses of the Koran. Each day a fresh rose is placed on the tomb. The Aga Khan's widow still visits Aswan every year and hers is the only *felucca* on the Nile allowed to have a red sail.

Pink rock: On the fringes of the Eastern Desert, in the southern perimeters of Aswan, lie the famous **granite quarries**, the main source of granite in Egypt. The quarries were exploited throughout ancient history right through to Graeco-Roman times. The Fourth Dynasty pharaohs who built the pyramids of Giza (2613–2494 BC) were among those who used stone from here. Nine great slabs of granite, 54 tons each, were extracted for the ceiling of the so-called King's Chamber of the Pyramid of Cheops (Khufu); red granite was chosen for the Temple of Khafre (Chephren), and black granite was quarried for the lower reaches of the outer casing of the Pyramid of Menkaure (Mycerinus).

The lofty obelisk of Queen Hatshepsut at Karnak, made of a single block of pink granite, was also quarried in Aswan and transported to Luxor. A further **"unfinished obelisk"** is still lying in the quarry attached to the bedrock. There is no indication of for whom it was intended but, had it been completed as originally planned, it would have weighed some 1,162 tons, and soared to a height of 126 ft (42 metres). It seems

Mausoleum of the Aga Khan.

to have been abandoned because of flaws in the stone.

The process by which the stone was extracted is readily visible in the quarry. Holes were bored along a prescribed straight line, and it was once thought that wooden wedges were driven into these, watered and left to expand and split the stone. Recent excavations, however, show that balls of dolerite, the hardest sort of stone, were attached to rammers and simultaneously and repeatedly struck with great force by the quarry workers until the stone separated. These dolerite balls, some weighing up to 12 lbs (5.5 kg), have been found in their hundreds in the area.

Island delights: Nubian boatman will sail you across to **Elephantine Island,** which is well worth visiting. An ancient **Nilometer** faces Aswan, although it is not as striking as some. It consists of a stairway on the river's bank constructed of regular-shaped stones so designed that the water, rising and falling with the ebb and flow of the flood, could register maximum, minimum and average wa-

ter levels. A text on a wall of the Temple of Edfu tells us that when the river rose to 24 cubits and three and a half hands at Elephantine, there was sufficient water to supply the needs of the whole country. The level of taxation was also fixed according to the level of the water, as a higher flood usually resulted in a better harvest. Plutarch, the Greek writer, recorded that the Nile once rose to a height of 28 cubits, or 47 ft (14.7 metres).

The Nilometer was repaired by the Khedive Ismail in 1870. A new scale was established and the ancient construction, unused for centuries, came into use once more. On the walls of the staircase are records in Demotic (fluid hieroglyphic hand) and Greek, showing different water levels.

There is a small **museum** on Elephantine in a colonial-style building originally built as a resting place for the British engineers engaged on building the original Aswan Dam. The exhibits include miscellaneous pre-dynastic objects from Nubia before it was inundated, some Old and Middle Kingdom

Monument erected by the Soviets on the High Dam.

objects, treasures from the Heqaib Sanctuary which is now being turned into an open-air museum, and various objects of the New Kingdom and Graeco-Roman period. The latter include sarcophagi containing mummies of a priest and priestess of Philae as well as a mummy of the sacred ram. (A new Nubia Museum south of Aswan near the Fatimid cemetery, opening in 1991, will house some of the objects from the Elephantine museum.)

The **Old Town**, on the southern tip of Elephantine island, is currently being restored. Among the monuments are a granite portal that once formed the entrance to a large temple, the foundations of a small temple built by Naktanebos II, the last native pharaoh, Julius Caesar and Trajan (AD 98–117), and blocks from the edifices of earlier temples. The most important piece of restoration underway is the elegant Temple of Satis, goddess of the Cataract Region, wife of Khnum, who guarded the "new water" of the rising of the Nile.

The dams: The first barrage across the Nile was built at the apex of the Delta north of Cairo in 1842. This was soon followed by others: at Assiut in Middle Egypt, at Esna and Aswan in Upper Egypt. The latter, the **Aswan Dam**, was erected above the first cataract between 1899 and 1902 when Egypt was still a British Protectorate. Its height was increased between 1908 to 1912 and again between 1929 and 1934. With each successive heightening, the thwarted waters built up and monuments and people alike were threatened.

The Nubians became somewhat fatalistic about the disappearance of their stark and beautiful land, which once linked Egypt with Africa. But when, in the 1960s, they learned that another bigger dam, the **High Dam**, would be built a couple of miles south of the Aswan Dam, and that the whole of their land would be totally lost, they seemed unable to absorb the awful truth. In fact, Lake Nasser, which was formed when the thwarted Nile swelled back upon itself, is the world's largest artificial lake, extending for 316 miles (510 km), a third in Sudanese territory. Its average width is 6 miles (10 km), and sometimes it spreads across 18 miles (30 km). Its storage capacity is 5,495 billion cubic ft (157 billion cubic metres).

The High Dam was the cornerstone of Egypt's development envisioned by President Gamal Abdel Nasser. It is a great rock-fill construction designed to control irrigation and increase Egypt's agricultural land in the face of its ever-increasing population. Its effect has been to increase agricultural land by 2 percent, reducing Egypt from 96 to 94 percent desert. Agricultural productivity has increased by over 25 percent since 1971. Electricity generated from the dam has powered numerous factories including one for fertiliser to compensate for the loss of flood-bourne silt.

The High Dam was largely financed and supervised by the Soviet Union after the withdrawal of US and British financial aid for the project when Nasser refused to commit himself to their side of the Cold War. A total of 595 million cubic ft (17 million cubic metres) of rock was excavated, and 1,495 million

Nubians in Aswan.

cubic ft (42.7 million cubic metres) of construction material was used, thus creating an artificial mountain of earth and rock over a cement and clay core. The dam is 10,800 ft (3,600 metres) long, 342 ft (114 metres) high and the width at the base is 2,940 ft (980 metres). It is said to be 17 times the size of the Great Pyramid.

A tall, elegant monument shaped like a lotus blossom was erected on the site by the Soviets. It symbolises friendship, and the interior is decorated with bas reliefs illustrating the benefits of the dam. There is also a visitors' lookout post halfway down the dam, containing the blueprints for its construction.

The dam's advantages – no flooding, twice-yearly cropping, more land availability and increased hydroelectric power – are balanced by disadvantages. The increase in agriculture, for example, has led to a corresponding increase in the incidence of bilharzia, which can now, fortunately, be controlled. And the loss of the annual flood, and the constant higher average water level, has resulted in increased salinity of the soil. This has adversely affected crops, especially in the Delta, which now requires constant irrigation and drainage. Moreover the ancient monuments throughout the land are suffering serious damage from seepage and salt erosion. It is also a moot point whether the dam has increased Egypt's military vulnerability (a breached dam could devastate the whole of Egypt).

Memories of Nubia: The people from Lower Nubia were resettled in Kom Ombo and Aswan. Those of Upper Nubia were taken to Qasr el Girba in the northern Sudan. Social studies on both in recent years have shown how well they have adjusted to their new conditions, although many older Nubians, especially around Aswan, remember with nostalgia "the land of our ancestors". Some have gravitated back to what little remains of their native land, to rebuild their simple villages at the edge of the lake, near where they imagine their old villages to have been.

It has always surprised Egyptians that, despite its stark and barren nature, the Nubian people had such a strong attachment to their land. In the 19th and early 20th centuries Nubians went northwards to Egypt to find employment as bargemen, door-keepers, cooks, or government clerks. They seldom married Egyptians and inevitably returned to Nubia bearing cloth, clothing, and food for their families.

They also brought pictures cut out of magazines and newspapers, mostly portraits of political leaders, athletes and film stars, which were used to adorn the walls of their houses, which were made of sun-baked brick, a mixture of clay and straw. The facade of each house was different from the next, not only individually shaped, but uniquely decorated by laying bricks at angles, in steps, or in lattice designs.

The houses were painted, both inside and out, with finger paintings of trees, chickens, boats, flags and sacred symbols, and most had porcelain plates (brought from Cairo) inserted into the clay. Coloured baskets woven from palm fronds hung around the inner doorway or adorned the spacious rooms. Nubia's date groves not only provided the people with food, but also with no fewer than 40 other commodities, such as fibre for ropes, timber for construction, and palm "spears" for a variety of uses.

Nubian settlements were grouped near the banks of the river. Whitewashed shrines of local saints and sheikhs broke the skyline. The groaning of the ox-driven waterwheels echoed along the Nile, to bring water to the tiny fields planted with barley, beans and castor plants. In the vast distances between villages were the great temples of Nubia: the great fortress of Kubban which once guarded the Wadi Alaki, one of the richest gold-mining areas in Nubia, and the richest source of Egyptian gold in ancient times, as well as the temples of Debod, Kertassi, Tafa, Kalabsha, and Beit el Wali, built atop jutting sandstone cliffs. And, of course, there was the great temple of Ramses II at Abu Simbel, a symbol of Egyptian power in Nubia in ancient times.

Travelling temples: In the decade during which the dam was being built,

Egypt sent out an international appeal through UNESCO to save the monuments doomed by the rising water. Nubia was subjected to the most concentrated archaeological operation ever mounted. It was the birth of "salvage archaeology".

Archaeologists, historians, architects, engineers, sociologists and photographers from over 30 countries fought against time in Nubia. They worked on ancient town sites, pre-dynastic cemeteries, churches and ancient monuments. "Ironically enough," commented one scholar, "as a result of the loss of Nubia, we now know more about it than many sites in Egypt!"

During a period of two decades, no fewer than 23 temples and shrines were saved, some to be reassembled far overseas. One complete temple, built by Queen Hatshepsut, was dismantled and transported to Khartoum in 59 cases aboard 28 trucks, there to be reconstructed in the National Museum of Khartoum. Another temple, that of Amada, was lifted as a unit of 800 tons, put on rails and dragged up a hill to safety, and yet others travelled across the sea to museums as far afield as Turin, Madrid and the Metropolitan Museum in New York. Some monuments were partially saved (the temples of Gerf Hussein and Aksha) and three were dismantled for reconstruction near the High Dam itself: the temples of **Kalabsha** and **Beit el Wali**, and the **Kiosk of Kertassi**.

Moving mountains: Two of the greatest salvage operations were the monuments of Philae, and the rock-hewn temples of Ramses II and Queen Nefertari at **Abu Simbel**. The latter were a tremendous challenge because, unlike the other temples in Nubia, they were not freestanding. They were, in fact, carved out of the heart of the mountain.

Moving Abu Simbel entailed sawing the temple into over 1,000 transportable pieces, some weighing as much as 15 tons, and placing them safely above the water level until they could be reassembled at a new site 192 ft (58 metres) higher than the original one.

While these blocks of stone were be-

ing treated and stored, the new site on top of the mountain was levelled. Explosives could not be used for fear of damaging the monuments, so compressed-air drills were employed. Studies were carried out on the bedrock to ensure that it could support the enormous weight it was destined to bear forever, not only of the reconstructed temple but also of the great reinforced concrete dome that would cover it and over which the mountain would be reconstructed. The dome is 80 ft (25 metres) high and the cylindrical part which is accessible from the northern facade of the temple is designed with a free span of some 192 ft (60 metres). This span was designed for a load of about 100,000 metric tons, and is a unique technological achievement.

The pylon, or entrance doorway, to the main **temple of Ramses II** at Abu Simbel was the cliff face itself, dominated by four seated statues of a youthful pharaoh. The central hall was flanked by eight more statues of the king in a double row facing each other, against a corresponding number of square pillars. He is portrayed in mummified Osirian form with crook and flail.

The ceiling is adorned with flying vultures in the centre, and with stars and the names and titles of the king on the side aisles. The walls teem with beautifully painted reliefs. Most are of religious ceremonies and battle scenes in which Ramses is depicted clasping his enemies by the hair and smiting them with a club in the presence of the great gods Amon-Ra and Ra-Harakhte, who hand him a curved sword of victory.

The northern wall of the hall was decorated with the Great Battle Scene, which is one of the most extraordinary and detailed reliefs to be found in the Nile valley. There are over 1,100 figures and the entire wall, from ceiling to bedrock, is filled with activity: the march of the Egyptian army, hand-to-hand combat, the flight of the vanquished, prisoners, and overturned chariots; there are scenes of camp life, inspection of officers, and also farmers anxiously driving their cattle into the hills.

The temple of Ramses II at Abu Simbel.

The royal camp is a square enclosure, a stockade of soldiers' shields. The royal tent can be seen, and at the centre of the camp is Ramses's pet lion, cared for by a keeper. Elsewhere the soldiers are shown eating from a common bowl as they crouch on their heels, and one officer is even depicted having his wounded foot dressed by a doctor.

Beyond the central court of the temple, carved out of the mountain to a depth of 183 ft (55 metres), was the sanctuary, which contained four seated statues of the god Ptah of Memphis, Amon-Ra of Thebes, the deified Ramses II, and Ra-Harakhte the sun-god.

The whole temple was so oriented on an east-west axis that the rising sun sent its rays to strike the rear wall of the sanctuary, 195 ft (61 metres) inside the mountain. At certain times of the year, after the autumnal equinox of 23 September and before the vernal equinox of 20 March, the rising sun illuminated the four seated statues, one after the other. The small **temple of Queen Nefertari**, which lay a little to the north,

was also saved. Nefertari was the most beloved of the wives of Ramses II and throughout the temple, on pillar and wall, and even in the sanctuary, the names of the royal couple are linked in their shared dedication to the goddess Hathor. The legend of the love of Ramses for his wife is enumerated along with his titles: "Ramses, strong in *maat* (truth), beloved of Amon, made this divine abode for his royal wife, Nefertari, whom he loves."

The terrace to the temple leads to a sloping facade that provides the frame for six recesses, three on each side of the central doorway. Within each there are beautifully carved standing figures: four of the king and two of the queen. They appear to be walking forward with spirited strides. Ramses wears an elaborate crown of plumes and horns, while Nefertari sports plumes and the sun disc. At their sides are figures of their children, with the princesses beside Nefertari and the princes beside Ramses.

The reconstructed temples of Abu Simbel have been aligned in their new

nside the emple.

position as in ancient times, and the sun still casts its rays on the sacred statues twice a year. Day visitors to the site come in by plane from Aswan, and access can also be made via a newly surfaced desert road, three and a half hours from Aswan. For those who wish to remain in Abu Simbel overnight, there are a couple of local hotels.

Island sites: The project to save the monuments of **Philae**, located on an island in the stretch of water between the two dams, presented a different problem altogether, because they were already overcome by the rising waters.

Although the sacred island was situated south of Aswan and, consequently, strictly belonged to Nubia, the goddess Isis was worshipped here by Egyptians and Nubians alike. Fantastic tales were told of her magical powers. It was believed that her knowledge of sacred formulae brought life back to her husband Osiris after he had been slain by his brother Set, and that her spells saved her son Horus from a poisonous snake.

Countless visitors came to the island

in Graeco-Roman times, to see the priests performing their sacred duties. They claimed a knowledge of the mysteries and if visitors were lucky, they could view the image of the goddess Isis during the spring and autumn festivals in her honour.

The monuments at Philae (particularly the grand **Trajan's Kiosk**) are covered in graffiti from almost every era of history. From a Greek inscription in the seclusion of the Osiris shrine above the sanctuary of the **Temple of Isis**, we learn that even as late as AD 453 the goddess was worshipped here by the Blemmys, tribes of the Eastern Desert, and their priests, long after the edict of Theodosius had declared that pagan temples should be closed.

The monuments of Philae, therefore, represent the last outpost of ancient Egyptian tradition on its native soil. Known as the "Pearl of the East", the temple is the only monument dedicated to a single goddess. "Seen from the level of a small boat," wrote Amelia Edwards in her *Thousand Miles up the Nile* in

Philae, rebuilt on Agilka island.

1873–74, "…those sculptured towers rise higher and ever higher against the sky. They show no sign of ruin or of age. All looks solid, stately, perfect."

Salvage job: This all changed following the construction of the first dam at Aswan, which inundated the island. Visitors like Amelia Edwards had to paddle around the upper parts of the temple in boats, and with the construction of the High Dam it seemed doomed to disappear altogether.

The salvage contract to rescue the temple from the water was awarded to an Italian company who started with the construction of a coffer dam in 1977. The stone blocks (47,000 in number) were then cleaned and stored. Meanwhile, 450 tons of granite were blown off the top of the neighbouring island of Agilka to accommodate the temples. Some of the granite was used to enlarge part of the island so as to resemble the shape of Philae.

The stones were then transported to their new home and, in a record time of 30 months, were re-erected in an even more perfection condition than before (although a water-level mark is clearly visible on the entrance pylons), because many of the reused or fallen blocks were replaced in the course of the reconstruction. In March 1980 Philae was declared open to the public again in its new location, and the nightly *son et lumière* tells the story of the rescue. The old island of Philae – a sandbank surrounded by the rusty remains of the coffer dam – is still visible from Agilka.

A relief that is particularly relevant to the Nile can be seen in a small monument known as **Hadrian's Gateway**, beside the temple of Isis. It relates to the source of the Nile. It shows blocks of stone heaped one upon the other, with a vulture (representing Upper Egypt) and a hawk (representing Lower Egypt) standing on top. Beneath the rocks is a circular chamber which is outlined by the contours of a serpent within which Hapi, the Nile-god, crouches. He clasps a vessel in each hand, ready at the appointed time to pour the water towards Egypt and bring goodness to the land.

A new island: Nubia has not passed into total oblivion. A site known as **Qasr Ibrim** rides high above the waters. Now an island, it was situated on the eastern bank of the Nile and was one of three massive peaks. Crowning the middle peak was a ruined town and fortress, whose imposing position commanded the valley for miles around in all directions. This Qasr (castle) is all that emerges above the level of the lake today, and is the only site in Nubia where archaeologists are still at work. Access to the site is possible via the Aswan/Abu Simbel road. A joint American/British excavation started here in 1986 and surviving documents in a host of languages, including Old Nubian (not yet deciphered), Arabic, Coptic and Greek, have been found.

Aswan is the focus of all these activities, of excavations in Nubia, of sidetrips to Abu Simbel, of excursions to the two dams, to the rescued temples of Philae, to the islands and to the monuments on the west bank. It is also the starting point of the navigable Nile and, for many, the beginning of the cruise downriver.

Moving Abu Simbel.

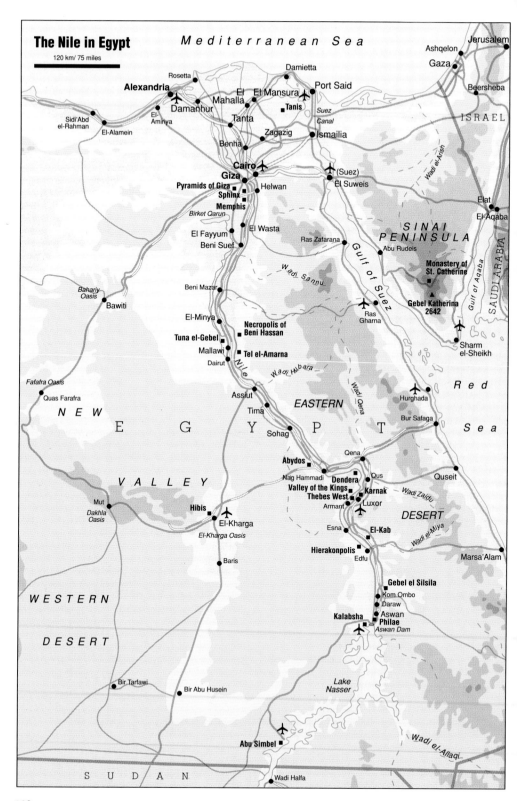

The Nile in Egypt

120 km/ 75 miles

Mediterranean Sea

Ashqelon
Jerusalem
Gaza

Rosetta
Damietta
Port Said
Alexandria
Beersheba
El
El Mansura
Damanhur
Mahalla
Tanis
El-Amiriya
Sidi'Abd
el-Rahman
Suez
Canal
ISRAEL
El-Alamein
Tanta
Zagazig
Ismailia
Benha

Cairo
Cairo
(Suez)
Giza
El Suweis
Pyramids of Giza
Helwan
Elat
Sphinx
El-Aqaba
Memphis
Birket Qarun

El Fayyum
El Wasta
Ras Zafarana
S I N A I
Beni Suef
P E N I N S U L A
Abu Rudeis
Wadi Sannu
Monastery of
St. Catherine

Bahariy
Oasis
Beni Mazar
Ras
Gharna
Gebel Katherina
Bawiti
2642

El-Minya
Necropolis of
Beni Hassan
Sharm
el-Sheikh
Tuna el-Gebel
Mallawi
Tel el-Amarna
Dairut
Wadi Hubara
Nile

Fatafra Oasis
Assiut
EASTERN
Hurghada
Quas Farafra
Tima
Bur Safaga
N E W
Sohag
Wadi Qena

E
G
Y
P
T

V A L L E Y
Qena
Quseit
Abydos
Nag Hammadi
Dendera
Qus
Mut
Valley of the Kings
Karnak
Dakhla
Hibis
Thebes West
Wadi Zaidu
Oasis
Armant
Luxor
El-Kharga
Esna
DESERT
El-Kharga Oasis
El-Kab
Wadi el-Miya
Hierakonpolis
Baris
Edfu
Marsa'Alam

Gebel el Silsila
WESTERN
Kom Ombo
Daraw
Kalabsha
Aswan
DESERT
Philae
Aswan Dam

Bir Tarfawi
Lake
Nasser
Bir Abu Husein

Wadi el-Allaqi
Abu Simbel

S U D A N
Wadi Halfa

Red

Sea

Gulf of Suez

SAUDI ARABIA

Gulf of Aqaba

Wadi el-Arish

ASWAN TO LUXOR

The Nile made Egypt, and Egypt is the Nile. The river flows past the back door of many modern Egyptians; but for ancient Egyptians – before roads and railways – the Nile flowed past their front door. Temples and palaces were built on the desert edge of the floodplain with materials that were floated down the river; those constructions which are today directly on the riverbank are likely to date from after the construction of the High Dam.

Modern cruises have an ancient pedigree. Greeks, Macedonians, Carians and Persians were the first travellers to Upper Egypt from as early as the 6th century BC. Then came Roman Emperors and their ladies, many of whom also went river cruising in plush and costly craft, followed more recently by turn-of-the-century European aristocrats. All succumbed to the legendary river, its fabled ruins and healthy climate.

The best way of seeing these monuments – and for seeing Egypt – is therefore on the Nile. If you have the time and the inclination, cruising can be done by *felucca*, but most people travel on sophisticated river boats which increase in number every year.

Ancient and modern: Another advantage to travelling by river is the opportunity to bridge time. Alongside ancient monuments and early Christian settlements along the banks are towns and modern factories that produce products ranging from fertiliser to molasses.

Though agriculture was probably introduced into the Nile valley in about 5,000 BC, a farmer today, as in ancient times, is hard-working. He rises with the sun and retires early (maybe not so early now that electricity has brought television to many rural areas). He tends his land with a wooden plough, transports produce from area to area on his faithful donkey, and draws water by such ancient devices as the water-wheel driven by patient buffaloes. In rural Egypt there have been few technical advances for thousands of years.

Keeping change and continuity side by side is not as paradoxical as it sounds. For although there have been very real political, social and ideological differences between the various periods of Egyptian history, much has stayed the same. Egyptian leadership, for example, has always been associated with the great source of life: the Nile. Through progressive civilisations efforts have been made to harness its waters. From the earliest pharaohs who ceremoniously wielded pickaxes to open new canals, to the present day, when the river has been harnessed by the High Dam, rulers – whether ancient Egyptians, Greeks, Romans, Mamlukes, kings or presidents – have built canals, barrages, aqueducts and dams. Faith in a leader who is provider, protector and controller of water is, therefore, one factor that has outlived change.

The farmers have adjusted their lives to the pace of the crop and the predictable rhythm of the seasons. The younger generation may aspire to an education and life in a large city, but for the vast

Preceding pages: temple carving from Kom Ombo. Right, travelling downstream.

majority of the rural population their livelihood reposes in the black soil beneath their feet. There is a timeless, almost Biblical quality to the scene that unfolds along the riverbanks.

The annual flood was the source of remarkable fertility. In ancient times there was no High Dam to harness its force. The swollen river flowed through Nubia until it reached Aswan, where it spread out over the valley and left its rich deposit on the land.

Egypt may, in the immortal words of Herodotus, have been "the gift of the Nile", but full exploitation of the land only came with unremitting toil. That is to say, unless the waters of the inundation were captured and retained for times of need, the fertility of the soil would last for only a few months. Without the farmer to create and mend water channels and carry the moisture to the outlying fields, the land would have continued to yield no more than the wild grain collected by the hunter-gathering communities of pre-dynastic times.

But the farmers worked. They waded into their fields and built their dykes, turning compact areas into natural reservoirs which retained a residue of mineral-rich sediment. They did not always agree on the limits of their land, and there were many disputes over water rights and boundary stelae; the latter were slabs of stone with rounded tops bearing text, on which they were in the habit of swearing an oath. Matters were usually set right by an overseer or, if necessary, in a Court of Justice.

Seasonal work: In the Sun Temple of the Pharaoh Nyusserre at Abu Sir (near Memphis), built about 2,300 BC, the life of the peasant farmer is graphically depicted during the seasonal operations in the course of a single year. The first season was the *akhet*, or season of the inundation, which started with the rising waters in June and reached its height by July, the start of the Egyptian New Year. Within a few weeks the water began to recede and the land was ready. This was the second season – the *perit* or "going forth" – and it began in mid-November. Although the farmer could

Left, farmer's breakfast. Below, water carriers.

simply cast the seed, reliefs of farming activities show that he frequently turned over the enriched soil by means of a hoe or a plough.

The hoe, one of the most ancient of agricultural tools, consisted of a broad, pointed blade of wood attached to a handle at an acute angle and held in position at the centre by a slack rope. It was enlarged into a plough by adding two long wooden arms on which the ploughman leaned to keep the furrow straight, and also to press the blade into the soil. A pole was provided with a yoke for attaching to draught animals to further facilitate the work.

The *shemu* (harvest) season began in mid-March. It was the third season and an important time for everyone in the land. Representations show that certain ceremonies were performed relating to cutting the first sheaf of grain with a sickle, and that afterwards there were harvest festivals of thanks. Because such festivals related to life reaffirmed on a regular basis, it was a time for merry-making and, right into the Persian pe-

Loading camels on to the ferry at Daraw.

riod in the 6th century BC, it was also a time for the taking of marriage vows.

The ancient Egyptians did not, as we do, orient themselves towards the north, but towards the south, the source of the flood which was the bearer of life. In sailing from Aswan, you are therefore moving northwards from Egypt's "first" Upper Egyptian province, which extended from the cataract region to a mountain chain north of Kom Ombo known as Gebel Silsila. From there, the 2nd to 4th provinces extended as far as Luxor. Aswan to Luxor is the first leg of the cruise journey, which explores the land, the people, the monuments, and ancient Egypt's mythological tradition.

Into the desert: As the vessel departs Aswan, you leave behind the granite rocks that are characteristic of the area. The desert here comes down virtually to the riverbank, and is still tinted with red ochre from the iron mines. The river is wide. And that great ball of fire, the sun, dominates the heavens. In a largely rainless country the sun is an insistent presence. In ancient times the centre of

the sun cult was ancient On, Heliopolis, northeast of modern Cairo, where the sun-god was known as Ra (the solar orb) or Atum (the setting sun). Under one priesthood he was Kheper (the beetle), under another Harakhte or Horus of the Horizon.

The sun was seen to sail across the heavenly ocean in a barge each day, from the pink-speckled dawn to the fiery sunset. With the last rays of the day, he transferred to another barge that continued the voyage through the underworld, bringing light to its darkened spheres. During the sun's absence the northern stars, the ones that never set, were "the eternal ones", the place of the afterlife. The ancient Egyptians had a delightful and imaginative concept of the universe. They saw their world as confined in something resembling a large box, with a narrow, oblong floor with Egypt as its centre. The river, arising from the eternal ocean in the south flowed towards the eternal ocean (the Mediterranean) in the north. The sky was conceived somewhat like an iron ceiling sprinkled capriciously with suspended stars. The people who lived within this protected area were *remej*, quite simply "people". All others were "sand wanderers", "desert wanderers" or people of the hill country. In other words, they were not the inhabitants of the flat land, the fertile, god-given land of Egypt.

The Egyptians also devised explanations about the environment. The land was Geb the earth-god who, in the beginning, was locked in an embrace with Nut, the sky-goddess. Then Shu, representing the atmosphere, emerged from the primeval waters and forcibly separated the two by slipping between them and raising Nut aloft in his outstretched arms to her new abode. Geb was left on the ground where the crops sprouted from his body.

Geb and Nut were father and mother of four deities: Osiris, who became associated with the Nile and the fertile lands bordering it, Isis his wife, Seth who was the god associated with the desert, and Nepthys his wife.

En route: After the arid beginnings of **Mill workers.**

the journey, the riverbanks begin to become more fertile at the village of **Daraw**, on the eastern bank of the Nile. Here you may catch sight of a caravan of camels kicking up the dust or crossing the river on the ferry (a recent innovation, before which the animals had to swim across). Hundreds of camels are brought regularly all the way across the desert from the Sudan for sale in Daraw, the scene of a weekly camel market.

The river now takes a curve towards the west and, on the eastern bank of the Nile, an imposing temple stands proud. It is the Graeco-Roman temple of **Kom Ombo**, constructed on what must surely be the most ideal location for a temple in Egypt, and cleared by the Antiquities Department in 1873. The town of Kom Ombo is some distance inland and the temple has been left to stand alone, unlike many others which have long since been swallowed up by more recent building. A newly-built pier enables vessels to moor immediately beneath it, on the inside of the island.

The ancient city of Ombos probably owed its foundation to the strategic importance of this site, on a hill ("kom" means hill) commanding both the Nile and the trade routes from Nubia to the Nile valley. Yet the town attained no great prosperity until Ptolemaic times (332–30 BC) when it became capital of a separate province and the Great Temple of Kom Ombo was built.

The temple was not dedicated to a single deity, as was usual in ancient Egypt, but to two gods: Horus, the hawk-god, and Sobek, the crocodile-god. The reason for this may have been because the Ptolemies, the heirs of Alexander the Great, saw how much of Egypt's tradition was presented in dualistic terms (a double crown for the pharaoh, who was called "Lord of the Two Lands", which were Upper and Lower Egypt), that they apparently saw nothing unusual in building this double temple to two hitherto unrelated deities.

Although, therefore, the temple is built on traditional lines with an entrance pylon, open court, hypostyle hall and sanctuary, there is an invisible division

Dominoes in Kom Ombo.

down the middle of the temple: two separate doorways extend its entire length, past the halls and antechambers, ultimately leading to the two sanctuaries where the sacred statues of the deities were kept.

Well worth noting is that between the two sanctuaries is a hidden corridor – now exposed – that was built into the thickness of the wall. This secret place could only be approached from a chamber situated immediately to the rear, where a portion of the floor could be raised to admit a priest to a passage below ground level. A priest whispering through the wall at the worshippers in the sanctuaries must have played an important part in the oracular power attributed to the two deities!

It is thought that a crocodile was kept in the small square pool in the middle of the courtyard. Hundreds of mummified crocodiles were found in 1960 during the construction of the Aswan to Kom Ombo road, a couple of which are in a chamber on the right side of the main steps. There were many more, but the smell became so overpowering that they had to be removed.

Sandstone belt: Leaving Kom Ombo and sailing northwards, **Gebel Silsila**, literally "The Hills of the Chain", soon appears on the eastern bank of the river, roughly halfway between Aswan and Luxor. This is the point at which the boat leaves the first province of Aswan, which physically belongs to the sandstone belt of Nubia, and enters the limestone plateau of Egypt proper.

As this is the last intrusion of sandstone in Egypt, it is not surprising that ancient architects quarried at Gebel Silsila for the stone that was so largely used in their building operations from the 18th Dynasty (1567 BC). The range was called Gebel Silsila (Hills of the Chain), because, according to legend, the Nile was once closed against river traffic from this point by a great chain that stretched across the river. The legend even points to two curiously shaped rocks as the posts to which the chain was secured in ancient times! There is no evidence of there ever having been such

The temple at Kom Ombo.

a barrier at Silsila, and the explanation may well have been invented just to suit the name.

This mountain range today forms the most northerly point of Nubian resettlement. It is as though the Nubian people only chose to live within the familiar sandstone environment of their native land, and the Nubian language is not spoken north of this point.

State of the art: The next port of call is **Edfu**. Its name is derived from the Coptic *Atbo* which, in turn, derived from the ancient name *Tbot*. The Greeks, who gave the site great importance, knew it as Great Appollinopolis.

The focus of interest at Edfu is the **Temple of Horus** (erected by the Greeks), which is the most well-preserved in the whole of Egypt. It was built over a period of 180 years, begun in 237 BC and completed in 57 BC.

The temple (usually reached by horse carriage from the riverside) was first cleared by the French Egyptologist Auguste Mariette in the 19th century, and gives a very clear picture of the layout and decoration of an Egyptian temple. From entrance pylon, through open court, to hypostyle hall and inner sanctuary, it is impressive. And the holy of holies where the sacred statue of the deity was kept is a rare carving of polished and speckled black granite.

Horus was the falcon (hawk) god, known in one form as Horus of Behedet. A large almost comical statue stands at the entrance to the temple, and the deity is represented in reliefs throughout either as a man with a falcon's head, or as a solar disc with outspread wings. Throughout the temple, inside and out, the walls, pylons, corridors, halls, antechambers, sanctuary, and inner chambers are embellished with reliefs that are considered among the most beautiful in Egypt, despite the defacings done by the Christians, who superstitiously concentrated on faces and hands lest the images should come to life to haunt their defacers. Around three sides of the sanctuary, separated from it by a corridor, is a series of shrines reserved for certain rites or belonging to various deities. All are adorned with reliefs,

many retaining their original colour.

One of the most interesting series of representations in the Temple of Horus relates to the New Year Festival. They show that each year the pharaoh, accompanied by priests bearing standards that represented Egypt's ancient provinces, mounted to the roof of the temple (the staircase still exists but is closed to tourists). He was followed by a long procession of priests of a lower order, chanting and reciting hymns, some shaking sistrums, burning incense or carrying offerings. Priests of a higher order carried two caskets, bearing the statues of Hathor the cow-goddess and Horus the hawk-god, towards the roof.

More priests are shown following the procession. They burn incense to safeguard the sacred statues from any evil spirit that might lurk in the temple. At the top of the staircase, priests with standards welcome the pharaoh who heads the procession. The caskets are placed on the roof of the temple to be revitalised by the rays of the rising sun.

Also depicted on the inner side of the

Horus statue
the temple
Edfu.

outer walls, on the left side facing the sanctuary, is the second part of the Horus legend, telling the story of the battles against his brother Seth, who is represented here both as a hippopotamus and a crocodile.

River traffic: As your boat slips under the bridge at Edfu, note the number of boats in the river. Many are the classical *felucca*, a flat-bottomed sailing boat that transports produce – mostly pottery, grain and limestone – and sometimes tourists. Sailing northwards they have the flow of the Nile underneath them, and southbound the prevailing north wind fills their sails. The smaller boats belong to boat people who live their lives on the water catching fish in long nets laid out in a semicircle with floats.

There are no more *dahabiyya* on the Nile. These were pleasure craft, popular in medieval times, which were first introduced in the 7th century after the Arab conquest of Egypt. They were large sailing boats with cabins, described by British Egyptologist and prolific writer Amelia Edwards as "the Rolls-Royce of the Nile", and it was these vessels which were used when the first Nile cruises for Westerners were introduced around 1830.

On the riverbanks you may catch sight of the ancient pumping methods that are still used today: the *shadouf* is a bucket and counterweight attached to the ends of a pile, operated by downward pressure to lift water from one level to another, which dates back to pharaonic times; the Archimedean screw comprises a screw thread in a cylinder dipping into the water at an angle of not more than 30 degrees; and the *sakiya* consists of a chain of buckets passing over a vertical wheel dipping in the water, geared to a horizontal wheel turned by a blindfolded buffalo walking in a circle. Of course, today there are also numerous electrical pumping devices of all shapes and sizes.

Crops cultivated on the riverside have remained largely unchanged since ancient times. They include vegetables, grains, lettuce, melons, cucumbers, onions, garlic and a sweet red carrot that **Fishermen at sunset.**

is peculiar to Egypt. Flax was the fibre formerly used for weaving, only to become obsolete with the arrival of cotton in the 7th century.

The Egyptian farmer has always taken great care of his livestock: several tombs have depictions of young farmhands feeding animals, milking them and aiding them through childbirth. Similar scenes are still enacted all along the Nile today. A farmer giving his charge a bath in a canal or on the banks of the river is not an unfamiliar sight. They house their animals in the courtyards of their homes, talk to them and give them names. An ancient Egyptian story relates how a farmer got to know his animals so well, often spending the night with them in the stable, that they told him where they found the best grazing.

Renewed site: Although **El Kab** (less than an hour from Edfu) is not yet on river cruise itineraries, it may soon be a stopping point for river craft. The ancient city, known as Nekheb, once ranked among the chief cities of Egypt and even under the Ptolemies was capital of the 3rd province. The site, which lies on the eastern bank, has recently been restored and prepared for tourists. The tombs have been made accessible by stairways and the surrounding area enhanced with trees and gardens.

El Kab was most prominent in the 18th Dynasty, around 1567 BC, when two of the city's brave sons were recruited to fight in the armies of Ahmose and Tuthmosis I. The two youths bore the same name as their pharaoh, Ahmose, who was the "Father of the New Kingdom". The first was Ahmose son of Ebana, and the other was Ahmose Pennekhbet. Their tombs are among the most individual and picturesque of ancient Egypt. Moreover, they date to the period in Egyptian history leading to the war of liberation from the hated occupying forces, the Hyksos, in the 2nd century BC. Consequently they are of considerable historical importance.

Ahmose Pennekhbet lived during the actual war of liberation from the Hyksos and the wars that followed immediately afterwards, and his tomb is a fascinating

The ferry home.

catalogue of military activities. For example, the warrior described, in somewhat exaggerated prose, how he personally took prisoners, captured horses and chariots, and, on one occasion, killed off the enemy because it was less trouble to do so than to take "living prisoners". As an aged warrior he was appointed to the most prestigious and responsible post of tutor to the eldest daughter of Queen Hatshepsut "while she was a child upon the breast."

Ahmose, son of Ebana, saw his nation through a similar period of crisis, but his tomb is more significant for its biographical data than its artistic merit. He claimed that he was a "soldier and sailor too" and was also a "warrior of the ruler". He described how he fought "more than what is true" during a campaign in Nubia, and "showed great bravery" in the pharaoh's wars in western Asia. He claimed, furthermore, that he was at the head of the troops under Tuthmosis I, and that his king "beheld my valour" and "presented me with gold in double measure" in recognition

of his worth. In his old age, Ahmose was apparently content in his retirement, happily reminiscing about his war years and his honourable record.

Opposite El Kab, on the western bank, is the ancient city of **Nekhen**, an important archaeological site which can only be visited by special permission. It was the pre-dynastic capital of Upper Egypt, where relics of the earliest kings of Egypt were found. These include some of the most famous treasures of the Cairo Museum such as the Palette of Narmer, the pharaoh traditionally known as Menes who unified Upper and Lower Egypt in 3100 BC and brought the whole of the Nile valley under his domination.

Dam town: The barrage through which steamers are locked at **Esna** was erected in 1908–09 to regulate irrigation as far as Qena, to the north of Luxor; today it is a major stumbling block for the cruise industry, as the lock is slow to operate and can only take one boat at a time. Moreover, at times of low water the river authorities sometimes close the lock altogether because it drains too much from the upper reaches. A new lock is currently being built.

Esna itself is a district capital and the largest town between Aswan and Luxor. Although some of the buildings hint at the prosperity of times long past, the town is not only uninspiring today but somewhat shoddy and the people are rather pushy. Were it not for the temple one would be hard-pressed to recognise this as one of the most important places in Upper Egypt in antiquity.

The Ptolemaic **Temple of Khnum**, the ram-headed deity, was almost totally obscured by the modern town until relatively recently and today lies in a large depression well below the level of the modern town, five minutes' walk from the river. The central court was excavated in 1842 by Mohammed Ali, not, it is recorded, for cultural reasons but rather "in order to provide a safe underground magazine for gunpowder." Literally dozens of houses were removed from its precincts, and the lip of the depression is still crowded with the modern town.

The most noticeable part of the temple is the Hypostyle Court, whose roof

Temple figures, Esna.

is still intact and supported by six rows of four columns, each with elaborately carved capitals. There are 16 different types for the 24 columns. The walls are decorated with reliefs which may not be the finest in execution but make up for that in content. They carry scenes of the various Roman Emperors depicted as Egyptian pharaohs sacrificing to the gods and carrying out various ritual observances. Among the most interesting is a relief near the bottom of the northern wall which shows the Emperor Commodus in the company of the hawk-headed Horus and the ram-headed Khnum drawing in a clap-net full of waterfowl and fish (the Nile perch was a recognised deity here), observed by the ibis-headed Thoth.

The temple is historically important because the Emperor Trajan Decius (AD 249–251) is the last Roman name to appear in a royal *cartouche* (an elliptical sign bearing the name of the pharaoh) in an Egyptian temple. Some of the hieroglyphs here have proved to be indecipherable.

Home strait: The last stretch of the journey towards Luxor is uneventful. In the background lie the hills of the Western Desert, with a foreground of extensive palm-groves interrupted by the smoking chimneys of brick factories. The town of **Armant**, the ancient Hermonthis, on the western bank of the Nile can hardly be seen from the river, but two summits, known as *Gebelein*, "two mountains", can be spotted. On the higher of these is the tomb of a holy woman called Sheika Musa. Armant is the site of one of many sugar factories in Upper Egypt. This important crop was introduced to Egypt at the beginning of the 19th century by the Khedive Ismail.

Approaching Luxor, the Nile begins to get wider, and the hills recede to the west and to the east, curving away from the river's bank and leaving broad plains on either side. This was the site chosen for Thebes: few spots in Egypt are so ideally suited for the growth of a great city; few places in the world have bequeathed to us more numerous or mightier monuments.

The Temple of Khnum, Esna.

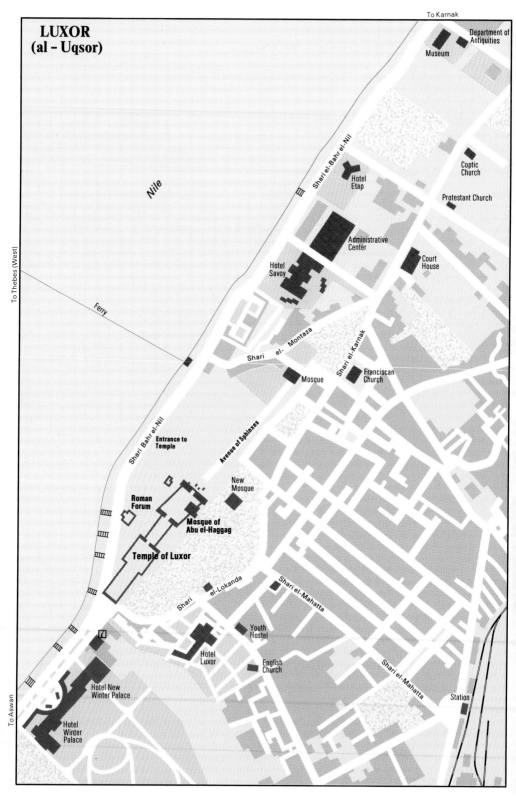

**LUXOR
(al – Uqsor)**

To Karnak

Nile

To Thebes (West)

Ferry

Department of Antiquities

Museum

Coptic Church

Protestant Church

Shari el-Bahr el-Nil

Hotel Etap

Administrative Center

Court House

Hotel Savoy

Shari el- Montaza

Shari el-Karnak

Mosque

Franciscan Church

Shari Bahr el-Nil

Entrance to Temple

Avenue of Sphinxes

New Mosque

Roman Forum

Mosque of Abu el-Haggag

Temple of Luxor

el-Lokanda

Shari el-Mahatta

Shari

Youth Hostel

Hotel Luxor

English Church

Shari el-Mahatta

To Aswan

Hotel New Winter Palace

Hotel Winter Palace

Station

LUXOR

Luxor, ancient Thebes, is like a huge open-air museum on both sides of the Nile, 420 miles (675 km) south of Cairo. On the eastern bank, the town side, are the Temple of Luxor and the Temple of Amon-Ra at Karnak. On the western bank, the necropolis or city of the dead, are the Valley of the Kings, the Valley of the Queens, hundreds of tombs of noblemen, and a semicircle of grand mortuary temples along the edge of the floodplain.

Modern Luxor is not the most exciting of Egypt's river cities. It is spared the harsh edge of industrialisation, but perhaps as a result it has been rather overrun by tourism. Luxor is often described by Egyptians as a "village" even though it has a population of 100,000 and an international airport where many charter flights bring in as many as 2,000 tourists a day; Aswan, with twice the population and proper commerce, has no international flights. Luxor has very little high-rise other than hotel accommodation; little commerce other than staple foods and that which is aimed at servicing tourism. Fundamentally it is a tourists' and farmers' town and once you get through the front layer of rather over-enthusiastic salesmen and *calèche* drivers – who probably do offer the best way of touring Luxor – it is friendly.

Women sometimes find Luxor taxing. "The people paw you, and hassle you and make vulgar remarks," said an American, adding, "they think that all Western women are available women." The fault might be theirs. Too many tourists, especially Europeans, show no respect for the decorum practised in a Muslim country.

From the river the town is almost hidden by the quantities of cruise boats and other craft which moor, sometimes five deep, along two or three miles of the eastern bank, many tied up alongside prestigious hotels. Two or three ferry crossings operate across to the western bank.

Inland from the tourist-oriented corniche are first of all the tourist *souq*, full of statuettes and Egyptiana, followed by the diverging street with the local *souq* of food and household goods. Beyond that is the railway station, and beyond that extensive but simple suburbs; that's Luxor.

Slumbering Thebes: Unlike Aswan which bears an aura of what it always was, a bustling border town, Luxor's monuments alone hint at its ancient glory. Its name is derived from the Arabic *El-Oksor,* "the palaces", in reference to the ruins that were, until the 1930s, half-buried. Mud dwellings had been built by the people alongside sculptured walls, and dovecots had been erected beside architraves and pylons. The much sought-after David Roberts prints of the ancient monuments, painted after his first voyage to Egypt in 1838, romantically show the temples thus, with columns toppling, architraves falling, and once lofty colonnades half-submerged in a sea of sand.

Now the monuments have been excavated and restored we can see some-

Preceding pages and below: the Temple of Amon-Ra at Karnak, Luxor.

thing of the ancient city of Thebes; a city that was once accepted as representative of the splendour and magnificence of the ancient eastern world. For over four centuries Thebes reigned without a rival in Egypt, and for part of that time the city was the virtual centre of the ancient world.

Thebes was of no particular significance for the first 2,000 years of ancient Egyptian history. It started off no different from hundreds of other unpretentious villages, and its inhabitants lived much as they do today in many isolated rural areas, in villages of sun-dried mudbrick houses separated by narrow lanes, caring principally about the agricultural cycle and little else.

During this time the Old Kingdom civilisation (2686–2181 BC) was making headway in the north. Zoser, the builder of the Step Pyramid at Sakkara, had complete control over the two lands of Upper and Lower Egypt. In his reign vessels over 150 ft (50 metres) long were constructed for river traffic, the copper mines in Sinai were exploited, commerce was carried out on the Phoenician coast, cedarwood was imported from Lebanon and slaves from Nubia. But ancient Thebes just slumbered. Even when the Fourth Dynasty powerful monarchs of the 4th dynasty built great pyramids at Giza which secured them undying fame: Snofru, Cheops, Khafre and Menkaure, Thebes was hardly affected.

The awakening: It was only when the unlimited power enjoyed by the pharaohs was partly passed to their officials and local governors sought to establish independence from the central government that political awareness started to develop in Thebes. This was what historians refer to as the First Intermediate Period, the Seventh to the 11th Dynasties (*circa* 2181–2133 BC), during which a powerful family of monarchs, whose capital was in Armant neighbouring Thebes (today Armant is a nearby industrial town), gained power and started to move northwards.

Little by little they extended their authority, annexing local provinces un-

A welcoming *calèche*.

til they clashed with the rulers of the north – and beat them. Theban supremacy was recognised, Amon-Ra was introduced as the local deity and Thebes began to develop at last.

But it only adopted its prominent place in Egyptian history following the wars of liberation from the hated Hyksos occupation. The Hyksos were tribespeople who came from the direction of Syria and ruled Egypt between about 1786 to 1567 BC, when an Egyptian prince called Sekenenre and his son Kamose rose against them. Kamose's brother Ahmose was able to establish the 18th Dynasty and what is now known as the New Kingdom, with Thebes at its centre. The Kingdom included the 18th, 19th and 20th Dynasties (*circa* 1567–1085 BC).

After ridding the country of foreign occupation, Thebes began to develop into the seat of a world power never before witnessed. Military conquests and territorial expansion went hand in hand with an artistic and architectural revolution of unparalleled grandeur. Greek visitors to Egypt were overwhelmed by the material wealth of the civilisation. In the words of the *Iliad, ix*:

Where, in Egyptian Thebes, the
heaps of precious ingots gleam,
The hundred-gated Thebes, where
twice ten score in martial state
Of valiant men with steeds and cars
march through each massy gate.

Tuthmosis III (*circa* 1470 BC), was the Napoleon of ancient Egypt. He conducted no fewer than 17 campaigns, which resulted in the creation of a vast empire that comprised almost all Western Asia including Palestine, Syria, Phoenicia, the western part of the Euphrates, Nubia, Kush (the Sudan today) and Libya.

Gods and glory: As a result of military victory, booty from conquered nations and tributes from the provinces of the then known powers poured into the gigantic storehouse of Thebes. The greater part of the wealth was bestowed upon Amon-Ra, who, with the aid of the influential priesthood, was established as "The King of Gods". The Theban triad, or group of three gods, comprised Amon-Ra, usually portrayed as a ram-headed sun-god, his wife Mut and son Khonsu.

The temples of Luxor were all built in honour of this Theban triad. They were elaborately embellished and adorned. It was both a duty and a privilege to serve the great god, and successive pharaohs systematically strove to outdo their predecessors in the magnificence of their endeavours.

When Amon-Ra was dishonoured by Amenhotep IV (Akhenaten), who opted to worship the life-giving rays of the full solar disc, the Aten, in place of the ascending sun Ra (*see chapter on the rebel Dynasty, pages 73–79*), this in retrospect affected Thebes but slightly. Although reliefs were defaced, shrines destroyed and the image of Amon-Ra hacked away, his dethronement was short-lived. Tutankhamun, on succeeding to the throne, started the restoration of damaged temples, and Haremhab, Ramses I, Seti I and Ramses II continued the work of rebuilding, reconstructing and renovating the temples, to restore the reputation of the king of gods.

Statue of Thutmosis III in Luxor Museum.

When Diodorus visited Thebes in 57 BC, the tradition of ancient splendour still survived. The inhabitants told him: "There was no city under the sun so adorned with so many and stately monuments of gold, silver, and ivory, and multitudes of colossi and obelisks cut out of one entire stone." The Thebans always boasted that they were the most ancient philosophers and astrologers in the world.

The advent of Christianity brought systematic destruction to the ancient monuments. It happened first in the tombs and shrines where the early Christians hid from Roman persecution. Later the "pagan" statues were uprooted, sacred sanctuaries mutilated, and attempts made to topple even obelisks and colossi to obliterate the visages of the "heathen gods". It wasn't until the 19th century that the pieces began to be put together again by modern archaeologists.

Temples in town: The two temples on the eastern bank of the Nile – the Temple of Luxor right at the edge of the river

near the centre of the city, and that of Amon-Ra at Karnak a little to the north – were once linked by a processional avenue lined with sphinxes. One of the projects of the Antiquities Organisation early in the 1950s was to excavate the whole road, but this has not proved possible. A mosque blocks the way, and the inhabitants of Luxor have not reacted favourably to plans to move it.

Both mortuary and national temples were usually decorated on the outside with battle reliefs, such as Ramses II's famous Battle of Kadesh where he tramples the enemy beneath the wheels of his chariot and captures the Hittite fortress (on the entrance pylon of the Temple of Luxor and in the Ramesseum on Luxor's western bank); Seti I in battle against Bedouin tribes of Libya, Palestine, and Syria (on the northern outer wall of the Hypostyle Hall at Karnak); or Ramses III in his naval battle against the "People of the Sea", who were probably Sardinians (on the northern, outer wall of the Temple of Ramses III at Medinet Habu).

Calèche on the Corniche.

The avenue of the sphinxes marches almost up to the entrance pylon of the **Temple of Luxor**, with its depiction of the Battle of Kadesh now rather faint. One of a pair of obelisks remains here; the other is in the Place de la Concorde in Paris. The temple was built by Amenhotep III, the great-grandson of the military genius Tuthmosis III. It is typical in the sense that the pavement rises progressively and the roof lowers from the entrance to the inner sanctuary, and it used to get progressively darker. Only the pharaoh, or the high priest in his stead, was permitted to enter the darkened inner sanctuary, and to behold the statue of the deity.

High up to the left, and easily missed at first, the **Mosque of Abu el-Hagag** is perched behind the entrance pylon in the first court. It is a Fatimid mosque constructed in the 11th century, dedicated to a local saint, and was originally built when the temple was almost covered in silt and sand; the temple has since been excavated, leaving the mosque stranded, perched about 40 ft (13 metres) above ground level, with all its foundations visible. Efforts by the Antiquities Organisation to rebuild it elsewhere have been to no avail. Local sheikhs claim that the tomb of Abu el-Hagag himself lies there and that it is a sacred site.

Festival carvings: The reliefs on the Luxor temple walls depict the great *Opet* Festival, when the sacred statue of the god Amon-Ra was taken out of the sanctuary at Karnak during the height of the flood and, amidst great pomp and ceremony, transported here, where it remained for certain festivities before being returned to Karnak.

Reliefs of preparations for the occasion are depicted on the right-hand wall of the temple's colonnade (some of which was reconstructed in the 1970s), which include a rehearsal by dancing girls. The procession began at the gate of Karnak Temple, which is shown complete with flagstaffs, from whence white-robed priests bore the sacred barge of Amon-Ra down to the water's edge.

An enthusiastic audience claps hands

Temple of Luxor, moonrise montage.

in unison, the boat is accompanied upstream by those along the shore, a sacrifice of slaughtered animals is followed by a group of acrobats, and finally offerings are made to the Theban triad at the Temple of Luxor. On the opposite wall are scenes of the festival's return procession. The barges are floated downstream, and the final sacrifice and offerings of flowers are made to the deities at Karnak Temple.

This magnificent series of reliefs is in a pitiful condition. The upper part of the wall is damaged, and the stone is suffering badly from pollution.

Today's Muslim *mulid* (annual celebration), closely resembles the *Opet* Festival. Muslim sheikhs emerge from the Mosque of Abu el-Hagag bearing three small sailing boats, which they place on carriages to traverse the city. Luxor is bedecked with flowers during the celebration, and dancing and clapping greet the procession.

Near the centre of the Luxor temple is the Court of Amenhotep III with a double row of columns on each side. They are of exquisite proportion and a fine example of the architecture of Egypt's golden age. Within this court an important discovery was made at the end of 1989. When the flagstones were being lifted to check on the tilt of the land and possible undermining of the columns, a hidden cache was found which contained, among other objects, life-size statues of various New Kingdom pharaohs. These are to be displayed in a special gallery of the Luxor Museum.

Beyond this court are several chambers, some of which were adapted by the Romans for Christian worship. Alexander the Great added the small end chapel, with reliefs of himself as an Egyptian.

The world's throne: The great **Temple of Amon-Ra** at **Karnak** is much larger than the Temple of Luxor. This huge and splendid complex which actually contains many separate temples covers 200 acres (80 hectares) and is styled as "The Throne of the World". Beneath its giant architraves and between bulky column and wall relief lie the records of its growth from a modest Middle King-

Avenue of the Sphinxes at Karnak.

dom shrine to a temple of splendid and unimaginable proportions. It owes a column to one pharaoh, a pylon to another; an inspiration here, a whim there. But each has the sole purpose of pleasing the god, Amon-Ra, who would ensure the builder a long, powerful and glorious life.

Unravelling the secrets of 2,000 years has been a major feat of Egyptology, made the more difficult by the fact that family rivalries and kingly jealousies were often the incentive behind new constructions. Often the reigning pharaoh would alter the royal cartouche of a predecessor and thereby take the credit for all the work that that predecessor had accomplished (which may be why Ramses II seems to have been so industrious in temple building). To add to the confusion, some parts of the buildings were raised from dismantled shrines or the walls of other temples. In addition, Karnak had to endure the degradation of Amon-Ra, first at the hands of the rebel pharaoh Akhenaten and then by the early Christians.

Where the car park and souvenir shops now stand outside the temple complex was once riverbank from where the builders' and the festival barges came and went. The double row of ram-headed sphinxes with sun-discs on their heads and statues of the pharaoh between their forepaws once led from the river bank to the main entrance.

The two blocks of the unadorned entrance pylon are unfinished (no carvings) and were added by Ethiopian kings in the last stage of its construction. Between, the entrance leads to the **Great Court**, which covers a massive area of 95,433 sq. ft (8,919 sq. metres), which was the one part of the temple accessible to the public. Within it are shrines, a single intact column, rows of ram-headed sphinxes, and columns, some of which are unfinished and give a clue as to how the ancient Egyptians conducted their work. They show that the roughly-shaped stones, heaved into position on ramps, were only shaped after erection, and that the polishing and decoration were performed from the top down-

Luxor market.

wards as the mud-brick ramps (a large mass of rubble behind one of the entrance pylons) were then removed layer by layer.

In front of the second pylon, which leads to the Great Hypostyle Hall, is a huge statue of the High Priest Panedjem (tour guides may tell you this is Ramses II). Whether this was its original position we do not know, as it was found inside the 3rd pylon. Through the entranceway the **Great Hypostyle Hall** itself is one of the great wonders of antiquity. It is one of the most massive of human creations, and covers an area of 53,318 sq. ft (4,983 sq. metres). To support the roof 134 columns were arranged in 16 rows, with the double row of central columns higher than the others. They have smooth shafts and are 67 ft (21 metres) high, topped with calyx capitals large enough, it is said, to accommodate 100 standing men.

The overall effect is awe-inspiring. Although some critics have commented on the fact that "you can't see the trees for the forest", its magnificence is indis-putable. It was noted by the learned *savants* of Napoleon Bonaparte's expedition to Egypt in 1798 that the whole of the cathedral of Notre Dame in Paris could comfortably be accommodated within its walls. At the time of the *savants* it, too, was half-submerged in sand and antique graffiti is clearly visible some distance up the columns.

Beyond the Hypostyle Hall are the third and fourth pylons, where the lofty **obelisk** erected by Queen Hatshepsut stands (the second and taller of the two obelisks still standing, which were both originally paired). This, the tallest obelisk in Egypt, was erected in the 16th year of the queen's reign and was carved from a single block of pink Aswan granite of the finest quality. The apex was once covered with a mixture of gold and silver. It was made in seven months, and one cannot but marvel at the tenacity required merely to quarry it, let alone cart it – it weighs around 323 tons – to the Nile, transport it along its waters, disembark it, and finally erect it with perfect accuracy on a pedestal. King

Left, Amenhotep II clutching the key of life. Below, the second pylon at Karnak.

Tuthmosis III, Hatshepsut's stepson, did his best to hide her obelisk by constructing a sandstone wall around it, the remains of which can still be seen.

The upper section of another, fallen obelisk, can be found near the **Sacred Lake** of the temple where the priests of Amon-Ra purified themselves in the holy water, piped through from the Nile in underground channels. Unfortunately too few of the hewn rocks survived the years to allow genuine restoration of the lake, but to the west is a bank of seats for part of the *son et lumière* performance, which is part tour and part spectacle. It covers ancient history, and mythological tradition, and re-enacts, against the splendid backdrop of the Karnak temple, the annual *Opet* festival. If you do attend in the evening don't forget warm clothing, particularly in the winter months, and be prepared for mosquitos emerging from the lake. On the temple side of the lake is a café (not usually open in the evenings).

Local collection: On the river's edge about halfway between the temples of Luxor and Karnak is the **Museum of Luxor**, which is usually open from late afternoon. It was designed by one of Egypt's leading architects, the late Mahmoud el-Hakim, to display works of art from the temples of Luxor and Karnak, as well as some selected pieces from the Cairo Museum. The delicacy of the collection and some of the workmanship contrasts strongly with the magnificence of the temples outside, filling in the detail that is missing from the open-air monuments. The selection, installation and illumination was done with the assistance of the Brooklyn Museum, and the difference between this designed environment and the warehouse approach of the Cairo Museum is particularly marked.

The approach to the museum up an inclined walkway is reminiscent of the primordial mound which is an architectural feature of ancient Egyptian temples. Some of the larger statues are displayed in the garden and in the recesses of the building's facade, forming a slatted wall along its outer face which serves to keep the museum cool. Among

them is the portrayal of Amenhotep II as an archer, sections of the red granite stela which were found in the 3rd pylon at Karnak (pylons are often hollow). Amenhotep is depicted demonstrating his ability by driving arrows through a copper target tied to a pole whilst galloping at full speed in his chariot, thus proving his athletic superiority.

Inside the museum, the first focal point is the magnificent head of the cow-goddess Hathor. This gold-leaf treasure from Tutankhamun's tomb is effectively displayed, and the lighting encourages the visitor to move towards the stairway to the rear of the main hall. In this long gallery the main objects include a seated statue of Amenhotep, Son of Hapu, who was one of the most important men in ancient Egypt, so respected that he was accorded special prerogatives during his life and was finally deified thousands of years after his death.

A major work of art in the main gallery is the huge alabaster statue of Amenhotep III, seated beside, and un-

der the protection of Sobek, the crocodile-god. This statue's discovery at the
bottom of a water-filled shaft in a canal
in Armant, south of Luxor, in 1967, was
one of the greatest finds of Thebes in
recent years. Interesting to observe is
the harmonious balance between two
figures of markedly different scale; the
artist has chosen to measure the much
smaller figure of the pharaoh against
Sobek's head, rather than his crown, by
eliminating a portion of the back slab
above the former's head. Also, in having Sobek present the *ankh* – the key of
life – to Amenhotep, the sweep of his
arm draws attention to the handsome
face of the king.

In the upper gallery two displays are
particularly noteworthy. The first is of
blocks, carved in relief, from the famous brown quartzite shrine of
Hatshepsut, which is also known as the
Chapelle Rouge. These were found in
the 3rd pylon at Karnak. Six long-haired
acrobats arch their supple bodies in a
backbend in the upper register, musicians are depicted in the lower, and a
harpist is shown accompanying them.

The other noteworthy display and one
of the most interesting reconstructions
of modern times is part of the famous
"Akhenaten Wall", a 54-ft (18-metre)
wall reconstructed on the upper floor of
the museum from some 300 of the 6,000
blocks of Akhenaten's sun temple extracted by the Franco-Egyptian Centre
at Karnak from Harmhab's ninth pylon.
These *talatat*, as the decorated and uniform sandstone blocks are known, were
discovered by a team of French excavators restoring the pylon. They soon realised that the fill inside the pylon had not
been deposited in a haphazard manner.
Rather, the upper courses had been dismantled and placed in the lowest level
with the middle courses on top, and the
lowest courses higher up the pylon. This
enabled the easy reconstruction of a
wall that had been deliberately dismantled 33 centuries earlier.

The Museum of Luxor also contains
monuments that date to the early centuries of the Christian era and to the Coptic
period. Among the former objects is a
headless limestone and marble statue of
the Greek goddess Demeter, an unusual
find to have made in Upper Egypt where
the worship of foreign gods was not as
prevalent as in other areas. There are
also examples of so-called Roman portraits, which were painted on linen. One
such portrait of what is thought to be a
Roman officer in a garrison at Luxor,
was found in an ancient tomb which had
been used for secondary burial in the
3rd century.

Before crossing to the other bank of
the river it is worth having tea or a
cocktail on the terrace of the **Old Winter Palace Hotel**, next to the Temple of
Luxor, which retains much of the style
of turn-of-the-century tourism. The **Savoy** also has a flavour of old, and refreshments on the terrace is a tradition.
Eating places outside the hotels are rare,
but two worthwhile places are the **New
Karnak Restaurant** (next to the New
Karnak Hotel) and the **Amun Restaurant** near the Temple of Luxor.

Aboudi's bookshop, near the Old
Winter Palace, has an excellent collection of books on Egypt.

Left, *Calèche*
driver and
assistant.
Right, donkey
with a
decorative
haircut.

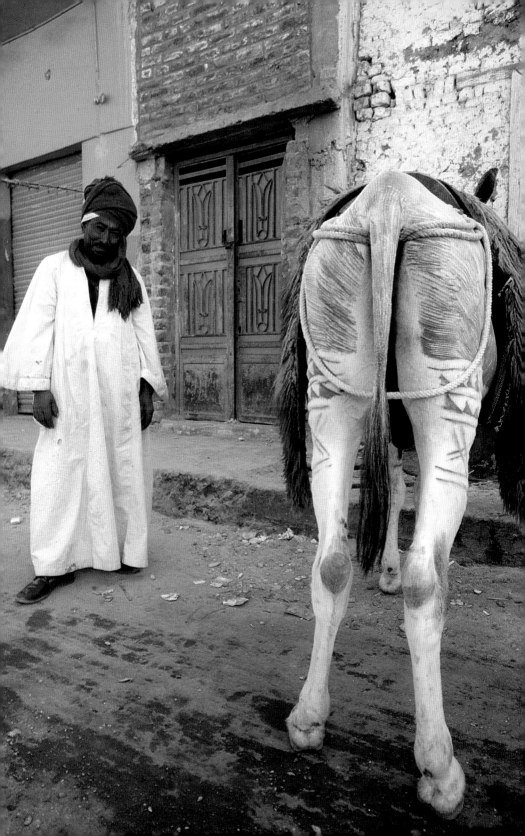

LUXOR:
THE WEST BANK

On the west side of the river at Luxor, where the tourist river boats dock, is a Ticket Office to the monuments of the Luxor necropolis. Be sure to make up your mind in advance which tombs or temples you wish to visit in a day (two or three is enough) because if you change your mind and want to see an extra monument it will mean coming all the way back to buy another ticket. Taxis are available for hire here, although it is advisable to ask someone other than a taxi driver what the going rate for a tour is before starting negotiations.

The necropolis starts where the floodplain ends, about 2 miles (3 km) from the river. The area was not always as arid and lifeless as it seems today. Beside each mortuary temple there were once dwellings for the priests and stables for the sacrificial animals. Nearby were the guardhouses and granaries, each with its superintendent. Surrounding or in front of each temple were lakes, groves and beautifully laid out gardens. Beside the mortuary temples there were also large palaces where the pharaohs took up temporary residence to supervise the progress of their monuments. Such palaces have been excavated beside the mortuary temples of Seti I, the Ramesseum of Ramses II, and the temple of Ramses III.

The approach to the necropolis is marked by two massive, sadly weathered statues known as the **Colossi of Memnon**, 54 ft (18 metres) high. They are all that remain of what was once the largest Mortuary Temple, that of Amenhotep III. It was probably damaged from a high flood, and further devastated by Ramses II and his son Merenptah who used the fallen blocks to build their own temples.

When cracks and holes appeared on the northern statue of the two Colossi, they created a musical sound at dawn when the breeze blew through them. Early Greek and Roman travellers explained this in their mythology by claiming that when Memnon fell at Troy he reappeared at Thebes as a singing stone statue and each morning he would greet his mother Aurora with a plaintive song. Aurora, on hearing the sound, shed tears in the form of the morning dew on the cold stone of the statue. But the cracks on the statue were filled in during the reign of Septimius Severus in AD 193 and the sound ceased.

Female pharaoh: The other mortuary temples are spead in a semicircle at the edge of the floodplain. The most spectacular is undoubtedly that of **Queen Hatshepsut (Deir el Bahri)**. The temple was built in terraces against the steep cliffs and it was styled in ancient times as "Most Splendid of All". It was built by the queen's architect, Senmut, who was also her political adviser and probably her lover. He was granted the unique privilege of constructing his own tomb beneath the temple of his queen.

Hatshepsut's famed voyage to Punt, on the Somali coast, is recorded in the carvings on one colonnade, and the legend of her "divine birth" by the god Amon-Ra is portrayed in another. This

was actually a device created by the beautiful queen to justify her position. Queen Hatshepsut was of direct royal lineage to the Great Royal Wife of Tuthmosis I, while his other (male) children were from minor wives. She consequently married her half-brother Tuthmosis II, assumed a throne name, Makere, and wore a royal skirt and ceremonial beard, which were the badges of kingship. To keep her right to the throne above dispute she commissioned reliefs that showed that her mother Ahmose had been impregnated by the god Amon-Ra by divine conception. After her death her stepson and successor, Tuthmosis III, did his best to erase her image.

The Polish Archaeological Mission has been carrying out a massive restoration project on the temple for many years and is also responsible for its illumination at night.

At the central point between the Valley of the Queens and the Valley of the Kings are the noble tombs at **Quornah**, a village of ochre-coloured houses on the hillside, where many tour buses oblige you to stop to look at the alabaster workshops. Attempts to relocate the villagers have so far been strongly resisted. That they are wealthy, despite their arid surroundings, is clear from the wall paintings on their houses, which depict their *haj* pilgrimages to Mecca. Some 30 years ago, Egyptian architect Hassan Fathy built a model village for the community on the floodplain between the river Nile and the Colossus of Memnon. Although designed with spacious homes, courtyards, schools, health care centre and all other facilities including a mosque, the people of Quornah never agreed to settle there. They chose, instead, to remain where they were on top of the tombs. The reason, it is said, was because they were living on income derived from illegal pillage (*see chapter on grave robbers, pages 67–71*).

This is not the whole truth. The people of Quornah are of Arab stock and although many such tribes today survive on agriculture, they do not mix with the *felaheen*, the Nile valley farmer

Left, alabaster shop at **Quornah**. **Below**, the **Colossi of Memnon**.

whom they regard disparagingly as "tillers of the soil". They traditionally live at the edge of the desert. (The owners of the horse stables at the foot of the pyramids is another such community resisting plans for relocation, and they, too, are of Arab stock).

Kingly ruins: Beyond the village is the mortuary temple of that most active of builders, Ramses II, known as the **Ramesseum**. Although half in ruin, it is a magnificent monument and contains remains of what was once a colossus of king Ramses II, which is one of the most massive granite statues ever fashioned to such perfection. Mathematicians who travelled to Egypt with Napoleon's army in 1798 made careful measurements of the chest, upper arm and foot. They calculated that the statue's total height must have been 51 ft (17 metres), and its weight over 1,000 tons.

Ramses II did an extraordinary amount of building during his 67-year reign. He had his state sculptors depict him repeatedly, and there is hardly a pylon, hall or chamber in the temples of Egypt that does not somewhere bear his name.

His favourite theme was his famous alliance with the King of the Hittites, as depicted on the great pylon that forms the eastern entrance to the Ramesseum. Another series of reliefs concerns the festival of Min. The pharaoh was borne on a richly-decorated carrying-chair, led by priests and soldiers, and followed by his sons and courtiers, to witness sacrifices and to watch the release of four birds to fly to the corners of the earth to carry the royal tidings.

To the north of the Ramesseum a road leads westwards up into the mountains to the Valley of the Kings. The road is scheduled to be widened following an incident where President Mubarak, while visiting the valley with some foreign diplomats, witnessed a near-collision between two tourist buses.

The **Valley of the Kings** is hidden a mile (2 km) inland from the edge of the floodplain. Otherwise known as *Biban el Muluk*, it contains 64 tombs belonging to the pharaohs of the 18th, 19th and 20th Dynasties (*circa* 1567–1080 BC),

Medinet Habu temple.

only nine of which are open to the public. More may well be discovered. A new tomb, the largest found so far and thought to contain 50 of Ramses II's 52 sons, was found in 1995.

To make life difficult for grave-robbers, little is visible above ground other than evidence of numerous underground warrens, holes in a hot and sandy valley. The tombs were hewn out of the bedrock and decorated throughout with scenes concerning the journey of the sun-god through the underworld. The deceased pharaoh, absorbed by the setting sun, travels in the barge of the sun-god through the 12 hours of night, each hour separated from the other by massive gates guarded over by serpents.

The solar barge, safeguarded from the hazards of the underworld by protective deities and emblems, finally reaches the Court of Osiris. Here the judge of the underworld, attended by Maat, goddess of truth and justice, and in the presence of 42 gods of the underworld, watches over the weighing of the heart of the deceased against the feather of truth. The ibis-headed Thoth, god of wisdom, records the verdict. If unfavourable, the deceased is consumed by a terrible animal or consigned to the fires. A favourable verdict gives access to a life ever after.

Some of the royal tombs (Ramses VI, for example) have burial chambers decorated with astrological signs. Others (Amenhotep II) are decorated to resemble papyrus texts pinned to the walls, while others again (Seti I) have wonderfully preserved painted reliefs, although the Tombs of the Nobles are on the whole more colourful.

Biggest and best: The **Tomb of Seti I** is a classical tomb that far surpasses all others both in size and in the artistic execution of the sculptured walls. Every inch of the wall space of its entire 300-ft (100-metre) length is covered with representations by the finest craftsmen. In the burial chamber (a long descent) was the sarcophagus of the pharaoh, made out of a single piece of alabaster carved to a thickness of two inches and with the exquisite reliefs filled in with blue paste.

Giovanni Belzoni, a circus strong-

Tomb entrances in the Valley of the Kings.

234

man who originally came to Egypt to market an irrigation pump he had designed in England, discovered the tomb in 1817. When Turkish officials in Egypt heard of the discovery they headed for Luxor bent on the delightful thought, no doubt, of acquiring priceless treasure. Down the corridors they went, ransacking every corner, only to find to their disappointment that the tomb contained no more than an empty sarcophagus. When Belzoni effected its transportation to England, the trustees of the British Museum considered the price set too high and the treasure was without a buyer until 1824. Sir John Soane paid £2,000 sterling for it and it now sits in the museum that bears Sir John's name in London.

The **Tomb of Tutankhamun** is the smallest and, surprisingly, least impressive of the royal tombs in the Valley of the Kings; it is difficult to imagine how his fabulous treasure fitted into it. It was discovered in 1922 by British archaeologist Howard Carter, working for the wealthy English Lord Carnarvon. During the first six fruitless years of Carter's search it was estimated that 200,000 tons of rubble were moved before he finally located the tomb immediately beneath that of Ramses VI, where roughly-constructed workmen's huts had been built on the fallen rubble, completely obscuring its entrance.

Whatever had been expected or hoped for, there is no doubt that the tomb's actual contents surpassed the wildest dreams. When Carter first looked into the tomb and was asked "What do you see?" he replied: "Wonderful things!" It must have been very hard for him to resist the temptation to enter the tomb before his sponsor arrived from England, and some believe he never did.

Tutankhamun was the only pharaoh to escape the grave robbers, who were so effective that the priests eventually removed 40 of the mummies for safety's sake and reburied them near the temple of Queen Hatshepsut, where they were subsequently discovered in 1899. The lengths to which the kings went to conceal their burial places is proved

Some tombs are hidden in the rock at the top of the valley.

most graphically by the **Tomb of Tuthmosis III,** hidden up in the crevice right at the back of the valley, and which has several twists, turns and traps in its construction to fool robbers. The wall decorations are in a more spare, graphic style that makes an interesting contrast to the richness of the others.

Queens and offspring: Back to the south beyond Quornah, the **Valley of the Queens** contains tombs of royal consorts and also of princes who died in the spring of youth. The most famous tomb is that of **Nefertari**, favourite wife of Ramses II. Having been restored with help from the Getty Foundation, this tomb, one of the most impressive monuments, was opened in 1995 for the first time since its discovery in 1904, albeit to no more than 200 people a day.

One of the most appealing tombs in the Valley of the Queens, however, is that of prince **Amon-hir-Khopshef.** He is portrayed being led by his father, Ramses III, through the mystical regions of the underworld. Ramses introduces the boy, one by one, to the various gods of the dead. The reliefs are of fine quality, in excellently preserved colour.

Lives of the noble: Just as the royal tombs on the Theban necropolis provide an insight into the realm of the dead, the 400 tombs in the **Valley of the Nobles** reveal aspects of the everyday life of important officials in the New Kingdom.

The **Tomb of Rekhmire,** for example, contains numerous painted scenes of jewellery-making, pottery manufacture, and carpentry as well as a court of law, in which tax evaders are brought to justice. Rekhmire was vizier under Tuthmosis III and his son, Amenhotep II. He was an outstanding official who was entrusted with so many duties that there was nothing, he wrote of himself in an inscription, "of which I am ignorant in heaven, on earth or in any part of the underworld."

The Tomb of Rekhmire was inhabited by a *felaheen* family for many years, and the wall decorations suffered somewhat. Nevertheless the tomb is a memorial to personal greatness and is, in the words of British Egyptologist James Breasted, "the most important private monument of the Empire."

The **Tomb of Ramose** is also historically and artistically noteworthy. Ramose was the vizier in the reign of Amenhotep III and his son, Amenhotep IV, later Akhenaten, leader of the rebel dynasty who promoted the worship of one god. Ramose's tomb provides a unique opportunity to see classical reliefs alongside the "realism" encouraged by Akhenaten.

One scene, for example, depicts Ramose standing before his seated pharaoh, who is depicted in the stylised majesty of traditional royal representations; on the opposite wall Ramose stands beneath a balcony in which Akhenaten and his wife Nefertiti stand in an informal posture beneath the symbol of the Aten, a solar disc with rays ending in hands holding the symbols of life and prosperity.

The **Tomb of Nakht,** though small, ranks as one of the finest in the group. The reliefs are executed with infinite charm and are in a good state of repair. Nakht was a scribe of the granaries under Tuthmosis IV and his tomb has reliefs of agricultural scenes including ploughing, digging and sowing, as well as stages of the harvest, especially measuring and winnowing the grain, reaping and pressing it into baskets. One of the most delightful scenes shows the nobleman on an outing with his family. He is depicted standing in a papyrus craft spearing fish and shooting fowl while his little daughter holds his leg to prevent him from falling into the water (*see picture on page 157*).

This tomb was recently the subject of an experiment that will not be repeated. Milan Kovac, a member of the Swedish Projection of Cultural Heritage Group, originated and installed a World Bank-sponsored pilot project to protect the tomb by means of a tube that isolated visitors from valuable reliefs.

The air-tight tube, made of safety glass, enables visitors to see the wall decorations while keeping their breath and exploring fingertips safely away. The temperature is controlled by the temperature of the tomb, not the outside air. Unfortunately, the project has received more criticism than praise. It was unflatteringly likened to a nightclub, a telephone booth, and "a far cry from the masterpiece of antiquity that it is." As a result, the Supreme Council for Antiquities has rejected the idea of repeating the experiment.

Endangered monuments: There are literally hundreds of tombs on the Theban necropolis, only a sampling of which are open to the public. Some have been "lost", that is to say, they were opened and partly recorded by early Egyptologists in the 19th and early part of the 20th centuries, but have since become filled with sand, all signs of their presence obliterated. Locating them again, properly recording and documenting them is one of the prime tasks of Egyptologists today.

One of the most important archaeological projects being carried out is a project to produce the first detailed map of the necropolis since 1921. Known as the Berkeley Theban Mapping Project it has made use of the most up-to-date equipment, and even hot-air balloons for low-level photographs of the hidden valleys and mortuary temples. Only when the monuments have been properly identified can steps be taken for their protection, and Luxor is today one of the most threatened archaeological sites in the world.

The threat comes from three sources: contamination, desecration and abuse – that is to say, environmental contamination from humidity and sub-soil water, plunder by grave robbers, and injury by tourists. The first is most difficult to control and although efforts to curb the environmental contamination have been carried out for many years now it seems to be a losing battle. As Egyptologist Michael Jones observed, "You cannot save a monument; all you can really do, in the long run, is to delay its rate of destruction." A sobering thought.

The deterioration of the reliefs on ancient monuments is even visible to the naked eye. The atmosphere – more humid as a result of water stored in Lake Nasser – and the air pollution from

Tomb paintings in the Valley of the Nobles.

factories is adversely affecting Egypt's ancient treasures. But worse still is the higher than average watertable since the construction of the High Dam, which results in salt-laden moisture creeping up the temple walls like some cursed disease, leaving the reliefs pimpled, festered and spoiled, after which they quite literally flake off.

Plunder of tombs is another serious problem. So long as there have been tombs, there have been robbers, but the tragedy of modern-day plunder is that the antiquities are lost to the world of art and scholarship, because they too often make their way out of the country through antique dealers and into private collections. The Egyptian government has clamped down on illicit digging and is working at many levels to curb or restore any damage, but with literally tens of thousands of monuments on both sides of the Nile, the task is a massive one. Meanwhile epigraphers are hard at work, accurately documenting whatever they can in order to have as accurate a record as possible on file.

The injury caused by tourists is being attended to on many levels. Alternative itineraries to different monuments in such popular places as the Valley of the Kings and of the Nobles is beginning to ease pressure on certain sites. Ground-rules for tourists – and, indeed, tour leaders – are being established. New access roads to the monuments are being constructed, as well as a bus terminus at a safer distance from the tombs and temples.

One recurring suggestion has been a project to keep tourists out of the most frequently visited royal tombs altogether. The possibility of building several concrete replicas of some of the most famous tombs (as with Tutankhamun's tomb), which will be buried in the cliff face, is being considered. The idea is to provide tourists with an opportunity to see the marvels of ancient Egypt while safeguarding the tombs themselves. The project was presented by the Switzerland-based Society of Friends of the Egyptian Royal Tombs, who have already carried out similar projects to threatened areas elsewhere in the world. "We have found a favourable response in Egypt," said a spokesman.

Tour companies and guides, however, are not so pleased with the idea. "Who wants to see a replica, when people come all the way to Egypt to see the real thing?" they say. "And to expect people to pay a huge entrance fee for an imitation tomb if they particularly want to see an original, is unrealistic," they add. "It will simply stop a lot of people from coming to Egypt."

The latter is extremely unlikely. Since Napoleon Bonaparte unlocked the door to the past in 1798, tourism to Egypt has steadily increased, and it is likely to continue to do so. After all, more is known about Egypt's heritage than any other ancient culture. Egypt has the only surviving wonder of the ancient world, the Pyramid of Cheops at Giza, and such monuments as the Colossi of Memnon, the Hypostyle Hall at Karnak, the Temple of Hatshepsut, and the royal tombs in the Valleys of the Kings and Queens. These are enough to lure human beings back to their ancient heritage.

Left, damaged carving in the Ramesseum. Right, endangered hieroglyphs at Medinet Habu.

DISCOVERING TUTANKHAMUN

The awesome sight which Howard Carter made out by flickering candlelight when he opened up Tutankhamun's disturbed but generally intact tomb in 1922 was all the more remarkable because, as royal tombs go, it probably was rather modest. The factor which had allowed it to go unplundered was the occupant's insignificance, a king stuck on the throne to keep it warm after Egypt's worst royal scandal. Tutankhamun was so forgettable that two of his successors chose to be buried practically on top of him.

The majestic pyramids of an earlier age than Tutankhamun's were altogether too conspicuous to be secure tombs for kings and their treasure. The later practice of building a monumental funerary temple in one place and discreetly burying the body in another, e.g. in the Valley of the Kings, was aimed at throwing grave robbers off the scent.

However, it became common knowledge that the Valley of the Kings was riddled with fabulous wealth and the chances of evading detection were slim. Tutankhamun's was probably the last undiscovered royal tomb in the valley, so the search for more had to turn elsewhere. It was known that the pharaohs of the 21st and 22nd Dynasties (Tutankhamun's having been towards the end of the 18th) were not happy with the arrangements near Luxor and had chosen to be buried near the old Hyksos capital of Tanis (the modern San el Hagar) in the Delta.

In 1939 the archaeologist Pierre Montet found five royal tombs near San el Hagar, two of them intact. The contents were priceless: lashings of gold, silver, precious stones, jewellery and, an unusual touch, a king (Psusennes I) wearing gold caps on his fingers and toes and a pair of solid gold sandals. The discovery was hailed as potentially greater than Carter's, but although the contents are on display in the Cairo Museum, the fuss over the discovery curiously waned. Montet's parting shot on his retirement in 1951 was that he had

unshaken faith in the existence of more royal tombs in the valley of San el Hagar.

Tutankhamun was as unfamiliar to ordinary people in 1922 as Psusennes, Osorkon, Takelot and Sheshonk – Montet's finds – were and probably still are. He grew up in the shadow of the Akhenaten heresy, a business so distasteful that the official king-list was quickly doctored to deny even the existence of the king concerned.

The succession was murky and there is doubt whether the caretaker "Smenkhare" was the lovely dowager Queen Nefertiti or the man who had usurped her husband's affection, possibly Tutankhamun's brother. In any case, the youthful Tutankhamun took over within a year, married Nefertiti's daughter, renounced his heretical upbringing, and died at a tender age.

When compared with Ramses II, for example, Tutankhamun was a very minor monarch, and when in 1907 a shallow pit in the Valley of the Kings was found to contain a bundle of tacky clothing, some stained linen and the remains of food in jars, it was thought likely that Tutankhamun's name on one of the jars meant that this was his tomb and represented what his peers thought of him.

Howard Carter, who had previously worked for the Antiquities Service in the valley, had other ideas which he was able to impress upon Lord Carnarvon, an authority on Egyptian antiquity in his own right and a man with money. Carter began work in 1915 and without much to show for it seven years later was advised by Carnarvon that his contract would not be extended. Carter had not been allowed to follow his instinct and dig in a certain area because it lay in the path of tourists wishing to visit the tomb of Ramses VI, who had lived some hundreds of years after Tutankhamun and usurped the tomb of his predecessor but one, Ramses IV.

On arriving for work on 4 November 1922, Carter was immediately aware that something out of the ordinary had happened. His diggers had been exploring the foundations of houses which had been built to accommodate the workers on the Ramses tomb, and they had just come across a step cut into the rock beneath. By the following afternoon they had exposed a flight of 16 steps and, at the bottom, a sealed door. The seal was merely that of some necropolis guard, not a royal one, but Carter dashed off a cable to Carnarvon, refilled the hole for security's sake, and sportingly waited 17 days for Carnarvon to arrive. Together they cleared the entrance and at the bottom of the door hit the jackpot. There, still intact, was the seal of Tutankhamun.

Beyond the door lay a sloping passage full of rubble which showed evidence of someone having wriggled a way through it – one of the dreaded robbers. About 30 ft (9 metres) along the passage Carter found another door which had ominously been opened and resealed. "The decisive moment had arrived," he later wrote. "With trembling hands, I made a tiny breach in the upper left-hand corner... widening the hole a little, I inserted the candle and peered in. At first I could see nothing, the hot air escaping from the chamber, causing the candle flame to flicker but presently, as my eyes grew accustomed to the light..."

Standing behind him, Carnarvon could no longer stand the suspense. "Can you see anything?" he asked. Carter's reply has joined the lexicon of quotable quotations: "Yes, wonderful things!"

The miserly proportions of the chamber reflected Tutankhamun's lowly status, but to Carter's astonishment it was packed with an untidy mess of three gilded beds, two golden chariots, various chairs and stools, two black and gold life-size statues and a huge assortment of objects including a trumpet which still works today.

That proved to be only the antechamber, and on 17 February 1923 began the exciting job of chipping away at the plaster to see what lay beyond. "I inserted an electric torch," Carter wrote. "An astonishing sight its light revealed, for there, within a yard of the doorway, stood what to all appearances was a solid wall of gold."

It was not a wall, but the side of a massive golden shrine. Carter managed to squeeze around it to find an open doorway which led to the treasury, a small room watched over by the life-size statue of a crouching guard dog. The gilded beds, statues and so forth were an understated clue to what lay in the treasury, an unbelievable collection of wealth. The box-like shrine provided the most exciting striptease ever performed. When a way was devised to open it up, it was found to contain another only marginally smaller. It came apart like a Russian doll, four shrines in all.

A whole year was taken to reach the fourth and final shrine, time enough to work out that the robbers, whoever they were, had got no further than the antechamber. They must have been caught as they were about to depart with the loot. The guards would have hastily restored the contents – no time to lay them out, just shove them in – and reseal the entrance.

The fourth shrine produced a yellow quartzite sarcophagus with a lid of pink granite. "The contents were completely covered with linen shrouds," Carter recalled. "As the last shroud was removed a gasp of wonderment escaped our lips, so gorgeous was the sight that met our eyes; a golden effigy of the young boy-king of most magnificent workmanship, filled the whole interior of the sarcophagus."

The weight of the coffin was such that a hoist was needed to move it. It contained, in a repetition of the multi-layered shrine, a second smaller coffin. On 17 October 1926, four years after Carter's cable summoning Carnarvon, the second coffin was opened, revealing what made the whole thing so heavy – a third and final coffin of solid gold, nearly 300 lb (110 kg) of it.

The mummy of the king was at last exposed: the now famous mask of gold with inlaid glass and lapis lazuli. The mask had protected the face well but the rest of the body had carbonised. The results of the postmortem on Tutankhamun's remains only compounded the mystery of why – and also how – such time, money and effort should and could have been invested in a king whose right of accession was at least dubious and whose death was swift.

The postmortem put his age between 16 and 17, and revealed a curious condition behind the left ear; Egyptology seems to produce as many questions as answers, and one intriguing question that may be added to the list is whether this seemingly inoffensive boy was launched to unintended and possibly unjustified fame by a sneaky crack on the back of the head. ∎

LUXOR TO ABYDOS

North of Luxor the river Nile sweeps to the northeast, flowing easily past verdant fields and the town of **Qift** (ancient Coptos) which is of no particular interest today, but was an important trading centre in ancient times. It was the starting point of a caravan route from the Nile valley to the Red Sea through the Wadi Hammamat.

Today a tarmac road connects the Nile valley to the Red Sea here, and travelling along it one can visualise the ancient traders, even after the Islamic conquest of Egypt, making their way along the dusty thoroughfare from the port of Quseir on the coast, laden with goods from the Far East.

"Qift only lost its importance after the Suez Canal was opened in 1869," explains a long-time resident of Luxor. "Now it has nothing to distinguish it, not even any ancient monuments." But Qift cannot be overlooked because it crops up again and again in the literature on ancient Egypt as the area sacred to the licentious god Min, a guardian of the Eastern desert.

Immediately to the south of **Qena**, the chief town of the province of the same name situated some 12 miles (20 km) further north, is the village of **Ballas** on the western bank of the Nile. This is where the distinctive *ballas* pottery is made from the large clay deposits in the region and, if you are lucky, you may see the pots lined along the bank of the river awaiting shipment. These, by the way, are the distinctive pots that women carry so gracefully on their heads as they go to draw water from the Nile. As you sail pass Qena, you may even catch sight of a sailing boat with a cargo laden with *ballas* being shipped northwards. Qena, like Qift, was a town with a link to the Red Sea in ancient times, with the port of Safaga, but today it is of no particular significance.

The river now takes a great curve to the southwest before continuing its flow towards the north. Within the curve is our first port of call, **Dendera**, famed for its great temple that cannot, unfortunately, be seen from the river. Although little less than a mile from the bank of the Nile, it is hidden by copious palm trees, and lies on the edge of the fertile plain with desert behind.

Finished by the Romans: This was the site sacred to the cow-goddess Hathor and the temple in her honour was built in Ptolemaic times (332–30 BC) and completed in the Roman period after 250 years of work. In dedicating a temple to Egypt's cow-goddess, the Ptolemaic kings were honouring one of Egypt's best loved deities. Usually depicted as a cow, Hathor was sometimes represented as a female figure with the head of a cow, and there are representations of her in most Egyptian temples.

The Temple of Dendera, like that of Edfu, is one of the best preserved in Egypt, even though it does show signs of the destruction carried out after it ceased to be used for worship. Indeed, some of the chapels and chambers were used by the local people for dwelling places through to the early part of this

century. The temple itself is surrounded by the rubble of its largely decaying outer walls.

Among the many noteworthy features of this temple is the **hypostyle hall**, where 18 Hathor-headed columns support a roof divided into seven registers and decorated with remarkable astrological scenes. The six signs of the Egyptian zodiac which are depicted are the crab, the twins, the bull, the ram, the fishes and the water carrier. Many can be identified because their original colour has been remarkably well preserved.

Another noteworthy feature is the series of reliefs that links the traditions of Hathor of Dendera with those of Horus of Edfu. Horus and Hathor were two deities of equal standing; husband and wife. At each site the triad consisted of Hathor, Horus and their son (who bore a different name at each place). Twice a year, on the occasion of the birthday of each deity, the "Festival of the Good Union" was celebrated. It must have been one of the most picturesque in the land and reliefs on the walls of the staircase leading to the roof – approached from the antechamber to the rear of the second hypostyle hall, and affording an excellent view of desert and floodplain – describe the event.

The sacred statues of the two deities would, at the start of the festival, be taken out of their respective shrines for the reunion. The vessel bearing the statue of Hathor would be carried upstream, while that of Horus would set off downstream, each in a splendid procession. Where the boats came together, they were encircled by a rope cast by other vessels, in a gesture of unity. Then the river craft would make their way to the appropriate temple to celebrate the reunion of husband and wife amidst joy, song and prayer.

In the Ptolemaic period Hathor was identified with the Greek goddess Aphrodite and began to enjoy immense popularity as "Mistress of music, dance and joy". However some of the dignity of Hathor as the mother-goddess sacred to the Egyptians was lost when her temple became the "home of intoxication and place of enjoyment". It is interest- ing to observe that among the Roman emperors depicted in the temple are Augustus, Tiberius, Caligula, Claudius and Nero.

A **Christian basilica** was built near the ruins of this temple. It, too, is worth noting because it is one of the earliest Roman basilicas and may possibly be the famous Christian centre of the 4th century where 50,000 monks assembled to celebrate the Easter Festival, which was described by St Jerome as being somewhere in the neighbourhood of Dendera.

Christian discoveries: The river Nile now continues its great sweep from east to west, so that the eastern bank of the Nile is to the north, and the western to the south. The tiny and inconsequential village of **Faw** can be spotted to the north, worth mentioning because it is the site of the basilica of St Pachomius, the father of the monastic way of life, who founded his first monastery in about AD 320.

As the Nile continues north, the rugged cliffs of **Gebel el-Tarif** become visible. They often appear murky against the skyline, especially when the sun is overhead, but look closely and you will see that they are of immense height. This was the range of hills where the Gnostic codices or books – as famous and as important as the Dead Sea scrolls – were discovered in 1947.

Accounts of the discovery differ. According to one, a huge boulder fell off a slope revealing a jar that was found by peasant farmers. In another account, two brothers chanced upon the jars while they were digging for fertiliser. Their discovery has proved to be vitally important to our understanding of the spread of Christianity in Egypt.

Perhaps the codices themselves were deliberately hidden when the Byzantine church stamped out what they regarded as heretical Christian groups around the year AD 400. At that time the Gnostics were hounded into silence in the name of orthodox Christianity, and until recently not much was known about them. Now the 12 codices, which are known as the Nag Hammadi Library, are housed in the Coptic Museum in Cairo.

Christian sites in this part of Upper Egypt become more numerous from this point on, although few can be seen as you sail along the river. Within an enclosed area created by the Nile describing a course to the south and then to the west before resuming its flow to the northwest again, the land is extremely fertile and picturesque. It remains to this day a predominantly Christian area, especially in the vicinity of the **Monastery of St Palomon**, whose bell-tower and latticed walls can usually be seen in the distance, rising above the surrounding agricultural land.

St Palomon, or *Anba Balamun* in Arabic, was one of the earliest anchorites in Upper Egypt. He was said to have eventually died from excessive fasting. A *mulid* or annual celebration is still observed in his honour.

On to the land: The most northerly point of most Nile cruises, **Nag Hammadi** is a large and sprawling provincial town whose population exploded in the 1960s when a large sugar refinery and an aluminium factory were built

there. A bridge crosses the Nile at this point, and the boats usually moor to the east, their passengers transferring to buses to visit the archaeological site of Abydos. Taxis can be hired by those who wish to venture even further north, to see the many sites of Middle Egypt. Remember in any negotiations with taxi drivers in Upper Egypt that bargaining is always part of the game.

Abydos is on the western bank of the Nile and an 18-mile (30-km) drive from Nag Hammadi. Balyana is its nearest riverside town for those who are travelling southwards by road, and a broad plain leads to the village of Kerba, which flanks the ancient site.

This latter village was where Umm Seti ("mother of Seti") lived for many years in the mid-20th century. She was known among the American community as a strange and rather eccentric Englishwoman who had come first to Egypt on holiday, but who had stayed on after some extraordinary and revelational experiences. She claimed to be able to speak with ancient gods and

The Temple of Abydos.

kings, and to be the mother of the pharaoh Seti in a previous life.

Umm Seti certainly had a great affinity with Abydos and knew its history intimately. She had come to Egypt as a young woman, married an Egyptian, learned Egyptology, and had worked in the Antiquities Department for many years. She bore a son whom she called Seti and it was among the local inhabitants of Kerba, where she lived for the latter years of her life, that she was affectionately known as Umm Seti.

Abydos was one of ancient Egypt's most sacred cities; a city to which annual pilgrimage was made in ancient times just as, today, Muslims journey to Mecca, and Christians and Jews go to Jerusalem. The temple was the cult centre of Egypt's most beloved hero and the central figure of the popular Osiris legend, repeated in the wall reliefs of many of their temples.

The Osiris legend: Osiris might have been an actual king of Egypt who was so loved by his people that his memory lingered on long after his death, passing from generation to generation. The Greek historian Plutarch was the first to record the Osiris legend in a coherent account. He described Osiris as the creator of law and agriculture, who, with his wife Isis at his side, ruled the world with justice. His brother Set, however, was jealous of his favours and conspired against him. At a banquet, he tricked Osiris into entering a chest which was then slammed closed, sealed and thrown into the Nile.

The broken-hearted Isis wandered far and wide in misery seeking the body of her loved husband. Accompanied on her sad mission by the goddess Nepthys, she eventually found the body entangled in a tamarisk bush in the marshes of the Delta. She carefully hid it, but the vicious Set, out boar-hunting, came across the body and cut it into 14 pieces, scattering it in all directions.

The dismayed Isis continued her mission. She searched out the pieces of her husband's body (at each spot where a part was found a monument was erected, which accounts for the widespread legend) and sought the help of the jackal-god Anubis – who became god of embalming – to prepare it for burial. While he carried out her orders, Isis wept then prayed; somehow her dead lord revitalised enough to give her his seed so that she could bring forth an heir.

In due course she had a son, Horus, whom she raised in the marshes of the Delta until he was strong enough to avenge his father's death by slaying Set. Horus then set out to seek his father and raise him from the dead. The risen Osiris, however, could no longer reign in the kingdom on earth and now became king of the underworld, while Horus took over the throne of his father on earth.

This widely known and most loved of ancient legends has been subject to many interpretations. One of the functions of mythology is to explain certain natural, social or political ideas, and the mythical Osiris (who was associated with settled community living and hence involved in agriculture and the annual rebirth of the land) falling victim to Seth (who was associated with the relentless desert) is thought to explain the physical environment and the constant battle against the encroaching desert.

Set's tearing the body of Osiris to pieces and scattering its parts up and down the Nile valley may be interpreted as the concept of sowing grain, following which, with the necessary incantations (like those performed by Isis and Nepthys), or rural festivals, the stalks of grain would be reborn as Osiris was reborn. Thus Horus, son of gods related to the rebirth of the land, triumphed over the desert (Set) and became the prototype of the pharaohs.

The myth of Osiris had become so well known by the Middle Kingdom, around 2,000 BC, that thousands of pilgrims from all walks of life annually came to Abydos to pay homage to their legendary ancestor. They would travel long distances to witness the ritualistic killing of Osiris by his brother Set, followed by several days of mourning and lamentation in the manner of Isis, his beloved wife. At a prescribed site a mock battle took place between Horus, son of Osiris and Isis, and Set his murderer. The death of Osiris was duly avenged, Horus became king and life would go on.

The temples: Abydos rose to the peak of its power as a holy city by the New Kingdom (1567–1080 BC), and pharaohs left signs of their devotion in the great monuments they erected there. The most frequently visited of these are the temples of **Seti I** and **Ramses II**. The former is one of the most beautiful in Egypt. Seti encouraged an artistic and architectural revival in his reign and the temple is decorated with finely carved and coloured reliefs, in a good state of preservation.

Noteworthy are the scenes (in the hypostyle hall on the eastern and northern walls) showing the pharaoh's active participation in the planning of a temple. He is depicted, in one scene, facing the goddess Seshat who was patron deity of records and archives. The goddess is shown driving stakes into the ground to measure out the ground-plan. Behind her is Osiris, who watches over the activities being conducted on his behalf. Above is a scene of Seti, assisted by Horus, stretching out a measuring rope, thus showing that he himself was personally involved in its construction.

In each of the shrines of the temple seven scenes depict daily ceremonies that were performed by priests. They include the burning of incense, perfuming and annointing the statue of the deity, adorning it with crown and jewels, and then withdrawing, backwards, while brushing away all footprints from the shrine before finally closing the door.

There is a certain naturalism in the reliefs in this temple that differs from the conservative canons of Egyptian art. The many representations of Seti, for example, may appear carbon copies of one another, but, on close scrutiny, they will be found to differ. As the king looks into the face of an honoured deity, his expression is one of reverence. Before a goddess, there is a look of loving trust. Facing one of the great gods, he bends slightly at the waist to indicate awe. Such emotional expression is not to be found in all temples, where the pharaoh

Excavations in progress at Abydos.

generally stands proudly erect and exalted. In the Temple of Seti, even the gods have human emotions: Osiris looks benevolent and majestic. Isis is gracious and tender. Horus is competent and direct.

To the rear of the temple is a wall which is covered with a list of Egypt's ancient rulers, a list which has been the basis of much of our reconstruction of pharaonic times. There are, however, notable omissions from the list: Queen Hatshepsut and Kings Amenhotep (Akhenaten) and Tutankhamun.

By the Graeco-Roman period, Abydos had came to be regarded as a place of healing. Sufferers from all over Egypt and, indeed, all over the Graeco-Roman world, gathered in the corridors and halls of the temple of Seti to make humble pleas for health or fertility. Graffiti on the walls in hieratic (a late form of hieroglyphics), Greek, Phoenician and Aramaic attest to this.

Unfortunately, the Temple of Seti, like others throughout Egypt, is suffering from sub-soil water and air pollution. One of the most seriously threatened parts of the temple is a separate structure that lies behind the main temple, known as the Osirion. It is sunk into a depression and has variously been called a cenotaph and a mortuary temple, though nobody knows for sure what it actually is. There is, however, a longstanding tradition of the sanctity of the area around the Osirion, and when the 13th-Dynasty Pharaoh Neferhotep (*circa* 1786 BC) erected a boundary stele at Abydos, it stated that none should set foot in the sacred place.

Up until the time of its recent restoration in the 1980s, the waters of the Osirion were regarded as advantageous to health. This recalls the hundreds of texts connecting Osiris with Abydos, with water, and with rebirth, in which this most beloved figure of ancient Egyptian tradition "sleeps in the midst of water". It is a pity that it is water seepage that is causing so much damage to the monuments up and down the length of the Nile valley.

Oldest cemetery: In the vicinity of

The desert from Dendera.

Abydos, slightly to the north, is the site of ancient **Thinis**, the home town of Narmer (Menes), the first pharaoh, who is credited with the unification of the two lands of Upper and Lower Egypt around 3100 BC. Narmer and his successors ruled from Memphis, the predecessor of Cairo, at the apex of the Delta, but they never forgot their ancestral home. Among the barren hills west of Abydos they constructed impressive cenotaphs where relatives and friends could make suitable offerings.

Generation after generation left offerings in pottery vessels, particularly at the cenotaph of the First Dynasty Pharaoh Djer, which was believed to be the actual tomb of Osiris. Today the site has acquired the name **Om el-Gaab**, or "mother of potsherds". It is not on the tourist track, but for those with time to spare, this archaic cemetery, approached from a track leading westwards from the village of Kerba, is worth seeing.

The huge funerary structures are believed to be the cenotaphs of Egypt's earliest kings who were buried in similar graves on the Sakkara plateau. The huge outer walls of the tombs were decorated with recessed panelling, and surrounding them were two enclosure walls also built of brick. The subterranean chambers, hewn deep in the bedrock, contained funerary equipment including tools, weapons, stone and copper vessels as well as jewellery. Surrounding many of the tombs were subsidiary graves for retainers of the deceased pharaoh, who, as and when they died, were buried in the vicinity of their monarch in order to serve him in the afterlife as dutifully as they had served him on earth.

Before leaving Abydos it should be mentioned that, according to some of the mortuary texts, the "afterlife" lay in a gap in the mountains to the west of here. Indeed, the afterlife is depicted as a long mountainous valley with a river running through it; the banks are lined with wheatfields, fruit orchards and gardens of flowers. Here the deceased would enjoy hunting and fishing forever in the "Field of Reeds".

An artist's impression.

MIDDLE EGYPT

The term "Middle Egypt" describes the area that lies between Abydos and Memphis. It is a long stretch of land where the river is wide and flows a smooth course through verdant fields, with good paved roads on both sides of the river. The road to the east runs through the desert while the west travels along picturesque canals, cultivated fields, and through towns and villages. Despite the tedious traffic, the latter route is the more interesting, especially as the farmers can be seen at work at much closer quarters than is possible on the river cruise.

Although the archaeological sites of Middle Egypt are less well known than those around Cairo and in Upper Egypt, Middle Egypt has four areas of special historic importance: Tel el-Amarna, Ashmounein, Tuna el-Gebel and Beni Hassan. There are tourist facilities at each of these places – regular barge services across the river and vehicles for transport to the sites – and the local officials, guards and guides are refreshingly informative and anxious to please.

An experience at Beni Hassan typifies the attitude. "Our young men and women," explains one of the old guards in a flowing *gallabiyya* at the resthouse, "are taking courses on ancient history at university and we, their parents, who have been *ghaffirs* (guards) all our lives and are used to dealing with archaeologists and tourists, are giving them practical training."

Middle Egypt is a delightful place to visit and the area is fast becoming popular among Cairenes for weekend excursions. But terrorist incidents can cause travel between Minia and Luxor to be restricted at times.

In ancient times, this central area was a separate political entity, one of three. It was the Middle Kingdom Pharaoh Senusert III (*circa* 1898 BC) who defined the first area, between Aswan and Abydos, as "the head" of Upper Egypt; the region from Abydos to Memphis as "Upper Egypt" (not Middle Egypt!), and the third region, as today, as the Delta.

The archaeological sites in Middle Egypt are of more than passing interest but they take time to reach. Those visitors keen to see the best of the region should, if circumstances permit, arrange overnight accommodation in **Minia**. This is the chief town of the province, about 155 miles (250 km) south of central Cairo. Minia is a sprawling urban area of about 200,000 people, with a choice of several hotels ranging from the turn-of-the-century Palace where there is more charm and atmosphere than comfort, to the 5-Star Etap. The Lotus and Nefertiti hotels have a reputation for "satisfying" meals. From here excursions to the sites are easily arranged.

Schism city: The first port of call from here is **Tel el-Amarna**, known today simply as Amarna. It lies on the eastern bank of the Nile opposite the modern town of Deir Mawas and was the site chosen by the Pharaoh Akhenaten (formerly Amenhotep IV) to found a city dedicated to the worship of a single god, the Aten (literally the sun's disc), rather than the whole pantheon of gods worshipped by his predecessors, who had founded Thebes.

Akhenaten's introduction of the worship of one god is frequently regarded as a form of monotheism. In Akhenaten himself, some scholars have seen metaphysical reasoning far ahead of the times, while others assert that his religion offered nothing new. Indeed, Akhenaten has been variously described as a mystic and an ascetic, or alternatively as a rebel and a fanatic.

In fact, worship of the Aten was not so much a new realm of thought, since worship of the sun in one form or another is apparent throughout ancient Egyptian history. The novelty lay in the recognition of the unlimited power of the sun-god as the creator and preserver of all mankind.

The celebrated hymn, which is inscribed in the tomb of one of his officials, has been ascribed to Akhenaten himself: "O... O living Aten... how manifold are thy works... thou sole god, like to whom there is no other. Thou didst create the earth after thy heart... even all men, herds and flocks, whatever is upon the earth, creatures that walk upon feet, which soar aloft flying with their wings…" (From a translation by Sir A. Gardiner in *Egypt of the Pharaohs*, Clarendon Press Oxford.)

When Akhenaten revolted against the priests of Amon-Ra at Thebes, he chose for his new capital this expansive crescent-shaped plain over 2½ miles (4 km) long and about half a mile (800 metres) across. The plain he had chosen was a site with no history of cult activity, no earlier settlement nor any existing priesthood. Akhenaten called it *Akhet-Aten*, the "Horizon of Aten".

At first sight Tel el-Amarna appears to be devoid of ancient structures and it is difficult to visualise a bustling city here. The site is a far cry from the legendary "hundred-gated Thebes" that we have already described. The reason for the lack of standing monuments is that Tel el-Amarna was totally razed after the pharaoh died. Once the priests of Amon-Ra had been reinstated and Luxor became the capital once more, all evidence of the religion of the Aten and the rule of "the heretic" were obliterated. All that was left of Akhenaten's unique city were a few walls and columns little more than waist high.

City planning: Yet it is from these ruins and from ground-plans that archaeologists have been able to study city-planning in ancient Egypt. Elsewhere those palaces and dwelling-places which had been built of sun-dried brick have since perished. The city of *Akhet-Aten*, however, was constructed on a plain above the level of the flood and was occupied for such a brief time (it was never returned to by further habitants) that it provides a unique opportunity to learn how an ancient city developed.

The site was designed with three main streets running parallel to the river. The central quarter, which spreads southwards from the modern village of el-Til to that of el-Hag Khandil, was the main residential area and also the site of the temple of the Aten. Some of the ruins of these can still be seen, though, visitors be warned, they are not very impressive to the layman!

The story of Tel el-Amarna, as told on site.

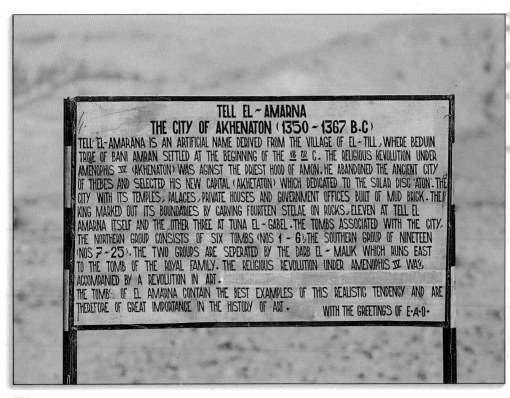

TELL EL~AMARNA
THE CITY OF AKHENATON (1350~1367 B·C)

TELL EL-AMARANA IS AN ARTIFICIAL NAME DERIVED FROM THE VILLAGE OF EL~TILL, WHERE BEDUIN TRIBE OF BANI AMRAN SETTLED AT THE BEGINNING OF THE 18 TH C. THE RELIGIOUS REVOLUTION UNDER AMENOPHIS IV (AKHENATON) WAS AGINST THE PRIEST HOOD OF AMON. HE ABANDONED THE ANCIENT CITY OF THEBES AND SELECTED HIS NEW CAPITAL (AKHETATON) WHICH DEDICATED TO THE SOLAR DISC 'ATON'. THE CITY WITH ITS TEMPLES, PALACES, PRIVATE HOUSES AND GOVERNMENT OFFICES BUILT OF MUD BRICK. THE KING MARKED OUT ITS BOUNDARIES BY CARVING FOURTEEN STELAE ON ROCKS, ELEVEN AT TELL EL AMARNA ITSELF AND THE OTHER THREE AT TUNA EL~GABEL. THE TOMBS ASSOCIATED WITH THE CITY, THE NORTHERN GROUP CONSISTS OF SIX TOMBS (NOS 1~6), THE SOUTHERN GROUP OF NINETEEN (NOS 7~25). THE TWO GROUPS ARE SEPERATED BY THE DARB EL~MALIK WHICH RUNS EAST TO THE TOMB OF THE ROYAL FAMILY. THE RELIGIOUS REVOLUTION UNDER AMENOPHIS IV WAS ACCOMPANIED BY A REVOLUTION IN ART.
THE TOMBS OF EL AMARNA CONTAIN THE BEST EXAMPLES OF THIS REALISTIC TENDENCY AND ARE THEREFORE OF GREAT IMPORTANCE IN THE HISTORY OF ART.   WITH THE GREETINGS OF E·A·O·

To the north and south were habitations for officials and priests. The side streets contained houses of the middle classes and servants. And the working classes, especially those employed on the necropolis, lived in special compounds to the east of the plain. Their houses were built on parallel streets and were uniform in size, apart from one larger house to each compound which probably belonged to the community's supervisor.

Akhenaten took up residence at *Akhet-Aten* with his family in the eighth year of his reign, about 1367 BC. He set up boundary stelae on the cliffs on both sides of the Nile, recording an oath in the name of his "father", the Aten, that neither he, his wife (Queen Nefertiti, whose famous bust is in the Berlin Museum) nor children would pass the limits he was setting, and that the land would remain sacred to the Aten forever. This was not to be. Shortly after the 14th year of his reign, Queen Nefertiti, for unknown reasons, took up residence in her northern palace. Akhenaten appointed his half-brother Smenkhare as co-regent, and died shortly afterwards. The sacred city, which was still under construction even then, was knocked to pieces.

Tomb scenes: Akhenaten's body has not been found, but his **tomb** is approached through a long narrow valley between the two mountain ranges to the east. Although not open to the public, it is worth mentioning because studies suggest that it was not a single tomb but a tomb complex; it may originally have been intended for the entire royal family. This would make it unique among royal tombs because kings were usually buried alone to ensure safety.

The tombs of the noblemen at Tel el-Amarna, however, can be visited, and it is from them that we get an insight into life during the short rule of Akhenaten. Although many were badly damaged, not all the reliefs were destroyed and the most important ones have now been carefully restored.

The tombs belonged to the refined citizens of the city and were hewn out of rock. One of the largest and best preserved belongs to a high priest called

Meri-Re (No. 4). In one of the reliefs Akhenaten can be seen at a palace window casting forth golden ornaments to the owner of the tomb. In another, he is depicted driving from his palace in a chariot, preceded by guards, and followed by the queen, the princesses and escorts, some in chariots and some on foot. Priests await their arrival at the temple, where, after the necessary prayers have been performed, the royal couple emerge and are greeted by other priests before inspecting the storehouses, barns and other chambers, some of which are enclosed in a garden.

These and other scenes were decorated in the unusual realism characteristic of what has become known as the "Amarna period". Unlike traditional art – in which the pharaoh ruled as a god and was symbolically depicted as a giant at temple entrance and in relief – Akhenaten was depicted quite naturalistically. He is often shown the same size as his people, as a mortal rather than as an aloof ruler, a family man who could delight in his daughters, eat a hearty meal, and demonstrate tender affection.

Fragments of slabs carved in relief were found in many homes at Amarna. They show figures of the royal family making offerings to the Aten, with a clear message: adore the one whom Akhenaten adores, and make offerings directly to the one to whom Akhenaten makes offerings.

Thoth worship: The ruins of the site of **Hermopolis** (modern **Ashmounein**) lie about 30 miles (50 km) north of Tel el-Amarna, on the western bank of the Nile. A good road from the nearest town of Mallawi across the fertile floodplain towards the site which, even in its ruined state, can be clearly seen in a picturesque palm grove.

This was the site of the ancient Egyptian city of *Khnumi* where Thoth, the beak-headed ancient Egyptian god of wisdom, was worshipped. Of the original pharaonic site, however, little remains apart from two gigantic statues of baboons, sacred animals of Thoth along with the ibis.

The elegant ruins at Hermopolis are,

in fact, a Greek *agora*, an area for an assembly of the people, and a market place. It had bazaars around the temples, and entrances and courtyards were adorned with carved statues of gods and heroes. The *agora* was the focus of social intercourse among the largely Greek community who lived in Hermopolis.

The Greeks identified Thoth with one of their own gods, Hermes, and under Greek rule the province was recharged with life. The annual Festival of Thoth was one of the most important in the land. It started at the beginning of the "season of the inundation", when the flood waters began to rise and Thoth, the "messenger of the gods", made announcements to the local priests.

From the surviving buildings – the columns, pedestals and open spaces – it is possible to visualise life in Graeco-Roman times: men, women and children milling round the bazaars where produce was sold; the stalls of fishmongers and bakers; craftsmen plying their wares; and, of course, the local population making their dutiful prayers and offerings at the main temple.

A few miles southeast of Hermopolis, situated just beyond the limits of the valley, is the necropolis of **Tuna el-Gebel**, a unique archaeological site where the galleries of the sacred ibis – also sacred to Thoth – are situated.

Ibis worship: This was the necropolis that the inhabitants of Hermopolis would visit. The ibis compound has been identified and near it is an extremely deep well which is fed by a waterwheel not unlike those that are still used for irrigation today.

The ibis galleries themselves are long underground passages that lead to chambers where the mummified ibis and baboons were interred. Although most of the remains have been placed in the nearby museum in Mallawi, many remain *in situ* and because the galleries are not very deep, light filters into the passages and creates a delightful, soft atmosphere within.

There is only one temple at Tuna el-Gebel, which may appear to be small

Boats on the river near Minia.

and insignificant compared to the ones already visited in Upper Egypt, but do not miss it. It is the **tomb of Petosiris**, a family tomb where eight generations of high priests of Hermopolis were buried. Although it is decorated on the facade with traditional Egyptian reliefs showing the deceased making offerings before the important deities, the inside is decorated with charming scenes, unlike any others in Egypt, that show particularly strong Greek influence in their workmanship.

The scenes themselves are traditional – farming, hunting and fowling – but the farmers are portrayed with thick jowls, muscular legs and togas that are decidedly non-Egyptian. Not only do the men have curly hair, but the branches of the trees also curl, and so even do the horns of the animals!

The local guard at Tuna el-Gebel seldom fails to draw the attention of the visitor to a small house-tomb which belongs to a girl who drowned in 120 BC. The name of the girl was Isadora, and the walls of her tomb are covered with stucco and painted with architectural themes such as imitation woodwork and marble.

Rock chambers: Some 13 miles (20 km) north of Mallawi, on the eastern bank of the Nile (almost opposite the modern town of Abu Kerkas), lies **Beni Hassan** – named after an Arab tribe that settled in the area in the 9th century – known for its famous Middle Kingdom tombs, dating to around 2000 BC.

Beni Hassan used not to be frequently visited because the site was not easily accessible, nor were the reliefs of the tombs in good condition; the tombs were frequented by Christian hermits during terrible persecutions by Decius and Diocletian in the 2nd and 3rd centuries AD and most of the wall paintings were blackened with soot from open fires, not to mention time and neglect. But all that has changed. Access to the site is now easy, and the paintings have been superbly restored, some of the colours appearing as fresh as on the day they were painted.

The tombs for which Beni Hassan is most famous are a long series of rock-hewn chambers about 655 ft (200 metres) above the floodplain, extending for several miles along the face of the cliff. The most interesting group of 39 chambers lies in the upper range. They belong to noblemen who governed the province some 4,000 years ago, and have simple facades. Some have elegant octagonal columns, and others 16-sided columns that flank the entrance doorways. Inside, the main chambers have triple-vaulted ceilings, with two rows of rock-hewn pillars purporting to support them. The walls are adorned throughout with unique scenes.

In the tomb belonging to a governor and commander-in-chief called **Amenemhat** (tomb No. 4) for example, is a scene (towards the centre of the left-hand wall) showing a caravan of Semites arriving in Egypt with their herds. They are characterised by their hook noses and multicoloured robes and their original arrival in Egypt is strongly represented in Biblical tradition.

That is to say, this representation dates to the time when Abraham, the "father of many nations", is believed to have lived (about 1900 BC). It was a time when there was scarcity of food in the land of Canaan, and "Abraham went down into Egypt to sojourn there; for the famine was grievous in the land" (*Genesis 12:10*). Egypt, by then, was a long settled monarchy with Egyptian governors at the seaports on the Phoenician coast and, as is clear from this representation, was willing to welcome strangers.

Another noteworthy representation painted in this same tomb above the doorway leading into the inner shrine, shows Amenemhat enjoying his leisure in a marsh scene. It shows the nobleman himself seated behind a blind made of reeds, from which concealed position he is able to observe hoopoes in a papyrus thicket.

These, and other vivid scenes of hunting, fishing, youths wrestling and women weaving, present a panorama of everyday life as it was enjoyed by governors, courtiers, and even princes who lived in Middle Egypt in the time of the Middle Kingdom.

PIGEONS AND HIPPOS, CATS AND CATTLE

In 1906 a party of British army officers were invited on a pigeon shoot by a landowner near the village of Denshawai in the Nile Delta. The inhabitants of Denshawai were keen pigeon-fanciers who raised birds in the characteristic, tower-shaped lofts made of unbaked brick. The previous year a dispute had broken out with the pigeon shooters in similar circumstances, and the village elder advised the shooting party to steer clear of Denshawai lest the villages should once again believe their own birds were being shot. Unfortunately it happened that, as the distant shots rang out, a threshing floor in the village caught fire.

The villagers jumped to conclusions and, wielding wooden staves, followed an elderly man named Hasan Mahfouz to confront the offenders. The senior British officer, a Major Pine-Coffin no less, instructed the party to lay down their guns to calm things down, but there was a scuffle in which a gun went off and four villagers, including one woman, appeared to drop dead. A Captain Bull then departed in a shower of sticks and stones to fetch help from a nearby army camp. In yet another astonishing coincidence, he died on the way – from heatstroke, not as a result of the injuries inflicted by the sticks and stones. British soldiers found a peasant beside his body, decided he was responsible for Bull's injuries (in fact, he was playing the Good Samaritan) and beat him to death.

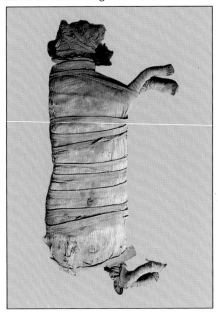

The affair blew up to colossal proportions: a trial of principle and strength between the British authorities and Egyptian nationalists. The British viewed it as "one more symptom of dangerous xenophobic fanaticism"; the Egyptian position was most succinctly put by George Bernard Shaw: "Imagine the feelings of an English village," he wrote, "if a party of Chinese officers suddenly appeared and began shooting the ducks, the geese, the hens, and the turkeys, and carried them off, asserting that they were wild birds, as everybody in China knew, and that the pretended indignation of the farmers was a cloak for hatred of the Chinese, and perhaps for a plot to overthrow the religion of Confucius and establish the Church of England in its place".

Hasan Mahfouz and three other villagers were sentenced to death, others to terms of imprisonment running from seven years to life, and others to 50 lashes each. The hangings and floggings were carried out in the village. The nationalist movement "gained a million new followers" and the Denshawai Incident, as it came to be known, went into the history books.

In a curious way, the pigeons at the heart of the Denshawai Incident were redolent of scores of battles, if not wars, in the history of Egypt, such was the importance of animals in the pantheon. Cats and cattle were famously revered, but fights could just as easily break out over fish, because one village might worship a particular type and the next village eat them. It ought to be said that pigeons were not conspicuously controversial; not, anyway, up until Mamluke times when they were highly prized as the key to a surprisingly effective express air mail system. "The number of animal species is limited," wrote Herodotus, "but I know few species which are not considered sacred." He thought it significant that "in my time... a goat had intercourse with a woman in the presence of many people."

The Hyksos invaders of about 1600 BC offended Egyptians with gratuitous jibes at the holy hippopotamus, but in Thebes, where the beasts in question were pampered in an artificial lake, there were paintings and sculpture which also showed how the hippo was hunted. It was crept up on, lassoed and played out on a line. Hunters then rushed up to get in their shots with javelins attached to lines. The instinct of this enraged pincushion was to find deep water, whereupon a tug-of-war commenced. The hippo would be hauled into a boat, break free, and the process would be repeated until the animal was exhausted.

At a more prosaic level, the ordinary *felaheen* would have had cause for misgivings toward the hippo long after it had disappeared from the Nile in Egypt. Its hide provided the business end of the dreaded *courbash*, the whip applied with such liberality that a pasha who once waved away a petitioner with a cry of "Give him 500!" left his officials in complete confusion as to whether he meant money or lashes. The *courbash* was the tax collector's trademark until abolished – but only for revenue purposes – by the British administration in 1883.

Like the hippo, the crocodile's fate depended on where it happened to be. Among the residents of Thebes, for example, it could hardly have asked for more: "It was fed and attended with the most scrupulous care; geese, fish, and various meats were dressed purposely for it; they ornamented its heads with earrings, its feet with bracelets, and its neck with necklaces of gold and artificial stones; it was rendered perfectly tame by kind treatment; and after death its body was embalmed in a most sumptuous manner."

The inhabitants of Apollinopolis, on the other hand, "held the crocodile in abhorrence, and lost no opportunity of destroying it." The Tenty-rite people provided entertainment for Roman tourists by leaping into the Nile to wrestle with crocodiles. Strabo reports that the performance went down so well that a troupe of Tentyrites were taken back to Rome for demonstrations in a tank with a shelving bank.

Crocodiles were also caught in certain places for eating. A hook baited with pork was thrown into the stream and the attention of lurking crocodiles drawn by beating a live pig into loud screams. The

crocodile was landed like a fish and, "its eyes being quickly covered up with mud, it was easily overcome."

Even in ancient Egypt, which is to say thousands of years before the Prophet Mohammed was born, a taboo on eating boar was widely observed although not, it seems, by the people of Damietta. Pigs were used for other purposes: to stamp seed into the residue of the annual inundation and as sacrifices at an annual festival which Herodotus compared with that of Bacchus when he paid his famous visit in 460 BC.

A considerable Greek community lived in Egypt in Herodotus's time, and they shamelessly ate pork. They were also unfussy about the heads of cattle, which most Egyptians would not touch. The correct treatment of cattle was for the Egyptians dominated by the goddess Isis, who took the form of a woman with a cow's head. That made the cow absolutely taboo; only bulls were sacrificed or eaten. If there were no Greeks about to take the head of a dead cow, Herodotus says, it was thrown into the Nile.

The Greeks were butchers, among other things, but a self-respecting Egyptian would no more eat beef slaughtered in the Greek manner than "kiss a Greek on the mouth". In some instances, cattle were buried with their horns sticking out of the ground to await the day when a raft arrived, collected all the bones, and carried them off for reburial on a sacred island called Atarbechis in the Delta. Apis, the sacred bulls of Memphis, had a special cemetery at Sakkara, the same facilities being provided for crocodiles at Kom Ombo, cats at Bubastis and ibis and rams at Elephantine.

Herodotus claimed to dislike obtuse subjects like the religious significance of animals, but he recognised his obligation to readers. Female Egyptian cats, he went on to say, were worked up to a state of high sexual excitement by their owners and then released into the company of males. If a fire was burning anywhere near when mating took place, the cats were seized by "a supernatural impulse" and leapt over the spectators ("standing at a distance") into the flames. Somewhat paradoxically, "when this happens great lamentations are made among the Egyptians". The death of a cat in normal circumstances required the family to shave off their eyebrows, whereas the death of a dog meant the whole head and the body as well.

Herodotus is less certain about Egypt's most famous bird, the phoenix. It was reputed to put in an appearance only once every 500 years, arriving from Arabia with the body of its father encased in an artifical egg of myrrh. The egg's size had to be carefully calculated: big enough for the father to fit in, but not too heavy for the flight to the temple of the Egyptian sun-god and the "rising from the ashes" ceremony. "This they say is done by this bird," is Herodotus's disclaimer, which implies that, unless the line is drawn somewhere, there is no knowing where the veneration of birds – no less than a friendly pigeon-shoot in Denshawi – may end. ∎

MEMPHIS, SAKKARA AND GIZA

The Mediterranean Sea once reached at least to the foot of the Muqattam Hills that shelter modern Cairo to the east, and probably even as far south as ancient Memphis. In other words, once upon a time there was a wide bay where the vast triangle of the Nile Delta stretches today. This bay was gradually filled up by ceaseless accumulation of alluvial deposits until the reclaimed land began to encroach on the sea. According to classical writers the river Nile flowed through seven outlets in ancient times: today there are only two such outlets; the Rosetta and Damietta branches of the river.

Memphis, the first capital of Upper and Lower Egypt, founded by King Menes, stood at the apex of the Delta. For 1,000 years it held the title of capital, and even with the growth of other cities, it retained its importance as a religious and commercial centre right through to Graeco-Roman times.

First city: Memphis is situated on the western bank of the Nile some 15 miles (25 km) south of Giza and almost opposite modern Cairo's suburb of Maadi. It was honoured by Egypt's most famous kings (some of whom built palaces there), as the place where they were traditionally crowned.

Memphis was lauded by classical writers in glowing terms, and was sought as a place of pilgrimage or a place of refuge. It was a city so great that any who sought control of Egypt knew that they first had to make themselves masters of Memphis.

Little remains of the ancient city today. Even the Temple of Ptah, one of the Great Gods of ancient Egypt, is in ruin. And most of that ruin lies beneath and around the mound on which the modern village of **Mit Rahina** stands. It is hard to imagine this derelict place as the former heart of one of the most important cities in ancient Egypt, as well as one of the most heavily populated.

Memphis is no more. It has suffered the ravages of war, fanaticism and time.

Its monuments have been torn down, usurped, pillaged and used as quarry material. Whatever remained of the ancient city was buried beneath alluvial soil that started to build up in medieval times when canals were neglected. Where once stood a mighty metropolis with river port, factories and settlements, modern-day villagers cultivate date-palm groves in the enriched earth.

French scholar Gaston Maspero described Memphis well when he said it was, in ancient times "what Cairo has long been for us moderns, the oriental city *par excellence*, the representation, the living symbol of Egypt."

It was one of the names of Memphis, *Hikaptah*, "house of the *ka* (spirit) of Ptah" that gave Egypt its name. This became *Aigyptos* in Greek and hence "Egypt" – just as, today, the Arabic word for Egypt (Misr) is also the word for Cairo.

In its position at the apex of the Delta Memphis was in an ideal position for local trade as well as foreign commerce, and coins and sculptures found in the ruins show that Carians, Lydians, Attic Greeks and Macedonians came in great numbers, as well as Semites, Syrians and Persians.

Essential monuments: A visitor to Memphis would do well to concentrate on the monuments in the **Museum Compound**, where the tourist buses park and where there is a cafeteria as well as a number of shops selling imitation antiquities.

The main feature of the compound is a statue of Ramses II in a special roofed enclosure. It is regarded as the finest statue of this pharaoh ever carved. It lies in a horizontal position and can only be viewed properly from a gallery. Part of the crown and the lower legs are missing but one can appreciate the fine craftsmanship apparent in the details of the king's mouth with indentations at the corners, the muscular shoulders and the sturdy torso. The royal name, in an oblong cartouche, can be seen on the right shoulder, the breast and on the pharaoh's girdle.

Ramses II built extensively at Memphis and erected his statues in pairs. It

Preceding pages: pyramid at Giza. Left, date palms in Memphis.

would not be unreasonable to suppose, therefore, that this limestone statue, as well as the red Aswan granite monolith from Memphis which today stands in Ramses Square in Cairo, and the fragments of statues in other qualities of granite, all had counterparts adorning entrances to the various monuments of Memphis.

Two other objects worthy of note in the museum compound are the **alabaster sphinx**, which is the largest statue ever found fashioned of this stone (it weighs some 80 tons and has been attributed to either Amenhotep I or Thutmosis I); and the huge round-topped stone slab, the Stela of Apries, erected by the 26th Dynasty pharaoh; it bears an important historical text, and the figures of the gods Ptah and Sokar.

Despite its importance and continuous occupation for thousands of years, not more than 10 percent of the central city of Memphis has ever been excavated. The Survey of Memphis is an Egypt Exploration Society project which is attempting to draw together all existing material including those relics which are now in museums worldwide, excavate the site systematically, and draw up a stratified map of ancient Memphis giving, where possible, ground plans of different structures at different stages of its history.

The word "Memphis" no longer exists in Egypt. It was a Greek derivation of *Men-nefer*, the name of the pyramid of Pepi I on the Sakkara necropolis. The villagers of Mit Rahina, however, still call their village *Menf* or *Manf*, and it is not known whether they adopted this name to please early archaeologists and travellers who talked about "Mennefer", or whether the original built-up area gradually crept beyond the site of Pepi's pyramid towards Mit Rahina.

First pyramids: To the northwest of Memphis on a very arid plateau is **Sakkara**, the ancient city's necropolis. It is a truly remarkable site, and one of the most important in Egypt. Its name is derived from Sokar, an agricultural god believed to dwell in the earth; the annual Festival of Sokar took place at the "White

Statue of Ramses II at Memphis.

Wall of Memphis". Herds of draught animals would be driven round the walls of the ancient city, as if going round and round a threshing floor, in a ritual to awaken the soil. Because Sokar lived in the earth he became regarded also as one of the gods of the dead; hence the adoption of his name for the whole necropolis.

Dominating the horizon of Sakkara is the **Step Pyramid**. It is the central feature of a funerary complex built by Imhotep for Pharaoh Zoser, the first king of the Third Dynasty in 2686 BC. Zoser's reign marks the beginning of the Old Kingdom or "pyramid age", an era of great vision and invention.

Until this time no stone had ever been used for large-scale construction and there was no architectural tradition from which to draw. But Imhotep, a brilliant innovator, builder, and "wise man" whose sayings were quoted for thousands of years, drew inspiration from contemporary buildings which were constructed of perishable materials: reeds, mud-brick and logs of wood. It is

thanks to his genius that we can see today, sculpted in stone, how bundles of reeds were tied together with the heads fanning out to form the earliest capital; how logs were laid across parallel walls to form a roof; and how reed fences separated property. In short, the detail of Sakkara mirrors the structures of the state capital of Memphis which, as already mentioned, have all but completely disappeared.

The Step Pyramid, which rises in six unequal tiers, originally had one single step. This was the superstructure over the burial chamber. But during the long reign of Zoser the structure underwent no fewer than five alterations: the ground plan was successively enlarged, and the height was increased in successive stages until, superimposed on top of one another, the six steps of the terraced structure emerged in their final form. The Step Pyramid is the forerunner of the true pyramid, which reached its apogee in the three magnificent Fourth Dynasty pyramids at Giza.

In visiting the Step Pyramid complex

Old and new transport at Sakkara.

it is as well to remember that the pyramid is a symbolic structure. That is to say, it was never meant to be used by man, as a temple would be used. It was a funerary structure in which the pharaoh could re-enact, in his afterlife, all his experiences on earth.

For this reason, the various courts (the main **Heb-Sed Court** to the east of the pyramid, for example) were not bulky and cumbersome. They have simple, pure lines with perfect proportions, and it is difficult to believe that such sophisticated forms were created so very long ago. For example, there are three engaged columns beyond the Heb-Sed court which are remarkably and realistically fashioned in the form of the papyrus plant. These delicate columns so accurately simulate nature that the triangular stem can clearly be seen, thickening at a point just above the ground, and then slimming gradually towards the fanning head of the plant.

Among the other structures on the Sakkara plateau are several Fifth and Sixth-Dynasty pyramids which were built of poor quality local limestone and fell to ruin when the outer casings were removed. Although unimpressive from the outside, they are of great interest and historical importance because many are inscribed with mortuary literature known as the Pyramid Texts. (The Giza pyramids, incidentally, were not decorated at all.)

These texts are long columns of inscribed hieroglyphics that include hymns, prayers and rituals for the deceased pharaoh, as well as lists of offerings of food, drink and clothing for the afterlife. They are beautifully carved into the stone and filled with blue or green pigment. In the Fifth-Dynasty **Pyramid of Unas**, for example, which was built about 2345 BC and situated outside the southwest corner of the Zoser pyramid complex, the texts cover all the available space in the tomb chamber, apart from the walls behind and beside the empty sarcophagus, which are themselves painted to represent the facade of a building.

What life was like: It is from the noblemen's tombs dotted around the plateau, however, that we gain a real insight into everyday life in ancient Egypt, especially from a group of tombs that date to the age of the pyramid builders. These are decorated with painted reliefs of everyday life, including agricultural activities, animal husbandry, hunting, various trades and industries, as well as family life.

The **Tomb of Ti**, a court dignitary, is one of the best preserved. It includes representations of the shipbuilding industry (in the sacrificial chamber) which are particularly interesting, depicting every stage of the work from the unloading of the cedarwood – which was brought all the way across the Mediterranean from Byblos on the Phoenician coast – to the shaping of the hull, the sawing and the preparation of the planks of wood. Finally, the ship is shown in full sail.

Also in the sacrificial chamber is a series of rural scenes, in one of which a grey cow gives birth with the help of a farmer, while, behind her, restive calves have their hind legs bound together or are tethered to pegs in the ground. Ti himself is charmingly depicted in the second corridor with his wife seated at his feet and being entertained by a flautist, two singers and two harpists.

The **Tomb of Mereruka** is a family tomb, with chambers belonging to the nobleman himself, his wife and children, and it is decorated with the largest number of diversified activities to be found in any single tomb. They include scenes of industrial activities like the manufacture of jewellery from gold that is weighed in a balance and registered by a scribe before use; pottery-making by workers who comment to each other on the excellence of the other's work; and life-size statues of the deceased being hauled to the tomb on sledges. (These are to be found in the first chamber leading off the entrance chamber to the right.) It is worth noting, in the latter scene, that men pour water on the earth just in front of the runners, to render the Nile clay slippery and enable the wooden sledges to be drawn more easily.

On the left-hand wall of the third chamber of this tomb is a representation of the estate headquarters. It shows clerks seated in a hall with lotus-bud columns, while village elders are forcibly dragged before them to give evidence on their apparently faulty tax returns. One man has been stripped, and his arms and feet are bound around a post where he is being beaten.

The standing statue of Mereruka, in the burial chamber, is one of the few Old Kingdom statues preserved intact. He is shown walking forward, out of his tomb and into the sacrificial chamber. The reason why the statue survived *in situ* is because the tomb had become filled with sand by Graeco-Roman times when the road leading to the Apis tombs, the Serappeum, was constructed. Unaware of what lay beneath, the workers preserved it by building over it.

The tombs of the Apis bulls: The **Serapeum**, as it was called in Graeco-Roman times, is a vast sepulchre of rock-hewn galleries for the internment of the sacred Apis bull of Memphis. It is within walking distance of the vast tent on the necropolis where refreshments are served and from where camels and donkeys are available for hire if you do not wish to walk to the site.

The tombs are hewn out of solid rock, and the flanking chambers contain mighty granite sarcophagi of an average weight of 65 tonnes each, and measuring some 13 ft (4 metres) long, by over 9 ft (3 metres) high. Most of the lids are of solid granite.

When the discoverer of this sepulchre, French archaeologist Mariette, first entered the galleries in 1851, he found that most of the sarcophagus lids had been pushed aside and the contents pillaged. Only one had been left intact because the robbers had been unsuccessful in their efforts to open it; Mariette actually had to use dynamite. Inside the sarcophagus he found a solid gold statue of a bull which is now in the Louvre; the mummy of the bull is in the Agricultural Museum in Cairo.

The monuments that can be seen on the Sakkara plateau today represent a mere fraction of what still lies beneath the sand. In fact, the whole plateau is

Tapestry from the Wissa Wassef workshop, off the Sakkara road.

literally riddled with sand-filled depressions, any one of which could be the top of a shaft leading to a tomb. Archaeological teams from many parts of the world are conducting excavations, restoring and clearing tombs. And the Supreme Council for Antiquities is planning to open up many others.

The pyramids: The great pyramids of **Giza** stand on a rocky plateau on the western bank of the Nile 15 miles (25 km) north of Sakkara, almost directly opposite Cairo. The Pyramids Road from Cairo is a dual carriageway that takes you to the foot of the plateau where the Mena Oberoi has fortunately escaped the fate of many other once-ancient hotels; it has been upgraded and modernised, not demolished.

It is not unusual for modern travellers who are used to skyscrapers, monumental stadiums, and the Olympic games, to observe the pyramids for the first time and say, "I thought they would be larger!" It is only when one has been on the plateau for several hours, looking at the mighty structures in relation to one-self and the surrounding desert, that one begins to realise how really remarkable they are. They are the most famous, intensely measured, studied and debated monuments in the world, and also, probably, the least understood. They are the imperishable landmarks to the geometrical accuracy and technical skill that went into their making.

The **Great Pyramid**, which was built in honour of the Fourth-Dynasty Pharaoh Cheops (Khufu) *circa* 2600 BC, is the sole survivor of the Seven Wonders of the Ancient World.

Originally 480 feet (147 metres) high and covering an area of 13 acres (5 hectares), the pyramid was constructed of some 2.3 million blocks of stone of an average weight of 2½ tonnes (some weighed as much as 16 tons), which were brought into contact to tolerances as close as one 5,000th of an inch. The sides of the pyramid themselves were oriented almost exactly true north, south, east and west, with the four corners again at perfect right angles. Incredibly, the maximum error in alignment has

Early photograph of the pyramids and the Sphinx.

been calculated as being a little over one-twelfth of a degree.

The outlines of the pyramids were once smooth and covered with limestone facing that was fitted and polished, nowhere betraying an entrance. The shape was inspired by the *ben-ben* stone, the sacred symbol of the sun-god at Heliopolis, and the purpose was funerary. That is to say, each pyramid was originally part of a complex that comprised the pyramid itself, its Mortuary Temple, and the Valley Temple which was situated at the edge of the cultivable land.

After the death of the reigning pharaoh, his mummified body would be brought by river to the Valley Temple, from there to be borne on the shoulders of white-robed priests to the Mortuary Temple where rituals and prayers were carried out before the internment of the body. The Valley and Mortuary temples were linked by a covered causeway.

The **Valley Temple** at Giza, which is also known as the **Granite Temple**, is part of the funerary complex of Chephren (Khafre), the builder of the second pyramid. To the right of its entrance is the famous **Sphinx**, a huge statue of a recumbent lion with a human head believed to be fashioned in Chephren's likeness. In front of the Granite Temple and the Sphinx, is the **Sphinx Theatre** where the *son et lumière* performance takes place every night. It is considerably shorter in duration than the performance at Luxor, but is no less entertaining. Check the newspaper for the times of the performances.

The suffering Sphinx: The Sphinx, fashioned out of the bedrock of the Giza plateau, is 840 ft (255 metres) long and some 65 ft (20 metres) high at its head. Between its outstretched paws is a red granite slab inscribed with a text relating that the pharaoh Thutmosis IV of the 18th Dynasty was sleeping in its shadow one day, when his "father", the sun-god Ra-Harakhte, appeared to him and instructed him to clear away the sand that was choking him. The sun-god declared that if Thutmosis hearkened to his words then he would be king and wear the

All forms of transport are available for visiting the pyramids.

crown of Upper and Lower Egypt – which, indeed, he did.

This inscription, which dates from *circa* 1400 BC, is the first record of any excavation on the Giza plateau, where wind-blown depressions are continually being filled with sand. The Sphinx itself was cleared of sand again in the Saitic period (600 BC), in the late-Ptolemaic (Greek) period, and again in Roman times. In the modern era Napoleon's team of *savants* cleared and measured the monument during the 1789 expedition to Egypt, and it has been successively cleared and restored by the Egyptian Antiquities Organisation (now the Supreme Council for Antiquities) since the 1920s.

Unfortunately, despite all these efforts, the Sphinx is suffering badly from age, environmental pollution and subsoil water seepage. Concerted efforts to restore and conserve the monument have been made in recent years. One cause of danger is currently being eliminated: a new sewage system in the nearby village of Neslet el-Siman will prevent water seepage.

In addition, current restoration measures include replacing earlier, poor quality repairs with "healthy stone"; and the Getty Conservation Institute of California is collaborating with the Supreme Council for Antiquities to collect data from a computerised weather station perched on the statue's rump. The data will include information on the direction and speed of the wind, humidity and pollutants which are contributing towards its decay. Once the data is to hand it should speed up decision-making on the next step to be taken in the preservation of the mounment. Zahi Hawass, Director-General of the plateau, optimistically said that the Sphinx "is not in any danger, its head and neck can live for another 1,000 years."

But the condition of the **funerary boat of Cheops** (the solar boat) on the Giza plateau, situated beside Cheops's Pyramid in a special museum, is not so assured. The museum itself, built in the early years of the Revolution, has proved not to be an ideal structure, and plans are underway to construct a new home for this monument, which was discovered in a rock-hewn pit near the pyramid in 1954 and is regarded as one of the most important finds of the 20th century. It is the oldest intact boat in the world.

The solar boat was built of cedarwood imported from Lebanon and the entire structure had been dismantled and laid in the pit. Reconstructed, it proved to be 141 ft (43 metres) long and 26 ft (8 metres) high. Although 4,500 years old it is still in near perfect condition, with a massive curving hull which rises to elegant prow and stern posts. The thick planks were "sewn" together by a system of ropes through holes that met in pairs on the inside.

A second, as yet unexcavated boat, is known to lie beneath the ground beside the boat museum. It, too, will be excavated once the new museum facility is completed, as there is evidence that the bedrock in which it lies is not hermetically sealed, and that the boat is, even now, deteriorating. A grant of $5 million was given by the Swedish government for this museum project, but opinions div-

The funerary boat of Cheops.

ided on whether it should be constructed west of Cheops's Pyramid, at the foot of the plateau, or near the resthouse that once belonged to King Farouk.

Tourist development: In the late 1980s a plan was set in motion to upgrade the Giza plateau as a tourist site; to clear and restore the monuments, open up tombs for tourists to visit, and set up facilities such as cafeterias, restaurants and souvenir shops in such a manner as not to detract from the natural and archaeological environment.

The plan was known as the "Pyramid Plateau Project" and stage one was quickly accomplished. Accumulated sand was removed from the Great Pyramid of Cheops, its inner corridors were cleared, and closed TV circuits, microphones, and suitable lighting and ventilation were installed.

Stage two involved clearing and restoring tombs on the necropolis, and Minister of Culture Farouk Hosni was able to announce in October 1990: "Fifteen tombs of nobility have seen their first visitors since they were discovered

in the last century." Stage three concentrated on the third and smallest pyramid, belonging to the Pharaoh Menkaure. Weakened parts were strengthened, and it, too, has been provided with TV closed circuits and adequate lighting.

Meanwhile, another project is also moving forward. Known as the Giza Mapping Project, it is an in-depth archaeological study of the plateau, its geology and topography. In the opinion of Egyptologist Mark Lehner, "It is not possible to understand the pyramids of Giza without understanding the geology of the land."

The aim of this project is to provide the first complete and detailed map of every feature of the plateau. It will enable, among other things, the identification of different qualities of stone used to build the pyramids with the bedrock from which they came. For example, while good quality limestone for its outer casing came from the Tura quarries on the eastern bank of the Nile, local limestone of mediocre quality was used for constructing the main body of the

Aerial view of both the Sphinx and the pyramids.

pyramids around a core of bedrock that was left intact. And where exactly this quantity of limestone – the volume of which must be equivalent to that used in the pyramid – came from, is one of the problems to which the solutions are being sought.

Perennial questions about the function and purpose of the pyramids are surface regularly (*see Pyramidology chapter, page 64*). That they were more than simple tombs seems certain. Were they also symbols of kingship and the prevailing solar worship? Or were they the main feature of a vast funerary complex associated with ancestor worship? In other words, a reliquary?

Building techniques: Whatever they were, the fact that 16 million tons of stone went into the construction of the Great Pyramid of Cheops alone is a remarkable fact that is even now not fully understood, nor how blocks of such enormous dimensions could have been elevated to a such a height. Scholars once thought that stone or mud-brick ramps sloped up to the top of the

pyramid, but that would have meant an incline of at least a mile long which would have left mountains of debris, "which," said Lehner, "just isn't there." What happened to the vast quantities of brick that must have been used to encase the mammoth ramp? No evidence remains, although there are huge mounds of stone chips and broken pottery on the plateau.

Lehner thinks it possible that the ancient Egyptian workmen dragged the stones up a short, broad ramp that actually rose with the pyramid structure itself. That is to say, it was a wrap-around ramp set against the sides of the main structure. Moreover, he and other Egyptologists now feel sure that the outer casing stones of Tura limestone were not added at the last stage of construction, but were put in position as the pyramid rose, and only dressed once the capping stone had been set and the workmen moved downwards towards the base.

The next few years will undoubtedly see new hypotheses, but the pyramids of Giza nevertheless remain an enigma. Scholars were once primarily interested in measuring them and speculating on their symbolic significance. Today, they have shifted their focus of interest. Members of the team of the Giza Mapping Project want to know how large a workforce was involved in the project of pyramid building; how long it took them, where they lived and what they ate. In other words, they want to know more about the pyramid-builders.

Herodotus the Greek traveller and historian estimated that 100,000 men laboured for 20 years to build the Great Pyramid of Cheops. Although never regarded as a reliable source, Herodotus's figure has nevertheless withstood the passage of time for want of any proof to the contrary. This may soon be available. A cemetery of ancient workers and overseers has been found on the Giza plateau, as well as evidence of a village to the southeast of the Sphinx. These may yet yield evidence on the number of workers that built the mighty structures, and throw more light on to the "pyramid age".

<u>Left</u>, montage of moon and Sphinx. <u>Right</u>, contemplating the pyramids.

274

CAIRO

Larger than any other city in the Middle East or in Africa, Cairo, the capital of Egypt, stretches along the east bank of the Nile for more than 20 miles (35 km), guarding the head of the Delta and marking the division between Upper and Lower Egypt. Across the river is Giza, technically a separate administrative district, but part of the same urban agglomeration.

In the river between Cairo and Giza are two islands: Rawdah, formed out of bed-rock, where there have been habitations since ancient times, and Gazirah, formed alluvially only within the past six centuries, where the suburb of Zamalek has grown up since 1870.

With a head-count of well over 15 million – there are more Cairenes than there are Scandinavians, Greeks, Dutch, Austrians, East Germans, or Hungarians – Cairo, Giza, and the islands constitute the most populous urban area in the world between America and India.

Beginnings: The city-site has been settled since Neolithic times. Memphis, the first political capital of Egypt, was founded on the west bank near the end of the 4th millennium BC and in later times expanded northward to occupy the entire site of modern Giza.

Some 15 miles (25 km) northeast of the Giza pyramids on the opposite side of the river, and thus directly north of Memphis, was the temple-city of On, the Old Kingdom's greatest religious complex, centre of the cult of the sun-god Ra. Mentioned in Genesis by its ancient Egyptian name, On was called *Heliopolis* ("Sun-City") by the Greeks, but its ancient site has no connection with the 20th-century suburb of Heliopolis (Misr al-Gadidah), some 3 miles (5 km) away.

At Giza the main road from Memphis to On crossed the river, using the island of Rawdah as a stepping stone. The small settlement at the landing place opposite Rawdah on the east bank was probably called something like *Per-Hapi-n-On* – "The Nile House of On" –

and became known to Greek travellers as *Babylon*. It became more important during the first Persian occupation of Egypt, when a canal was opened from the Red Sea to the Nile.

When Egypt became a Roman province in 30 BC, one of the three legions controlling the whole country was garrisoned in the fortress at Babylon (now Old Cairo). It is probably the place where St Peter wrote his first Epistle. Under the Roman emperor Trajan (AD 98–117) the old Persian canal was reopened and extended through the centre of the fortress. Later repaired by the Emperor Arcadius (395–408), the fortress of Babylon stood largely complete until near the end of the last century, when British army engineers demolished half of it.

By the time of the Arab invasion in 641, Memphis had declined into a large town and Heliopolis had virtually disappeared; Alexandria had taken over the mantle of the most important city in Egypt. The Delta, however, the country's richest region, remained impassable in any direction except north or south along one of the branches of the Nile, which also provided the only route between Upper Egypt and the Mediterranean. Babylon (as the embryonic Cairo was still called at the time) controlled not only access to the Delta, but also access to Upper Egypt, and was thus a gateway to the entire country.

After a brief siege the fortress fell to the Arabs under their leader Amr ibn al-As, who then founded the city of Al-Fustat ("The Tent" or perhaps "The Earthworks"), where he settled his troops. For their spiritual needs he built the large congregational **Mosque of Amr ibn al-As** (today situated a couple of hundred metres north of the Roman fortress in Old Cairo, on the main road parallel to the Metro line). Originally constructed in 641 or 642, this was the first mosque in Africa. It has since been rebuilt many times, and the latest work on it, finished in 1983, sought to recreate its appearance as it might have been in its early years.

For 500 years Al-Fustat was the centre of a trade network that spread from

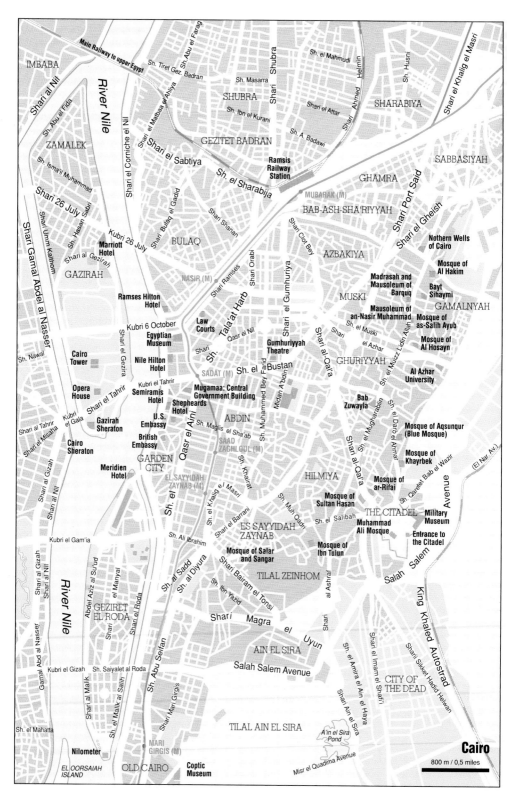

IMBABA

Main Railway to upper Egypt

Sh. Tiret Gez. Badran

Sh. Abu el Farag

Sh. el Mahmudi

Sh. Husni

Sh. el Khalig el Masri

Shari al Nil

River Nile

Sh. Abu el Fida

Sh. el Matbaa el Ahliya

Shari Shubra

Sh. Masarra

SHUBRA

Shari el Attar

Sh. Ahmed Helmin

SHARABIYA

Shari el Corniche el Nil

ZAMALEK

Sh. Isma'il Muhammad

Shari el Sabtiya

Sh. Ibn el Kurani

GEZITET BADRAN

Sh. A. Badawi

Ramsis Railway Station

SABBASIYA

Shari 26 July

Sh. el Sharabija

MUBARAK (M)

GHAMRA

Shari Port Said

Shari Gamal Abdel al Nasser

Sh. Hasan Sabri

Kubri 26 July

Shari Bulaq el Gadid

Shari Shanan

BAB-ASH-SHA'RIYYAH

Shari el Gheish

Shari al Gezirah

Marriott Hotel

BULAQ

NASIR (M)

Shari Clot Bey

AZBAKIYA

Nothern Wells of Cairo

GAZIRAH

Ramses Hilton Hotel

Kubri 6 October

Shari Ramsés

Shari Orabi

Shari el Gumhuriya

MUSKI

Mosque of Al Hakim

Madrasah and Mausoleum of Barquq

Bayt Sihaymi

Sh. Nawal

Cairo Tower

Egyptian Museum

Law Courts

Qasr el Nil

Shari

Mausoleum of an-Nasir Muhammad

Sh. el Muski

Mosque of as-Salih Ayub

GAMALNYAH

Shari el Gezira

Nile Hilton Hotel

Kubri el Tahrir

SADAT (M)

Sh. el Bustan

Gumhuriyyah Theatre

Shari el Qal'a

Shari el Azhar

GHURIYYAH

Mosque of Al Hosayn

Opera House

Semiramis Hotel

Mugamaa: Central Government Building

Shari Muhammed Bey Farid

Midan A'bidin

Shari

el Azhar

Sh. el Mu'izz l'din Allah

Al Azhar University

Kubri el Gala

Shari el Tahrir

Shepheards Hotel

U.S. Embassy

ABDIN

Sh. Maglis el Sha'ab

Bab Zuwayla

Shari al-Mugharablin

Shari el Darb el Ahmar

Mosque of Aqsunqur (Blue Mosque)

Shari al Tahrir

Gazirah Sheraton

British Embassy

SAAD ZAGHLOUL (M)

Sh. Khairat

Mosque of Khayrbek

Shari el Darb el Ahmar

Shari el Misaha

Cairo Sheraton

GARDEN CITY

Meridien Hotel

EL SAYYIDAH ZAYNAB (M)

Qasr al Aini

Sh. el Khalig el Masri

HILMIYA

Shari al-Qal'a

Mosque of ar-Rifai

Shari Qaréfet Bab el Wazir

(El Nar. Av.)

Kubri el Gam'ia

Shari al Gizah

Shari al Nil

Sh. el

Shari el Barrani

Sh. Ali Ibrahim

Sh. al Sadd

Sh. al Diyura

ES SAYYIDAH ZAYNAB

Sh. Muh Qadri

Sh. el Salibah

Mosque of Sultan Hasan

Mosque of Ibn Tulun

Muhammad Ali Mosque

THE CITADEL

Military Museum

Entrance to the Citadel

King Khaled Autostrad

Mosque of Salar and Sangar

TILAL ZEINHOM

Shari Bairam el Tonsi

Sh. Ibn Yazid

Shari al Astraf

Salah Salem Avenue

Kubri el Gam'ia

River Nile

Gamal Abd al Nasser

Shari al Gizah

Shari al Nil

Abdel Aziz al Su'ud

el Manyal

GEZIRET EL RODA

Shari al Roda

Shari

Shari Magra

el Uyun

Shari

Sh. el Amira el Ain el Haya

Shari el Imam el Shafi'i

AIN EL SIRA

Shari Sikket Hadid Helwan

CITY OF THE DEAD

Kubri el Gizah

Sh. Saiyalet al Roda

Sh. Abu Seifan

Shari al Malik

Sh. el Malik al Salih

Shari Mari Girgis

Salah Salem Avenue

Shari Ain el Sira

Sh. el Mahatta

Nilometer

MARI GIRGIS (M)

TILAL AIN EL SIRA

A'in el Sira Pond

EL OORSAIAH ISLAND

OLD CAIRO

Coptic Museum

Misr el Quadima Avenue

Cairo

800 m / 0,5 miles

Spain to China; very little of the original city remains (the site is behind Old Cairo to the east but is closed to visitors) but many of the most beautiful and interesting items excavated from the ruins are in Cairo's **Museum of Islamic Art** on Shari Port Said.

Cairenes themselves do not call their city "Cairo". They call it "Misr", which means "metropolis", "capital", "that which is inhabited and civilised", but also means "Egypt". When Fustat became the capital of the country under the Arabs, it was called "Misr-Fustat", and every succeeding settlement that has been added to the agglomeration has simply been absorbed into Misr. It was the Fatimids, who arrived from Tunisia in the 10th century, that built the royal enclosure called "Al-Qahirah" north of the original city, and it was this new area which was then mis-pronounced by Italian merchants as "Gran Cairo", a name which caught on throughout Europe.

Old Cairo: The fortress of Babylon, the mosque of Amr and the ruins of Fustat are all situated in the quarter thus called **Misr al-Qadimah**, a district which is referred to by Western visitors as **Old Cairo**, though it has no historical or topographical connection with Al-Qahirah and offers only the dimmest foretaste of the city's true splendour, which is its medieval architecture. Misled by the name, in fact, some visitors have left Cairo without ever seeing the heart of its historic zone, with all of its monuments, which is much further north than Old Cairo.

Old Cairo has separate attractions. Useless for military purposes after the Arab conquest, the fortress of Babylon evolved into a Christian and Jewish enclave and many churches were built within its walls. The easiest way to reach Old Cairo is by Metro, which stops by the modern Greek Orthodox Church of St George (Mar Girgis), constructed on the remains of one of Trajan's two great circular towers.

Originally created to flank the old canal mentioned above, they now frame the entrance to the garden of the **Coptic Museum**. The museum contains many of the finer details of decoration which were originally in the surrounding churches, but its pride is a fine collection of manuscripts, including the earliest known copy of the Book of Psalms and the Nag Hammadi codices, nearly 1,200 papyrus pages of Gnostic texts in Coptic, which were bound into books – the most ancient leather-covered ones known – and hidden in an Upper Egyptian cave in the 4th century. Also important are objects from the monastery of Apa Jeremiah at Sakkara, which suggest what the interior of an ancient church looked like.

A portal in the south wall of the museum garden leads up to the **Church of the Blessed Virgin Mary**, known as "Al-Muallaqa" ("The Suspended"), built atop the bastions of another Roman gate. Tradition gives this foundation a 7th-century date, but like all Old Cairo's churches it has been repeatedly rebuilt, especially in recent times. Much old furniture has been preserved, however, including a particularly fine marble *ambon* or pulpit (11th century) and a

screen of ebony inlaid with ivory (12th or 13th century).

A stairway near the museum's ticket office leads from the garden down to the stone-paved alley that is the main street of the enclave. The **Church of St Sergius** is down the street to the right. Traditionally regarded as the oldest in Misr al-Qadimah, it is said to have been built in the 5th or 6th century over a cave where the Holy Family stayed during their sojourn in Egypt. The **Church of St Barbara** is further down the main alleyway, then to the left. Though continuously rebuilt, it still has a fine inlaid medieval iconostasis, one of the few surviving medieval icons of St Barbara, and an extraordinarily beautiful 13th-century icon of the Virgin with Child Enthroned.

A few steps away is the **Ben Ezra Synagogue**, used as a church in the 8th and 9th centuries, closed under the fanatic Caliph Al-Hakim (996–1021), then sold to the Sephardic community. From the 11th century onward it served as a *geniza*, a repository for discarded documents, which were discovered when it was rebuilt in the 19th century and have since provided a wealth of information.

The shortest route back to the main road outside the fortress returns past the Church of St Sergius, then goes around a corner to the **Convent of St George**, which contains a remarkable room with wooden doors 23 ft (7 metres) high. Clearly the reception hall of a 12th-century house incorporated into the convent, it has become the subject of a pious legend which links it with Roman persecution.

On the island: Across a narrow branch of the Nile from Old Cairo onto the island of Rawdah is the earliest Muslim structure still extant in the city: the Rawdah **Nilometer**, built in 861 by the governor of Egypt at the order of the Abbasid caliph. The building's conical dome is not part of the original Nilometer, but a replica of the Ottoman-style dome that covered it in the 17th and 18th centuries. In the middle of a square stone-lined shaft that descends below the level of the river is the

The Church of St George, Old Cairo.

Nilometer itself, an octagonal column divided into cubits, which stands on a millstone at the bottom of the shaft. A stairway around the walls of the shaft leads past inlets at three levels: the level of the uppermost inlet is indicated by recesses outlined with what a Gothic architect would have recognised as "tiers-point" arches, but they were built three centuries before the earliest European example.

The so-called **Manastirli Palace**, next to the Nilometer, is the *salamlik* or reception kiosk of a palace complex built in the 1830s by the founder of a distinguished Cairene Turkish family. Restored in 1990, it offers a romantic view of the Nile and is used by the Ministry of Culture for receptions.

Vanished quarter: Like all the rulers of Misr, the invading Abbasids built a new quarter to the city. Called "Al-Askar", theirs was occupied by a succession of governors, the most famous of whom was Ahmed ibn Tulun, who declared his independence in 872 by having the caliph's dedicatory inscription removed from the Nilometer. The autonomous state he established – the first in Egypt since 30 BC – soon became an empire.

North of both Al-Askar and Fustat he founded a regal new city, naming it "Al-Qatai" (The Wards), because of its division into separate districts, which were defined by class and kind of inhabitant. Al-Qatai covered a square mile (260 hectares) and contained palaces, governmental buildings, markets, and even a hippodrome. At its centre was – and is – the gigantic **Mosque of Ibn Tulun**, one of the great masterpieces of world architecture. Ibn Tulun's vast congregational mosque was meant to contain an army for Friday prayers. Erected between 876 and 879, it is now all that remains to testify to the magnificence of the Al-Qatai quarter. Echoing the architecture of Baghdad, it consists of a square enclosed by a massive flat-roofed arcade of baked brick, which is covered with fine plaster and surmounted by anthropomorphic cresting.

In the centre of the mosque is a massive courtyard of more than four acres

Inside the Nilometer at Rawdah.

(nearly two hectares) with an ablution fountain in the middle.

The arcading consists of elegant Syrian-style pointed arches, less elaborate than the arches of the Nilometer, but still two centuries earlier than any European equivalent. The arcade is five rows deep on the eastern or Mecca-facing side, where several *mihrabs*, ornamental recesses or wall-treatments, indicate the direction of prayer.

On this side also is a wooden *minbar* – a structure like a staircase, which serves some of the same function that a pulpit fulfils in a church – the oldest (1296) still in use in Cairo and one of the finest. Carved stucco decoration is used throughout with wonderful inventiveness and a band of sycamore wood carved with Koranic verses runs around the building's whole interior circumference – more than 1 mile (2 km).

The minaret was built in 1296 as a replacement for Ahmed ibn Tulun's original, which was modelled in turn on the minaret of the Great Mosque at Samarra near Baghdad. Though well worth the climb, the view it offers over the surrounding neighbourhood is disrupted by ugly new buildings and marred – for those who are not prepared for it – by the rubbish that litters Cairene rooftops. Built against one end of the mosque are the two old houses that compose the interesting **Gayer-Anderson Museum**.

The Citadel: Looking eastward from the Ibn Tulun minaret, the most obvious shape on the horizon is that of the Muqattam Hills, with the **Citadel** just below, easily identifiable from the Hollywood-Oriental outline of the Ottoman-style Mosque of Mohammed Ali, completed nearly 1,000 years later than Ibn Tulun.

Both a fortress and a royal city, the Citadel continued the tradition among Cairo's rulers of building enclosures for themselves and their retainers. It was begun by Salah ad-Din ibn Ayyub (1171–93), founder of the Ayyubid dynasty, the "Saladin" of the medieval Western chroniclers and Scott's novel *The Talisman*. The original walls and **The walls of Ibn Tulun.**

towers were erected between 1176 and 1183. Between 1200 and 1218 Salah ad-Din's round towers were encased in massive new constructions and square keeps were planted around the perimeter. His nephew Al-Kamil (1218–38) became the first sultan to live in the Citadel, which remained the seat of government for the next 650 years.

After the Bahri Mamlukes overthrew the Ayyubids in 1250, their first great sultan, Baybars al-Bunduqdari (1260–77), divided the fortress into two enclosures linked by an inner gate, the **Bab al-Qullah**. During the various reigns of the Bahri Mamluke **Sultan An-Nasir Mohammed** (1294–95, 1299–1309, 1310–41), most of the buildings in the Southern Enclosure were torn down and replaced by much grander structures, such as the **Mosque of an-Nasir Mohammed**, finished in 1335. Standing next to the Bab al-Qullah, it is one of the finest arcaded mosques in Cairo, as well as the only Mamluke building in the Citadel to survive. Its inner court is a virtual museum of reused pharaonic and Roman-period columns, while its two minarets show Persian influence in their upper pavilions, which are covered in green tiles. The marble that adorned its walls was stripped off by the Ottoman conquerors in 1517 and shipped to Istanbul.

The other three of the four mosques in the Citadel date from between 1517 and 1914, when Egypt was an Ottoman province. One Ottoman landmark is the massive tower facing the Muqattam, the **Burg al-Muqattam**. Another is the fortified gateway called the **Bab al-Azab,** which has been well restored.

Under the rule of Mohammed Ali Pasha (1805–48) the outer walls of the Citadel were rebuilt to suit the needs of a modern army and the decaying medieval buildings in the interior were replaced by new palaces, barracks, military schools, armament factories, and his own colossal **Mosque of Mohammed Ali**. Alien to the architectural style and spirit of the rest of the city, this mosque was built between 1830 and 1848 and imitates the great religious structures of Istanbul, though the deco-

Rooftops of Cairo.

ration is a hybrid of European, pharaonic and Islamic motifs. Its size, setting, and ease of access, however, have made it a popular tourist site; and the Pasha himself is buried here under a marble cenotaph. The clock tower in the outer court was given to him in 1846 by Louis Philippe, in belated exchange for the obelisk set up in the Place de la Concorde in Paris in 1833.

South of the mosque are the remains of Mohammed Ali's **Gawharah ("Bijou") Palace**, completed in 1814, the seat of the viceregal court and the centre of government from then until 1874, when the Khedive Ismail, Mohammed Ali's grandson, moved his family and administration to the vast new Abdin Palace. A museum for decades, the Gawharah was gutted by fire in 1972. The administrative wing has not been rebuilt, but a refurbished audience hall and private apartments display furniture and curios that once belonged to the Ali dynasty. The name "Bijou" refers only to the style of its amenities: it contains no collection of jewellery.

The **National Police Museum**, opposite the Mosque of an-Nasir Mohammed, consists of displays around the terrace that Mohammed Ali built over the site of a Mamluke palace. The terrace was originally intended as an artillery platform from which to bombard the city and thus offers a spectacular panorama of medieval Cairo's minarets and domes. On a rare clear day it is possible to see as far as the pyramids of Giza and Sakkara.

Dominating the Northern Enclosure is Mohammed Ali's **Harim Palace**, constructed in 1827, now housing the **Egyptian Military Museum**. Especially attractive is the Summer Room, built around a cooling system of marble fountains, basins, and channels. Beyond the Harim Palace is a small **carriage museum**, containing eight carriages formerly used by the Mohammed Ali family, borrowed from the larger Carriage Museum in Bulaq. At the far end of the Northern Enclosure is the **Mosque of Sulayman Pasha**, erected in 1528 to serve the Janissary regiment which was

Left, Mohammed Ali Mosque. Below, the Citadel.

quartered in the Northern Enclosure, a charming example of Ottoman provincial architecture.

The Red Way: The glory of Cairo is its medieval architecture, plentifully visible below the Citadel. Northwest is the 10th-century royal enclave of Al-Qahirah, built by the Fatimid dynasty. Between the Citadel and Al-Qahirah is the district developed as an aristocratic quarter in the 14th century by the relatives and retainers of the prolific Sultan an-Nasr Mohammed. It is named **Darb al-Ahmar** (The Red Way), after its major thoroughfare. On the *maydan* (square) immediately below the Citadel, for example, opposite the Bab al-Azab, soar the walls of the **Tomb and Madrasah of Sultan Hasan**, the seventh son of An-Nasir Mohammed.

The noblest outstanding example of Bahri Mamluke architecture, this mosque was begun in 1356 and not finished until seven years later. Sultan Hasan himself disappeared in 1361, presumably murdered, and therefore never saw it completed. In contrast with the congregational mosque of Ibn Tulun, it combines four residential colleges (*madrasahs*) with a mausoleum. The towering main entrance has a canopy of stalactites and carved peonies show Chinese influence.

A bent passageway leads to the cruciform central court. Here four great arched recesses or *iwans* create sheltered spaces for instruction in each of the four schools of Islamic jurisprudence, the Hanafi, the Shafii, the Maliki and the Hanbali. Multistoreyed living quarters for teachers and students are built into the corners of the court. From the domed tomb chamber behind it six ground-level windows offer a splendid and unobstructed view up to the mosque-topped Citadel.

Across the street is the **Rifai Mosque**, begun in 1869, six centuries later than the Sultan Hasan mosque and completed in 1912. Because it was planned as a complement to its Mamluke neighbour in scale, fabric, and architectural style, tourists frequently mistake it for an ancient monument. In it are interred the

Tomb and Madrasah of Sultan Hasan.

Khedive Ismail, his mother, two of his daughters, three of his wives, four sons including Sultan Husayn Kamil and King Fu'ad, Fu'ad's son King Farouk, whose body was moved here from the Southern Cemetery, and Mohammed Reza Pahlevi, the last Shah of Iran, whose first wife was Farouk's sister. The roofed and carpeted interior is magnificently adorned with Mamluke-inspired motifs.

The Darb al-Ahmar runs from the Citadel to **Bab Zuwayla**, the southern gate of Al-Qahirah, and is lined with medieval buildings. Visitors are sometimes taken to see the mosque of the amir **Aqsunqur** (1347), which contains the tomb of Kuchuk, the brother of Sultan Hasan, murdered in 1341 at the age of six.

Three hundred years later (1652) it was half-heartedly done up by an Ottoman officer, who had the walls partially covered with Damascene tiles. Guides consequently call the building the "**Blue Mosque**," but anyone expecting it to resemble the famous Blue Mosque in Istanbul will be extremely disappointed.

Far more beautiful is the **Mosque of Altunbugha Maridani**, built in 1339 by a son-in-law of An-Nasir Mohammed. Demarcated by a superb 14th-century wooden *mashrabiyyah*, its sanctuary contains a marble dado that is exceptionally fine, though badly damaged by rising damp, and a *mihrab* decorated with coloured marble, mother-of-pearl and blue faïence. Between these two mosques are the *mashrabiyyah* casements of an 18th-century townhouse called **Bayt ar-Razzaz**, constructed around a 15th-century core. As the Darb al-Ahmar curves westward towards Bab Zuwayla, the exquisite **Mosque of Qijmas al-Ishaqi** (1481) appears on the right. Its carved stucco windows and varicoloured marble panelling were restored in 1981.

Just outside Bab Zuwayla itself is the covered-in 14th-century **Souq al-Khiyamiyyah (Tentmakers' Bazaar)**, where the tentmakers still sit cross-legged on raised platforms in tiny shops on either side of the street, stitching away at the bright appliqué from which temporary pavilions are made. A continuation of the Darb al-Ahmar, which now changes its name to **Shari Ahmed Mahir**, heads past Bab Zuwayla westward to the **Museum of Islamic Art**, which contains over 75,000 objects, many of them inscribed with the names of Cairo's princes, kings and caliphs.

Inside Al-Qahirah: Massive **Bab Zuwayla**, finished in 1092, marks the southern boundary of Al-Qahirah, the walled royal enclosure founded by the Fatimids in AD 969. Enclosing a bit less than a square mile, sections of its stone walls still stand, pierced by Bab Zuwayla in the south and two other fortified gates in the north, **Bab al-Futuh** (1087) and **Bab an-Nasr** (1087). Except for the objects preserved in the Museum of Islamic Art, the Fatimids' almost unbelievable material wealth – including 120,000 manuscripts, the greatest library of the medieval world – was dispersed when they were overthrown by Salah ad-Din, who opened up their enclosure to ordinary folk.

Inheriting the commercial role of

The "Blue Mosque" of Aqsunqur.

Fustat, Al-Qahirah became an international entrepôt specialising in Eastern luxuries. *Wakalahs* – warehouses with long-term residential accommodation – sprang up throughout the city and many are actually still in use. Three important mosques from the Fatimid golden age survive, however, within what was their royal enclosure; and a fourth – the **Mosque of As-Salih Tala'i** (1160) – stands just outside Bab Zuwayla.

Running in a straight line between Bab Zuwayla and Bab al-Futuh, thus bisecting Al-Qahirah, is a street that has various names in short stretches, but is conveniently known as the **Qasabah** or High Street. It has been a vital artery since medieval times, since it continues beyond both Bab al-Futuh and Bab Zuwayla and links up the entire city. The modern street called **Shari Al-Azhar**, which was cut through the district in 1927, crosses the Qasabah at right angles and divides Al-Qahirah into northern and southern zones.

Just inside Bab Zuwayla is the **Mosque of Sultan Muayyad Shaykh,** begun to fulfil a vow in 1412. To serve this last great courtyard mosque, the Burgi Mamluke sultan erected two minarets on the top of the adjacent Fatimid gate and built an adjoining bath complex that is palatial in scale. The interior is decorated in marble and stucco, ebony, mother-of-pearl and blue faïence and the doors came from the Mosque of Sultan Hasan.

Sections of the Qasabah are bazaars and therefore have names derived from the particular trades or occupations carried on in them. From Bab Zuwayla northwards the street offers all manner of household goods: brass bedsteads, tarbooshes (felt hats with tassels), feather dusters, and cheap shoes.

Just before Shari al-Azhar is the area called the **Ghuriyyah,** thanks to its having been owned by Qansuh al-Ghuri, one of the last Mamluke sultans. In 1504 he built the mausoleum and *madrasah* that stand on opposite sides of the Qasabah here, with the **Souq al-Haririyyin (Silk-Mercers' Bazaar)** occupying the basement vaults of both

Perfume shop.

buildings and the space between them. Al-Ghuri also built a superb *hammam* (bath), recently restored, a *wakalah*, where ground-floor rooms now display examples of traditional crafts, and a palace, of which the remains are still visible behind the mausoleum, which today serves as a cultural centre.

Part of the **Souq al-Attariin (Herbalists' Bazaar)** is here and it extends north of Shari Al-Azhar, which cuts through Al-Qahirah at this point and can only be crossed by using a green-painted iron bridge or a tunnel. Slashing across the Qasabah, it brings heavy traffic right past the main entrance of the **Mosque of Al-Azhar** ("The Resplendent"), founded in 970, the most famous seat of learning in the Muslim world. Now a university, its centre is the original congregational mosque built by the Fatimids, a courtyard surrounded by keel-arched arcading.

Khan al-Khalili: Opposite the university on the other side of Shari al-Azhar, in the northern zone of Al-Qahirah, is the popular shrine of **Sayyidna (Our Lord) Husayn**, grandson of the Prophet, murdered in AD 680, which is used by the President and members of the government on state occasions. Between Sayyidna Husayn and the Qasabah is the city's most famous tourist market, the **Khan al-Khalili bazaar,** which takes its name from the fact that it is housed in and around the ruins of a 14th-century *khan* or *wakalah* (warehouse). Most people enjoy browsing through its welter of wares, though better quality and more variety are offered elsewhere in the city.

The stretch of the Qasabah right beside Khan al-Khalili is the **Souq as-Sagha (Goldsmiths' Bazaar).** Gold and silver are sold by weight, as are brass and copperware in the neighbouring **Souq an-Nahhasiin (Coppersmiths' Bazaar)**, which has occupied the same place since the 14th century.

Between the palaces: Northward the Qasabah widens out into a space that was once the most important in the city: **Bayn al-Qasrayn.** The name means "Between the Two Palaces" and refers

Bread-making in Khan al-Khalili.

DEALINGS WITH THE NATIVES

In 1885, which is to say 16 years after the opening of the Suez Canal and the 10th anniversary of Stanley's pronouncement on the true source of the Nile, tourism in Egypt had reached such a volume that Karl Baedeker of Leipzig rushed out a second edition of his guide to Egypt. The urgency is reflected in a kind of stop press at the conclusion of the historical section. The British army had despatched a rescue mission up the Nile, it reported. "Though an absolutely trustworthy account of the fate of General Gordon has not yet been received, there is almost no room to doubt that he perished at the capture of Khartum."

Under the rather brisk heading of "Dealings with the Natives", Baedeker warns that the traveller "will find it exceedingly difficult to deal with the class of people with whom he chiefly comes in contact. The extravagance of their demands is boundless, and they appear to think that Europeans are absolutely ignorant of the value of money."

Many of these petty annoyances could be eliminated, according to Baedeker, by the employment of a suitable dragoman (as guides used to be known), although "most of the dragomans are fond of assuming a patronising manner towards their employers, while they generally treat their own countrymen with an air of vast superiority."

Although both nominally illegal and a "pernicious and degrading custom", the smoking of hashish – "the strong and unmistakeable smell of which is often perceptible even in the street" – is dealt with in some detail: "Hasheesh is to be obtained not only at some of the coffee shops: there are shops of a smaller and more private description solely appropriated to the sale of this and other intoxicating preparations: they are called *mahsheshehs*. It is sometimes amusing to observe the ridiculous conduct, and to listen to the conversation, of the persons who frequent these shops. They are all of the lower orders…"

Travellers were advised not to expect too much of the local music: "The Egyptians consider themselves a highly musical people, and the traveller will indeed often be struck by the frequency of their singing. The Egyptian sings when indulging in his kef (i.e. while relaxing after a bath), whether sitting on his heels or stretched out on his mat, when driving his donkey, when carrying stones and mortar up a scaffolding, when working in the fields, and when rowing.

"A peculiarity of the Egyptian songs, however, is that they have no tune… They are sung through the nose on seven or eight different notes, on which the performer wanders up and down as he feels inclined. The character of this so-called music is exceedingly monotonous. The songs are all of a lyrical description, most of them are erotic and often grossly obscene, and many are at the same time pointless and meaningless."

Baedeker moves on to other forms of entertainment: "The female dancers… were formerly one of the chief curiosities of Egypt, but for some years past they have been prohibited from performing in the streets. Really good dancers are said to be now rare, but on the Nile voyage the traveller will have an opportunity at Keneh, Luksor, and Esneh of seeing very curious and elaborate, though to his taste often ungraceful performances…"

On the plainly-stated business of "Intercourse with Orientals", not meant quite as it now sounds but hovering on the brink, "Europeans, as a rule, should never enquire after the wives of a Muslim, his relations to the fair sex being sedulously veiled from the public. Even looking at women in the street or in a house is considered indecorous, and may in some cases be attended with danger.

"Intimate acquaintance with Orientals is also to be avoided… Beneath the interminable protestations of friendship with which the traveller is overwhelmed, lurks in most cases the demon of cupidity, the sole motive of those who use them being the hope of some gain or bakshish."

After having been thoroughly alerted to all the pitfalls, the reader is regaled with a comforting summary: "the most ordinary observer cannot fail to be struck with the fact that the degraded ruffianism so common in the most civilised countries is unknown in Egypt." ∎

to the two enormous Fatimid palaces that stood on this site.

Dominating Bayn al-Qasrayn is the splendid monumental ensemble built by a succession of Mamluke sultans. The largest element is the complex erected in 1284 for the Bahri Mamluke sultan **Qalawun**, who founded a dynasty that lasted almost a century. It includes a *madrasah*, a mausoleum, a mosque, and the remains of a hospital (a clinic still operates on the site).

Qalawun is buried in a majestic tomb chamber. His son An-Nasir Mohammed – who had the longest reign of all the Mamlukes – chose to be buried here with him, rather than in the next door **Madrasah of An-Nasir Mohammed** (1326), which was originally intended to be his mausoleum. The Gothic-looking doorway was brought from a Crusader church at Acre; the Spanish-looking stucco-work on the minaret was carved by Andalusian craftsmen, refugees from Christian persecution.

The third building in the ensemble is the **Mausoleum and Madrasah of**

Barquq, the first of the Circassian Mamluke sultans. Barquq's son Farag built another and far grander mausoleum in the Northern Cemetery where Barquq is actually buried, but this one, built in 1384, is nobly proportioned.

Almost across the street is the **Kasr Beshtak**, the five-storey palace built by Amir Beshtak, one of an-Nasir's sons-in-law, in 1339. The remains of a water-raising system that supplied running water to every floor are still in evidence. At a corner a few metres further on stands the charming little 18th-century *sabil-kuttab* (fountain-school) of **Abd ar-Rahman Katkhuda**.

The Qasabah goes to the left here, leading past the badly restored Fatimid **Mosque of Al-Aqmar, "the Moonlit"** (1125), which sits below street-level a few metres further along. At number 19 in the Darb al-Asfar, the first large lane to the right beyond Al-Aqmar, is **Bayt as-Sihaymi**, a charming 17th-century townhouse, open to the public.

Another hundred metres up the Qasabah stands the great congregational **Mosque of Al-Hakim** (1010), the second Fatimid caliph, rebuilt in the early 1980s by a Shi'ite sect from western India who claim descent from the Fatimids. The Al-Hakim mosque stands against a surviving section of the **North Wall** that connects the round-towered **Bab al-Futuh** ("Gate of Conquest") with the square-towered **Bab an-Nasr** ("Gate of Victory"). The wall and both towers are well worth exploring and the views southward take in a thousand domes and minarets. Northward is the Bab an-Nasr cemetery, in continuous use since Fatimid times.

Important graves: Cairo's key burial places – and part of the living city because more than a million people live in and around the tombs – are the Northern and Southern Cemeteries.

Principal monuments in the **Northern Cemetery** northeast of the Citadel, for example, include the **Khanqah of Farag ibn Barquq** (1410), one of the most impressive buildings in Cairo. Two other huge complexes just north of it, built by Sultan Inal (1456) and Amir Qurqumas al-Kabir (1507), are part of **One of the Qasabah's medieval sidestreets.**

long-term projects undertaken by the Polish-Egyptian Group for Restoration of Islamic Monuments.

A hundred metres south of the Khanqah of Farag ibn Barquq is the complex of **Sultan Ashraf Barsbay** (1432) and further down the same road is the **Mosque of Qaytbay** (1472), an architectural jewel that is depicted on the Egyptian one-pound note. With this building, the most exquisite of the Circassian Mamluke monuments, the art of stone carving in Cairo reached its pinnacle.

In the larger and older **Southern Cemetery**, to the south of the Citadel, is the **Mausoleum of Imam ash-Shafii**, the founder of the Shafiite school of Islamic law, whose tomb was first built by order of Salah ad-Din in 1180. Salah ad-Din's carved teak cenotaph for the saint still stands in the tomb chamber.

Nearby is the **Hawsh al-Basha**, constructed by Mohammed Ali in 1820 as a family tomb, though he himself is buried at the Citadel. Many Bahri Mamluke princes are buried here in elegant tombs which can be distinguished by their domes and minarets.

Downtown attractions: Modern Cairo, what is regarded today as the city's centre, contains fewer major historical attractions than the areas mentioned above. At its heart, though, is the **Egyptian Museum**, by the river just north of Maydan at-Tahrir. Displays on the ground floor are arranged clockwise more or less chronologically. Thus Pre-Dynastic and Old Kingdom objects are left of the entrance, from which the conscientious visitor can work his way round to Roman-period objects, ending with a replica of the Rosetta Stone next to the entrance on the right.

The **treasures of Tutankhamun** occupy two large galleries on the floor above, but the queue to see them often extends down the stairs. Other galleries upstairs are also worth seeing. In Room 27, for instance, are models found in an 11th-Dynasty tomb showing life as it was in 2000 BC. And in the foyer at the head of the stairs near the entrance is Case H, containing some of the muse-

The Egyptian Museum.

um's particular prizes, most of them made famous from postcards or photographs in books that give no idea of their diminutive size: the ivory statuette of Cheops from Abydos; the black bust of Queen Tiyi; the statuette of a Nubian girl with a single earring; the gilded statuette of Ptah; the ivory pygmies who dance to the tug of a string; and the blue faïence hippopotamuses that have been reproduced all over the world.

The museum gazes across a row of bus-stops into **Maydan at-Tahrir** ("Liberation Square"), which was originally called Maydan Ismailiyyah and boasted a statue of the Magnificent Khedive in its centre. After the 1952 Revolution the square was renamed and the statue was hauled away, though its massive plinth was not finally dismantled for 25 years. Its site marks the approximate centre of modern Cairo, most of whose streets, squares, and parks appear in the master plan for the city, modelled on the Paris of that time, that Khedive Ismail's ministers developed between 1867 and 1873.

Island retreats: Congestion, traffic, and air pollution have tended to make touring modern Cairo either on foot or by car increasingly unpleasant. The islands, however, offer modern attractions that are worth a specific visit. On Rawdah, for example, is the **Manyal Palace complex**, which can be visited in combination with Old Cairo and the Nilometer mentioned previously. Built by Prince Mohammed Ali, younger brother of Khedive Abbas II Hilmi, first cousin of King Farouk and Heir Apparent until 1952, it contains a huge *salamlik* or reception palace, the two-storey *haramlik* that was the prince's residence, a model throne room, a museum with superb collections of furniture, calligraphy, glass, silver, textiles, costumes, and porcelain. A hunting museum is to the right of the main entrance.

On the island of **Gazirah** the most important structure is the Japanese-built **National Cultural Centre**, known as the **New Opera House,** at the Gazirah Exhibition Grounds. Opened in 1988, the New Opera House contains three stages, as well as exhibition halls and

<u>Left</u>, local attraction. <u>Below</u>, downtown hotel pool.

practice rooms, and has hosted troupes from all over the world. Ballet is particularly popular.

Also within the Exhibition Grounds are the **Museum of Modern Egyptian Art** and the **Nile Hall**, where the work of contemporary artists is displayed. In the Planetarium building next to the New Opera House is a curious **Museum of Egyptian Civilisation**; one floor above it is the **Gazirah Museum**, a display of miscellaneous paintings and *objets d'art*, some inherited from the now defunct Museum of Modern Art, some confiscated from the Mohammed Ali family, much of it interesting, all of it in need of lighting, cataloguing, dusting, cleaning, and redisposition in an intelligible order.

The garden of the **Gazirah Palace,** built by Khedive Ismail between 1863 and 1868, is now the grounds of the **Cairo Marriott Hotel**, which incorporates the palace in its central structure and contains much of the furniture the Khedive brought back from the Paris Exposition of 1867.

The suburb of **Zamalek** occupies the northern half of Gazirah and offers art galleries and upmarket boutiques, as well as more than half of this capital city's embassies and consulates. Originally a luxury suburb, it has become increasingly commercialised and its main streets now exhibit a fascinating mixture of wealth and poverty, cosmopolitan trendiness and folk tradition. The new suburbs on the Giza side of the Nile – Mohandisiin, Aguza, Duqqi – have all grown up since 1965 and look, by contrast, pretty much like the new suburbs of any city, anywhere.

In **Gizah**, on the Gizah Corniche, the **Muhammad Mahmud and Emilienne Luce Khalil Museum** houses the **Khalil Collection**. This bequest to the nation concentrates on French 19th-century painting – Ingrès, Delacroix, Daumier, Corot, Courbet, Renoir, Sisley, Pissarro, Degas, Manet, Monet – but also includes some sculpture, chinoiserie, japonaiserie, and turquoiserie. The house, confiscated from the Mohammed Ali family, is worth visiting for its own sake.

Gazira island (foreground) and Giza.

THE DELTA

After the noise of Cairo, the River Nile is ready for the peace of the sea. In its hurry to get there it splits, first in two, then into the myriad canals and streams of the Delta. But in this densely populated region of Egypt, so named by the Greeks for its similarity on the map to their triangular letter D, the river has yet to endure its most intensive use by man.

A hundred miles (160 km) wide at its Mediterranean base and 100 miles long, the flat, rich Nile Delta contains more than half Egypt's agricultural land and much of its industry. Fifteen million Egyptians live in its thousands of villages, cultivating extensive mango and citrus orchards, cotton, wheat and vegetables for the stomachs of the insatiable capital. Roads, railways, bridges and canals crisscross the land. To the east and west the once impenetrable desert is giving way to mammoth land reclamation projects.

Unsurprisingly, the people of the Delta are known chiefly for their industriousness, particularly as compared to their libidinous Upper Egyptian cousins. Yet despite proximity to cosmopolitan Cairo and Alexandria and a relatively advanced economic base, patches of the Delta are still pretty backward, as can be seen from the vintage taxis that chug along its byways.

A watery past: The Delta was once part of the sea. Millennia of Nile alluvia washing down from Ethiopia created first swamps, then fabulously fertile farmland. During the annual flood river water turned the Delta into a vast lake. Consequently the Ancient Egyptian inhabitants built their towns on hills and hummocks which appeared like islands when the inundation was at its height.

Early in history the Delta was a relatively wild region whose people were distinct from their cousins in Upper Egypt. Some 5,000 years ago the first pharaohs joined Egypt's marshy north to the niparian south in a united kingdom, symbolised in their elaborate headdresses that combined the crowns of Lower and Upper Egypt. In the course of time the Delta grew tamer, and by late antiquity its cities – Tanis, Sais, Naucratis, Bubastis – had largely overtaken Thebes, Memphis and other southern capitals in importance.

But sadly for us, whereas Upper Egypt enjoyed an accessible supply of sturdy building stone, the Delta had to make do with mudbrick. As a result, little of the glory of its past has endured. Although many of the most precious individual objects in the Egyptian Museum were found there, the ancient sites of the Delta are for the most part mounds of mud and shards intelligible only to the most patient of excavators. The greatest of them, Tanis in the Eastern Delta, is nothing but a desolate heap of dirt littered with chunks of masonry.

Because of their lack of standing structures, the Delta sites have until recently received little attention from archaeologists. But with the intensification of agriculture that followed the building of the High Dam at Aswan, waterlogging has become a serious worry to Egypt's

Antiquities Organisation, which now actively promotes excavation in the Delta to save what they can before its too late.

Environmental concerns: Indeed, the Delta environment is perhaps the most fragile and threatened of any in the Nile basin. Overuse of irrigation has caused serious drainage problems, pushing salts to the surface and reducing the fertility of the soil – which is no longer replenished by the Nile's flood-borne silt. Pollution from untreated waste and agricultural chemicals has sharply reduced the fish catch, particularly in the nothern lakes where fishing was once a major source of livelihood. Attempts to control some hazards have exacerbated others: government use of weedkiller on the water hyacinth, a pestiferous plant that clogs canals, was found to be decimating aquatic fauna.

Worst of all, the Mediterranean Sea is swelling with the melting of polar ice caps caused by global warming, and threatens to drown the low-lying Delta. Where the Nile flows into the sea at Damietta and Rosetta, gigantic concrete dykes are being built to prevent shore erosion. Already lighthouses built onshore have been swamped. In the resort of Ras al Bar a whole row of beach houses has gone and high tide now laps in the living rooms of the next row.

A Delta tour: The Delta begins in Cairo itself, where the first of its canals branches eastwards, heading ultimately to the Suez Canal at Ismailia along the route of the ancient seaway built by the Persians in the 6th century BC. But the great city's industrial suburbs do not end until the river itself divides. This spot is marked by the multiple arches and sluices of the **Barrages** built in the 19th century to control the annual flood. Here extensive parks, now somewhat frayed, are a favourite destination for summer outings.

Northwards the plain broadens continuously, dotted with tiny hamlets and the remnants of the huge estates that were divided up by the revolutionary government of the 1950s. Sadly, a loss of local pride seems to have accompanied the decline of the landed gentry

that once built stylish villas and parks here. Provincial towns like Shibin el Kom, Damanhur, Kafr el Sheikh, Benha and Mansura are overgrown and have little to offer. Even Zagazig is not as prepossessing as its name suggests.

On a smaller scale the Delta towns suffer the same problems as Cairo: overpopulation, housing shortages, inadequate public services, lack of planning. However, the state bureaucracy's preoccupation with impressing government ministers and foreign visitors means that provinces receive far less attention than the capital.

The largest city of the Delta is **Tanta**, a ramshackle place that marks the halfway point between Cairo and Alexandria. Every October its half-million inhabitants are swollen to four times their number during the Islamic saint's day of Ahmed al Bedawi, a 13th-century mystic who founded Egypt's most numerous Sufi brotherhood. Despite its ancient, even pre-Islamic origins, this biggest *mulid* of the Egyptian calendar is now a modern affair complete with

A Delta farmer's wife.

megaphones, strobe lights and riot police. By day pilgrims flood to the grandiose tomb and mosque of the saint, which is ringed by graphically advertised circumcision booths and vendors of sweets, whistles and party hats. By night increasingly rowdy revellers throng the streets.

Other towns hold similar festivals for local Christian, Muslim and even Jewish saints. But these days Delta cities are better known for their industries. **Talkha** is dominated by its mammoth fertiliser plant, **Kafr al Dawar** and **Mehalla al Kubra** are restive centres of the textile industry based on Egyptian cotton. **Damietta,** an ancient seaport near the mouth of the river that bears its name, has grown prosperous producing the lurid rococo furniture so beloved of Egyptian mothers-in-law.

Alone among its sister towns, **Rosetta**, where the famous stone that provided the key to deciphering hieroglyphics was found, still has much charm. Its neat, narrow lanes lined with brick houses, some dating back to its time of glory in the Middle Ages, run down to a waterfront lined with fishing vessels and primitive boatyards.

The Nile meets the Mediterranean: Five miles (8 km) downstream, the Rosetta branch of the Nile, much reduced by man's uses, slides quietly and undramatically into the sea. To the west, the Damietta branch does the same, entering the Mediterranean at Ras el Bar. In between, the windswept coast is largely barren.

Along the Delta shore lies a series of wide, marshy lakes: **Maryut, Edku, Burullus** and **Manzala.** Accessible only by elegant pointed punts, these wetlands have long been hideouts for fugitives from justice. They also provide refuge for the migrating waterfowl of Europe.

The Bride of the Sea: Although it is not strictly of the Nile – indeed the river is only linked to it by canal – no description of Egypt would be complete without some sort of mention of its second city, **Alexandria**.

To Egyptians this great and ancient port is known as the Bride of the Sea.

Raising water at sunrise.

THE ROSETTA STONE

Pierre Bouchard, a Frenchman working for Napoleon, was strengthening a fort at Rosetta when he turned up a stone about the size of a small gravestone, whose implications were immediately obvious even to an army engineer. He announced his discovery in the armed forces newspaper which Napoleon's specially imported printing presses were producing in Cairo: "a stone of very fine granite, black, with a close grain, and very hard... with three distinct inscriptions separated in three parallel bands."

Two of the bands were in the meaningless scripts to be seen on monuments all along the Nile. No one had been able to understand the hieroglyphs since the 4th century AD, and the few words which had passed into the Coptic language were no help. The Arabs insisted, and others accepted, that each hieroglyphic sign represented a whole idea, not a letter of some alphabet.

The exciting part of Bouchard's discovery was the last of the parallel bands, which was in readable Greek. That much was easy: the stone identified itself as a proclamation issued by Ptolemy V in 196 BC and actually said that the other languages were Egyptian. One was the classic form of hieroglyphs, the other a more manageable demotic script derived from it. The stone was hurried to Cairo where Napoleon immediately had casts made, some of which were despatched to France for scholars to ponder.

Napoleon later sneaked back to France, and in due course his abandoned army surrendered to the British. One of the terms of surrender was that Britain would take everything the *savants* had collected in Egypt. The French scholars were understandably appalled and threatened to dump the whole lot. Happily the British were willing to negotiate – but not over the Rosetta Stone. On this point the British army officers were being strenuously lobbied by two civilians who knew a thing or two about Egyptian antiquity, one of them being William Hamilton, on whose advice Lord Elgin had carted off large chunks of the Parthenon in Athens, the still controversial "Elgin Marbles".

A French general had the stone hidden in his house in Alexandria and had no intention of letting it go, but a British colonel learned of its whereabouts, broke in at night and seized it. The colonel, Thomas Turner, then watched over it all the way back to the British Museum in London.

The decipherment of the Rosetta Stone became something of a race, albeit at a snail's pace. A Swede named Akerblad spotted that royal names in the Greek part had fairly obvious equivalents in the demotic. He also recognised three words: "his", "Greek" and "temple".

In England the pioneering work was done by a grown-up child prodigy, Thomas Young, who could read English perfectly at two years of age, understand a dozen languages at 14, and went on to become the *Encyclopaedia Britannica*'s authority on no fewer than 400 languages. He made quick work of the demotic signs, establishing that the "rope-loops" now called cartouches were the names – almost the coats of arms – of kings. Recognising that all three versions had letters which spelt out P-T-O-L-E-M-Y meant that hieroglyphs were a kind of alphabet and had a grammar.

Young forwarded his findings to Jean-François Champollion in France, another prodigy who at 16 had presented a paper arguing that Coptic was the language of the ancient Egyptians. He had progressed to a professorship at Grenoble University and was still under the impression that hieroglyphic symbols represented whole ideas when Young put him on the right track, a debt he never acknowledged.

Nevertheless, full credit is due to Champollion for the conclusive decipherment which he announced in what is known as *Lettre à M. Dacier*, the Secretary of the French Royal Academy of Inscriptions. "I have now reached the point where I can put together almost a complete survey of the general structure of these two forms of writing," he declared confidently.

Unluckily he died in 1832 at the age of 42 before the publication of his historic grammar, after which, instead of being mere decoration on walls and papyri, hieroglyphs sprang to life as the deeds, words and thoughts of people who had been muted for 1,500 years. ∎

The name seems corny, but Alexandria's intimate relationship with the Mediterranean makes it strangely appropriate. The city of 6 million inhabitants is slender – only a few miles wide from north to south. But it reclines along the shore, stretching from east to west for 30 miles (48 km). So one is never far in Alexandria from the sound of the surf or the smell of fresh fish. In summer, hordes of festive Egyptians live on the beaches of Maamoura, Montaza, Stanley Bay and Agami. In the winter a dozen fierce sea storms rinse the city and rust away the wrought-iron balconies of the seafront Corniche.

The presence of the sea lends Alexandria a meditative air that is notably absent elsewhere in Egypt. The city has much to reflect upon: its history is one of unrivalled opulence followed by penury followed by renewed splendour.

Founded by Alexander the Great, Alexandria grew under his successors in Egypt, the Greek-speaking Ptolemies, into the most illustrious centre of Hellenic culture in the Mediterranean. The wealthy Ptolemies embellished their capital with fine buildings, including the lighthouse of Pharos which was considered one of the Seven Wonders of the World.

Alexandria's famous institutions, the **Library** and the **Mouseion**, carried the baton of Greek science and literature until the fall of the Roman Empire. It was here that the earth was shown to be round, that the Old Testament was translated, that geometry was invented, that medical science was advanced more than in the succeeding thousand years.

In the late Roman age the city declined amid squabbles between its polyglot religious communities. In a sign of decay, the Pharos itself disappeared sometime in the Middle Ages. When Napoleon invaded Egypt at the end of the 18th-century Alexandria was little more than a fishing village.

Alexandria's fortunes were to rise again only in the past two centuries as the importance of Egypt's Mediterranean trade – and especially that in cotton – grew. By the 1920s it was an attractive town of parks and squares, Italianate villas, banks and department stores where Greek, Italian or French were as likely to be heard as Arabic. Its louche mores and Levantine atmosphere were to inspire the writings of Cavafy, Forster, Durrell and others.

Modern Alexandria is less cosmopolitan and more industrialised. Foreign communities have dwindled in numbers while heavy industries – rubber, cement, chemicals, steel – have prospered. Of its pre-Revolutionary heyday some of the faded charm survives in high-ceilinged cafés and outdoor restaurants. But with its seafront high-rises the city of today has begun to resemble Chicago more than Naples. And of Alexandria's glorious ancient past there is little to be seen outside the superb little **Greco-Roman Museum** (which houses one of the world's greatest coin collections). Aside from some interesting catacombs and other ruins, all of the ancient city lies underground, its artefacts unearthed on occasion by construction crews erecting tower blocks for holidaying Cairenes.

Naval customers at a café in Alexandria.

INSIGHT GUIDES
Travel Tips

Your vacation.

Your vacation after losing your wallet in the ocean.

 Lose your cash and it's lost forever. Lose American Express®
Travelers Cheques and get them replaced. They can mean
the difference between the vacation of your dreams and
your worst nightmare. And, they are accepted like cash
worldwide. Available at participating banks, credit unions, AAA offices
and American Express Travel locations. *Don't take chances. Take American Express
Travelers Cheques.*

do more

**Travelers
Cheques**

Getting Acquainted

The Place 306
The Climate 306
The Economy 306
Government 306
Geography & Population 306
Etiquette 306

Planning the Trip

What to Bring 307
What to Wear 307
Entry Regulations 307
On Arrival 307
On Departure 307
Health 307
Money 308
Public Holidays 308
Getting There 308
Specialist Tours 309
Special Facilities 309
Useful Addresses 309

Practical Tips

Business Hours 309
Religion & Religious
Services 309
Media 310
Postal Services 311
Telephone 311
Internet 311
Embassies
& Consulates in Egypt 311
Emergencies 311

Getting Around

Orientation 312
From the Airport 312
Public Transport 313
Private Transport 313
On Foot 314
Hitchhiking 314

Where to Stay

Hotels 314

Eating Out

Where to Eat 317
Drinking Notes 318

Attractions

Culture 319
Historical Sites 321
Other Attractions 322
Cruising the Nile 324
Festivals 324
Photography 325

Outdoor Activities

Participant 325
Spectator 325

Shopping

What to Buy 326

Language

Conversation 327

Further Reading

The Nile 328
Other Insight Guides 328

Art/Photo Credits 329
Index 330

Getting Acquainted

The Place

Area: Egypt is 1,002,000 sq. km (386,874 sq. miles)
Capital: Cairo
Highest mountain: Mount Katherine (2,637 metres/8,650 ft)
Longest river: The Nile (6,670 km/ 4,145 miles)
Population: 55,163,000
Language: Arabic, Nubian, Berber, French and English.
Religion: Sunni Muslim (90 percent) and small Coptic Christian minority.
Time zone: GMT plus two hours.
Currency: Egyptian pound, of 100 piastres.
Weights and measures: metric
Electricity: 220 volts.
International dialling code: international access code + 20

Popular Saying

When God created all things
He gave each a companion.
"I shall go to Syria," said Reason.
"I shall go with you," said Rebellion.
Poverty said, "I am going to the desert."
"I'll come along too," said Health.
Abundance said, "I am going to Egypt."
"And I will accompany you," said Endurance.

The Climate

Summers are hot and dry in Upper Egypt, humid in the Delta and along the Mediterranean Coast. In recent years the humidity has spread to Cairo and the city swelters in August. Winters are mild with some rain, but usually there are bright, sunny days and cold nights.

Spring and autumn are short and during the 50 days (khamseen) between the end of March and mid-May dust storms can occur sporadically.

Average Year-round Temperatures
max/min in Fahrenheit (Celsius)

	winter	summer
Alexandria	69/51 (20/10)	86/69 (30/20)
Cairo	69/51 (20/10)	96/68 (35/20)
Luxor	79/42 (26/05)	107/72 (41/22)
Aswan	79/49 (26/09)	108/77 (42/25)

The Economy

Since 1979 there has been a massive influx of foreign aid into Egypt. As a result there are new roads linking all areas of the country, villages up and down the Nile and in the deserts have been electrified, new schools, hospitals and other services have sprung up by the dozen, telephone systems continue to undergo massive renovation and expansion, and the private sector has been encouraged to invest heavily in Egypt's future. The change in Egypt has been dramatic. Everything connected with the infrastructure has improved.

For the tourist there are dozens of new hotels and restaurants, monuments have been restored and their environments spruced up, tour guides are licensed, and retail shops are bursting with good quality products.

The Egyptian pound has been floated, with an exchange value fixed daily and has shown itself to be remarkably stable. For Egyptians, however life is expensive. Rents are high, food though abundant is costly, and salaries lag behind the cost of living.

The major source of income for the country as a whole has been remittances from Egyptians working abroad. Domestically, tourism has become vitally important and visitors are encouraged to spend freely.

Government

Egypt is officially known as the Arab Republic of Egypt (ARE). Its capital city is Cairo and other major cities include Alexandria, Giza, Port Said, Asyut, Suez, Minya, and Aswan. It is a republic with an elected president who is commander in chief of the Army, and leader of the National Defence Council. The prime minister and cabinet are appointed by the president.

There is one legislative body: the National Assembly, composed of elected representatives from all districts of the country, 50 percent of whom must be from the working class or farmers. Copts and women are elected according to a quota. The Shura Council is an advisory body with 140 elected members and another 70 appointed members.

Geography & Population

Egypt links the northeastern corner of Africa and the southwestern edge of Asia.

The country is approximately 1 million sq. km (386,900 sq. miles) in size. Its longest distance north–south is 1,025 km (640 miles) and widest distance east–west is about 1,240 km (775 miles).

The northern border is the Mediterranean Sea and the southern boundary is with the Sudan, at latitude 22 degrees north. Israel, the Gulf of Aqaba, and the Red Sea flank the eastern border, while the whole of the western border is with Libya.

The River Nile stretches 6,670 km (4,145 miles) through Africa, from the Blue Nile in Ethiopia to the White Nile in Sudan. By the time the river crosses the Sudanese border into Egypt it has travelled 5,000 km (3,000 miles)

Egypt's 60 million people live primarily in the Nile Valley, leaving the rest of the land sparsely populated. Cairo, the largest city in Egypt, is estimated to have a population of over 15 million people which is growing at an alarming rate.

Etiquette

Whether Muslim or Copt, the Egyptians as a whole tend to be religious and piety is important in their daily lives. So is commitment to the extended family. Each family member is responsible for the integrity of the family and for the behaviour of other members. Certainly, one result of these concerns is that the city of Cairo is safer than any Western metropolis.

Yet when Westerners visit Egypt they are often apprehensive. Their views of Egyptians and Arabs, fomented by unkind and untrue media stories, often bear no relation to reality. Travellers normally receive friendly, hospitable treatment everywhere and take home with them good feelings about the warmth and goodwill of the Egyptian people.

Planning the Trip

What To Bring

Almost everything is available in Cairo, but may be cheaper at home. Special medication should be brought with you. A small supply of plasters, antibiotic ointments and anti-diarrhoea tablets may well come in handy. If you have a favourite sun lotion, make-up, toothpaste, or shampoo that you cannot possibly live without, bring some with you. A torch or flashlight would be useful for some tombs and *son et lumière*.

What To Wear

Be modest, be sensible, and travel light. Egypt is a conservative country. It is an affront to your hosts to appear in a mosque or even on the street in clothing that is considered immodest. Women should keep shoulders and upper arms covered. Neither men or women should wear shorts except at resorts or on the tennis court. No topless or nude bathing is permitted.

On the practical side, leave your synthetics at home as they will prove to be too hot in summer and not warm enough in winter. Cotton is suitable for all seasons; wool for winter and many summer nights.

Loose and flowing garments are not only modest, but also practical in a hot climate. Hats are vital and necessary, to protect against heat stroke and so are sunglasses, to defend the eyes against the glare.

Bring stout, comfortable shoes. You will be doing a lot of walking and neither Cairo's streets nor Luxor's temple floors are friendly to feet.

Entry Regulations
Visas & Passports

All travellers entering Egypt must have the appropriate travel documents: a passport or other legal pass and a valid visa. Lost or stolen passports must be reported to the police immediately. New passports can be issued in a matter of hours at the consular office of your embassy in Egypt but procedures will require a copy of your police report. Tourist visas are also routinely issued at the Cairo International Airport and the Port of Alexandria, but may be acquired in advance of your visit at any Egyptian consulate.

Types of Visas

Single entry visas are good for one entry into the country for one month. If you require a longer stay, request it at the time of application.

Multiple entry visas should be requested if you plan to exit and re-enter Egypt during your visit.

Student visas for people studying in Egypt are valid for one year and are not issued until the student can verify registration at an Egyptian university.

Business visas are issued to persons with business affiliations in Egypt.

Tourist Residence visas are extended to persons wishing to visit Egypt for an extended period of time. They are not permitted to work in Egypt and must be prepared to present evidence of having exchanged $180 a month for up to six months at a time. This type of visa is only issued in Egypt at the Passport Department of the Mugama'a (central administrative building). Persons holding a Tourist Residence visa must apply for a re-entry visa whenever they plan to leave the country.

All visas may be renewed up to 15 days beyond their expiration date. If not renewed during that time a fine is imposed and a letter of apology from your embassy must be taken to the Mugama'a.

Customs

A visitor is permitted to enter the country with 250 grammes of tobacco, or 50 cigars, one litre of alcohol and their personal effects. Animals must have a veterinary certificate attesting to their good health as well as a valid rabies certificate.

Duty-free purchases of liquor (3 bot-

tles per person) may be made within a month of arrival twice a year at ports of entry or at the tax-free shops in Cairo.

Persons travelling with expensive electronic equipment such as cameras, video cameras, or computers may be required to list these items in their passports to ensure that they will be exported upon departure.

Animal Quarantine

It is not wise to bring a pet to Egypt on vacation. Rabies is a problem in the country and most hotels do not have facilities for animals.

On Arrival

A notice stamped in passports on entry into Egypt says "registration within 7 days" but arrivals in Cairo should in fact be registered within 48 hours, either at the nearest police station or at the Mugama'a, with re-registration at each new city visited. Hotels perform this service routinely, but visitors staying in private houses must make other arrangements to be registered. Their hosts may be held responsible for failure to do so.

On Departure

Although the traveller is free to buy and export reasonable quantities of Egyptian goods for personal use, the export of large quantities of items requires an export license. Egyptian-made items over two years old are not permitted to leave the country. Nor are foreign-made items deemed to have "historic value". Exportation of carpets, Egyptian-made or not, is restricted. Travellers may be requested to show bank receipts as proof of payment for other valuable items. Egyptian currency may not be taken out of Egypt. Travellers may exchange their extra pounds at the airport provided they have valid bank receipts.

Health

Evidence of yellow fever and cholera immunisation may be required from persons who have been in an infected area within six days prior to arrival.

Money

Airport Exchange

Banks are available at the airport for currency exchange. Egyptian money, with both Arabic and English numerals, consists of these denominations:
Pound notes (LE): 100, 20, 10, 5, 1.
Piastre notes: 50, 25.
Coins: 20, 10, 5.

Credit cards are used in most major hotels, but not always in shops. Bring some traveller's cheques.

Public Holidays

There are currently six official government holidays a year when banks, government offices, many businesses and schools are closed. In addition there are Islamic and Coptic holidays spread throughout the year.

New Year's Day. Public holiday.

Coptic Christmas, January 7. Copts observe the birth of Christ on the same date as all other Orthodox churches except the Armenian. Prior to the feast they abstain from animal flesh and animal products for 43 days.

Feast of Breaking the Fast, Id al-Fitr, celebrates the end of Ramadan, the month of fasting. During daylight hours, Muslims will have abstained from food, drink, sex and violence for some 30 days. Business hours are shortened during Ramadan and social life, centering on the meal eaten after sunset, called *iftar*, becomes nocturnal and intense. The Id al-Fitr is a happy celebration with new clothes, gifts, and plenty of good food. Festivities usually last for three days.

Feast of the Sacrifice, Id al-Adha, begins approximately 70 days after the end of Ramadan and commemorates Abraham's sacrifice of a sheep in place of his son, Isaac. It is traditional to kill a sheep and share the meat with the extended family, neighbours, and the poor. Festivities last for four days.

Coptic Easter ends the Coptic Lenten season. It is usually celebrated one week after Western Easter. Coptic businesses are closed.

Sham an-Nissim, "sniffing the breeze", is a holiday celebrated the Monday after Coptic Easter. Dating from Pharaonic times, it is celebrated by all Egyptians regardless of religious affiliation. The entire population goes to the countryside or to some urban green space for a day long outing, with picnic baskets filled with hard boiled eggs and pickled fish. Businesses are closed.

Liberation of Sinai Day, April 25. Public holiday.

Labour Day, May 1. Public holiday.

Islamic New Year, Ras al-Sana al-Higriya. Public holiday.

Anniversary of the 1952 Revolution, July 23. Businesses are closed.

Prophet's Birthday, Mulid eh-Nabi, is celebrated in honour of the Prophet Mohammed. A traditional parade complete with drums and banners is held in the historic area of Cairo. Public holiday.

Armed Forces Day, October 6. Public holiday.

Getting There

By Air

Egypt is served by international airports at Alexandria, Cairo, Luxor, and Hurghada on the mainland, and at Sharm el Sheikh on the Sinai peninsula. The largest and most active airport is at Cairo.

There are non-stop flights from African, Asian and European cities. Return tickets must be confirmed before returning home. Check with a travel agent in your hotel or contact the airline office in Cairo. Most major airlines have offices at the Cairo International Airport and downtown in and around Midan Tahrir.

In recent years Cairo I**nternational Airport** has expanded into a first-class facility. Despite being located to the north of the city, most airlines from Europe approach the airport from the south. In daylight passengers are offered a spectacular view of Cairo, the Nile, and the Giza pyramids.

Terminal 1: Egyptair domestic and international flights.

Terminal 2: International airlines.

Terminal 3: Saudia Arabia Airline.

Terminal 4: International cargo.

English-language information, tel: 291-4255, 291-2266. Quarantine, tel: 666-688.

Alexandria airport is served by Olympic Airlines and Egyptair. **Luxor** Airport now has direct flights from several European cities via Air France and Lufthansa. **Hurghada** Airport is also serviced by Lufthansa while **Sharm el Sheikh** Airport receives charter flights from Germany and France.

Other airports are Asyut, Aswan, Abu Simbel, Al Arish, St Catherine's, Kharga Oasis, Siwa Oasis.

DOMESTIC AIRLINES

Egypt has two national carriers for internal flights, Egyptair and Air Sinai. Egyptair flies daily from Cairo to Alexandria, Luxor, Aswan, Abu Simbel, and Hurghada and twice a week to Kharga Oasis. Air Sinai flies from Cairo to Hurghada, Al Arish, Taba, Sharm el Sheikh, St Catherine's Monastery, El Tor, and to Tel Aviv, Israel.

EGYPTAIR OFFICES

Alexandria: 19 Midan Zaghloul, tel: 492-0778.

Cairo: 6 Adli Street, tel: 920-000; 12 Kasr el Nil Street, tel: 750-600; Nile Hilton Hotel, tel: 759-703; Cairo Sheraton, tel: 985-408.

Heliopolis: 22 Ibrahim el Lakani, tel: 668-552.

Luxor: Winter Palace Arcade.

Aswan: Corniche.

By Sea

Alexandria and Port Said on the Mediterranean Sea and Suez and Nuwayba on the Red Sea are ports of entry. For sailings, check with your travel agent or the following operators:

Adriatic Lines, Castro and Company, 12 Talaat Harb, tel: 743-213/144 (passengers and shipping).

The Egyptian Navigation Company, 26 Sherif, tel: 393-8278; 1 Hurria, Alexandria, tel: 472-0824.

Favia Shipping Lines, 18 Adli, tel: 393-8983.

Federal Arab Maritime, 27 Gazira el Wosta, Zamalek, tel: 341-5823, 340-6351.

The International Agency for Tourism, Navigation and Trading Services, 13 Midan Tahrir, tel: 762-892, 779-452.

International Transport & Maritime Service Co, 26A Asma Fahmi, Kulliet el Banat, Heliopolis, tel: 661-783.

Misr Edco Shipping Company, Menatours, 14 Talaat Harb, tel: 776-951.

North African Tourist Shipping, 171 Mohammed Farid, tel: 391-3081/4682; or el Takkadom, Medinet Nasr, tel: 608-417 (only from Port Said to Cyprus and Haifa).

By Land

With some restrictions all borders are now open to travellers.

From Israel: Private vehicles are not permitted to enter Egypt from Israel; however, travellers may use public transport and enter Egypt via Rafah on the northern coast of Sinai or from Eilat on the Red Sea. Buses run regularly from Tel Aviv and Jerusalem to the border at Rafah. At the border passengers disembark from the Israeli vehicle, go through customs, and take an Egyptian bus or taxi. There are no facilities for issuing visas at the Rafah border. In Eilat, Israeli buses are permitted to enter Egypt and travel as far as Sharm el Sheikh at the southern tip of Sinai.

From Sudan: There is a twice-weekly steamer that ferries cars the length of Lake Nasser, from Wadi Halfa in the Sudan to Aswan in Egypt. Information is available from the Nile Navigation Company Limited, Ramses Square (in the railway station) and Nile Maritime Agency, 8 Kasr el Nil, both in Cairo; and the Nile Company for River Transport, 7 Atlas Building, Aswan. All arrangements to enter Sudan, including visas, must be made in Cairo. You must have a valid passport and either a transit or tourist visa to Sudan. If you plan to pass through the Sudan you must have a valid visa for your next destination.

From Libya: The border with Libya is open and buses and taxis make regular runs between Alexandria and Sollum. There are some travel restrictions for Westerners. Consult your embassy or the nearest Libyan Embassy for details.

Motoring to Egypt

All private vehicles entering Egypt must have a trip *tyque* or *carnet de passage en douane* from an automobile club in the country of registration or pay customs duty which can be as high as 250 percent. Emergency *triptyques* are available at the port of entry via the Automobile and Touring Club of Egypt. This permits a car to enter Egypt for three months with one extension. The extension is available from the Automobile and Touring Club of Egypt, Kasr el Nil, Cairo. All persons travelling in the vehicle must have a valid passport and the driver must have an International Driver's Licence. The latter is available from automobile clubs in the country of registration (See Getting *Around*, *Private Transport* for additional details on driving in Egypt).

Specialist Tours

There are hundreds of tour operators in Egypt offering a variety of packages. This list of Cairo-based companies services travellers along the Nile.

Amarco Tours, 5 Talaat Harb, tel: 759-146.

American Express, 15 Kasr el Nil, tel: 75044.

Bestours, 37 Kasr el Nil, tel: 392-4741.

Eastmar, 13 Kasr el Nil, tel: 753-147.

Egypt Panorama Tours, 11 Tourist Center, Mohandisiin, tel: 344-9590.

Misr Travel, 1 Talaat Harb, tel: 392-4737.

Thomas Cook, 4 Champollion, tel: 743-955.

Additional details of tour companies can be found under Travel *Packages*.

Special Facilities

Disabled Travellers

Few hotels or cruise boats, and no public buildings, restaurants, theatres or historical sites provide any facilities for the infirm or disabled. Major airlines, however, provide services both entering and leaving the country that match worldwide standards.

Useful Addresses

Embassies and Consulates

The Eygptian representatives in your own country can provide useful tourist information:

Canada: 3754 Côte de Nièges, Montreal; 454 Laurier Avenue M.E. Ottawa.

Switzerland: 11 Rue de Chantepoulet, Geneva.

United Kingdom: 2 Lowndes Street, London SW1.

United States: 2310 Decatur Place, N.W. Washington, DC 20008; 1110 Second Avenue, New York, NY 10022; 3001 Pacific Avenue, San Francisco, CA 94115; 505 N. Lakeshore Drive, 4902, Chicago, IL 60611; 2000 West Loop So., Houston, TX 77027.

Practical Tips

Business Hours

Banks: 8.30am–1.30pm daily; closed Friday, Saturday and most holidays.

Businesses: Business hours throughout the week are flexible. Few businesses function before 8am; many are open until 5pm, but some close during the afternoon and then re-open at 5pm. Clinics are customarily open from 5pm to 8pm.

Government offices: 8am–2pm daily, closed Friday, Saturday, most holidays.

Shops: Shops keep hours according to demand. In central Cairo many shops, including those owned by Muslims and Jews, are closed on Sunday.

Khan al Khalili (the Cairo souq): 10am–7 or 8pm daily, closed Sunday.

Religion & Religious Services

Islam is the official religion of Egypt, but there is a large Coptic community and other Christian sects are represented in the country. There is also a small Jewish community.

Islam is part of the Judaeo-Christian family of religions and was revealed to the Prophet Mohammed in what is now Saudia Arabia. Islam has five major principles, known as "pillars", which form the foundation of the religion. The first is the belief that there is only one God and that the Prophet Mohammed is the messenger of God. The second is prayer, which should be performed five times a day. Almsgiving is the third principle and Muslims often donate a percentage of their earnings to others.

The fourth pillar is fasting during the holy month of Ramadan. The fifth pillar is pilgrimage to Mecca, haj, which all Muslims hope to perform at least once. The pilgrimage is performed during the month of Dhu'l-Higga, which begins 70 days after the end of the Ramadan fast.

Coptic Orthodox: The Copts, a large minority in Egypt, are a Christian sect which separated from the Byzantine and Latin churches in AD 541 over a disagreement in religious doctrine. Copts founded the world's first monasteries, and the continuing monastic tradition is an important part of the Coptic faith.

Religious Observances

Visitors may attend any Coptic service. Non-Muslims should not enter mosques while prayers are in progress, and may be asked, in mosques listed as antiquities, to pay entry fees at other times. Muslims may enter any mosque at any time free of charge.

Following is a small selection of Christian services. Hours should be checked in the weekend newspapers.

CATHOLIC CHURCHES

Church of the Annunciation, 36 Mohammed Sabri Abu Alam, near Midan Talaat Harb, tel: 393-8429. Armenian Rite. Holy Liturgy Sunday 8.15am (in Coptic with Arabic readings); 9.30am, 10.30am and 6.30pm.

Our Lady of Peace (Melkite, Greek Catholic), 4 Midan el Sheikh Yusef, 96 Qasr el Aini. Byzantine Rite in Arabic. Holy Liturgy Sunday at 8.30am, 10.30am, and 6pm.

Holy Family Catholic Church, 55 Road 15, Maadi. Latin Rite. Daily Mass in French 8am Friday. Family Mass 10am Saturday in English. Saturday Mass 6pm in German, 7pm in French. Sunday Mass 9.30am in French 10.30am and 6pm in English.

St Joseph's Church (Italian and Egyptian Franciscan Friars), 2 Bank Misr at corner of Mohammed Farid, tel: 393-6677. Latin Rite. Holy Mass Sunday 7.30am in French; 8.30am in Arabic; 10am in Italian; 12.30pm in French; 5.30pm in English; 6.30pm in French. Weekdays 7.30am and 6.30pm in French.

St Joseph's Roman Catholic Church, 4 Ahmed Sabri, Zamalek, tel: 340-8902/9348. Latin Rite. Holy Mass Sunday 8.30am in Arabic; 11am in English; 6pm in French. Weekdays 6pm in French. Saturday 6pm in Italian (sometimes Spanish).

ORTHODOX CHURCHES

Armenian Orthodox, Cathedral of St. Gregory the Illuminator, 179 Ramses near Coptic Hospital. Armenian Rite in Armenian. Holy Liturgy Sunday 9–11am.

Abu Serga Church, Old Cairo. Coptic Rite in Coptic and Arabic. Holy Liturgy Sunday 8am–12 noon.

St Mark's Cathedral, 222 Ramses, Abbassiyah. Coptic Rite in Coptic and Arabic. Holy Liturgy Sunday 6–8am.

Church of the Virgin Mary, 6 Mohammed Marashli, Zamalek, tel: 340-5153. Coptic Rite in Coptic and Arabic. Holy Liturgy Sunday 7.30–9.30am and 9.30–11am.

PROTESTANT CHURCHES

All Saints' Cathedral, 5 Michel Lutfallah, Zamalek, behind the Marriott Hotel Episcopal/Anglican. Services in English Sunday 8am.

Christian Science Society, 3 Midan Mustafa Kamil. Service and Sunday School, Sunday 7.30pm. Testimony Meeting Wednesday 7.30pm. Reading Room with Bible references and Christian Science literature open Wednesday and Sunday 6–7.20pm and Friday 11am–2pm.

Church of Jesus Christ of Latter-Day Saints (Mormon), 44 Road 20, Maadi. Weekly sacrament service Friday at 9.30am.

Maadi Community Church (The Church of St John the Baptist), corner of Port Said and Road 17, Maadi. Services in English Friday 8.30am and 11am, with nursery; Sunday 7pm, no nursery.

Saint Andrew's United Church, 38, 26 July and Ramses. Service in English Sunday 9.30am.

Seventh Day Adventist Church, 16 Kubba, Roxi Heliopolis, tel: 258-0292/0785.

Media

Radio

European Radio Cairo: 557 AM and 95 FM, 7am–midnight, is a music station playing European classical, pop and jazz music. News in English at 7.30am, 2.30pm and 8pm; in French at 8am, 2pm and 9 pm; in Greek at 3pm; in Armenian at 4pm; in German at 6pm.

Radio Cairo Overseas: broadcasts to Egypt on 639 KHz and 1323 KHz. The higher metre band provides a better reception between sunrise and sunset. There are also shortwave alternatives.

BBC: World Service Middle East broadcast is on 639 KHz from 6.45–10.15am, 1–2pm, 3pm–9pm; and 1325 KHz from 5pm–1.15am News is on the hour.

The **VOA** (Voice of America) broadcasts on a variety of wavelengths from 3am–10am daily.

Television

Channel 1: on the air from 3.30pm–midnight (local time) and found on 1 and 5 on the dial, is mainly in Arabic.

Channel 2: broadcasting from 3pm–midnight daily and also from 10am–noon on Friday and Sunday, has many foreign language programmes.

Channel 3: is a Cairo-only station broadcasting in Arabic from 5pm–9pm.

CNN: this station arrived in Egypt in January 1991. It broadcasts to subscribers 24 hours a day with an uncensored programme.

See the *Egyptian Gazette* for daily television schedules. Schedules vary during Ramadan and in the summer.

Newspapers & Magazines

In Cairo all major English, French, German and Italian daily newspapers are available at larger hotels and at newsstands in Zamalek and Maadi usually a day late. The two most important local dailies are *Al Ahram* and *Al Akhbar*. *Al Ahram*, "The Pyramids", was established in 1875, making it the oldest newspaper in Egypt. Published daily, it also has a UK edition and a new English-language edition, *Al Ahram Weekly*. *Al Akhbar al Yawm*, "The News", established in 1952, also has a weekly edition.

The Egyptian Gazette, established in 1880, is the oldest foreign-language newspaper still in operation in Egypt. In the past decade several new English-language newspapers have emerged including the *Middle East Times*, published weekly, the *Arab World*, which caters more to news of Arabia, and the newly created *Al Ahram Weekly*.

In French there is *Le Progrès Egyptien* and *Le Journal d'Egypte*. In Greek, *Phos* and in Armenian, *Arev*.

Hosts of foreign-language newsletters serve the foreign residents in Egypt: the *British Community Association News* for the British community; *Helioscope*, serving the residents of Heliopolis; the *Maadi Messenger* for foreigners in Maadi, *Papyrus* for the German community.

English-language magazines include *Arab Press Review*, a biweekly political magazine, *Business Monthly*, featuring business news, *Cairo's*, a monthly what's on, *Cairo Today*, a monthly general interest magazine, *Places in Egypt*, designed for tourists, and *Prism*, a literary quarterly.

Postal Services

The Central Post Office at Midan al Ataba in Cairo (tel: 912-356) is open 24 hours a day except Friday and occasional holidays. All other post offices are open from 8.30am–3pm daily, except Fridays. Mailboxes found on street corners and in front of post offices are red for regular Egyptian mail, blue for overseas airmail letters and green for Cairo and express mail within Cairo. Allow seven days for airmail post to Europe, 14 days to America.

Express Mail Services

DHL: 20 GAmal el Din Abul Mahasen, Garden City, tel: 355-7301/7118; 34 Abdel Khalek Sarwat, tel: 392-9198, 393-8988; 35 Ismail Ramzi, Heliopolis, tel: 246-3571/0324.
Federal Express: 1079 Corniche el Nil, Garden City, tel: 355-0427; 24 Syria Mohandisiin, tel: 349-0986; 31 Golf, Maadi, tel: 350-7172.
IML Air Couriers: 2 Mustafa Kamel, Maadi, tel: 350-1160/1240.
TNT Skypac International Express: 33 Duqqi, Duqqi, tel: 348-8204/7228.

Telephone, Telex & Fax

Most 5-star hotels offer direct dial service in your room and via the telephone operator in the hotel. The Central Telephone and Telegraph Offices (8 Adli; Midan Tahrir; 26 Ramses) are open 24 hours a day, as are many branch exchanges. Others are open from 7am–10pm daily. Telex and fax services are also available from the above, and fax facilities in particular are available at business centres dotted around the city.

If you have an at&t calling card it is possible to charge a call from Egypt to the United States to a US account. You may place a call with a New York operator by dailing 356-0200/510-0200. You must supply both the American number and the number of your AT&T account.

The following telephone codes are used within Egypt:

Alexandria	03
Aswan	097
Asyut	088
Cairo	02
Fayoum	084
Hurghada	062
Ismailia	064
Luxor	095
Port Said	066
Suez	062

Internet

Internet facilities are available through both commercial offices and educational institutions.

Embassies & Consultates in Egypt

Afghanistan: Embassy of India, Afghanistan Interests Section, 59 Oruba, Heliopolis, tel: 666-653.
Algeria: Embassy of India, Algeria Interests Section, 14 Brazil, Zamalek, tel: 340-2466.
Australia: Cairo Plaza, Corniche el Nil, Bulaq, tel: 777-900/994.
Bahrain: 8 Gamaiyet el Nasr, Mohandisiin, tel: 706-202.
Bangladesh: 40 Syria, Mohandisiin, tel: 349-0646.
Bourkina Fasso: 40 Thawra, Medinet el Zobbat, Duqqi, tel: 709-754.
Burundi: 13 Israa, Mohandisiin, tel: 346-2173/9940.
Cameroon: 42 Babel, Duqqi, tel: 704-843/622/954.
Canada: 6 Mohammed Fahmi el Sayed, Garden City, tel: 354-3110/9.
Central Africa: 13 Shehab, Mohandisiin, tel: 350-2337, 713-291.
Chad: 31 Adnan Omar Sidki, Duqqi, tel: 704-726.
Djibouti: 157 Sudan, Mohandisiin, tel: 349-0611/5.
Ethiopia: 59 Evan, Duqqi, tel: 705-372/133.
Gabon: 17 Makka el Mokarama, Duqqi, tel: 348-1395.
Great Britain: 7 Ahmed Ragheb, Garden City, tel: 354-0850-9.
Iran: Embassy of Switzerland, Iran Interests Section. 12 Rifa'a, Duqqi, tel: 348-7641/7237.
Iraq: 9 Mohammed Mazhar, Zamalek, tel: 340-9815/2633.
Ireland: 3 Abu el Feda Tower, Zamalek, tel: 340-8264/8547.
Jordan: Embassy of Pakistan Inter-

ests, Section of Jordan. 6 Gohaini, Duqqi, tel: 348-5566/6169.
Kenya: 20 Boulos Hanna, Duqqi, tel: 704-546/455.
Kuwait: 12 Nabil el Wakkad, Duqqi, tel: 716-091.
Lebanon: 5 Ahmed Nessim, Giza, tel: 728-315/454.
Mali: 3 Kawsar Madinet el Attaba, Duqqi, tel: 701-641/895.
Morocco: 10 Salah el Din, Zamalek, tel: 340-9677/4718.
Niger: 1010 Pyramids, Giza, tel: 856-617/607.
North Yemen: 4 Ahmed Shawki, Giza, tel: 737-398.
Oman: 30 Montaza, Zamalek, tel: 340-7811/7942.
Qatar: 10 Themar, Mohandisiin, tel: 702-176.
Rwanda: 9 Ibrahim Aswan, Mohandisiin, tel: 346-2587/1126.
Saudi Arabia: 2 Ahmed Nessim, Giza, tel: 729-805.
Senegal: 46 Abdel Meneim Riad, Mohandisiin, tel: 346-1039.
Somalia: 38 Abdel Meneim Riad, Mohandisiin, tel: 704-577.
Sudan: 3 Ibrahim, Garden City, tel: 354-5034.
Tanzania: 9 Abdel Hamid Lotfi, Duqqi, tel: 704-286.
Turkey: 25 Falaki, Bab al Louk, tel: 354-8364.
United Arab Emirates: 4 Ibn Sina, Giza, tel: 729-107.
USA: 5 Latin America, Garden City, tel: 355-7371, 354-8211.
Zaire: 5 Mansour Mohammed, Zamalek, tel: 341-1069/7954.
Zambia: 22 Nakhil, Duqqi, tel: 709-620/67.

Emergencies
Security & Crime

Like many other countries, such as Italy and the USA, Egypt has been troubled in recent years by right-wing extremists. Like the US in the late 1960s and more recently, Germany in the 70s, the UK and France throughout the 70s, 80s, and early 90s, it has also suffered from terrorist violence. The terrorists' campaign in Egypt, however, was amateur, half-hearted, unorganized, and short-lived; and even during a six-month period, from September 1991 to March 1992, when tourists were supposed to have been specifically targeted, a tourist was statistically much safer from violence in Cairo than in Miami, several million times less likely to be assassinated than an American President. Ironically, however, the Western myth of Egypt as a politically unstable country about to transform itself into a theocracy run by religious fanatics has been largely the creation of American media. Since 1979, for example, the *New York Times*, has regularly used "Islamic fundamentalism" as a bugbear to provide dramatic background for otherwise unsensational stories about the discovery of tombs or the opening of new discothèques.

Such being the case, visitors from abroad should nevertheless be warned that restrictions still pertain on travel into or through Middle Egypt, the zone along the Nile in Upper Egypt between Minya and Luxor. This region is Egypt's equivalent to Appalachia, Sicily, or the Balkans: beautiful, but poverty-stricken, and historically given to violence, much of it directed against officialdom or formal authority. Since it also contains many of Egypt's most interesting and least spoiled ancient sites, some of them only recently opened to visitors, one hopes the restrictions will be increasingly relaxed.

In Luxor the volatile male temperament characteristic of Upper Egypt may become overt in sexual aggressiveness. A century or so of casual adventuring by female tourists has fostered belief in the universal concupiscence and generosity of Western women. Unaccompanied women of any age or configuration should therefore not be surprised, especially on the West Bank, at sexual exhibitionism or vehement advances.

Elsewhere, common prudence is advised, of the kind appropriate in a crowded country where human nature flourishes in all its variety. Serious difficulties should be reported immediately to the nearest police station.

Police

Tourist Police wear a green armband and stand guard at the major tourist sites and hotels. Traffic Police wear black and white in winter and white in summer and can be found on major street corners. The Central Security policemen wear black and guard embassies, hotels and public buildings.

Health & Medical Services

Called Montezuma's Revenge in Mexico, Pharaoh's Revenge in Egypt, and a host of other names in other countries, a stomach upset can spoil any holiday. No matter what your precautions, a change in water and diet can result in diarrhoea and nausea. It is best to stay away from raw fruit and vegetables, and drink plenty of liquids.

Amoebic dysentery, caused by a microscopic single-celled animal, an amoeba, is a much more serious matter. The amoebae are ingested with unclean food or drink. Symptoms are similar to gippy tummy but the condition persists and can cause serious damage. With proper treatment recovery is quick. Although an amoeba can be ingested in even the finest restaurants, it is best to stay away from street stalls or other suspect places where hygiene is questionable. Drink bottled water, which is inexpensive and readily available.

Malaria is not a problem in Egypt, although it is on the increase throughout the world. Rabies, however, is endemic. Stay away from the stray dogs around monuments. Rabies can be contracted not only from a bite, but from the saliva of the sick animal contacting an open wound. It is fatal if not treated in time.

All hotels have references for medical services and some have a doctor on call 24 hours a day. All Egyptian doctors speak some English. Embassies can also be consulted. The red crescent is the symbol of medical services in Egypt equivalent to the red cross seen in many countries. It designates hospitals, ambulances and other medical services.

Hospitals

There are good hospitals in Cairo and Alexandria. However they operate on a cash basis and patients cannot use foreign medical insurance plans (pay first, claim on insurance later). Some hospitals in Cairo are:

Anglo-American Hospital Zohoreya, next to the Cairo Tower, Zamalek, tel: 341-8630.

As Salam International Hospital, Corniche el Nil, Maadi, tel: 363-8050/4196/8424/8764.

Arab Contractors Hospital Autostrade, Nasr City, tel: 828-907,

832-534, 838-642, 833-501/408.
Italian Hospital, Abbassia, tel: 821-433.
Nile Badrawi Hospital, Corniche el Nil, Maadi, tel: 363-8688/8167/8.
Al Salam Hospital, 3 Syria, Mohandisiin, tel: 346-7062/3.

Pharmacies

Pharmacies are usually open from 10am–10pm and are staffed by competent professionals. Both locally made and imported medication is subsidised by the government and is inexpensive. Some medications requiring prescriptions abroad are sold over the counter in Egypt.

24-HOUR PHARMACIES IN CAIRO

Attaba: Attaba Pharmacy, 17 Midan Attaba, tel: 910-831.
Central Cairo: Isaaf Pharmacy, 3 Sharia 26 Yulyu (July), tel: 743-369; Seif Pharmacy, Qasr el Aini, tel: 354-2678.
Maadi: As Salam International Hospital, Corniche el Nil, tel: 842-188; Esam Pharmacy, 101 Road 9, tel: 350-4126; Mishriki Pharmacy, 81 Road 153, tel: 350-3333.
Zamalek: Zamalek Pharmacy, 3 Shagaret el Dorr, tel: 340-2406.

Getting Around

Orientation

The Nile flows through the country from south to north. Upper Egypt is therefore the south, Lower Egypt the Delta. Upstream is south, downstream north. Many good maps are available.

From the Airport

All airports in Egypt have a taxi service to city centres, operated on a flat fee basis (ask your airline). In Cairo transport includes limousine, taxi and bus. Curbside limousine service is offered by Misr Limousine (tel: 259-9831).

Official Cairo taxis are predominantly black and white and Alexandria taxis are black and orange. There are also Peugeot taxis in a variety of colours and sizes, but they all have an emblem and number painted on the driver's door. Fees are the same as the limousine service.

The Airport Bus Service operates from Terminal 1. The bus leaves when full and stops at Midan Tahrir in downtown Cairo, in Mohandisiin, and along Pyramids Road in Giza.

Porter Service

For the cost of the LE, baggage trolleys are available for use at Cairo International airport. There are also porters with larger trolleys to service individuals and groups. Porters should be tipped.

Left Luggage

At the airport luggage is claimed via airline offices. In hotels consult the manager.

Public Transport

By Rail

The Egyptian State Railway is a government-owned system founded in 1851 which services the entire Nile Valley down to Aswan, the Red Sea cities of Suez and Port Said, the Delta and Northern Coast cities of Alexandria (two stops) and Mersa Matruh. There are at least half a dozen through trains a day on major routes. Fares are inexpensive, but unless one is travelling with a tour, tickets must be purchased at the main railway stations (in Cairo at the Ramses Station at Midan Ramses).

There is one privately-owned train operating in Egypt, the Wagon Lits sleeper with first, second and third-class compartments. The train travels overnight from Cairo to Aswan and back again, leaving Cairo at around seven in the evenings and arriving in Aswan at nine the following morning. Bookings are one week in advance through a travel agent or from Compagnie Internationale des Wagons Lits Egypte, 9 Sharia Menes, Heliopolis, tel: 290-8802/4; 48 Sharia Giza, Giza, tel: 348-7354, 349-2365.

By Bus

Air-conditioned buses link most parts of Egypt to Cairo and Alexandria. Seats may be reserved up to two days in advance. There is also a fleet of cheaper non-air-conditioned buses. Al-though bus times may change without notice, departures are so frequent that schedule changes are not usually a problem.

The principal carrier to Aswan and Luxor is the Upper Egyptian Bus Company, 4 Yussef Abbas, MN, tel: 260-9304/9297. Departures are from 45 al Azhar and the terminal at Midan Ahmed Helmi. Two buses a day complete the run to Aswan, departing early morning and arriving in the evening.

Metro & Tram

Both Alexandria and Cairo have tram systems that run through at least part of the city. Cairo also has a Metro. Trains run every few minutes from early morning (5.30am) to 10.30pm and sometimes later. Fares are inexpensive, usually under a pound to the farthest destination.

In **Cairo** the metro system is identified by circular signs with a big red M. The system runs north–south with over 30 stops from Heliopolis to Helwan through the heart of the city. Additional routes, planned east and west, are currently under construction. Useful stations:

Mubarak Station, Midan Ramses Square with access to the main train station and bus stations to Upper Egypt and the Oases.

Urabi Station, Sharia Gala'a.

Nasser Station, Midan Tawfiqiyyah.

Sadat Station, Midan Tahrir with ten entrances and access to Egyptian Antiquities Museum, the American University in Cairo, Nile Hilton, major airline offices, and the Mugama'a.

Mar Girgis at Old Cairo with access to the Coptic Museum, Coptic churches, and Roman fortress.

Zaghlul Station, The National Assembly. Zaghlul monument.

Heliopolis is served by six tram lines. The three major ones are:

Abd el Aziz Fahmi line (green) from Midan Abd el Monim Riad (behind the Egyptian Museum) via Ramses to Roxi, Merryland, Mahkama, Heliopolis Hospital to the Shams Club;

Nuzha line (red) runs Midan Abd el Monim Riad, Ramses, Roxi, Heliopolis Sporting Club, Salah el Din, and Midan el Higaz to Nuzha;

Mirghani line (yellow) Midan Abd el Monim Riad, Ramses, Roxi, Sharia el Merghani, Saba Emarat, Midan Triomphe, Military College.

By Taxi

For one of the experiences of your life, take an Egyptian taxi. Taxi drivers seem to need to fill every empty space on the road (and sometimes the pavement). All taxis have orange license plates and are identified by a number on the driver's door. Drivers are required to have their license and identity numbers displayed on the dashboard. Sharing a taxi is not unusual. In Cairo and Alexandria taxis ply the streets at all hours of the day or night and can be flagged down. There are also taxi ranks at all the major hotels and public squares.

Official or metered prices are unrealistic and meters are seldom used. The fare should be agreed beforehand. The majority of taxi drivers are honest, but some try to cheat unwary foreigners, especially between five-star hotels and such destinations as the pyramids or Khan al-Khalili. Do not hesitate to ask for assistance from the tourist police. At your destination, pay the fare in exact change and walk away. No tip is expected.

Taxi drivers are friendly, many speak English, some are college graduates moonlighting to supplement their incomes, and most are very eager to be hired by the day. The fee is negotiable. Such an arrangement is ideal for shopping or for seeing several scattered monuments.

Taxis in Luxor and Aswan are easier to find (they line up at all hotels), but for distance travelled they are more expensive than those in Cairo.

Private Transport

By Car

The roads from Cairo to Upper Egypt are the longest, most congested, and most dangerous in Egypt. Most traffic moving south from Cairo must travel a route along the western shore of the Nile. It is not advisable to drive on any major road at night; vehicles stop dead on the road and turn out their lights; unlit donkey carts move at a snail's pace and are usually not seen until it is too late, and long-distance taxis and overloaded trucks travel too fast, often without lights, and are driven by drivers who use "stimulants".

There are petrol stations throughout the country, with those operated by

Mobil, Esso, and Shell offering full service with mini-markets on the premises. Fuel, which is inexpensive and sold by the litre, is available in 90 octane (*tisa'iin*) which is super, or 80 (*tamaniin*), regular. 90 is better for most purposes.

Road signs are similar to those used throughout Europe. Driving is on the right-hand side of the road. Speed limits are posted on major highways and are enforced by radar.

Distances between Cairo and other cities:

CITY	MILES	KILOMETRES
Alexandria	140	225
(Delta road)		
Alexandria	138	221
(desert road)		
Damietta	119	191
Barrages	15	25
south to Minya	151	236
Asyut	224	359
Luxor	415	664
Esna	449	719
Edfu	484	775
Kom Ombo	521	835
Aswan	550	880
east to Port Said	137	220
Ismailia	87	140
west to Fayoum	64	103
Bahria Oasis	197	316
Farafra Oasis	262	420
Dakhla Oasis	413	690
Kharga Oasis	366	586

Car Rental

As driving in Egypt demands complete attention the best alternative is to hire a driver and car together, thus freeing you to enjoy the scenery. Car rental agencies exist at most major hotels. Foreigners must have an International Driver's Licence and be at least 25 years of age to rent a car in Egypt. Some agencies offer four-wheel drive vehicles, with or without driver, for desert travel. You will need your passport, driver's licence, and a prepayment. Credit cards are accepted.

RENTAL AGENCIES

Avis: 16 Maamel el Sukar, Garden City, tel: 354-8698.
Bita: 15 Mahmud Bassiouni, tel: 774-330/753-130.
Budget: 5 Sharia el Maqrizi, Zamalek, tel: 340-0070/9474; 85 Road 9, Maadi, tel: 350-2724; 1 Mohammed Ebeid, Heliopolis, tel: 291-8244.

Max Rent-a-Car: 27 Sharia Lubnan, Mohandisiin, tel: 347-4712.
Sunshine Tours & Services: 106 Mohammed Farid, tel: 760-559, 393-1955.

Limousines are available for those who want to travel in style:
Bita Limousine Service: Gazirah Sheraton, tel: 341-1333/1555. Marriott Hotel, tel: 340-8888.
Budget Limousine Service: Semiramis Intercontinental Hotel, tel: 355-7171 / 8991.
Limousine Misr: 7 Aziz Bil-Lah, Zeitoun, tel: 259-9813/9814.
Egyptrav: Nile Hilton, tel: 755-029, 766-548, 393-2644.

On Foot

Even in their few green spaces, Alexandria and Cairo are crowded cities, and walking through their business areas is too slow to be satisfactory as exercise. There are plenty of distractions, however, and no-one is ever bored by a stroll through Cairo's historic zone, which should be a highlight of an Egyptian trip. Walking in Luxor and Aswan, however, is a pleasure. These towns are not crowded and there is a pleasant country atmosphere. Hiking as a pastime is not popular in Egypt and should not be undertaken in remote areas without a guide. Local people may be willing to act as guides in the Eastern Desert, Sinai and the Oases.

Hitchhiking

Hitchhiking is not a common practice in Egypt and is not recommended, especially for women.

Where to Stay

Hotels

Price ranges for double rooms with bath are PPPPP $60–$400; PPPP $35–$60; PPP $20–$40; PP $10–$30; P $6–$20. In three, four, and five star hotels, payment for non-Egyptians and non-resident foreigners must be made in foreign currency by credit card, or in Egyptian currency with a bank exchange receipt.

Motels do not exist in Egypt.

Alexandria

☆☆☆☆☆
Muntazah Sheraton, Corniche, Muntazah, tel: 968/969-220, 968-550. Overlooking the sea, outlets include Café Coquillage Coffee Shop open 24 hours; Grillade, terrace on the roof for continental dining; L'Entrecote, French cuisine; El Phanar Night Club, Aquarius Disco. Swimming pool.
Helnan Palestine Hotel, Muntazah Palace Grounds, tel: 861-799, 958-554. Occupying what was once part of the summer residence of the Mohammed Ali family, the Palestine Hotel is surrounded by beautiful gardens. Outlets include the Dahabeya Restaurant, Sea Horse Restaurant, Pizzeria for Italian specialities, the Dolphin Night Club, and Salamlek Lounge. Private beach.

☆☆☆☆
Pullman Cecil Hotel: 16 Midan Saad Zaghlul, tel: 480-7055/7758. One of the grand hotels of yesteryear, the Cecil is still a nice place to stay. Outlets include El Amira for continental dining; El Mahroussa for buffet and seafood; El Sultan Cocktail lounge; and Layali Night Club.

☆☆☆ *and under*
Agami Palace: El Bitash, tel: 433-0386, 422-0230. Located on the beach in the small resort town of Agami.

Cairo

☆☆☆☆☆

Cairo Concorde, Cairo International Airport, tel: 664-242. Located on the fringes of the airport, the Concorde is handy for people who need airport facilities, but far from the centre of Cairo.

Cairo Marriott, Sharia Saray al Gazirah, Zamalek, tel: 340-8888. The Marriott chain has installed itself in and around one of the palaces built by the Khedive Ismail. Antique furniture graces the halls and public rooms. Restaurants include: Almaz Nightclub operating in the garden during the summer months; Empress Nightclub, open year round in one of the rooms of the palace; Eugénie's Lounge, an elegant cocktail bar; Garden Promenade, open-air café in the Khedive Ismail's garden; Gazirah Grill, French cuisine served in the former billiard room; Omar's Café, coffeeshop with good snacks and dining; Roy's, a salad bar, with hamburgers and other fast foods; the View, a pleasant lounge at the top of the hotel with a panorama of the city.

Cairo Sheraton, Midan el Galaa, Duqqi, tel: 348-8600/8700. One of the first international hotels in Cairo, near city centre. Aladdin, Middle-Eastern cuisine and entertainment; Alhambra, a nightclub with excellent oriental floor show; Arousa al Nil, continental and Middle-Eastern cuisine; La Mamma, one of the best Italian restaurants in Cairo.

Gazirah Sheraton, Gazirah, tel: 341-3442/1333/1555. South of the Cairo Opera House, the Gazirah Sheraton has a superb view of the Nile. Gazirah Andalus Café, 24-hour coffeeshop; Abu Kir, seafood out of doors on the Nile; outdoor summer nightclub with an oriental show; Le Gandool Bar; Paradise Island, a floating restaurant on the Nile offering barbecues and *mazzah*. The Grill has a Nile view and international cuisine. Kebabgy al Gazirahh offers oriental cuisine.

Heliopolis Mövenpick, Hurriyyah, Heliopolis, tel: 664-242, 247-0077, 679-799. Near the airport. In Mövenpick tradition it offers good food: Al Sarraya, French restaurant; Il Giardino, an Italian *taverna* with snacks and live entertainment; Orangerie, buffet breakfast, lunch and dinner; Gourmet Shop, a pastry shop with Swiss sweets; Karawan, Middle Eastern cuisine and barbecues in a garden atmosphere; Mövenpick, for Swiss and Middle Eastern meals and snacks with a special ice cream menu. Papillon disco; St Germain bar.

Swissôtel El Salam Cairo, 61 Abdel Hamid Badawi, Heliopolis, tel: 245-5155/2155. Although El Salam is far from the centre of town, it is housed in a former palace with lovely grounds. Restaurants include Café Jardin Coffeeshop, with a buffet; Marquis for light snacks; Ezbetna, for traditional Egyptian foods; Whispers, a bar offering a happy hour. Ya Salam is the Nightclub and Vito's is the disco.

Mena House Oberoi, end of Sharia al-Haram (Pyramid's Road), Giza, tel: 855-444, 857-999, 855-174. An historic landmark refurbished by the Oberoi chain, the Mena House is the only hotel in Egypt to have a golf course. Outlets include: the Greenery Coffeeshop, a buffet in the garden; Khan al Khalili, a coffeeshop featuring international and Middle-Eastern entrées; the Mogul Room offers Indian food and is one of the best restaurants in Egypt; the Rubayyat is the main dining room with continental and Middle-Eastern meals and live entertainment. Bars include the Mameluke Bar and El Sultan Lounge. Nightclubs are Oasis Summer Nightclub and Abu Nawas Nightclub. The disco is The Saddle.

Forte Meridien, Rawdah Island, entered from the Corniche in Garden City, tel: 362-1717. A river front hotel in the heart of the city. Fontana Coffeeshop offers international and Middle Eastern meals and snacks. Kasr al Rashid provides a Middle Eastern atmosphere, food and entertainment. La Belle Epoque is a nightclub and restaurant. La Palme d'Or offers French dining to live music. Nafoura is a summer restaurant with Middle Eastern specialities.

Forte Meridien Heliopolis, 51 Oruba, Heliopolis, tel: 290-5055/1819. Located on the busy airport road. Outlets include Le Marco Polo Restaurant for Italian food and Café St Germain for snacks. Cakes and pastries at La Boulangerie.

Nile Hilton, Corniche, Midan Tahrir, tel: 750-666, 740-777. One of the first international hotels in Cairo, the Hilton, located on the Nile in the city centre, has an authentic ancient Egyptian statue in the lobby. Abu Ali's Café serves *sheesha*, green tea, and light snacks on the terrace; Belvedere is the winter nightclub while the Tropicana is the summer nightclub around the pool; Ibis Cafe has continental cuisine; Jackie's is the popular disco. The main dining room is the Rotisserie, which offers international cuisine. La Pizzeria offers Italian pizzas and an open buffet; Le Gateau is a pastry shop. Bars include the Safari Bar, Lobby Bar, and the Taverne du Champ de Mars, an Art Nouveau pub offering drinks, snacks, and daily buffet.

Pullman Maadi Towers, Corniche, Maadi, tel: 350-6092. On the Nile to the south of the city centre, the Pullman offers a wonderful panorama of the desert plateau on the west bank of the Nile including the pyramids of Giza, Sakkara, and Dahshur. Outlets include Le Clovis for international cuisine; Maadi Café, open 24 hours; and Darna for traditional Egyptian food.

Ramada Renaissance, Cairo/Alexandria Desert Road, tel: 538-995/6. North of the pyramids in a former citrus and palm grove, this hotel has excellent grounds. Outlets include: Garden Coffeeshop featuring continental meals and snacks; Les Fontaines offers continental food and Sultan Middle Eastern food. Habiba is the nightclub. Golden Club is the disco.

Ramses Hilton, 1115 Corniche, Maspero, tel: 777-444, 758-000, 744-400. Located on the Nile in one of the busiest sections of the city, the 36-storey Ramses Hilton has no grounds, but its upper floors offer an interesting panorama of Cairo. Citadel Grill offers elegant dining with seafood and grills; Falafel offers Middle Eastern foods and snacks; La Patisserie coffeeshop has excellent cakes and ice cream specialities. Terrace Café coffeeshop presents international and Middle Eastern meals and snacks. Bars include Club 36 with piano entertainment and a panorama of the city.

Safir ETAP Hotel, 4 Midan Misaha, Duqqi, tel: 348-2424/2828/2626. In a residential square not far from the city centre, the Safir is a favourite hotel for visitors from the Gulf states. Diar El Andalos caters Lebanese and Middle Eastern cuisine with *sheesha*; Filaka coffeeshop has an excellent daily buffet; Gazirat al Dahab offers French and Middle Eastern food. Khan Morgan is the bar.

Semiramis Intercontinental, Corniche, Garden City, tel: 355-3900/3800. Built on the Nile-side site of the legendary Semiramis Hotel the current hotel offers good facilities but no grounds. Restaurants include: Feluka Brasserie featuring Middle Eastern and continental open buffets; Far East offering oriental foods; Semiramis Grill with French cuisine; Sultana's Disco offering international live shows.

Helnan Shepheard Hotel, Corniche, Garden City, tel: 355-3804/14. Planned as a replacement, it now has neither the name, the site, nor the glamour of the original and famous Shepheard's Hotel which burnt down in 1952. Caravan offers international and Middle Eastern meals and snacks; Asia House offers oriental foods; Régence offers French cuisine; and Italiano has pastas and pizzas.

Siag Pyramids, 59 Mariutia, Sakkara Road, tel: 856-022/623, 857-399. Near the desert with a view of the Giza pyramids, the Siag is host to the Pharaoh's Rally every October. Dining room only, but excellent food.

Sonesta, 4 Tayaran, Nasr City, tel: 611-066, 609-444. Le Café for pastries and breads; the Garden Grill is an open-air summer restaurant featuring grills; Gondola offers Italian dining; Borobodur offers Indonesian food; Greenhouse coffeeshop has international meals and snacks; Rib Room is a steakhouse. Bars include Arabic Lounge and Speke's Bar. The disco is Sindbad.

☆☆☆☆
Atlas Zamalek, 20 Gam'at al Dowal al Arabiya, Mohandisin, tel: 346-4175/ 5782/6569. Chez Zanouba is Middle Eastern dining while Kahraman is French dining. Tamango is the hottest dance spot in Cairo.

Baron Hotel, Heliopolis off Oruba, Heliopolis, tel: 291-2468/7/5757. Le Baron coffeeshop features international and Middle Eastern meals and snacks; the Terrace caters an international buffet each evening; Le Jardin is the daily buffet. Pasha is the bar.

Bel Air Cairo Hotel, Muqattam, tel: 922-685/816/884. The only hotel on the Muqattam hills, but you must leave the grounds to have a view of the city.

Mövenpick Jolie Ville, Cairo/Alexandria Desert Road, tel: 855-118/539/ 612. Reopened after a fire. Mövenpick Restaurant offers daily buffets; Orangerie, breakfast, lunch, and dinner buffets; Pavillon des Pyramides, French dining. Terrace, snacks.

Novotel, Cairo Airport, Heliopolis, tel: 671-715, 679-080, 661-330.

☆☆☆
Cairo Inn, 26 Syria, Mohandisin, tel: 349-0661/2/3. Eagle Arms English pub; Taberna Espanola with Spanish entertainment in the evening. Excellent Spanish food.

Cleopatra, 2 Bustan, Midan Tahrir, tel: 708-751.

Egyptel, 93 Merghani, Heliopolis, tel: 661-716.

El Borg, Saray al Gazirah, Zamalek, tel: 341-7655.

El Nil, 12 Ahmed Ragheb, Garden City, tel: 354-2808.

Khan al Khalili, 7 Bosta, Attaba, tel: 900-271.

President, 22 Dr. Taha Hussein, Zamalek, tel: 341-6751/3195. Cairo Cellar, excellent food. Lebanese *mazzah* a speciality.

☆☆
El Hussein, Midan Hussein, al-Azhar, tel: 918-664/089.

El Nil Garden, 131 Abdel Aziz al Saoud, Manial, tel: 985-767, 983-931.

Viennoise, 11 Mahmoud Bassiouni, tel: 751-949, 743-153.

Windsor, 19 Alfy Bey, tel: 915-277, 915-810.

UNCLASSIFIED

Anglo-Swiss Pensione, 14 Champollion, tel: 751-479.

Bodmin House, 17 Hasan Sabri, Zamalek, tel: 340-2842.

Duqqi House, 42 Madina al Munawara, Duqqi, tel: 705-611/713.

Garden City House, 23 Kamal el Din, Garden City, tel: 354-8126. Rub elbows with archaeologists and anthropologists.

Hotel of Youth & Sports, Masaken, Madinat Nasr, tel: 260-6991/2.

Mayfair Pension, 9 Aziz Uthman, Zamalek, tel: 340-7315.

Pensione Roma, 169 Mohammed Farid (Emad ad-Din), tel: 342-0055, 341-8447.

Minya
☆☆☆☆☆
PLM Azur Nefertiti, Corniche, tel: 326-281. Offers a view of the Nile.

☆☆
Akhenaten, Corniche, tel: 325-918. View of the Nile. Clean and inexpensive.

Ibn Khasib, 5 Sharia Ragib, tel: 24535. In a garden.

Palace, Main Square, tel: 327-071. A surrealistic experience in a clean place.

Asyut
☆☆☆☆☆
Badr Hotel, Salah Salem. The only recommended hotel in Asyut.

Luxor
☆☆☆☆☆
Club Mediterranée, Sharia Khalid ibn Walid, tel: 377-7575. Typical Club Med facilities overlooking the Nile.

Hilton International Luxor, Village of New Karnak, north of Luxor, tel: 384-933. Hilton hospitality overlooking the Nile.

Mövenpick Jolie Ville, Crocodile Island, south of Luxor, tel: 384-855. Excellent food and accommodation in a pastoral setting.

PLM AZUR, Corniche, tel: 382-166. The former ETAP in the heart of the city.

Sheraton, Awamiya, tel: 384-544. Offering several restaurant outlets overlooking the Nile.

Winter Palace, Corniche, tel: 382-222/000. The granddaddies of hotels in Luxor, the Winter Palaces, both old and new, have recently been renovated by the Pullman Hotel chain.

☆☆☆☆
EGOTEL, located behind Luxor Temple.

Isis, Sharia Khalid ibn Walid, tel: 382-750.

☆☆☆
Horus, Sharia. Suk, tel: 382-165.

Phillip, Sharia Nefertiti, tel: 282-284.

Windsor, Sharia Nefertiti, tel: 382-847.

☆☆ *and under*
Happy Home, off Mahatta. Cheap, friendly and clean.

New Karnak, across from the railway station, tel: 382-427.

Aswan

☆☆☆☆☆
Aswan Oberoi, Elephantine Island, tel: 762-835. An aggressive, rather ugly, modern tower offers a fine view of the river.
New Cataract, Corniche el Nil, tel: 333-222. Next to the Old Cataract.

☆☆☆☆
Amon Village, Sahara City, tel: 24826.
Cleopatra, Sharia Saad Zaghloul, tel: 322-983.
Old Cataract, Corniche el Nil, tel: 323-222. Grand, exotic and colonial, worth visiting even if you're not going to stay there.

☆☆☆
Hapi Hotel, Abdel el Tahrir, tel: 322-028.

☆☆ **and under**
Abu Shelib Hotel, Abdel el Tahrir, tel: 323-051.
Hathor Hotel, Corniche el Nil, tel: 322-590.

Eating Out

Where to Eat

In addition to their regular fare, five star hotels often fly in European chefs for week-long extravaganzas. See the hotel section for listing of hotel restaurants. The list below tries to provide a good cross section of restaurants outside hotels. By international standards, even the most expensive restaurants in Egypt are inexpensive. No restaurant has a good wine list – local beer is the preferred option and some establishments do not serve alcohol.

Insight Guide codes (for a three-course meal with drink):

Expensive (Ex)	–	LE30+.
Average (Av)	–	LE15–30
Inexpensive (Inex)	–	LE5–15

Cairo

MIDDLE EASTERN

Egyptian food makes the mouth sing.

Breakfast: *Fuul*, brown beans slow cooked in special copper pots, and *tamiya* (*falafel*), a deep fried mixture of ground beans, coriander, and garlic are the main breakfast foods in Egypt. Either can be served separately or in the form of a sandwich. *Fuul* can be mixed with oil, garlic, tomatoes, yoghurt, and other condiments.

Mazzah: The Egyptian meal begins with a series of salads and appetizers served in small dishes and accompanied by either white or brown flat bread. One can make a meal of good *mazzah*, which can include sausages, meatballs, and chopped salads. Types of *mazzah* include: *tehina*, a dip of sesame seed paste; *babaganouh*, tahina mixed with eggplant; *torshi*, a variety of Egyptian pickles including carrots, turnips, and sometimes lemons; *kobeiba*, a fried meatball of meat, onions, and nuts; green olives; chicken livers; white beans, white cheese, and beets. *Mashi* can be a *mazzah* or accompany the main course; it can be peppers, tomatoes, aubergines, courgettes, or grape leaves stuffed with a mixture of rice, or rice and meat.

Main Courses: *Shish kebab* is perhaps the most famous Middle Eastern main course. In Egypt it is heavily spiced and accompanied by *kofta*, ground grilled lamb. *Kusheri*. is made of layers of rice, macaroni and dark lentils covered in a rich tomato sauce and garnished with fried onions. *Fattah* is a delightful combination of layers of rice, dried bread soaked in broth, and grilled lamb or chicken topped by yoghurt and nuts and soaked in vinegar (or lemon for chicken).

Desserts: Sweet and sticky, Egyptian desserts are delicious. *Aish Saraia*, bread of the palace, is a bright orange cake soaked in syrup and covered in cream. *Baklawa*, famous throughout the Middle East, is filo pastry layered with nuts and sometimes custard and cottage cheese. *Basbousa* is a cake made of semolina, soaked in syrup and often filled with cream and nuts. *Konafa*, a speciality of Ramadan, is shredded batter stuffed with nuts, cream, or cheese.

Lukmet el Adi is the Rum Baba of Egypt, fried dough soaked in syrup. *Um Ali* is a bread pudding soaked in milk and garnished with nuts and sometimes coconut.

Four- and five-star hotels have small coffee shops and restaurants from ethnic eateries to smart supper clubs with live music. Outstanding in Cairo are:

Al Fanuws (Moroccan), Burg Riyadh, 5 Sharia Wissa Wasif (off Gizah Corniche, Sharia Gamal Abd an-Nasir) 6th Floor, Gizah. Tel: 737-595/592. No alcohol.
Al Mashrabiyyah (Egyptian), 4 Sharia Ahmad Nissim, Duqqi. Tel: 348-2801.
Al Ruwsha (Lebanese), 3 Sharia Gamiat ad-Dawal al-Arabiyyah, Maydan al-Hor, Muhandisiin, Tel: 344-5773, 345-5100. Fax: 345-8866.
Al-Rifai, Sayyida Zaynab.
Aladin (Lebanese). Cairo Sheraton Hotel, Duqqi. Tel: 348-8600.
Cairo Cellar. President Hotel, 22 Sharia Taha Husayn, Zamalek. Tel: 341-3195/341-6751.
Darna (Egyptian). Sofitel Maadi Towers Hotel, Maadi. Tel: 350-6092.
Felafel, Ramsis Hilton Hotel, Tel: 744-400, 758-000.
Felfela (Egyptian), 15 Sharia Hoda Sha⁼arawi with an entrance at 15 Sharia Tal⁼at Harb, Cairo. Tel: 392-2833. Corniche at Sharia al-Nahda, Ma⁼adi. Tel: 350-3327. Maryutiyyah Canal Road, Gizah. Tel: 854-209. 27 Cairo-Alexandria Desert Road, Gizah. Tel: 850-234.
Florencia. Flamenco Hotel, tenth floor, 2 Gazirat al-Wusta, Zamalek. Tel: 340-0815.
Gazirat al Dahab (Lebanese), Safir ÉTAP Hotel, Maydan Missaha, Duqqi. 348-2828, 348-2424.
Ibis Café (Egyptian/International). Nile Hilton Hotel. Tel: 765-666, 767-444. Lunch or light supper: central, fast, efficient, and reliable.
Il Yotti (Lebanese/International), 44 39 Muhiy ad-DIn Abu'l-Izz St. Duqqi Tel: 349-4944. Ring the bell for admittance.
Johnny's Pub (Lebanese *mazzah*), On **Le Pacha 1901** boat, Zamalek. Tel: 340-6730.
Kebabgy, El Gezirah Sheraton Hotel, Gazirah. Tel: 341-1333, 341-1555.
La Gondola (Italian/Turkish). Sonesta Hotel, 4 Sharia at-Tayaran (Airport

Road), Madinat Nasr. Tel: 609-444.

Le Bistro (French). El Gezirah Sheraton Hotel, Gazirah. Tel: 341-1333, 341-1555.

Le Champollion (French). Forte Méridien Hotel, Rawdah opposite Garden City. Tel: 362-1717.

Lebanon Corner (Lebanese *mazzah*). El Gezirah Sheraton Hotel, Gazirah. Tel: 341-1333, 341-1555.

Marco Polo. Forte Mériden Heliopolis Hotel, Sharia at-Tayaran (Airport Road), Heliopolis (Misr al-Gadidah). Tel: 290-5055, 290-1819.

Moghul Room (Indian). Mena House Oberoi Hotel, Pyramids Road (Sharia al-Haram), Gizah. Tel: 85-5444/7999 Ext. 661.

Naguib Mahfouz Café, 5 Sikkat al-Badistan, Khan al-Khalili, Cairo. Tel: 590-3788, 932-262. No alcohol.

Nubian Village, Forte Méridien Hotel, Rawdah opposite Garden City. Tel: 362-1717. Summer only.

Papillon (Lebanese; catering, delivery service), Sharia 26 Yulyu (July), Tersana Shopping Centre (Suq Nadi at-Tirsana), Muhandisiin. Tel: 347-1672.

Paprika (Lebanese), 1129 Corniche, near the Radio and Television Building, Maspero. Tel: 749-447.

Rôtisserie. Nile Hilton Hotel, Cairo. Tel: 765-666, 767-444.

Spaghetteria. Semiramis Intercontinental Hotel, Garden City. Tel: 355-7171. Do-it-yourself pasta dishes with a wide choice of sauces.

Tekeia (Egyptian), 12 Maydan Ibn al-Walid, Muhandisiin. Tel: 711-470.

The Grill. Semiramis International Hotel, Garden City. Tel: 355-7171.

Tikka Grill, 47 Sharia Al-Batal Ahmad ᶜAbd al-ᶜAziz, Muhandisiin. Tel: 340-0393, 345-5985. 85 Sharia 9, Maᶜadi. 7 Sharia Dr. Sayyid Abd al-Wahid, Roxy, Heliopolis (Misr al-Gadidah).

Yamato (Japanese). Ramses Hilton Hotel Annexe, Maspero. Tel: 752-3999.

Zahle (Lebanese), Siag Pyramids Hotel, Saqqarah Road, Gizah. Tel: 385-6022, 385-3005, 385-6623.

WESTERN FOOD

Il Camino (Italian), Burg Riyadh, 5 Sharia Wissa Wasi, Giza, tel: 737-592/595. No alcohol. Home made Italian pastas. (Av)

Caroll 12 Sharia Qasar an-Nil, tel: 746-739. Excellent dining in 1950s style. (Av)

Flying Fish 166 Sharia an-Nil, Aguza, tel: 349-3234. Specialising in seafood. (Av)

Il Capo 22 Sharia Taha Husayn, Zamalek, tel: 341-3870. Pastas, pizzas and antipastos. (Inex)

Justine 4 Sharia Hasan Sabri, Zamalek, tel: 341-2961, 340-1647. Elegant formal dining at Four Corners. French cuisine. (Ex)

La Cloche d'Or 3 Sharia Abul-Feda, Zamalek, tel: 340-2314/2268. French cuisine. (Ex)

Mama Lola 15 Sharia 9B, Maadi, tel: 351-5587. French cusine with an emphasis on seafood. (Ex)

Steak Corner 8 Midan Amman, Duqqi, tel: 349-7326. Steaks and salad bar. (Av)

Swissair Le Chalet 31 Sharia al-Nil, Giza, tel: 348-5321, fax: 672-191. Authentic Swiss food. Try the ice cream. (Av)

Tirol 38 Sharia Gaezirat al-Arab, Mohandisiin, tel: 344-9725. Austrian food. (Inex)

ORIENTAL

Burg Riyadh 157 Sharia 26 Yulyu (July), tel: 340-6761/5473. Cantonese food. (Av)

Chandani 5 Sharia Wissa Wasif, Giza, tel: 737-592/595. No alcohol. Excellent Indian cuisine. (Ex)

Burg Riyadh 5 Sharia Wissa Wasif, Giza, tel: 737-592/595. No alcohol. Jacket required. Japanese Teppan-Yaki table. (Ex)

Tandoori 11 Sharia Shihab, Mohandisiin, tel: 348-6301. No alcohol. Indian curries and grills. (Av)

FAST FOOD & ICE CREAM

Al Mastaba 65 Mohi el Din Abu el Ezz, Duqqi, tel: 249-1157. Kebab, kufta and other Middle Eastern dishes. (Inex)

Egyptian Pancakes 7 Khan el Khalili, tel: 908-623. Made to order *fitir*. (Inex)

Free Times 75 Mosaddaq, Duqqi, tel: 348-0006. North American food: subs and burgers. (Inex)

La Dolce Vita 21 Sharia Misr Helwan, Maadi. Excellent homemade ice cream and cones. (Inex)

McBurger 16 Gamat el Dowal el Arabiya, Mohandisiin, tel: 344-24109. Burgers, pies, onion rings, the works. (Inex)

Wienerwald Batal Ahmed Abdel Aziz, Mohandisiin, tel: 346-6940. Bavarian

chain with German and Austrian dishes. (Inex)

FLOATING RESTAURANTS

Nile Pharaoh docks at 31 Nil, Giza, tel: 726-713. Lunch cruise 2.30–4pm. Summer early dinner cruise 7.15–9pm. Dinner cruise 9.30–midnight. Pharaonic boat complete with lotus decor.

Scarabée docks across from Helnan Shepheard's Hotel, tel: 984-967. Lunch at 2.30pm and dinner at 9.30pm.

Luxor

In Luxor and Aswan travellers usually dine in hotels. However, there are a few places to eat scattered throughout.

Marhaba Corniche. Middle Eastern. Try the *sharkasayyia*. (Inex)

Hatey Sharia el Mahatta, tel: 382-210. Middle Eastern. Try the *shish kebab*. (Inex)

New Karnak Restaurant Variety. (Inex)

Amun Sharia Karnak. Middle Eastern. (Inex)

Aswan

Mona Lisa Corniche. Middle Eastern. Try the baked fish. (Inex)

Moon Corniche. Middle Eastern. Grilled chicken and ice cream. (Inex)

Madina Sharia el Souq. Middle Eastern. Grilled chicken and meat. (Inex)

Drinking Notes

The traditional **hot and cold drinks** served in coffeehouses are delicious and thought to be health-giving. The usual idea of American coffee is instant Nescafé. As for decaffeinated coffee, you have to bring your own.

Fresh juices such as orange, mango, strawberry, pomegranate, lime or whatever, depending on the season, are available everywhere *except* in major hotels.

Internationally formulated drinks made and bottled locally under licence include a range of Schweppes and Canada Dry mixes, Coca-Cola, Seven-Up, Sport, and Pepsi-Cola.

The local **beer** is Stella, a lager that comes in four varieties: Stella Export or ordinary Stella, which is less sweet and therefore usually preferred to Export; the increasingly rare Stella

Aswali, a dark beer from Aswan; and seasonal Stella Marzen, a bock or Märzenbier. The adventurous may encounter a mild home-brew called *buza*, which is recorded to have been made as long ago as the Third Dynasty.

Egyptians were making **wine** even earlier. Since 1986, however, Egyptian wine has deteriorated disastrously, despite the importation of new hardware. Whereas previously bottles varied unpredictably in quality, they are now almost uniformly unfit even for cooking purposes, thanks to heavy-handed introduction of chemical preservatives. Reds include Omar Khayyam, Pharaons, and Château Gianaclis; there is one one rosé, called Rubi d'Egypte. Among the whites – Gianaclis Village, Cru des Ptolemées, Castel Nestor, Nefertiti, and Reine Cléopatre – one label or other is occasionally drinkable for a brief period. Caution is therefore advised when dining out: no bottle is likely to be good, but if there is a risk of spoiling an evening, the worst should be sent back immediately. Mediocre French or Italian wine is available in the major hotels, of course, at prices roughly ten times their maximum value on the western market.

Imported spirits are also available. Local spirits are quite popular among Egyptians, they include several kinds of brandy and various versions of **zibeeb** or **araq**, the Arab World's heady equivalent to *ouzo, raki, anisetta*, or *pastis*.

Most crucial to know are the two brands of **mineral water**, popular and available in hotels: **Baraka**, bottled in association with Vittel, and **Mineral**, bottled in collaboration with Evian.

Coffeehouses

The coffeehouse is a Middle Eastern tradition and there are thousands in Egypt. They are famous for sheesha smokers, shoeshine boys, backgammon, checkers, cards, newspapers and, of course, their good Turkish coffee, served black and ordered sa*ada*, with no sugar; *arriiha* with half a teaspoon of sugar; *mazbut* with one sugar; and *ziyaada* with one and a half sugars. Some coffeehouses mix cardamon, mastika, or nutmeg in the coffee for added flavour. These traditional shops also offer strong Egyptian tea while continental coffeehouses serve espresso and cappuccino. Some coffeehouses offer *erfa*, a cinnamon tea; *ersos*, a licorice juice also sold by street vendors; *karkadee*, a tea brewed from the petals of the hibiscus flower; *sahlab*, an exotic drink of arrowroot usually served in winter; and *tamr hindi*, a tea brewed from the fruit of the tamarind.

Some of the more distinguished coffeehouses can be visited at:

Atelier, 2 Karim el Daoula, off Talaat Harb, tel: 746-730. Continental. Frequented by literary personalities.

Café Saint Germain, 41 Babel, Duqqi, Cairo, tel: 704-519. European bakery and coffeeshop. Branches also at 97 Higaz, Heliopolis, and 59 Zahraa, Mohandisiin.

Fishawi, Khan al Khalili, Cairo, tel: 906-755. 24-hr. Traditional. Founded in 1773. Much changed, but never closed.

Groppi, Midan Talaat Harb, Cairo, tel: 743-244. Famous English-type coffeeshop, now rather downmarket.

Groppi Garden, 2 Abdel Khalek Sarwat, Cairo, tel: 391-6619.

Pastroudis, 374 Sharia al Gaysh, Alexandria, tel: 586-4470. Featured in *Alexandria Quartet*.

Phoenix, Emad el Din, Cairo. Traditional. Coffee and backgammon.

Simonds, 112 Sharia 26 Yulyu (July), Zamalek, Cairo, tel: 340-9436. Small coffeeshop with pastries, espresso and cappuccino.

Attractions

Culture
Museums

CAIRO

The most famous of the city's museums is the Egyptian Antiquities Museum, but many others are well worth visiting. The usual hours are from 9am–4pm daily except Friday, when all museums are closed between approximately 11.30am and 1pm.

Bayt as-Sihaymi Darb al-Asfar, Gamaliyyah. An Ottoman-period townhouse, largely intact, with Chinese porcelain made for the Arab market.

Coptic Museum Mar Girgis, Old Cairo (Misr al-Qadimah), tel: 841-766. Arts of Egypt's Christian era: textiles, metalwork, woodwork, ceramics, glass.

Egyptian Antiquities Museum Midan at-Tahrir, tel: 754-319. The world's greatest collection of Pharaonic antiquities, including the Menkaure triads, the finds from the tomb of Hetepheres and the treasures of Tutankhamun.

Gayer-Anderson House adjoining Ibn Tulun Mosque, tel: 354-6950. Two houses, 16th and 17th century, joined together and furnished with his collections by Major Robert Gayer-Anderson Pasha, who lived here between 1935 and 1942.

Gawharah Palace Museum (Qasr al-Gawharah): Citadel, tel: 926-187. Mohammed Ali's Citadel *salamlik* (reception palace), restored since 1971 and fitted with furniture formerly owned by the Mohammed Ali family. The name of the palace means *bijou* or jewel, but there has never been a "jewel collection" in it.

Gazirah Museum planetarium building, Gazirah Exhibition Grounds, next to the National Cultural Centre, tel: 806-982. Paintings, bibelots, and *objets d'art*, some inherited from the defunct Museum of Modern Art and some confiscated from the Mohammed Ali family.

Islamic Art Museum, Corner of Sharia Port Said, Sharia Qala'a (Sharia Mohammed Ali) and Sharia Sami al-Barudi, Abdiin, tel: 341-8672. Important collections of arms and armour, ceramics, coins, carpets and textiles, manuscripts and printed papers, metalwork, stonework and woodwork from the period of the city's greatest glory.

Manastirli Palace and the Nilometer, southern end of Rawdah. Restored in 1990, this early 19th-century *salamlik* is the public portion of a palace complex that belonged to a distinguished Cairene Turkish family. The Nilometer is the oldest intact Islamic monument in Cairo.

Manyal Palace Museum, Rawdah Island, tel: 936-124. A complex of gardens and buildings constructed between 1901 and 1929 and bequeathed to the nation in 1955 by Prince Mohammed Ali, younger brother of Khedive Abbas II Hilmi and first cousin of King Faruq. Apart from the prince's residence with all its furnishings, there are buildings housing splendid collections of family memorabilia, costumes, calligraphy, glass, porcelain, silver, and trophies of the hunt. **Mohammed Mahmud and Emilienne Luce Khalil Collection**, was installed between 1971 and 1991 in the Amir Ibrahim Palace, but has been returned to the **Mohammed Mahmud and Emilienne Luce Khalil Museum** on the Giza Corniche (Sharia Gamal Abd an-Nasir) in Giza. Paintings, chiefly 19th and 20th-century French, including works by Ingres (2), Delacroix (8), Corot (12), Daumier (4), Courbet (4), Millet (6), Renoir (6), Degas (2), Fantin-Latour (2), Manet, Monet (5), Pissarro (6), Sisley (5), Toulouse-Lautrec, Gauguin (3), Van Gogh and others; sculpture (Houdon, Barye, Carpeaux, and Rodin); chinoiserie, japonaiserie, and turquoiserie. Bequeathed with their house to the nation by Mohammed Mahmud Khalil (died 1955), landowner, industrialist, and politician, and his French wife, Emilienne Luce Khalil (died 1962).

Museum of Modern Egyptian Art, (Museum of Twentieth-Century Egyptian Art). Gazirah Exhibition Grounds. Not to be confused with the defunct Museum of Modern Art.

Royal Carriage Museum, 82 Sharia 6 Yulyu (July), Bulaq, tel: 774-437. Entry from behind the Ministry of Foreign Affairs on the Corniche or from next to the Abu'l-Ila mosque on Sharia 26 Yulyu (July). A world-class collection of 78 viceregal, khedivial, and royal horse-drawn vehicles representing 22 types, with displays of harness, livery and trappings.

Shawqi Museum, 6 Sharia Ahmad Shawqi, between Sharia Giza (Sharia Murad) and the Giza Corniche (Sharia Gamal Abd an-Nasir), tel: 729-947. Elegant residence of Ahmad Shawqi (1868–1932), court poet to Khedive Abbas II Hilmi, exiled by the British between 1915 and 1919.

Boat Museum, beside Cheops Pyramid, Giza, tel: 857-928. Houses the Old Kingdom funeral boat found on the site and painstakingly reassembled.

State Railway Museum, Sharia Bab al-Hadid (Main Railway Station), tel: 977-393. Splendid collection of viceregal rolling stock and British-made models.

Luxor Museum, on the Corniche. A small but excellently laid out museum which features a collection of Armana art and royal statues of the 18th Dynasty. Open 4–9pm in winter and 5–10pm in summer.

Art Galleries & Studios

El Patio, 6 Road 77c, Maadi. Tel: 351-6654. Occasional exhibits in the upstairs gallery. 10am–6pm, closed Sunday.

Mashrabia, 8 Champollion, near Thomas Cook. Tel: 778-623. Group and individual shows. 11am–2pm and 5.30–8pm.

Music

Arabic Music Troupe, (Shirket al Musiqa al Arabia) al Galaa Building, Sharia Galaa, tel: 742-864. Also known as the Classical Orchestra and Choir of Arabic Music, this all-male choir performs songs for mixed voices, solo and group, and classical pieces.

Cairo Conservatoire, City of Art, Pyramids Road, tel: 851-475/561. Egypt's leading music school provides instruction in composition, musicology, percussion, piano, singing, string, and wind, and offers concerts at the Sayed Darwish Concert Hall.

Cairo Symphony Orchestra, the orchestra performs at the Cairo Opera House every Friday at 8.30pm from September to mid-June.

Ballet & Dance

Cairo Ballet, located on Pyramids Road in the City of Art complex, the Cairo Ballet was founded in 1966. Dancers are trained at the National Ballet Institute, which was created with the help of Russian experts in 1960, and then enter the ballet company which performs in the new Opera House.

Folk Dance Troupes, folk dancing is very popular in Egypt and there are over 150 troupes throughout the country. Among the most prominent are the National Troupe and Reda Troupe which perform regularly in Cairo and Alexandria.

Opera

Cairo Opera Company, from 1869 to 1971 Cairo was regularly visited by foreign opera troupes, which performed in the old Opera House. A local company has performed in Arabic since 1961, and features fine individual singers. Performances are at the Cairo Opera House.

Theatre

The theatre season in Cairo is from September to May and there is a summer season in Alexandria. Curtain is at 9.30pm, 10.30pm during Ramadan. Theatres are dark on Tuesdays or Wednesdays. Except at the American University, all performances are in Arabic.

Al Warsha (The Workshop), 10a Abdel Hamid Sayed, tel: 779-261. The repertory of this exploratory theatre troupe includes translated and new Egyptian plays.

The American University in Cairo Theatre Company, tel: 354-2964. Performs in the Wallace Theatre and Howard Theatre on the AUC campus.

Cairo Puppet Theatre, Azbakkiyah Gardens, tel: 910-954. Dialogue is in Arabic, but the gestures and meanings of the local and visiting performers are not too difficult to follow. Thursday–Saturday at 6.30pm, Friday and Sunday at 11am.

Comedy Theatre. Star-studded casts perform at the Mohammed Farid Theatre, Sharia Mohammed Farid, tel: 770-603, and the Floating Theatre, next to University Bridge, Manyal, tel: 849-516.

Modern Theatre. Al Salam Theatre, 101 Qasr al Aini, tel: 355-2484, 354-3016. The hardworking cast performs contemporary Arabic plays in three nightly shows beginning at 5.30pm.

Samir Ghanem Troupe. Named after the famous Egyptian comedian who is often the star of the show, this troupe performs comedies at the Bab al Luq Theatre, Midan Falaki, tel: 355-3195.

Cinema

Most of Cairo's cinemas are old with poor acoustics and sound systems. A few new venues have opened in recent years, most featuring Western films. Films are shown at around 10am and 3, 6 and 9pm. Some of the better cinemas are:

Swissôtel el Salam Cairo, Abdel Hamid Badawi, Heliopolis, tel: 245-5155. Foreign films at 6 and 9pm Thursday–Saturday, during Ramadan at 9pm and midnight.

Karim I, Karim II, Emad al Din, tel: 924-830, two new theatres offering current international films.

Bookshops

Cairo is the publishing capital of the Middle East and there are hundreds of bookshops. English-language books can be found in all major hotels. For rare books try The Orientalist on Qasr al Nil Street, Cairo. Second-hand books, in Arabic and English, can be found at the stalls in Opera Square, Cairo. Some bookstores that offer foreign-language publications are:

Al Ahram Outlets: 165 Mohammed Farid; Cairo Sheraton; Cairo International Airport; Meridien Hotel; Semiramis Inter Continental Hotel; Nile Hilton Hotel; Ramses Hilton Hotel Annex; Maadi Club.

American University in Cairo Bookshop, 113 Kasr el Aini. Excellent collection of English-language books on Egypt.

Lehnert and Landrock Bookshop, 44 Sherif, tel: 392-7606. German and English books, maps, and old postcards.

Reader's Corner, 33 Abdul Khalek Sarwat, tel: 392-8801, and Nile Hilton. General English

Zamalek Bookshop, 19 Shagaret el Dorr, Zamalek, tel: 341-9197.

Gambling

Gambling is available in Egypt, but only for foreigners and only in 5-star hotels. Casinos are mainly in Cairo, but there is a casino at the Hilton International in Luxor. The hotel casinos offer the traditional games (roulette, blackjack, *chemin de fer*, slot machines) and are open until the early hours. (Note: the word casino otherwise in Cairo traditionally and normally means "teahouse".)

Historical Sites

No matter where you go along the Nile there is something spectacular to see. From the Pyramids of Giza and the tombs of Sakkara, to the temples of Luxor and the lush natural environment of Aswan, this is the greatest outdoor museum in the world. The tourist with limited time will have a problem deciding what not to see.

Alexandria

So much of ancient Alexandria is lost to us: the great library with over 500,000 scrolls; the Pharos lighthouse, one of the seven wonders of the ancient world; the obelisks of Cleopatra, which now reside on foreign shores; and the grave of Alexander himself, which may or may not be there. But Alexandria remains an essential city to visit.

ANCIENT MONUMENTS

Pompey's Pillar, Sharia Ahmed el Sawari, in the southwestern part of the city. This Aswan rose granite pillar, built in AD 297 in memory of the Roman Emperor Diocletian, stands on the site of the Serapeum, one of the greatest temple complexes of the ancient world. Open 9am–4pm daily. Small entrance fee.

Catacombs of Kom esh-Shawqafa, south of Pompey's Pillar in the southwestern section of the city. Discovered in 1900, the catacombs are dug one hundred feet into the rock bed and date back to the second century AD. The reliefs are a blend of Greek and Egyptian symbolism. Open 9am–6pm daily. Small entrance fee.

MEDIEVAL MONUMENTS

Fort of Qaitbey, located at the northern tip of the eastern harbour, the 15th-century fort stands on the site of the Pharos, the ancient lighthouse. Open 9am–3pm daily. Small entrance fee.

PALACES

Antoniadis Villa and Gardens, in the southern central section of the city along the Mahmoudieh Canal. Mansion and gardens open daily 8am–4pm.

Muntazah Palace Complex, set in a seaside park, was a summer residence of Abbas II Hilmi (1874–1944, Khedive 1892–1914). At the outbreak of World War I, the British deposed Abbas and seized his estate which they used as a military hospital until 1919. It later belonged to King Fa'ad. The park is open to the public.

DAY-TRIPS

Abu Qir, located to the east of the city of Alexandria along the shore of the Mediterranean. This was the site

where Nelson destroyed Napoleon's fleet in 1798.

Al Alamein, 62 miles west of Alexandria along the Mediterranean coast, was the site of the decisive battle for North Africa in World War II. Commonwealth, Italian and German cemeteries open during daylight hours, if closed look for the guard. No entrance fees.

Cairo

PHARAONIC MONUMENTS

Cairo did not exist as a city during pharaonic times, but the area surrounding was dominated by Memphis, one of the most important administrative centres of ancient Egypt.

Sakkara, 15 miles (26 km) southwest of Cairo along the western bank of the Nile, is part of a long cemetery which runs from Giza to Maidum. It is the greatest burial site of ancient Egypt. Included in standard tours are the Funerary Complex of Zoser with the Step Pyramid, The Pyramid of Unas, the Tombs of Ptah-Hotep, Ti, and Mereruka, and the Serapeum. Open daily from dawn to sunset. Allow at least 4 hours to tour Sakkara. Photography restrictions within the tombs. Fees for videos. Entrance fee.

A few miles south and east of Sakkara, **Memphis** was the capital of the Old Kingdom. Most of this once magnificent city is buried under the village of Mit Rahina, but sites to visit include the Colossus of Ramses II, Temple of Ptah, and the Temple of Hathor. Open daily from dawn to sunset. Allow 1 hour to tour Memphis. Small entrance fee.

South of Sakkara along the same road, the four pyramids of **Dahshur** represent royal burial sites of the Old and Middle Kingdoms. The most interesting complex contains the Bent Pyramid.

The highlight of any tour of Egypt, the Giza Plateau is located at the end of Pyramids Road. Sites include the three pyramids, Boat Museum (special fee), the Sphinx, and various tombs. Allow at least 4 hours to tour the area. Photography permitted in outdoor areas. Fees for videos. Entrance fee.

Old Cairo

Most of the monuments of early Christianity in Egypt are found in Old Cairo, to the south of the modern city. Accessible by Metro (Mari Girgis Station), sites to see include the **Fortress of Babylon**, the **Convent of St George**, **Hanging Church**, **church of Abu Serga**, the **church of Saint Barbara**, and the **Coptic Museum**. Area open 24 hours. Churches open from dawn to sunset, but discretion is advised during religious ceremonies. Allow 2–3 hours. Small entrance fees at various sites.

North of Fustat is a crowded area filled with modern and medieval buildings called the **Southern Cemetery**. The most important monuments in the area are the **Mausoleum of Imam al Shafi'i**, a shrine, a pilgrimage site and a functioning mosque originally built by Salah el Din in 1211, and **Hauosh al Basha**, a multi-domed tomb housing the graves of the Mohammed Ali dynasty. Both buildings are open from sunrise to sunset. There is an entrance fee for Hosh el Basha.

Medieval Cairo

Cairo was founded by the Arab invaders in the 7th century and its fortunes grew with their successes. They ruled the city for nearly 1,000 years and left behind a dynamic legacy in stone. Left to languish when the city expanded and came under Western influence in the 19th century, many of the architectural features have recently been restored and rise gloriously from the medieval streets. Tourists touring the medieval city should dress modestly (no shorts, no sleeveless dresses, no short skirts) and use common sense when taking photographs. Although most mosques are open to visitors, non-Muslims should not enter when religious services are taking place.

The **Mosque of Amr ibn al-As** (Old Cairo) was the first to be built in Egypt. It was named after the Arab soldier who conquered Egypt and founded Cairo. It is a functioning mosque and open from sunrise to sunset. Allow 1 hour. Entrance fee.

The graceful and serene Mosque of Ibn **Tulun** is one of the most impressive buildings in the world. It is an architectural masterpiece of Islamic art. Beside it is the Gayer-Ande**rson Museum**. Allow 1–2 hours. Entrance fee.

The **Citadel**, begun by Salah el Din in the 12th century, was the headquarters of government until the 19th century. Located on a spur of the Muqattam Hills overlooking Cairo, it houses a host of museums and mosques. In the square below, once used as a race course, stand the **Madrasah of Sultan Hasan** and the **Rafa'i Mosque**, where Khedive Ismail and the Shah of Iran are buried. Allow 3–4 hours. Open daily 9 am–4pm. Entrance fees.

The **Bab Zuwayla** is one of the main gates to the medieval city. The area around the gate is rich in medieval architecture including the **Qasaba of Ridwan Bey**, the last existing example of a covered bazaar, and the **Mosque of Maridani**, one of the most exquisite 14th-century mosques in the city. The area is open 24 hours a day. Allow at least 3 hours. Photograph at will, but be aware of people's sensitivities. Entrance fees to some of the monuments.

The **Northern Cemetery** is the best place to see an oriental skyline. Minarets and domes from mortuary buildings of the 14th and 15th centuries stretch for several miles. Two monuments must not be missed: the Mausoleum of Barquq and the Mausoleum of Qaitbey. In the **Mausoleum of Barquq** everything is in duplicate: two minarets, two domes, two *sabils*, and two delicate wooden screens. The **Mausoleum of Qaitbey** was built near the end of the mamluke era and epitomises the power and exquisite taste of Egypt's slave dynasty. Area open 24 hours. Monuments open 9am–4pm. Do not enter during religious services. Photograph with discretion. Entrance fees to monuments.

Other Attractions

Cairo Tower, Gazirah, near the Exhibition Grounds, tel: 341-0884. A modern tower offers a wonderful panorama of Cairo.

Cairo Zoo, Sharia Giza, Giza, tel: 726-314. The main zoo in Egypt, this facility, founded in 1891, sits on 52 gardened acres and features over 400 animals. Open 9am–5pm daily. Small entrance fee.

Camel Market. One of two major animal markets in Egypt, the camel market at Embaba operates on Friday and Sunday from dawn to dusk and sells camels, goats, horses, donkeys, and other livestock.

Dr Ragab's Papyrus Institute, 3 Sharia el Nil, Giza, tel: 348-8676. The original papyrus institute in Egypt, Dr Ragab revived the craft this century. Tour includes an exhibition of how papyrus is made. Articles for sale. Open 9am–7pm daily.

Egyptian National Circus, Sharia el Nil, Aguza, tel: 346-4870. The big top is located south of the Balloon Theatre. Performances at 9pm.

Fish Garden, Sharia Wadi el Gazirah, Zamalek, tel: 340-1606. Fish and grottos in a 19th-century atmosphere. Open 9am–4pm daily. Small entrance fee.

Gazirah Planetarium, Gazirah Exhibition Grounds, Zamalek, tel: 341-2453. Nightly skyshows in Arabic only. Open 7pm nightly. Closed Friday.

Orman Botanical Gardens next to the Cairo Zoo, Giza, tel: 728-272. Created in the 19th century by Barillet-Deschamps. A spring flower show is held in March. Open 8am–5pm in summer, 8am–4pm in winter.

Pharaonic Village, Jacob Island, Giza, tel: 729-186. Tourists circle the island by boat and observe re-enactments of life in ancient Egypt. Open 9am–4pm daily.

Nile Barrages, Qanater. Two 19th-century dams block the river as it diverges into the Rashid (Rosetta) and Dumyat (Damietta) branches at Qanater, 15 miles (24 km) north of Cairo. Around the highly ornate dams a park has been created with cycling, boating, and carriage rides.

Sound and Light, Giza Plateau in front of the Sphinx. Two shows nightly beginning at sunset. Saturday, English and French; Sunday, French and German; Monday, English and French; Tuesday, French and German; Wednesday, English and French; Thursday, Arabic and English; Friday, English and French. Performance about one hour. Photography permitted. No videos. Entrance fee.

Minya

Travel and tourism in the zone between Minya and Luxor is currently restricted though it includes some of the most interesting and least spoiled sites in Egypt.

Beni Hassan is located on the east bank of the river. Signs along the main highway mark the way to the river crossing. A local *felucca* watertaxi crosses the river. On the east bank one may walk the mile or so to the tombs or ride a donkey, tractor, or car. The 39 tombs of the 11th and 12th Dynasty are cut into the side of the mountain. Area open 24 hours. Monuments: 9am–4pm. Allow half a day. Photography permitted. Videos for a fee. Entrance fee.

Tel el Amarna is the most important site in Middle Egypt. The area contains the site of the town of **Akhet-Aten**, the capital of ancient Egypt during the short reign of Amenhotep IV, the Pharaoh Akhenaten. Now a ruin, foundations of palaces, temples and houses can be seen. In the tombs located in the mountains to the east are wall illustrations executed in the naturalistic style of the Armana period. The most interesting tombs are the **Tomb of Aye** and the **Tomb of Meri-re**. To get to Tell el Amarna one must cross the river by ferry and take donkeys or tractors or walk around the site. Area open 24 hours. Monuments: 9am–4pm. Allow half a day. Photography permitted. Entrance fee to tombs.

Abydos

The most impressive monument is the **Temple of Seti I**, with a hypostyle hall, seven shrines, and the Corridor of Kings. Abydos is often included on tour itineraries combined with a visit to Dendera. Area open 24 hours. Monuments: 9 a.m–4pm. Allow half a day. Photography permitted. Fee for video. Entrance fee.

Dendera

Parts of the Graeco-Roman temple of **Hathor** at Dendera (4th century BC) still stand. The zodiac on the roof and the crypts below the temple are particularly interesting. There is also the ruin of a Christian basilica, one of the earliest structures of the Christian era. Dendera lies on the west bank of the Nile 37 miles (60 km) north of Luxor and can be visited from the latter city by bus or taxi. Allow a day for Dendera and Abydos. Area open 24 hours. Monuments: 9am–4pm. Photography permitted. Fee for video. Entrance fee.

Luxor

Great Temple of Amun at Karnak, Not to be missed are the first pylon, the temple of Ramses III, the hypostyle hall, the obelisks of Hatshepsut, the sacred lake, and the festival hall of Thutmosis III. Karnak is north of Luxor and can be reached by car, horse carriage or bus along the Corniche. Allow 3–4 hours. Open 9am–4pm. Photography permitted. Fee for video. Entrance fee.

Luxor Temple, In the heart of modern Luxor. Allow 1 hour. Open 9am–11pm. Photography permitted. Fee for video. Entrance fee.

The West Bank, One can cross the river to the west bank via tourist or local ferry. Tickets are available to all sites at the kiosk near the tourist ferry. Tickets cannot be purchased at the various sites. Taxi, donkey, and bicycles can be rented to visit the West Bank at the ferry landings. A superficial tour visiting 1 mortuary temple, 3–4 tombs in the Valley of the Kings, a quick trip to Deir el Medina, and 2–3 tombs in the Valley of the Nobles is all that can be accomplished in a day. It would take weeks to really explore the area.

Valley of the Kings, There are 62 known tombs in this desert valley. Several have electricity and are open to the public on a continuous basis. Among the most famous tombs are: Tutankhamun, where the famous treasures were found; Ramses VI, with its vaulted ceiling; and Seti I, the largest and finest tomb in the valley.

Valley of the Queens, Although there are over 70 tombs of queens and royal children of the 18th and 19th Dynasties in this valley, only a few are open to the public.

Tombs of the Nobles at Qurnah, Many of these 400 noblemen's tombs are closed to the public but not to be missed (if open) are the tomb of Nakht with scenes of planting, harvesting, banqueting, hunting and fishing; the tomb of Menna with fishing and fowling scenes; and the tomb of Ramose with the famous mourning scene.

Mortuary Temples, Four mortuary temples remain standing: Seti I with very good reliefs; Ramses II, called the Ramesseum, Ramses III, the most intact; and Deir el Bahri, the elegant temple of Hatshepsut. Of the Mortuary Temple of Amenhotep III, once the largest on the West Bank, only a stela and the two statues of the king remain. The latter are known as the Colossi of Memnon.

Dawn and sunset hot-air balloon excursions, complete with champagne and elegant meals, quietly and slowly sail over the green plain of the West Bank, giving travellers a bird's-eye view of the monuments below. Book at the Mövenpick Jolie Ville and Hilton International.

SOUND & LIGHT

Held at the Karnak temple, it is one of the best sound and light shows you will see or hear. Two performances nightly at 6pm and 8pm. Duration is 90 minutes and some walking is required. Sunday, French and German; Monday, English; Tuesday, French and German; Wednesday, English and French; Thursday, Arabic; Friday and Saturday, English and French.

From Esna to Kom Ombo

Most tour boats ply the river between Luxor and Aswan stopping at the Ptolemaic temples along the way. Visits are usually an hour long and entrance fees are included in the package. Open 9am–4pm. Photography permitted. Fee for videos.

From north to south they are: the Temple of Esna, the least impressive of the group; the Temple of Edfu, the best preserved Ptolemaic temple in Egypt; and the Temple of Kom Ombo.

Aswan

PHARAONIC

Elephantine Island, accessible by *felucca* which docks at the quay of one of the few remaining Nubian villages, Elephantine Island was the original site of ancient Aswan. Modern excavations have unearthed several interesting sites including the Temples of Khnum and Satis, the complex of Hekayib, and the Necropolis of the Sacred Rams. Also on the island is the ancient Nilometer and the Aswan Museum. Allow 2–3 hours. Site open dawn to dusk, museum from 9am–2pm. Photography permitted. No entrance fee to the island, small entrance fee to the museum.

Tombs of the Nobles, on the west bank of the river along the mountain called Qubbet el Hawa, Dome of the Wind, are tombs of noblemen from Aswan. The best are the Tomb of Kehayib, Tomb of Harkhuf, Tombs of

Mekhu and Sabni, Tomb of Sarenput II, and Tomb of Khunes. Allow half a day. Accessible by *felucca* and a steep climb. Open 9am–4pm. Photography permitted. Small entrance fee.

Philae, Philae rises from the lake on its new home between the High Dam and the Aswan Dam. Sites to see include the Temple of Isis, the Gateway of Hadrian, the Temple of Hathor, and the Kiosk of Trajan. Allow half a day. Open dawn to dusk. Accessible by motor launch. Photography permitted. Entrance fee. Sound and light show at sunset.

MODERN

Mausoleum of the Aga Khan, located on a hilltop across the river from the city of Aswan. Accessible by felucca and camel or on foot. Open dawn to dusk. No entrance fee.

Kitchener's Island, a botanical paradise of exotic plants and trees. Access by *felucca*. Open dawn to sunset. Photography permitted. Small entrance fee.

Aswan Dam and High Dam, the Aswan Dam was the first to harness the river at Aswan. Today it is joined by the much larger and more effective High Dam. Between them is a small lake and beyond the High Dam is the Lake Nasser. Accessible by vehicle. Open 24 hours. No photography. No entrance fee.

Abu Simbel

Abu Simbel is south of Aswan on the western shore of the Lake Nasser. Two magnificent temples await the visitor, the Temple of Ramses II and the Temple of Nefertari. This site was the object of the greatest salvage operation in history. Abu Simbel is serviced by flights from Cairo, Luxor, and Aswan. It is also accessible by car. Allow at least 2 hours. The temple is open 9am–4pm, but the grounds are accessible from dawn to dusk. Photography permitted. Entrance fee.

Cruising the Nile

Scores of Nile cruise-companies offer packages to suit every pocket and taste. Most offer 4-, 5- and 7-day tours between Luxor and Aswan. Trips are as comfortable and often cheaper if they are arranged outside Egypt. Here are some of the boats and operators:

☆☆☆☆☆
Alexander the Great, Jolley Travel and Tour Company, 23 Qasr el Nil. Tel: 393-9390. This cruise ship was featured in the American series *The Love Boat*.
Anni, *Aton*, *Hotp*, and *Tut*, Sheraton Management Corporation, 48B Sharia Giza, Dokki. Tel: 348-8215.
Golden Boat, International Nile Cruise, 87 Sharia Ramses. Tel: 760-198.
Isis and *Osiris*, Hilton International Company, Nile Hilton Hotel. Tel: 740-880. The first modern day cruise boats on the Nile, these sister ships offer 5-day cruises.
Neptune, Trans Egypt Travel Company, 37 Qasr el Nil. Tel: 392-4313. Seven-, 10-, and 11-day cruises.
Nile Admiral, *Nile Emperor*, *Nile Legend*, *Nile President*, *Nile Princess*, *Nile Ritz*, *Nile Symphony*, Presidential Nile Cruises, 13 Marashli, Zamalek. Tel: 340-0517; 4-, 7-, and 10-day cruises.
Nile Majesty I, *Nile Majesty II*, Mo Hotels Travel and Nile Cruises, 41 Sherif. Tel: 392-5674.
Nile Queen, *Nile Sphinx*, Sphinx Tours, 2 Behler Passage, Qasr el Nil. Tel: 392-0704.
Oberoi Shehrayar and *Oberoi Shehrazad*, Oberoi Corporation Ltd. Mena House Hotel. Tel: 387-1225.
Ra, Eastmar Travel, 13 Qasr el Nil. Tel: 753-216.
Seti II, *Seti III*, Magdy G. Henein, 16 Ismail Muhammad, Zamalek. Tel: 341-9820.

☆☆☆☆
Atlas and *Nile Star*, Eastmar Travel, 13 Qasr el Nil. Tel: 753-216.
Fleur, International Nile Cruises Company, 3 Monshat el Katab. Tel: 392-4656.
Horus, International Company for Hotels and Nile Cruises, 23B Ismail Muhammad, Zamalek. Tel: 340-0675/6.
Seti I and *Seti IV*, Magdy G. Henein, 16 Ismail Muhammad. Tel: 341-9820/2. Part of a fleet of six ships ranging from 5-star to unclassified.

☆☆☆
Abu Simbel, *Aswan*, *Nile Delta*, Hapi Travel and Tourism Company, 17 Qasr el Nil. Tel: 393-3611/93, 393-3562. Seven- and 14-day cruises.
Karnak, *Pyramids*, *Queen Nefertiti*, and *Akhenaten*, Pyramids Nile Cruise Company, 56 Gamet el Dowal el Arabia, Mohandeseen. Tel: 360-0146/7.
Nefertari, Eastmar Travel, 13 Qasr el Nil. Tel: 753-305; 13-day cruises.

Unclassified
Unclassified cruise ships may be 3–5 star and above. This is a selected list.
Aida I and *Aida II*, Nile Valley Tours, 80 Gamel el Dowal el Arabia, Mohandeseen. Tel: 349-5482, 349-3768.
Ambassador I and *Ambassador II*, Ambassador Nile Cruises Company, 33 Hosny Saleh, Mohandeseen. Tel: 347-1015.
Excelsior and *Seti the Great*, Magdy G. Henein, 16 Ismail Muhammad, Zamalek. Tel: 341-9820/2.
Nile Pullman Fleurette and *Nile Pullman L'Egyptien*, Pullman International Hotels, 9 Menes St, Heliopolis. Tel: 290-8802/3.

Felucca Trips

You can hire a *felucca* to sail between Luxor or Aswan, taking 2–4 days and visiting the temples along the way. Ask along the Corniche in either Luxor or Aswan.

Festivals
Calendars

The business and secular community in Egypt operates under the Western (Gregorian) calendar. But other calendars have official status in Egypt. The Islamic calendar, used to fix religious observances, is based on a lunar cycle of 12 months of 29 or 30 days. The Muslim year is thus 11 days shorter than the year according to the Gregorian calendar and months move forward accordingly.

In the Gregorian calendar, for example, April is always in the spring, but in the Muslim calendar all months move through all seasons in a 33-year cycle.

The Coptic calendar is the Julian calendar which was replaced in the West by the Gregorian calendar between 1582 and 1752, but the months carry their current Egyptian names. The Coptic year consists of 12 months of 30 days and one month of 5 days. Every four years a sixth day is added to the shorter month. An adaptation of the Coptic calendar is used by many farmers for planting and harvesting crops. It is used by the authorities of the Coptic Orthodox Church.

Muslim	Coptic
Muharram	Toot (begins Sept 11 or 12)
Safar	Baaba
Rabi' il-awal	Hatour
Rabi' it-tani	Kiyaak
Gamada-l-uula	Tuuba (mid-Jan)
Gamada-l-ukhra	Amshir
Ragab	Baramhat
Sha'aban	Barmuda
Ramadan	Bashans
Shawal	Bauna
Dhu'l	Abiib
Dhu'l	Misra
	Nasi (5-6 days)

Photography

There's no doubt about it: Egypt is a photographer's paradise. The best film speeds for daylight outdoors are low (100 and under), but fast film (400, 1000) is necessary for interiors, high-powered lenses and night shots like the moon over the Nile or the sound and light at the pyramids or Karnak. Photography is forbidden in security zones, often curiously defined, and a variety of rules pertains to Pharaonic monuments. Signs are usually posted in restricted areas. Heed them. In other areas you are permitted to take photographs if you pay a fee. Fees for still cameras run as high as LE50, for video cameras up to LE200. There are no restrictions on photography anywhere in the historic zone of Cairo.

Scholars and professional photographers working on projects may apply for a special permit to take pictures from the Supreme Council for Antiquities. The procedure may well take some time, and passes are not given out freely.

Photographing individual people requires a bit of common sense and consideration. The Egyptian people are constantly having cameras pushed in their faces, so be courteous and ask first. If a person does not want you to take his or her photo, do not take it. If he or she wants to be paid, pay. If you don't want to pay, don't take the picture. You will find plenty of good shots elsewhere.

Processing of colour film is fast but perfunctory. Professionals prefer to take all their films back for processing. No studio offers top-quality processing, slides or transparencies can only be handled by two or three establish-

ments and Kodachrome has to be sent to Europe.

Outdoor Activities

Participant

Fishing

The Nile, Lake Nasser and the lakes along the northern coast support commercial fishing. However, fishing is a thriving sport on the Mediterranean and Red Sea. For information about international tournaments contact the Shooting Club, Sharia an Nadi as Sayd, Duqqi, tel: 704-333.

Gliding

For a spectacular view of the pyramids and portions of the city of Cairo, gliding excursions are available on a hit and miss basis Thursdays and Fridays at the Imbaba Airfield to the west of Cairo. The Egyptian Gliding Institute and the Egyptian Aviation Society offer motorgliders and lessons.

Golf

There are two nine-hole golf courses in Cairo, one at the Gazirah Club in Zamalek and the other at the Mena House Oberoi in Giza (with the pyramids as a backdrop). Equipment can be rented but the courses are extremely busy.

Riding

There is little to compare with a dawn or dusk gallop through the desert. The Bedouin at the Giza pyramids have been catering for eager riders for generations and there are several good stables in the area. Horses and camels are on offer. Lessons are available. Overnight trips to Sakkara can be arranged. Stables include MG, KM, SA, AA (850531), and FF.

Shooting

Large mammals are increasingly rare, but the migration of wild-foal attracts legal and illegal sportsmen. Would-be hunters must have a local hunting li-

cence and respect protected areas. It is extremely difficult for the authorities to control the sport and illicit hunting trips are sometimes offered to travellers. Illegal hunters face severe penalties and unwanted publicity. For trapshooting, target-shooting and advice on hunting contact the Shooting Club, Sharia an Nadi as Sayd. Tel: 704-333.

Rowing

There are 10 rowing clubs in Cairo, and almost all are located on the west bank of the Nile from Giza to Imbaba. Competitions start in November and run through April. They are held every Friday on the Nile. Schedules can be obtained from any rowing club and lessons are available at some clubs. For information see the Egyptian Rowing Club, 11 Sharia al Nil, Giza, near the Cairo Sheraton, tel: 731-639.

Yachting

Docking facilities exist at major ports in Egypt and along the Nile at major cities. Yachts may enter the country through the various ports provided they have the proper documentation. The Egyptian Tourist Information Centres throughout the world have a small booklet for yacht enthusiasts entitled Egypt for Yachtsmen giving entry information and maps.

Spectator

Horses

There are several spectator sports that revolve around horses. Horse racing takes place on Saturday and Sunday from mid-November through May at the Heliopolis Hippodrome Course in Heliopolis, in Cairo, and at the Smouha Race course in Alexandria. Races begin at 1.30pm. Betting is allowed.

The Arabian horse is known throughout the world for its beauty, stamina, and intelligence. It was originally bred on the Arabian Peninsula, but stud farms for Arabians now exist all over the world. Characteristics include a compact body with a straight back, a small head, wide eyes, wide nostrils, a wide forehead, small ears and a wide jawbone.

There are many stud farms in Egypt, but only four major ones. The biggest, with 300 horses, is the government-owned Egyptian Agricultural Organisation (EAO), El Zahraa Station, Sharia Ahmad Esmat, tel: 243-1733. This farm has only pure-bred bloodlines and is the home of the most famous Arabian stallion of this century, Nazeer. Every important stud farm in the world has some of his offspring.

Soccer
Every vacant lot in Cairo is a soccer field and young enthusiasts have been known to use just about anything for a ball, including an unlucky hedgehog. Professional soccer has been known to cause traffic jams, slow down service in restaurants, and empty the streets. It is the national pastime of Egypt. Three leagues compete at 3pm each Friday and Sunday afternoon from September to May at various stadiums throughout Egypt. Among the top teams in Egypt are Ahly, Zamalek, and the Arab Contractors.

Shopping
What to Buy
If you buy items that cannot be easily carried it is best to let the merchant handle the export. Items over LE200 require export licences.

Amber
Pale yellow, honey, brown, red, white, and almost black amber can be found in shops in Cairo's Khan al-Khalili in the form of beads, necklaces, pipe parts and cane handles.

Antiquities and Antiques
Pharaonic and Islamic antiquities can be exported only through a few shops. Each sale should be accompanied by a letter of authenticity and permission to export the item. Street vendors selling antiquities are selling fakes, worth

purchasing for their own merit, but not as authentic articles. In fact, the best buys in Cairo are European antiques. There are many little antique shops in Cairo around Sharia Hoda Shaarawi in Zamalek and Maadi. In Alexandria the Attarine district around the street of the same name is popular with antique hunters.

Baskets
Every region in Egypt has its own distinct type of basket. Best places to buy are in the village *souqs*. In Aswan, the typical flat Nubian baskets are still available.

Brass & Copper
The Suq au-Nahhasiin in the Qasabah near Khan al Khalili is the best place in Egypt to buy brass and copper, both antique and modern. But a good alternative is Sh. q in Maadi.

Weaving
Kirdassah, on the western fringes of greater Cairo, has a large market where weaving is sold. Harraniyyah, on the Saqqarah road, is world-famous for its tapestries, woven by villagers using naturally-dyed wools. Bedouin rugs, made on small looms in the desert, vary in design between tribes. The most popular are red and white striped from the northern coast; the most difficult to find are green and orange diamond patterns from the Sinai.

Clothing
Ready to wear clothing is beautifully designed and well-made. The world's finest cotton is Egypt's major export. For sleeping, lounging, or informal wear there is nothing like an Egyptian *gallabiyyas*. They come in all sizes and designs or can be made to order in a day. Bedouin dresses are handmade and most have a great deal of embroidery on them. Those from Northern Sinai are cross-stitched in reds, oranges and yellows, or blues and pinks. They can be bargained for in the villages on the way to Al Arish, or in Khan al Khalili, or at Kirdassah.

Jewellery
From modern pharaonic cartouches to antique Turkish, Art Deco, and Art Nouveau pieces, jewellery is one of the best buys in Egypt. Gold is sold up to 21 carat for traditional jewellery,

and 18 carat for modern jewellery of chains and charms. One of the best places to shop is the Suk el Sagha in the Khan al Khalili. Here you will find traditional designs coveted by the farmers' wives in the form of necklaces, earrings and bracelets. Special shops sell 21-carat handtooled or stamped Nubian designs. Shops that sell gold plate are identified by a large gilded camel in the window. Modern designs are found in jewellery stores throughout the city. Many are found on Abdel Khalek Sarwat west of Opera Square in Cairo. In Luxor the jewellery bazaar is just behind Luxor Temple to the north of the Luxor Hotel. In Aswan look for jewellery shops in the souq.

Although gold is the preferred metal today, silver traditionally dominated the market. Designs tend to be large and heavy, and are therefore too costly to be made in gold. If one is interested in Bedouin ware one must ask, for these wonderful items are often hidden away in giant sacks under the counter. Silver items are sold in all shopping areas and souqs in Egypt but predominate in the Khan al Khalili in Cairo.

Leather
Everything from large and small pieces of luggage to clothing is found in an abundance of designs. Leathers include buffalo, gazelle, crocodile, serpent, lizard, cow, moose and goat.

Musical Instruments
Middle Eastern musical instruments of all qualities are made in Cairo. The people who make them and those who sell them are all found along Sharia Mohammed Ali near the Citadel.

Muski Glass
Glass made of recycled bottles in traditional factories comes in five main colours: navy blue, brown, turquoise blue, green, aqua, and purple. The glass is hand-blown into pitchers, beakers, cups, tumblers, vases, dishes, Christmas ornaments, and amulets. The imperfections, cracks, and bubbles make this inexpensive glass very fragile.

Papyrus
A few decades ago the particular reed from which papyrus is made was virtually extinct in Egypt, but its cultivation

was revived by the Dr Raghab Papyrus Institute. There are now shops all over Egypt selling hand-painted papyrus sheets. Designs are quite stunning and many duplicate famous ancient Egyptian wall paintings.

Perfume

Perfume shops with their beautifully decorated bottles are easy to spot and exist in all shopping areas of the country, especially the *souqs* in Alexandria, Cairo, Luxor, and Aswan. Egypt grows and exports jasmine, geranium, rose, violet, camomile, and orange for the major perfumiers in France, from whom essence is then re-imported. Shelf life, however, is a problem.

Appliqué

The Tentmakers' Bazaar (Souq al Khiyamiyyah), the only covered bazaar left in Cairo, is the place to buy appliqué tenting. This wonderful craft, probably traceable to ancient Egypt, when appliqué banners billowed from the tops of temple gates, comes in pharaonic and Islamic designs in the form of pillow cases, tablecloths, and wall hangings. It is one of the best buys in Egypt.

Furniture and Woodwork

Mashrabiyyati, traditional screens of turned wood, covered the windows of old-fashioned Cairene houses and shielded the sanctuaries of mosques. Expensive, but top quality work is available at NADIM, the National Art Development Institute of Mashrabia, 47 Suliman Gohar, Dokki. Tel: 715-927.

Language

Conversation

Many sounds in spoken Arabic do not get represented by transliteration. A particularly characteristic Arabic sound, however, is represented in the following list: *c*ayn, represented as ᶜ.

All Arabic-speakers, native and otherwise, delight in producing the appropriate noise, described as a guttural hum or a voiced emphatic "h", which occurs in such common names as ᶜAbbas, ᶜAbdallah, Ismaᶜil, and ᶜAli (which is not, incidentally, accented on the last syllable). Non-Arabic-speakers generally find pronouncing ᶜ impossible without instruction and practice; and if it seems too difficult, it may be ignored. One will merely be marked as a non-Arabic-speaking foreigner or as having a speech impediment.

Most Cairenes know a few words of English, though real ability to use languages other than Arabic is confined to the educated. A few words of colloquial Egyptian Arabic are therefore useful. The words and phrases listed below are not transliterated, but spelled more or less phonetically, according to the following rules:

Vowels

ᶜ = ᶜ*ayn*, as explained above
' = glottal stop
a = a as in *father*
aa = a as in Standard English *bad*, *mad*, *glad*
e = e as in *very*
i = i as in *if, stiff*
ii = ee as in *between*
o = o as in *boss*
u = u as in *put*
uu = o as in *fool*

Consonants

(All emphatic consonants have been omitted.) All consonants are pronounced individually and as in English with the following exceptions:
kh = ch as in Scottish *loch*
sh = sh as in *shut*.
gh = Arabic *ghayn*, usually described as resembling a (guttural) Parisian *r*.
q = Arabic *qaf*, frequently pronounced in Cairo as a k or a glottal stop.

Vocabulary

airport	matár
boat	mérkeb
bridge	kubri
car	ᶜarabiyya, sayára
embassy	sefára
hospital	mustáshfa
hotel	fúnduq
post office	bosta
restaurant	matáam
square, maydan	midan/midáan
street	shaariᶜ

right	yemiin
left	shemáal
and/or	wa/walla
yes/no	aywa/laa'
please/thank you	minfadlak/shukran
big/little	kibiir/sughayyar
good/bad	kwáyyis/mish kwáyyis
possible	mumkin
impossible	mish mumkin
here/there	hena/henáak
hot/cold	sukn/baarid
many/few	kitiir/olayyel
up/down	fo' (foq)/taht
more/enough	kamáan/kefáya
breakfast	íftar
dinner	asha
today	innahárda
tomorrow	bokra
yesterday	embáareh
morning	is-sobh
noon	id-dohr
afternoon	bᶜad id-dohr
at night	belayl
next week	il esbuul-iggáy
next time	il mara-iggáya
last time	il-mara illi fáatit
after a while	bᶜad shwayya
I/you	ana/enta
he/she	huwwa/hiyya
they/we	humma/ehna
Hello, welcome	ahlan wa sahlan
Good morning	sabáh-il-kheyr
Good evening	masáal-kheyr
Goodbye	mᶜas-saláama
What is your name? (to a male)	íssmak ey?
What is your name? (to a female)	íssmik ey?
How are you? (to a male)	izzáyak
How are you? (to a female)	izzáyik
I am fine	kwayiss (M), kwayíssa (F)

NUMERALS

1	wáhid
2	itnéyn
3	taláatah
4	arbᶜá
5	khamsa
6	sitta
7	sébᶜa
8	tamánya
9	tíssa
10	áshara
11	hedásher
12	itnásher
13	talatásher
14	arbatasher

15	*khamastásher*
16	*sitásher*
17	*sabatásher*
18	*tamantásher*
19	*tissᶜatásher*
20	*ashríin*
30	*talatíin*
40	*arbaᶜíin*
50	*khamsíin*
60	*sittíin*
70	*sabaᶜíin*
80	*tamaníin*
90	*tissaᶜíin*
100	*miiya, miit*

MONEY

money	*filúus*
50 piastres	*khamsíin ᶜersh (qersh)*
75 piastres	*khamsa wa sabaᶜíin 'ersh (qersh)*
change/no change	*fakka/ mafiish fakka*
the bill	*il hesáb*
this/that	*di/da*
how much?	*bekáam?*
how much do you	*ᶜayiz kaam?*
want? (to a male)	
how much do you	*ᶜayza kaam ?*
want? (to a female)	
all/half	*kull/nus*

DAYS/MONTHS

Sunday/Monday
yowm al had/yowm al-itnéyn

Tuesday/Wednesday
yowm it-taláat/yowm al-árba

Thursday/Friday
yowm al-khamíis/yowm ig-gómᶜa

Saturday
yowm is-sabt

January/February/March
yanáyer/febráyer/máris

April/May/June
abreel/mayuu/yuunyuu

July/August/September
yiilyuu/aghustus/sibtímbir

October/November/December
októbir/nofímbir/disímbir

Thank God
il-hamdo li-lah (standard reply)

Often heard is "*insha'Allah*," which means "God willing" and is a reminder that all things are ultimately in the hands of Providence. The standard reply to a casual "See you tomorrow," for instance, is "*Insha'Allah*".

☞☞☞
Further Reading

The Nile

Moorehead, Alan. *The White Nile*.
Moorehead, Alan. *The Blue Nile*.
Vivian, Cassandra and others. *Father of Rivers: A Traveler's Companion to the Nile Valley*. Trade Routes Enterprises, 1989.

Flora

Bircher, Warda. 1960. *Gardens of the Hesperides*. Cairo: Anglo-Egyptian Bookshop.
Chaumes. 1899. *Les promenades et les jardins du Caire*.
Delchevalerie, 1970. *G. Culturs Egyptiennes*, Namru.
El Hadidi, Nabil. *Street Trees of Egypt*. Cairo: American University in Cairo Press.
Tackholm, Vivi and Mohamed Drar. 1969. *Flora of Egypt*. Cairo: Cairo University.
Tackholm, Vivi. 1974. *Student's Flora of Egypt*. Cairo: Cairo University.

Fauna

Bruun, Bertel and Sherif Baha el Din. 1990. *Common Birds of Egypt*. Cairo: American University in Cairo Press.
Hollom, Porter, Schristensen, and Willis. 1988. *Birds of the Middle East and North Africa*. London.
Goodman, Meininger, Baha el Din, Hobbs, and Mullie. 1989. *Birds of Egypt*. Oxford University Press.
Houlihan, Patrick F. *Birds of Ancient Egypt*. 1988. American University in Cairo Press.

Other Insight Guides

Other books in the 190-title Insight Guides series which highlight destinations in this region include *Insight Guide: Egypt, Cairo, Jordan, Israel* and *Jerusalem*.

Apa Publications also produces two other series of guidebooks: *Insight Pocket Guides*, which provide detailed itineraries for the short-stay visitor and include full-size pull-out maps, and *Insight Compact Guides*, which are mini-encylopaedias packed with facts and information and perfect for on-the-spot reference.

Insight Compact Guides

Insight Compact Guide: Egypt is a companion to this book. All text, pictures and maps in its information-packed pages are carefully cross-referenced.

Art/Photo Credit

Photography by
Apa Photo Agency/D&J Heaton 46, 82, 261
Marcus Brooke 70, 187, 208, 233, 244, 304
Christie's Colour Library 89, 91
Thomas Cook Ltd 44, 47, 50
Andrew Eames 23, 48 , 51, 53, 98, 168/169, 182/183, 192, 212, 213, 249, 250, 251, 267, 270
Tor Eigeland 12/13, 18/19, 49, 60, 61, 85, 121, 146/147, 151, 152/153, 179, 180, 181, 191, 198, 200/201, 209, 210, 211, 214/215, 224(L), 224(R), 226, 228/229, 230, 234, 242/243, 245, 247, 254, 256, 264, 266, 273, 291, 294(R) 296/297, 300, 301
Guild Home Video 26/27, 33, 174/175
Robert Harding Picture Library 66, 102, 144/145
Axel Krause/Apa 1, 2
Lyle Lawson 54/55, 164/165, 276/277, 287, 295
Mansell Collection 86
National Maritime Museum 110/111
Richard Nowitz cover, 14/15, 20, 24, 25, 52, 64, 68, 69, 72 80/81, 84, 150, 166/167, 170/171, 172, 189, 195, 196, 197, 204(L), 206, 219, 220, 221, 222, 223, 225, 232(L) 235, 237, 240, 252/253, 269, 271, 272, 274, 278, 281, 284, 290, 292, 294(L)
Christine Osborne 31, 156(R), 176, 177(R), 184/185, 262/263
Eddy Posthuma de Boer 7, 16/17, 190, 193, 204(R), 207, 211, 217, 218, 227, 231, 232(R), 238, 239, 258, 275, 285, 289, 298, 299, 303
Topham Picturepoint 41, 42/43, 45, 57, 71, 74, 83, 99, 103, 126/127, 132, 135, 137, 138, 140, 142, 143, 148, 149, 154(R), 158, 159, 160, 161, 178, 199, 260
Wallace Collection 100/101
Marcus Wilson-Smith 21, 130(L), 141, 154(L), 156(L), 203 205, 282, 283, 286(L), 286(R), 288, 293
Cassandra Vivian 155

Maps Berndtson & Berndtson

Visual Consultant V. Barl

Index

A

Abbas I 64
Abbas II 134
Abbassids 283
Abd el-Latif 50, 63
Abdelsalem Shadi 161
Abdin Palace 133
Abdullah Al Mamun 63
Aboukir Bay 103, 125
Abu el-Hagag 221
Abu Simbel 46, 85, 181, 195–198
Abydos 247–251
Aga Khan 187
agriculture 155, 203–205
Ahmed Arabi 133
Ahmed el Bedawi 300
Ahmose Pennekhbet 211, 212
Ahmose, son of Ebana 211, 212
Akhenaten *see* Amenhotep IV
Al-Kamil 285
Al-Salih Ayyub 93, 95
alabaster sphinx, Memphis 266
Alexander the Great 303
Alexandria 116, 301–303
Almasy, Ladislous 142
Amenemhet II 148
Amenhotep I 266
   tomb of 70
Amenhotep II 225
   tomb of 234
Amenhotep III 74, 236
Amenhotep IV (Akhenaten) 74, 78, 79, 219, 223, 236, 255–257
American Civil War 132
Amin, Idi 177
Amon (later Min) 76, 78
Amon-hir-Khopshef (tomb of) 236
Amon-Ra 196, 219, 223, 232, 256
An-Nasir Mohammed 285
animals (sacred) 261
Antony, Mark 89–91
Anubis (god of the dead) 153, 248
Apis bull of Memphis 261, 269
Armana Letters 74
Armant 213, 218
Ashmounein *see* Hermopolis
Aswan 185–199
   Corniche 185
   Elephantine Island 186, 192–193
   granite quarries 191
   Kitchener's Island 186
   Mausoleum of Aga Khan 191
Nilometer
   Pullman Cataract Hotel 47, 187
   unfinished obelisk 191

Aswan Dam 25, 151, 193
Aswan granite 148, 191
Aswan High Dam 25, 151, 153, 185, 193, 238, 299
Atbara 180
Awakening, The (film) 161
Ayyubid dynasty 284, 285

B

Baedeker, Karl 291
Bahri Mamlukes 95
Baker, Sir Samuel 24, 36, 37–39, 113–114, 178
Balyana 247
banana trees 155
Baring, Sir Evelyn 117
Barrages, the 300
Battle of Aboukir 108
Battle of Chaldiran 98
Battle of Kadesh 83, 84, 85, 220
Battle of the Nile 103
Battle of the Pyramids 93, 99, 104
Baybars al-Bunduqdari 96, 285
Belzoni, Giovanni 69, 235
Beni Hassan 259
Bent Pyramid 61
Berkeley Theban Mapping Project 237
birdlife 154, 157
Bisharin tribe 188
Blood from the Mummy's Tomb (film) 161
Blue Nile 21, 23, 25, 30, 179–180
Bonaparte, Napoleon 32, 46, 63, 64, 65, 93, 99, 103–109, 149, 224, 233, 238, 272, 302
Borchardt, Howard Ludwig 79
British, the 103, 123–125, 133–134, 139, 179, 260, 302
Bruce, James 25, 29–31
Brugsch, Emile 70
Burckhardt, John Lewis 32–33
Burton, Richard (actor) 160
Burton, Richard Francis 23, 33, 34, 35, 37, 162
Burullus 301

C

"Curse of the Pharaohs" 64
Cabinet of Dr Caligari, The (film) 160
Caesar and Cleopatra (film) 159
Caesar, Julius 87, 88, 89
Cairo 279–295
   Abd ar-Rahman Katchuda 292
   Amr Ibrahim House 295
   Bab al-Azab 285
   Bab al-Qulluh 285
   Bab an-Nasr 288, 292
   Bab Zuwayla 288
   Bayn al-Qasrayn 290
   Bayt ar-Razzaz 288
   Bayt as-Sihaymi 292
   Ben Ezra Synagogue 282
   Blue Mosque (Mosque of Aqsunqur) 288
   Burg al-Muqqatam 285
   Cairo Marriott Hotel 295

   Church of St Barbara 282
   Church of St George (Mar Girgis) 281
   Church of St Sergius 282
   Church of the Blessed Virgin Mary 281
   Citadel 284–287
   Convent of St George 282
   Coptic Museum 281
   Darb al-Ahmar 287
   Egyptian Military Museum 286
   Gawharah Palace 286
   Gayer-Anderson Museum 284
   Gazira 294
   Gazira Museum 295
   Harim Palace 286
   Hawsh al-Basha 293
   Kasr Beshtak 292
   Khan al-Khalili bazaar 290
   Khanqah of Farag ibn Barquq 292
   Madrasah of An-Nasir Mohammed 292
   Manastirli Palace 283
   Manyal Palace 294
   Mausoleum and Madrasah of Barquq 292
   Maydan at-Tahrir 294
   Mosque of Al-Azhar 290
   Mosque of Al-Hakim 292
   Mosque of Altunbugha Maridani 288
   Mosque of Amr ibn-al-As 279
   Mosque of an-Nasir Mohammed 285
   Mosque of As-Salih Tala'i 289
   Mosque of Ibn Tulun 283
   Mosque of Mohammed Ali 285–286
   Mosque of Qaytbay 293
   Mosque of Qijmas al-Islaqi 288
   Mosque of Sulayman Pasha 286
   Mosque of Sultan Muayyad Shaykh 289
   Museum of Egyptian Civilisation 295
   Museum of Islamic Art 288
   National Cultural Centre (the New Opera House) 294
   Northern Cemetery 192–293
   Old Cairo (Misr al-Qadimah) 281–282
   Qalawan 292
   Rawdah Nilometer 282
   Shari Ahmed Mahir 288
   Shari Al-Azhar 289
   Shrine of Sayyidna Husayn 290
   Souq al-Attarin (Herbalists' Bazaar) 290
   Souq al-Hariyyin (Silk mercers' Bazaar) 289
   Souq al-Khiyamiyyah (Tentmakers' Bazaar) 288
   Souq as-Sagha (Goldsmiths' Bazaar) 290
   Tomb and Madrasah of Sultan Hasan 287
   Zamalek 295
Carnarvon, Lord 67, 235, 240–241
Carter, Howard 67, 70, 79, 235, 240–241
Cataract Hotel, Aswan *see* Pullman Cataract Hotel

cataracts 180, 187
Champollion Jean-François 302
Cheops (Khufu) 62
  pyramid of, see Great Pyramid
    of Cheops
Chephren 63
  pyramid of, 63, 271
Christianity 220, 223, 246–247
Christie, Agatha 45, 161
Churchill, Winston 121, 136
Citadel 96, 98, 99
Cleopatra (film) 160
Cleopatra 87–91
conservation of ancient
  monuments 237–238
Cook, Thomas 24, 45, 120
cotton industry 132, 211, 303
cow, the (*see also* Hathor) 261
Crocodile Island, Luxor 156
crocodiles 153, 261
Cromer, Lord 113, 151
Crusaders 93

D

du Camp, Maxime 45
da Gama, Vasco 22, 97
dahabiyyas 46, 210
Damietta 301
Daraw 207
date palm, the 155
Davis, Bette 161
de Breuys, Admiral 106
de Lesseps, Ferdinand 131,
  133, 149
Death on the Nile (film) 161
Delta region 299–303
Dendera 245
Denon, Dominique Vivant 105–109
Denshawai 260
Diodorus 220
Djer, Pharaoh 251
Dongola 181
Drovetti, Bernardino 69
Duff Gordon, Lady 187

E

Ed Debba 181
Edfu 209
Edku 301
Edwards, Amelia 46, 83, 199, 210
Egypt Exploration Society 84
Egyptian cat 261
Egyptian Museum, Cairo 293
El Kab 211
El Obeid 116
Elephantine Island, Aswan 186, 187,
  192–193
Elgin, Lord 302
Empress Eugénie 132, 133
Eppler, John 142

F

Fahmy, Hekmet 142–143
Faidherbe, the 123–125
falconry 157
Farouk, King 22, 135–140, 142,
  273, 294
Fashoda 24, 115, 122–125
Faw 246
Fayyum 148
Festival of Sokar 266
Festival of Thoth 258
films set in Egypt 159–162
First Cataract 187
flax 211
flora 155
foul sudani 188
Fu'ad, King Ahmed 134–135, 288

G

Gardiner, Sir A. 256
Gayer-Anderson Museum, Cairo 284
Geb (earth-god) 206
Gebel Aulia Dam 179
Gebel Bakal 181
Gebel el-Tarif 246
Gebel Silsila 205, 208–209
Germany 139, 142–143
Giza 270–274
  funerary boat of Cheops (the solar
    boat) 272–273
  Great Pyramid of Cheops 270
  Pyramid of Chephren (Khafre) 271
  Sphinx Theatre 271
  Valley Temple (Granite Temple) 271
Giza Mapping Project 273, 274
Glubb Pasha (John Bagot) 93, 94
gods of ancient Egypt 77, 153, 188
  Amon (tutelary god of
    Thebes) 76, 78
  Amon-Ra (*see also* Amon)196, 219,
    223, 232, 256
  Anubis (god of the dead) 153, 248
  Apis bull of Memphis 269, 261
  Aten (sun-god) 78
  Geb (earth-god) 206
  Hapi (the Nile-god) 188, 199
  Harakhti 206
  Hathor (cow-goddess) 209, 225,
    245–256
  Horus (hawk-god) 198, 206, 207,
    209, 213, 246, 248, 249
  Isis 198, 207, 248
  Khnum (god of Cataract
    region) 188, 213
  Khonsu (moon-god) 219
  Maat (goddess of truth and
    justice) 234
  Min (god of the desert; see also
    Amon) 76, 245
  Mut (consort of Amon) 219
  Nepthys (protector goddess of the
    dead) 207, 248
  Nut (sky-goddess) 206
  Opet (the hippopotamus-goddess)76
  Osiris (judge of the dead) 60, 198,
    206, 234, 248, 250

Ptah (god of Memphis) 197
Ra (form of sun-god; *see also* Ra-
    Harakhte) 206, 279
Ra-Harakhte (form of the sun-god;
    see also Ra) 271
Seshat (god of records and
    archives) 249
Seth (god; son of Nut and Geb)
Shu (air-god) 206
Sobek (crocodile-god) 153, 207, 226
Sokar (god of the dead at
    Memphis)
Statis (goddess of Cataract
    Region) 188, 193
Thoth (god of wisdom) 153, 213,
    234, 257
Golding, William 45
Gondokoro 22, 24, 36, 114, 178
Gordon, General Sir Charles 24, 114–121
  murder of, 179
Grant, Captain James 35–36
grave robbers 67–70
Great Pyramid of Cheops (Khufu) 45,
  59, 61, 62, 64, 68, 238, 270–271
  granite for, 191
Greaves, John 22, 64

H

Hapi (the Nile-god) 188, 199
Harakhti 206
Haremhab 219
Harkhuf 189–190
Harrison, Rex 160
Hathor (cow-goddess) 209, 225,
  245–246
Hatshepsut, Queen 76, 224, 231
  obelisk of, Karnak 191, 224
  temple of (Deir el Bahri) 47, 76,
    231–232
Heliopolis (ancient) see On
Hermopolis 257
Herodotus 22, 31, 62, 77, 147, 148,
  149, 204, 260, 261, 274
Hetepheres, Queen 61
Heyerdahl, Thor 48
Hicks, Colonel William 116
High Dam Lake see Lake Nasser
High Dam, Aswan see Aswan High Dam
hippopotamus, the 153, 260
Hittites 83, 233
Horus 198, 206, 207, 209, 213, 246,
  248, 249
Hosni, Farouk 273
Houssaye, M. Henry 88
Howard-Vyse, Colonel 63
Husayn Kamil 288
Hyksos 74, 211, 219, 260

I

Imhotep 60, 267
Ismail Pasha Ayyub 115
Ismailia 132
Ibn Khaldun 187
Isis 198, 207, 248
ibis worship 258

J

Janissaries 98, 286–287
Jarvis, H. Wood 99
Jewel of the Seven Stars, The
(film) 161
Jinja 176
Johnston, Sir Harry 29
Julius Caesar (film) 160

K

Kitchener, Herbert Horatio 24, 120,
122, 124–125, 179, 187
Kabalego Falls (formerly Murchison
Falls) 24, 177
Kafr al Dawar 301
Kagera River (formerly Murchison
Park) 176
kakaday 188
Kamal el-Mallakh 49
Kamose 219
Karma 181
Kerba 247
Khalif Canal 149
Khalifa Abdullah 120
Khartoum 24, 114, 115, 117–121,
179, 195
Khedive Ismail 113, 115, 130,
131–133, 192, 213, 286, 294, 295
Khnum (ram-headed god of Elephan-
tine) 188, 213
Khonsu (son of Amon-Ra) 219
Khufu (*see* Cheops)
Killear, Lord *see* Lamson, Sir Miles
Kiosk of Kertassi 195
Kitchener's Island, Aswan 186
Kom Ombo 207
Kosti 179
Kovak, Milan 236
Kush 180

L

Lake Victoria 36
Legh, Thomas 32
Livingstone, Dr David 23, 39, 40
Luxor 60, 217–226
Amoun Restaurant 226
Colossi of Memnon 231
Mosque of Abu el-Hagag 221
Museum of Luxor 225–226
New Karnak Café 2256
Old Winter Palace Hotel 226
Quornah 232
Ramesseum 233
Savoy Hotel 226
Temple of Amon-Ra, Karnak 222
Temple of Luxor 221–222
Temple of Queen Hatshepsut
(Deir el Bahri) 231
Valley of the Kings 233–236
Valley of the Nobles 236–237
Valley of the Queens 236
West bank 231–238

M

Maat (goddess of truth and
justice) 234
Mahdi, the *see* Mohammed Ahmed
Ibn el-Sayyid
Mahfouz, Hasan 260
Mahmoud el-Hakim 225
Mallawi 252
Mamlukes 93–99, 103, 104, 285
Manetho 73
Manzala 301
Marchand, Jean-Baptiste 122–125
Mariette, Auguste 209, 269
Marriott Hotel, Cairo 132
Maryut 301
Maspero, Gaston 265
Mausoleum of the Aga Khan,
Aswan 191
McLeave, Hugh 131
Mehalla al Kubra 301
Meidum Pyramid 61
Memnon 69
Memphis 60, 265–266, 279
Menes (Narmer) 60, 147, 212, 251
Merenre 189
Mero 180
Middle Kingdom 248, 269
Milner, Lord 131
Min (Amon) 76, 245
Mit Rahina 265
Mohammed Ahmed Ibn el-Sayyid 24,
116–121, 125, 179
Mohammed Ali 22, 99, 109, 113,
129–131, 149, 150, 285, 294
Monastery of Apa Jeremiah 281
Monastery of St Paloman 247
Monastery of St Simeon 190
Moorehead, Alan 22, 23, 25, 29, 36,
40, 107, 115, 118, 119
Mougel Bey 150
Mountains of the Moon
(film) 162
Mubarak, President 233
mummification 71
Mummy, The (film) 160
Murad Bey 94, 99, 104, 106–107,
108, 109
Murchison Falls *see* Kabalego Falls
Murchison, Sir Roderick 36, 39
Mut (goddess; wife of Amon-Ra) 219
Mutesa, King 35, 38

N

Nag Hammadi 247
Nag Hammadi Library 246
Nahas Pasha 139
Napoleon *see* Bonaparte, Napoleon
Nasser, Gamal Abdel 140, 151, 193
Nazli, Queen 135
Neferhotep 250
Nefertari 85, 297, 236
tomb of 236
Nefertiti 74, 79, 257
Nekheb (ancient city) 211
Nekhen 212
Nelson, Sir Horatio 106

Nephthys (goddess: wife of
Set) 207, 248
New Kingdom 73–79, 83–85, 249
Night of Counting the Years, The
(film) 161
Nile
controlling 147–151
flooding of 21, 147, 187, 192,
204, 300
in search of the source 23, 25,
29–40, 176
irrigation 210
navigation 48
varieties of boats 48
nilometers 149, 282
Nubia 25, 151, 193, 195
Nubian migration 188–189, 209
Nubians 194
Nut (the sky-goddess) 206
Nyussere, Pharaoh 204

O

Octavian (Augustus) 89, 90
Old Kingdom 59–63 189–190, 218,
267, 269, 279
Om el-Gaab 251
Omdurman 24, 118, 120, 179
On (Heliopolis) 206, 279
Opera House (old) 133
Opet (hippopotamus-goddess of
Thebes) 76
Osiris (god; judge of the dead) 60,
198, 206, 234, 248, 250
Ottomans, the 98–99
Owen Falls Dam 176
Ozymandias (poem by Percy Bysshe
Shelley) 83

P

Paez, Pedro 29
Palaearctic African Bird Migration 154
Palmerston, Lord 113
papyrus canoes 49
Pascal, Gabriel 159
Pentaour 83
Pepi I 189
Pepi II 190
Pettigrew, T.J. 71
Philae 151, 198–199
phoenix, the 261
Pliny 59
Plutarch 90, 248
pollution 300
Pompey 87
Psusennes I 240
Ptah of Memphis (god) 197, 266
Ptolemies, the 87–91, 207, 245, 303
Ptolemy V 303
Ptolemy XIV 88
Ptolemy XV 88
Ptolemy, Claudius 22, 32
Pullman Cataract Hotel,
Aswan 47, 187
pumping methods 210
Pyramid of Cheops *see* Great Pyramid
of Cheops

Pyramid of Chephren (Khafre) 271
Pyramid of Mankaure (Mycerinus)
  granite for 191
Pyramid of Unas, Sakkara 268
Pyramid Plateau Project 273
pyramid building 274
pyramidology 64
Pythagoras 65

Q

Qansuh al Ghori 98
Qasr Ibrim 199
Qena 245
Qift 245
Qubbel el-Hawa 189
Quornah, Luxor 69, 232

R

Ra (the sun-god) 206, 279
Ra-Harakhte (the sun-god) 271
Rafelson, Bob 162
Ramesseum 85, 233
Ramses I 84, 219
Ramses II 83–85, 195, 196, 219,
  220, 233
  statue of, Memphis 265
  tomb of 70
Ramses III 220
Ramses VI (tomb of) 234
Ras el Tin Palace 131
Rassul family 47, 69
Rawdah 149, 282
Rawlinson, George 85
Ripon Falls 176
Rommel, Erwin (the Desert Fox) 143
Rosetta 301
Rosetta Stone 68, 362
Rosetta Stone 108, 109
Rossellini, Roberto 161
Royal Geographical Society 35, 36, 39

S

Sabni 190
Sadat, Anwar 140, 143
St Peter 279
Sakkara 60, 266–270
Saladin (Salah ad-Din ibn Ayyub) 94,
  284, 293
Saleem the Grim 99
Satis (goddess of the Cataract region)
  188, 193
Scott-Moncrieff, Sir Colin 150
Seif ed-Din 134
Senmut (Queen Hatshepsut's
  architect) 231
Senusert III 255
  pyramid of, Dahshur 50
Serappeum, Sakkara 269
Seshat (patron deity of records and
  archives) 249
Sesostris III 148
Seth (god, son of Nut and Geb) 207,
  210, 248
Seti I 84, 219, 220, 249
  tomb of 70, 234

Severus, Septimius 231
Seymour, Admiral Sir Beauchamp 133
Shelley, Percy Bysshe 83
Shendy 33, 180
Shepheard's Hotel (former) 47, 140
Shepheard, Samuel 131
Shu (god of the air) 206
Siemens, Sir W. 64
slave trade 33, 40, 113–114, 115
Smelt, Reverend Charles 32
Smenkhare 257
Smith, Sir Sidney 109, 129
Snofru, King 61
Soane, Sir John 235
Sobek (crocodile-god of Fayyum and
  Kom Ombo) 153, 207, 226
Sokar (god of the dead at Memphis)
  266, 267
solar boat (funerary boat of Cheops)
  272–273
solar boat, Giza 49–50
Soviet Union 193
Speke, John Hanning 23, 34–37,
  162, 176
Sphinx, Giza 271, 272
Stanley, Henry Morten 23, 40
Stanwood, August 71
Step Pyramid, Sakkara 267–268
Stoker, Bram 161
Strabo 68, 187, 261, 64
Sudan, the 113–121, 178–181
Sudd, the 24, 114, 178–179
Suez Canal 22, 113, 122,
  132–133, 245
Sufism 300
sugar cane 155
Suleiman the Great 99
Sultan Hasan Mosque, Cairo 63
Survey of Memphis, the 266

T

Talkha 301
Tanta 300
Taylor, Elizabeth (actress) 87, 91, 160
Taylor, John 64
Tel el-Amarna 73, 78, 255–257
Temple of Amon-Ra, Karnak 222–225
Temple of Beit el Wali 195
Temple of Dendera 245–246
Temple of Horus, Edfu 209
Temple of Isis, Philae 151, 198
Temple of Kalabsha 195
Temple of Khnum, Esna 212
Temple of Luxor 221
Temple of Queen Hatshepsut (Deir el
  Bahri) 231
Temple of Queen Nefertari,
  Abu Simbel 197
Temple of Ramses II, Abu Simbel 196
Temple of Ramses II, Abydos 249
Temple of Ramses III, Medinet
  Habu 220
Temple Seti I, Abydos 249, 250
Ten Commandments, The (film) 159
Tewfik 116, 133–134
Thebes *see* Luxor
Thinis, Abydos 251

Thoth (god of wisdom) 153, 213, 234,
  257, 258
Toman Bey 99
Tomb of Amenemhat, Beni Hassan 259
Tomb of Mereruka, Sakkara 268–269
Tomb of Meri-Re, Tel el-Amarna 257
Tomb of Nakht 236
Tomb of Petosiris, Tuna el-Gebel 259
Tomb of Ramose, Valley of the
  Nobles 236
Tomb of Rekhmire, Valley of the
  Nobles 236
Tomb of Ti, Sakkara 268
Trajan Decius 213
Trajan's Kiosk, Philae 198
Treaty of London 131
Tuna el-Gebel 258
Turan Shah 95
Turf Club 140
Turkey 129, 133, 134
Turner, Thomas 302
Tutankhamun 74, 219, 235, 240, 193
  discovery of tomb 67, 160, 235,
  240–241
  tomb of 67, 235, 240–241
Tuthmosis I 232, 266
Tuthmosis II 232
Tuthmosis III 75–77, 219, 225
  tomb of 70, 236
Tuthmosis IV 63, 236, 271

U–V

Umm Seti 247–248
unfinished obelisk, Aswan 191
Valley of the Kings, Luxor 233–236
  grave robbers in 69
Valley of the Nobles 236–237
Valley of the Queens, Luxor 236
Victoria, Queen 118, 120, 121

W–Z

Wadi Halfa 180
White Nile 21, 23, 30, 114, 176–179
wildlife 153–157
Winter Palace Hotel, Luxor 47
Wolseley, Sir Garnet 117
World War II 139, 142, 143
Wright, Patricia 123
Young, Thomas 302
Zoser, King 61, 218, 267

A
B
C
D
E
F
G

I
J
a
b
c

e
f
g
h
i
j
k
l

The Insight Approach

The book you are holding is part of the world's largest range of guidebooks. Its purpose is to help you have the most valuable travel experience possible, and we try to achieve this by providing not only information about countries, regions and cities but also genuine insight into their history, culture, institutions and people.

Since the first Insight Guide – to Bali – was published in 1970, the series has been dedicated to the proposition that, with insight into a country's people and culture, visitors can both enhance their own experience and be accepted more easily by their hosts. Now, in a world where ethnic hostilities and nationalist conflicts are all too common, such attempts to increase understanding between peoples are more important than ever.

Insight Guides:
Essentials for understanding

Because a nation's past holds the key to its present, each Insight Guide kicks off with lively history chapters. These are followed by magazine-style essays on culture and daily life. This essential background information gives readers the necessary context for using the main Places section, with its comprehensive run-down on things worth seeing and doing. Finally, a listings section contains all the information you'll need on travel, hotels, restaurants and opening times.

As far as possible, we rely on local writers and specialists to ensure that the information is authoritative. The pictures, for which Insight Guides have become so celebrated, are just as important. Our photojournalistic approach aims not only to illustrate a destination but also to communicate visually and directly to readers life as it is lived by the locals.

Compact Guides
The "great little guides"

As invaluable as such background information is, it isn't always fun to carry an Insight Guide through a crowded souk or up a church tower. Could we, readers asked, distil the key reference material into a slim volume for on-the-spot use?

Our response was to design Compact Guides as an entirely new series, with original text carefully cross-referenced to detailed maps and more than 200 photographs. In essence, they're miniature encyclopedias, concise and comprehensive, displaying reliable and up-to-date information in an accessible way.

Pocket Guides:
A local host in book form

However wide-ranging the information in a book, human beings still value the personal touch. Our editors are often asked the same questions. Where do *you* go to eat? What do *you* think is the best beach? What would you recommend if I have only three days? We invited our local correspondents to act as "substitute hosts" by revealing their preferred walks and trips, listing the restaurants they go to and structuring a visit into a series of timed itineraries.

The result is our Pocket Guides, complete with full-size fold-out maps. These 100-plus titles help readers plan a trip precisely, particularly if their time is short.

Exploring with Insight:
A valuable travel experience

In conjunction with co-publishers all over the world, we print in up to 10 languages, from German to Chinese, from Danish to Russian. But our aim remains simple: to enhance your travel experience by combining our expertise in guidebook publishing with the on-the-spot knowledge of our correspondents.